ON THE CHARIOT WHEEL

J.C.M., aged 80, from the portrait by Alan Gwynne-Jones, R.A., in Christ
Church Hall

ON THE
CHARIOT WHEEL

An Autobiography

J. C. MASTERMAN

*It was a pretty conceit of Aesop's, as Bacon said,
to speak of the fly on the axle wheel,
and his cry, 'What a dust I raise.'*

OXFORD UNIVERSITY PRESS
1975

Oxford University Press, Ely House, London W.1

GLASGOW NEW YORK TORONTO MELBOURNE WELLINGTON
CAPE TOWN IBADAN NAIROBI DAR ES SALAAM LUSAKA ADDIS ABABA
DELHI BOMBAY CALCUTTA MADRAS KARACHI LAHORE DACCA
KUALA LUMPUR SINGAPORE HONG KONG TOKYO

ISBN 0 19 951048 2

© *J. C. Masterman 1975*

*Printed in Great Britain
by William Clowes & Sons, Limited
London, Beccles and Colchester*

ACKNOWLEDGEMENTS

To the many who have helped me in the composition of this book I wish to express my gratitude. Worcester College have allowed me to reproduce the portrait by Edward Halliday, and Christ Church that by Alan Gwynne-Jones. The *Daily Mail* permitted the reproduction of a cartoon by Tom Webster which appeared in 1923. I am especially grateful to Lady Herbert for allowing the late Sir Alan Herbert's rhymed speech to appear in full, and to the Revd. Anthony Harvey for according me the same privilege with regard to a poem of his father's, which is printed as Appendix II. I am also most grateful to *The Times* for leave to quote their Law Report of 8 December 1965, and to the Literary Estate of the late Charles Morgan and Messrs. Chatto and Windus for permitting the use of a quotation from *The Gunroom*.

It is impossible to name all the many friends who have (sometimes unwittingly) assisted me in the writing of this book. They will, I hope, be content with a general acknowledgement of their help. To one, however, I owe a very special debt. It would be difficult to exaggerate all the help and co-operation which I have had from Mr. I.G. Philip, Deputy-Librarian of the Bodleian. He constructed the notes, verified many of the dates and references, and read, critically, the whole of the text. Most important of all, he advised me, with kindliness and candour, which parts of my MSS. to retain and which to excise. For those faults which remain I alone am responsible, but I have relied so much on his help and judgement that it gives me pleasure to acknowledge the debt which I owe him.

CONTENTS

LIST OF ILLUSTRATIONS

I

FAMILY HISTORY

We much revere our sires.
They were a noble race of men.
For every glass of wine we drink
They nothing thought of ten.

G. O. TREVELYAN

ALL my life I have followed the conventional course. To do the right thing—or rather what public opinion regarded as the right thing—was a stronger influence with me than the dictates of reason or even of morality. A sad confession, but true. Accordingly I begin these reminiscences in the conventional manner—that is, with some account of my forebears. Even those who cavil at 'ancestor worship' and belittle the importance of inherited qualities and talents cannot deny altogether the influence which our forebears have upon our lives, nor can they persuade the orthodox (of whom I am one) to abandon their belief that there is no privilege so great as that of being born of worthy and healthy parents and of starting life with the benefit of inherited traditions of conduct and behaviour. It is for this reason that I begin by looking at my four grandparents and the families from which they came.

The name 'Masterman' has no underlying aristocratic significance. Indeed, rather the opposite. In early times it was written 'Maisterman', and it means not the master-man but the master's man, that is to say the bailiff or factor or perhaps even, in industrial terms, the charge-hand. Not, I hasten to add, the gentleman's gentleman of a more recent and vulgar period, but still only the assistant or right-hand man or lieutenant and not the master or commander. The Mastermans of the sixteenth and seventeenth centuries were yeoman stock, settled for a long time in the Cleveland district of the North Riding of Yorkshire—as well as in the City of York and its neighbourhood. The continued use of the same Christian names is an obstacle to the proof of direct succession. From the year 1606 onwards the name appears frequently in the Jury lists at the Quarter Sessions; from 1605 to 1745 the Freemen's register of the City of York shows entries of fourteen names which, up to 1657, were written Maisterman and after that date Masterman. They represented at least three different families. A search for a common ancestor has not been successful. In that branch of the family to which I belong the first certain entry is that of Thomas Masterman of Nunthorpe, in the Parish of Great Ayton in Cleveland, County York. From that date the records are reliable, for the Mastermans of this branch were from 1665 (probably before) Quakers, as an entry in the register of the Society of Friends of the birth of a son to Thomas Masterman proves. The family prospered; they moved to London and became traders, and from trade they moved into banking. William Masterman, born 1758, died 1845, married Lydia, daughter of Daniel Mildred, and the bank of Mildred, Peters, and Masterman was formed. Under the administration of his son John the bank attained considerable prosperity, and John, my great-grandfather, became a figure of importance. He was born in 1781 and was the first of the family to dissociate himself from the Quakers. A note in the Friends' register states that 'John Masterman having so far deviated from the religious principles of our Society as to take up arms we therefore hereby disown the said John Masterman as a member of our Society.' There follows the usual formula about hoping he would come to see the error of his ways. Yet he must have retained the respect of his former co-religionists, for—whether readmitted or not—he was buried in the Friends' burial ground at Barking. I have often blamed myself because I did not in my youth inquire about him. It would have been easy to talk to many who had known him—both relatives and friends—for he lived until 1862. I neglected the opportunity, but perhaps the omission is another reason for the writing of this book. As things are, I am dependent upon the few family traditions and upon the newspapers and journals of the time. He was, without doubt, a man of considerable reputation and importance both in the City of London and at Westminster. He was the head of the family bank, a bank which later absorbed the Agra bank. He was a director of the Honourable East India Company—in a word, a city magnate during the middle years of Victoria's reign. He was also Member of Parliament for the City of London for nearly fifteen years, elected in three successive elections—in 1841, 1847, and 1852. These three elections were all exciting and full of interest. In 1841 according to *The Times* the Guildhall 'presented such an appearance as has not been witnessed (according to the evidence of some of the oldest members of the Livery) since the days of Wilkes'. John Masterman, 'a Conservative in favour of free trade', came at the head of the poll with 6,339 votes, but even the last of the eight candidates (there were four places to be filled) polled 6,017. Lord John Russell secured the fourth place by the narrow margin of nine votes. In 1847 the contest was equally exciting though more orderly. On 30 July *The Times* recorded that all four Liberals had been returned with Lord John Russell at the head of the poll. *The Times* was in error, as this entry on the following day shows:

Yesterday the official declaration of the final state of the poll took place in Guildhall, which was densely crowded. For some time after the announcement of the numbers, considerable excitement prevailed on its being discovered that Mr. Masterman, by the reckoning of the Sheriffs, had polled a larger number of votes than Sir George Larpent.

The numbers were exhibited, opposite each candidate's name, on a black board, at the top of the hustings, and were announced by the Sheriff—for

Lord J. Russell	7,137	(Great cheering)
Pattison	7,030	(Great cheering)
Rothschild	6,792	(Great cheering)
Masterman	6,722	(Groans and hisses)
Larpent	6,719	(Loud cheers).

[Other Candidates' names follow]

(*The Times*, 31 July 1847)

Once again John Masterman had stood as a Conservative in favour of free trade, adding on this occasion that he was 'prepared to resist any further concessions to popery'. In 1852 the result was very different for he was once more at the head of the poll with a majority of 558 over Lord John Russell who came second. In the City itself the most lasting record which he left was the foundation of the City of London Club. This club was founded by a group of prominent bankers, merchants, and ship-owners who formed a committee under his chairmanship. In the centenary notes on the *History and Traditions of the Club* published in 1932 it is erroneously stated that my great-grandfather was 'then Member of Parliament for the City'. It is, however, true that he was chairman of the club from 1832 to 1858. His portrait by Pickersgill hangs in the club opposite to that of the Duke of Wellington by the same artist. The Duke and Sir Robert Peel were both original members and continued their membership till their deaths. In 1848 John Masterman received an honorary D.C.L. at Oxford in the company of Gladstone. I have always regarded this with special pleasure, for it must have been unusual to confer the degree on a banker and politician who had no connection with the University. My gratification was a little damped, but only a little, when I realized that the then Vice-Chancellor, Benjamin Parsons of Wadham, was married to John Masterman's daughter, Lydia. But subsequent experience has taught me that the Vice-Chancellor is very far from being an autocrat in matters of this kind and that an honorary degree is one of those distinctions which only personal merit can secure—or perhaps in some cases philanthropy. The honorary D.C.L. was the only public honour which my great-grandfather received but it was a legend in the family that he had refused a peerage or a baronetcy. This may or may not be true. It is not improbable that he should have been offered some mark of distinction after fourteen years at Westminster; nor is it improbable that his Quaker upbringing should have led him to refuse any such offer.

And so I come to the first of my grandparents, Henry Masterman. He was the fifth of seven sons; there were also five daughters but of those senior to him three died young and the fourth left no heirs. Henry himself died in 1883, eight years before I was born. All that I know of him, therefore, depends upon oral tradition and upon dimly remembered remarks of my parents and uncles—yet the picture is clear enough. He was a solicitor and a typical representative of the Victorian paterfamilias of his day, always referred to by his sons as 'the Governor', respected and obeyed in his family and a figure of reputation and some importance in the City of London. The picture painted by Galsworthy in the Forsyte Saga of the growth of a family in London seems to repeat itself in the case of the Mastermans though the latter were a generation in advance of the Forsytes. I must confess that much of this is the product of imagination. Once in the Cathedral at Oxford I heard the Professor of Ecclesiastical History preach on St. Frideswide's day. A year previously I had listened to another Canon who had indulged in the usual eloquent and detailed eulogy of the Saint, full of what appeared to be historical details of her life. This had given no pleasure to the Professor of Ecclesiastical History who began his sermon with the words: 'About St. Frideswide nothing is known whatsoever. We can only assume that she was good.' Alas! I have little more personal knowledge of my grandfather's character than that; I know only that his reputation stood high and that he was respected, and perhaps admired by his family and his intimates.

My paternal grandmother, on the other hand, I came to know well, for she lived until 1911. She was born in 1817, a member of another large Victorian family. Her father, Nathaniel Snell-Chauncy, had sixteen children, only one of whom died in infancy, and of the rest all but three married. The family of Chauncy descended from William de Chauncy who held lands in the County of York in the reign of King Henry I. Some of his descendants moved to Hertfordshire early in the fifteenth century where they held considerable estates. Among them two were of especial interest. Charles Chauncy (1592–1672), after running foul of Laud and the Court of High Commission, migrated to America and became for nearly twenty years the second President of Harvard. The second was Sir Henry Chauncy (1632–1719) who published the *Historical Antiquities of Hertfordshire* in 1700, and in his judicial capacity was notorious for his arrest of witches.

As a small boy I used to be taken—together with my brother—to visit my grandmother. She was small, and must in her youth have been vivacious but, by the time that I knew her, her great days were far behind her. She regarded herself, I think, very much as the head of the family and, though keenly interested in her grandchildren, held firmly to the view that children should be seen and not heard and that nothing of importance should be discussed in their presence. It was, in consequence, something of an ordeal to sit in her Victorian drawing-room, especially when one knew that one's parents were nervous lest 'London granny', as we called her, should be disturbed by noise or untoward movements. She had a kind heart and a sweet smile but her remarks were sometimes touched with acid. We were fond of her and in a curious way rather proud of her; she occupied in our minds a place not unlike that accorded to Queen Victoria.

She must have had many tales to tell, but by the time that I realized this she was already ninety, for she had been born in 1817. Once, indeed, she did tell me something of her youth and related the tale of the annual journey of her family from the country to London in the early summer. Her father would fuss over every detail of the departure of the family coach. Was everyone present and ready? Had anything been forgotten? And finally a question to the coachman: 'John, is the blunderbuss loaded?' Only when assurance was given that this rite had been duly performed was the journey allowed to begin.

My grandparents on my mother's side were both known to me, although my maternal grandfather—the Revd. J. Roydon Hughes—died when I was very young. In the case of the Hugheses I am on firmer ground for my great-grandfather Thomas Hughes and his younger brother wrote in 1795 'Memoirs of the Families of Hughes and Bridges' (their mother was one Elizabeth Bridges), which I have in manuscript beautifully written and sumptuously illustrated by their coats of arms.

Of their earlier ancestors more still is to be found in Sir Joseph Bradney's monumental *History of Monmouthshire* (11 volumes 1904–32). My great-grandfather's account really begins about 1600, but before that William Hughes of Cillwell had married as his second wife Mary, the illegitimate daughter of William Somerset, third Earl of Worcester, a direct descendant, through John of Gaunt, of the Conqueror William I. By the beginning of the seventeenth century an earlier Thomas Hughes was living 'in splendour' at Moyne's Court, Mathern, just outside Chepstow. The house had been built by Francis Godwin, Bishop of Llandaff, and from him passed to Thomas Hughes who was, as his will shows, a very wealthy man. He left two sons, Thomas and Charles, whose activities during the Civil War are of interest. Thomas, the elder, who succeeded to Moyne's Court, became a colonel in the Parliamentary

My grandparents

2. Henry Masterman

3. Ellen Masterman (née Chauncy)

4. The Revd. Roydon Hughes

5. Susan Hughes (née Worsley)

6. My father and mother on bicycles, Donaghadee 1896

7. My father, Captain J. Masterman, R.N., J.P.

8. My brother, Sir Christopher Masterman, C.S.I., C.I.E., Deputy High Commissioner for the U.K., Madras 1947

9. My mother, aged 75, from the drawing by J.B. Soutar

10. Preparatory school age. My mother, brother, myself, and our two servants, Sarah Maulden and Clara Figgins

11. Lord Charles Beresford presenting the Channel Fleet Golf Cup to H.M.S. *Britannia*

army and was Governor of Chepstow town and castle. Charles, the second son, on the other hand, was a major in the royalist forces and took a leading part in the defence of Raglan Castle. It would appear that Thomas was able to protect Charles during the time of the Protectorate and Commonwealth, whilst Charles was able to return the compliment when the Restoration came. Thomas died in 1664 leaving an only daughter, and Moyne's Court therefore passed out of the family, but Charles, in the meantime had married an heiress Jane Jones and succeeded to the estates of Trostrey. Jane must have married young for she died at the age of thirty-one in childbed, leaving her husband with fourteen children.

The history of the family in the next century is similar to that of many other families, which have met alike successes and disasters. Charles was a rich man, for he left estates to all his many children; his second son Charles was equally prosperous and was, apart from his legal offices, Steward of all the Beaufort estates, a Deputy-Lieutenant of the County, and, on the appointment of Queen Anne, Receiver and Appreciator of the estate of the Duchy of Lancaster in the Counties of Monmouth, Hereford, and Gloucester. Unfortunately he died whilst his son Robert was still a minor. Robert Hughes (1701–39) is at once the most attractive and the least fortunate of the family. He was a Gentleman Commoner at Christ Church and settled early on his paternal estate. What followed is thus related by my great-grandfather:

He lived there in great hospitality much beloved and respected and in habits of particular intimacy with the Beaufort family. Political dissensions at this time were at a great height. In Monmouthshire the Whig interest prevailed under the auspices of the Morgan family, and the Jacobite or Tory interest, supported by the house of Somerset, was not a little pleased to have so popular a man as Robert Hughes of Trostrey to set up against their opponents. He accordingly stood a warmly contested election against Major Hanbury and Mr. Morgan of Tredegar. The superior weight and more popular cause of the latter prevailed and my grandfather was left, though by a small majority, in the situation too frequently consequent on such contests, in the pleasant remembrance of the personal attachment of many friends and with an impaired and injured fortune.

Had Robert lived he might well have recovered, but he died

in 1739, when his affairs were still in confusion and the estate heavily mortgaged to an old Christ Church friend, Dr. Secker, afterwards Archbishop of Canterbury. It is a clear case of the popular, acquiescent, generous but improvident man whose affairs declined proportionately with the growth of his popularity. The sons were not the men to restore the family fortunes. I cannot tell the tale better than by quoting again from my great-grandfather's narrative: 'Of the sons, Charles the eldest was educated at Westminster School, but he was not afterwards sent to either of the universities, probably from an apprehension that his propensity to expenses would have too large opportunity of being indulged at these seats of dissipation.' Instead he was sent to an attorney at Bath to study the law but 'he soon felt the confinement of the desk degrading to his pride or restraining to his liberty and he left to lead an idle life at home'. The event was inevitable. Trostrey had to be sold, most disadvantageously; the purchaser after recouping himself for almost all of the purchase price by selling the timber for £9,000, resold the estate for £30,000. Again I quote the narrative: 'His estate sold, his family dispersed, his attention unoccupied, to a man of Charles Hughes's spirit and vivacity the army was the only resource.' Here the good Dr. Secker came to his assistance and procured him a commission. He died of a fever at the siege of Pondicherry in 1762. The second son had a similar career; he, too, after leaving Winchester 'was put to an attorney'; he too quickly left the office and entered the army where, owing to the support of the Duke of Cumberland, his rise was rapid. He fought in Germany and at Culloden and was then sent to the Highlands where he died of the smallpox in 1750. Some of his letters were published in the *English Historical Review* in 1893. Perhaps the chief point of interest in them is that he records the belief in the army that Dettingen was a greater victory than Blenheim.

Thomas, the only surviving son (and my great-great-grandfather), settled in the practice of the law at Cheltenham. For two centuries almost all the male Hugheses were in some way connected with the law and most of them were 'of the Middle Temple'. He married Elizabeth Bridges of Keynsham Abbey and prospered in his law business. He left two sons of whom Thomas Bridges, my great-grandfather, was the elder. My grandfather, James Roydon Hughes, was his son and to him I now turn. He was born in 1810 and educated at Winchester and New College where he matriculated in 1827, becoming at once a Fellow of the College. He was a Fellow from 1827 to 1843 when he married and was given the living of Newton Longville. Thence he moved to Long Ditton, of which parish he was Rector until 1889. He died in 1894 but I remember him well for he seemed to me to be full of kindness and human sympathy. He had been a stout Evangelical, active in youth in working for the erection of the Martyrs' Memorial, an enemy of all hatred—in short a good man whose goodness was self-evident. In the family he was referred to as 'the Rector' or 'the old Rector'. I could wish that I had been able to learn more from him but I treasure one tale of his youth. When Prefect of Hall (i.e. head of the school) at Winchester he had narrowly escaped expulsion. The reason? His mother had sent him tea for his breakfasts and this was considered an insult to the small beer which was provided for that repast.

My grandmother (Kingston granny as we called her) I knew much better, for a good deal of my time as a small boy was spent in her house. She, like my other grandmother, was something of a matriarch but we knew her well enough to have no sort of fear of her. She was Susan Worsley, a member of an old and honourable family, tracing direct descent from Sir Elias Workesley, in the time of William I of Workesley in Lancashire. A warrior in the Crusades, he died at Rhodes. A branch of the family came to the Isle of Wight early in the sixteenth century and Sir James Worsley, who died in 1538, was Governor of the island. This line seems to have divided in the next century into Worsley of Appledurcombe and Worsley of Gatcombe. My grandmother was descended from the junior branch and her grandfather was Rector of Gatcombe and her father also in Holy Orders. It was therefore very much a clerical family for my grandmother had been, when I knew her, already nearly fifty years—'the Rector's wife'. I spent much of my time as a small boy in her house and her influence on me was no doubt considerable. To some she may have seemed formidable, but not to us for she had a very soft spot in her heart for her grandchildren. All her sons and her only daughter, my Mother, regarded her with a deep affection. She died in 1900.

The families of Masterman and Hughes had a pleasant symmetry and were doubly united. There were five Masterman sons and one daughter. The Hugheses had six sons and a daughter but of these one son died in infancy and another as a boy from a fall from stilts. The oldest Hughes son, my uncle Charles, married the only Masterman daughter and the second Masterman son, my father, married the only Hughes daughter. My Father was born in 1847 and joined *Britannia* as a naval cadet in early youth. He nearly died, but was saved by the energy of my grandmother, who succeeded in having one of the Queen's physicians sent down to inspect and suggest improvements in conditions on board.

My Father was of all men the most reserved, even shy, and the most modest and reticent. He never spoke of himself and seldom of the things which he had seen and experienced. I have the impression that he was disappointed in his naval career, for he retired at the age of fifty—but perhaps this is not altogether surprising for he was constitutionally incapable of pushing his own interests or of asking for or working for preferment. Besides the period was not one well suited to his gifts and capabilities. The Navy was passing from sail to steam during his period of service and he was a natural conservative in his views. The *Warrior* was the first all-metal battleship, and in 1860 the year of her construction the Navy stood committed to masts and sails, counting the screw as a useful adjunct.

The twenty-five years succeeding her launch must be described as a transition period. Yet my Father had seen much of the world—China, the Mediterranean, South Africa, Newfoundland, and the West Indies, and sometimes, as though by chance, he would let fall some memory or reminiscence. How, for example, all Newfoundland ratings could be given cod to eat for seven days in the week but that mutiny threatened if they were given salmon more than once weekly; or how the Admiral in command in the West Indies would arrange his gunnery practice. He had observed that by dint of hard work all the ammunition issued for the year could be expended in one day. Alas, on one occasion, a petty officer gun-layer hit the target on his first shot and destroyed it. The consequent delay, whilst a fresh target was made ready hopelessly upset the time schedule and the gun-layer lost a stripe. Later, though perhaps this was only *ben trovato*, the Admiral realized that by using the last day of one year and the first of the next he could get rid of his unwanted supply of ammunition for two years in two consecutive days and thus save much trouble and vexation. It all sounds irresponsible, but in those years the Navy policed the world and brought security and peace over the greater part of the globe. One sad episode in my Father's life at sea is also on record; I have the sailing orders given to him to bring back the body of the Prince Imperial from Africa in *Boadicea*, of which ship my Father was then in command. In spite of the disappointment which I have mentioned he was a happy man in his retirement for he spent his time in an unceasing round of unpaid but useful work in which he excelled. He was church-warden, treasurer of the Benefit Nursing Association, a Rural District Councillor, a member of the Board of Guardians, and a Justice of the Peace. For the rest he was a more than competent painter in water colours, an enthusiastic gardener, and a skilful carpenter. As a father he had every merit except one. Fond though he was of his sons he was too shy and reserved to give us, my brother and me, the full benefit of his counsel and advice.

My Mother was married to him in 1888. I think that there had been a long engagement as my Father was still serving in the West Indies. Towards the end of her life I was driving my Mother from Oxford to Eastbourne and on the road between Henley and Wargrave she quite suddenly said, 'That is the hotel where I became engaged to your Father; I was staying with the Mastermans for the Henley Regatta, and I have never seen it since.' In my life she played so great a part that I hesitate to attempt a description, lest it should appear extravagant and fulsome. In the reminiscences of an old friend I came upon this sentence: 'Ours was not a rich home, except in love.' The same was true of my home and my Mother was the centre of it. As a boy I could not imagine anyone who could match her and I have never had cause to change that opinion.

In my parents I was fortunate indeed. Of course as a young man I was sometimes impatient of their judgements and thought myself quicker and cleverer than they were, but never in my wildest moments did I think that they were not acting, as they thought, in my best interests. It would have seemed against nature had they ever acted otherwise. It is not always easy to obey the ten commandments but at least I have never been tempted to disobey the fifth. To honour my Father and Mother was as natural as to breathe. If the commandment is taken to mean, as some would have us believe, that we should honour and respect all constituted authority, I hesitate. Has this been in fact a weakness? Some rebellion, some revolt, some independence of outlook in early days might have made me a better man, though not, I fancy, a happier one. With forebears from trade and banking, from the Church and the Law, from the rich or landed gentry I was, perhaps irrevocably fixed on the side of the Establishment.

II

BOYHOOD AND PREPARATORY SCHOOL

The mournful period of boyhood when eccentricities excite attention
and command no sympathy.

BENJAMIN DISRAELI

I was born on 12 January 1891. According to my nurse the † 1977
doctor who presided over my birth walked across the frozen
Thames to my grandmother's house. 'True or false?' as the
modern quiz-master would ask. It could be true, for 1891 was
one of the hard winters. The very early years of anyone are apt
to be of little interest to any but the person involved and I must
pass over them quickly. For my first three years my Mother had
a small semi-detached house close to one of the entrances to
Richmond Park and then a few hundred yards off my grandmother's house—Crescent Lodge on Kingston Hill. My Father
was for part of this time still serving in the West Indies and I
think that much of our time must have been spent with our
grandparents. Few memories remain; I recall only the trees
and fallen leaves in Richmond Park; of lying under the table
whilst my brother,[1] eighteen months older than myself, was
being taught to read (with the happy result that when my turn
came I was able to read almost at once and without effort); of
an optimistic attempt, inspired by my brother, to dig a hole
through to Australia—he having been apprised of the fact that
the earth was round. A change came when I was three, for
my Father was appointed to a coastguard command in Northern
Ireland and the family was transported to Donaghadee. We
lived there till 1897 and in that time memories are more vivid
and more numerous, though it is trivialities which remain in
the mind when more important things are forgotten. I remem-

---

[1] Sir Christopher Masterman, C.S.I., C.I.E., Deputy High Commissioner for
U.K. Madras, 1947.

ber nothing of our journeys to and from Ireland; hardly anything of our lessons or games; very little of our daily life. Yet
some few trifles are crystal clear—a troublesome but good-
tempered mob plucking all the orange lilies in the garden on
Orange Day; a mighty battle between the rooks who built their
nests at the bottom of the garden and invading sea-gulls; a
passionate and insistent desire that my curls should be cut off
(a wish not granted until near the end of our stay in Ireland).
More clearly a wreck on the coast and the paintings of the
shipwrecked vessel which my Father made afterwards. I
remember too the first sweepstake in which I took part. My
brother and I persuaded my Father to invest a shilling in a
sweepstake (allegedly for some good cause) in which the first
prize was a silver watch. We were greatly excited when we
received a letter to say that we had won the prize, but our
enthusiasm was a little damped when we read at the end of
the letter the announcement that the watch would be sent to us
if we dispatched £1 to pay for the chain that went with it.
Strangely enough my Father refused to let us accept our prize.
The most vivid of all my Irish recollections is that of our clergyman the Revd. R.H. Coote. He was a rumbustious man and it
was his habit when he came to the house to seize my brother
or myself and hold the one or the other high above his head and
wave him to and fro—an experience which filled me with both
terror and exhilaration. He was a happy extrovert but about his
spiritual ministrations I have my reservations. One day, as my
Father used to relate, the summer meeting on the golf course
and the local regatta both concluded, he decided that he must
visit some of his parishioners and that he would begin with two
of the oldest, a married couple James and Mary, both in their
late eighties. He found Mary alone and burst into her house
with the cheerful greeting: 'Good evening to you, and how's
James the day?'

'Shure, your honour, and isn't it yourself that had the burying
of him last Saturday?'

'Dear me—no, Saturday was medal day on the golf course so
I got the Baptist minister to do the burying for me. And was
that James? Well, never mind, Mary, better luck next time.'

For a long time I thought of Coote whenever I heard speak
of a typical Irishman and when an uncle referred to someone

being 'bald as a coot' I protested vehemently that Coote was not bald at all.

In 1897 my Father retired with the rank of captain, and we all returned to England. There was a long debate as to where we should live and much viewing of houses before we settled in that corner where Hampshire, Surrey, and Berkshire meet. Heathcroft was in the parish of Yateley, though the address was 'Blackwater, Hants'. In point of fact the house lay about mid-way between Yateley and Blackwater on the edge of Darby Green and was below the Hertford Bridge Flats. Heathcroft was my home for a quarter of a century and I must describe it as it appeared to the eyes of a very small boy. The Aldershot country, on the edge of which it was, has suffered hardly from the pens of writers ever since the days of George Borrow, but at the turn of the last century it had much to recommend it. The summer's day on which I first saw Heathcroft is unforget-table. The garden was large, and outside it lay the common, a stretch of gorse and heather (where white heather was not infrequent) with firs and pines and a great wall of foxgloves near the gate. Moreover, we had, as it were, the best of both worlds, for where our garden began, the Aldershot country melted into the richer agricultural land, and fir and pine gave way to oak and ash and elm. And the garden! If ever trees were made to be climbed it was here, and the common offered almost unlimited possibilities of adventure. Almost always there was a gipsy encampment which tempted us to approach it with fearful yet enticing pleasure, terrified that the gipsies might kidnap us as in the stories, yet half hoping that this thrilling experience would come our way. There was one tremendous occasion on the common in, probably, 1898, for it was before what we came to call the 'great' Boer war. A military exercise was held along-side Hertford Bridge Flats and as it seemed to us a mighty battle was staged between two rival armies, the one dressed in scarlet and the other in blue. For most of the day figures appeared, easily distinguished by their vivid colouring, from behind gorse bushes and from under hedges. In the evening the affair ended with a grand cavalry charge of the blue forces over the heather upon the serried ranks of the red infantry. To us watching boys it seemed impossible that the surging wave of cavalry would not ride over and destroy the infantry—unless indeed the latter did not first shoot them all down. Waterloo, we thought, must have been something very like the battle we were watching. Alas! the bright colours and the massed cavalry were soon enough to be shown as unsuitable for the conditions of South African warfare.

They were happy years. We spent most of the time at Heath-croft, but there was always a summer visit to the seaside or to some of our relatives. It was at this time that two of my uncles came to fill a big place in my mind. Uncle Will was my Father's eldest brother and was County Court Judge at Nottingham. He lived outside the town first at Wilford and then at the Old Rectory at Clifton. To him our family used to go in August and to us boys he was indeed the ideal uncle and Clifton the ideal holiday home. This was the house that figures largely in Rosslyn Bruce's *The Last of the Eccentrics*. The garden was splendid, rich in lawns and trees, and distinguished by the glass-houses full of the most mouth-watering fruit. With all the solemnity of children we would debate whether the nectarine was superior to the peach and whether the great black grapes could surpass the muscats. At Clifton Uncle Will gave us our first bicycles and as soon as we had learned to ride them we were allowed to accompany him on his rides before breakfast—on weekdays the 'trivial round', on Sundays a longer journey, for he was free of his duties. He was afraid of growing too fat and the bicycle was the most convenient form of exercise. On weekdays after breakfast he would drive himself or be driven in a dog-cart to his court and we, my brother and myself, would spend long days playing endless games of cricket in the garden. On some days there were greater thrills. If Nottinghamshire was playing a home match we two boys would be driven in the dog-cart to Trent Bridge and there, sitting on the top of the pavilion, we would watch every ball that was bowled. And what a side Notts. were! J.A. Dixon and A.O. Jones were the two leading amateurs, with Arthur Shrewsbury, William and John Gunn to back them. Oates was the wicket-keeper and Tom Wass the fast bowler. It is curious, if one has a good visual memory, how a man's bowling action stays fast in the mind. I believe that, were it possible to see them, I could name most of the bowlers I have seen and played with over fifty years, even though their faces were all masked. The same is true of the lawn-tennis

players; disguise them in their dress and mask their faces—
their shots would still at once betray them. Perhaps today this is
less true than formerly, for the service at least, like many other
things in life, has tended to become stereotyped. Occasionally
there were even greater thrills than a visit to Trent Bridge.
When visiting sides came to Nottingham some two or three of
the amateurs would sometimes stay with my uncle. On one
memorable occasion G. L. Jessop, Sewell, and another whom I
have forgotten were staying at the Old Rectory and in the
evening they strolled out to watch us playing cricket on the
lawn. Afterwards Gilbert Jessop sent a book to my brother and
myself from the Yorkshire ground where he was playing his
next match. It was called *Giants of the Game* and I have it still
with the card which he wrote to us stuck inside. Small wonder
that he became the first of all our cricket heroes!

Uncle Will had many claims to be considered the perfect
uncle. He had a notable stamp collection which received some
notice in *The Times* when it was sold after his death, he was
Master of the Skinners' Company and several of the great
square boxes of sweetmeats which the Company used to present
to its guests found their way to his nephews. He must too have
been a very good lawyer. He was County Court Judge at
Nottingham for eleven years during which time, as the Nottingham papers recorded, no single one of his judgements was upset
on appeal. He died at the early age of fifty-seven when I was
twelve years old.

The other uncle of whom I spoke had a much greater effect
on my life. My Mother's second brother, Thomas Bridges
Hughes, had a rather curious career—curious because of the
things which he had failed, or rather omitted to do. Like his
father he was Prefect of Hall at Winchester and both there and
at New College he had many triumphs both in the Schools
and on the playing fields. Though a notable cricketer he did not
get into the University side, but he played in the first University
soccer match and in that Oxford side which won the F.A. cup.
In 1874, a year after the Law School list was separated from
that of Modern History, his name stood alone in the First Class.
The examiners were the formidable trio of Dicey, Holland, and
Maine. He was called to the Bar and then abandoned all
pursuit of the glittering prizes of success. Instead he became and

remained throughout his working life, a preparatory-school master at Evelyns, where the headmaster was his cousin Godfrey Worsley. The truth seems to be that he was without ambition and that he disliked responsibility, belonging in fact to that class of men who, in wartime, although competent and utterly reliable, refuse to take a commission and serve with complete self-abnegation and devotion in the ranks. Even at Evelyns he resolutely refused on more than one occasion to take a partnership, preferring to remain an assistant master. All that was clear to me very much later. He spent a part of most of his holidays with us and at the time he represented to me exactly the sort of man that I wished to be and I took immense pride when I was told that I was very like him. He taught me not only to love books and reading but also to love games and the men who played them. He lived until 1940, becoming gradually less the uncle and more the confidant and friend.

When does childhood end and boyhood begin—that 'mournful period of boyhood', as Disraeli terms it, 'when eccentricities excite attention and command no sympathy'? Perhaps there is no clear dividing line, but with arrival at school the period of childhood is certainly over. My own school-days were not mournful, for I shunned eccentricities—indeed I was almost obsessively anxious to conform to expected standards and to do the right thing—but I cannot say that school-days were the happiest days of my life. Holidays were immensely more agreeable than term time. In my preparatory school I was fortunate. Godfrey Worsley, the headmaster at Evelyns, was my grandmother's first cousin and his school at that time one of the leading preparatory schools in the country. I was too young to appreciate two things; the first that my parents were determined to give my brother and myself the best education which was to be had, the second that money was scarce and that sacrifices had to be made if this was to be done. My Father gave up his club and drank only beer instead of wines or spirits, my Mother spent hardly anything upon herself. Such things were never mentioned and my parents took no credit for what seemed to them natural and inevitable sacrifices, but it would be a failure of *pietas* not to remember and record the debt. I went to Evelyns when I was about nine and I think that Godfrey

Worsley generously remitted a great part of the fees for my brother and myself. He himself was a formidable figure. He had no degree, for his early life had been spent in Canada. In appearance he seemed to the boys like an incarnation of God the Father—with a long white beard above a tweed knicker-bocker suit with stockings and spats. His vacations were devoted to golf and shooting but on Sundays when he preached to us in Chapel he had all the dignity and conviction of the clerical family from which he sprang. His staff was carefully chosen and packed with good and able men. My uncle Tom was the second master and even after seventy years I can recall how sound the teaching was.

A preparatory school at the turn of the century was a strange mixture of the hard and the easy life. Of course we were well housed and reasonably well fed (though we thought not), but we always started the day with a plunge into a rather cold swimming-bath, at 6.30 in the summer and 7 in the winter, and the classrooms were grim and cheerless, lacking the bright fittings and pictures of today. The gaslights and their smell and the carpetless passages are a vivid memory. No sweets were allowed and hampers, except gifts of fruit, were banned. Out-side events touched us little. We were too young to discuss the rights and wrongs of the Boers and the war for us was chiefly a matter of collecting boxes and emblems which bore the portraits of the Generals—Buller, White, Methuen, Baden-Powell, and the rest. The copies of the *Illustrated London News* in the library made Rorke's Drift and Omdurman as near to us as Colenso or the relief of Ladysmith. The death of Queen Victoria seemed like the end of an age but our interest in it was quickly swallowed up in excited anticipation of the Coronation. When the time came we were promised leave for three or four days and great was our despondency when the news of the King's illness began to trickle through to us. Godfrey Worsley assembled the school and told us in grave and measured tones of the monarch's dangerous illness—for appendicitis was then regarded with fear and awe. 'But', he said, 'I have decided that as your parents expect you, you shall be allowed to have your holiday as arranged.' Boylike we unthinkingly began to cheer and were sternly reproved for our insensitivity and lack of proper feeling for our beloved monarch.

A modern observer would probably condemn the school as a hotbed of snobbery and class prejudice. It is true that save for a thin stream of Wykehamists and Harrovians everyone was being prepared for Eton. It is true also that we had an instinctive, or perhaps inherited, feeling that, as gentlemen, we were to some extent above and better than our less fortunate contemporaries. But our snobbery was not of the obnoxious kind. Boys are usually shrewd judges of character and character was a better passport to respect than rank or wealth. Worsley always refused 'royalty' for the school out of mistrust of the effect which the presence of royal personages might have on the rest of the school. As for wealth, that in 1900 was suspect. No boy would have liked to admit that his parents had made their money in recent years by trade or business. Still, when all allowances are made it was a snobbish and restricted world. Had we been older that would have done us harm; as it was it made no sort of difference to us. We were in fact quite unconscious of it.

At Evelyns occurred the first great crisis in my life. There had never been any question in the family about the future career of my brother Chris and myself. He would go to Winchester and Oxford and then either take Orders or pass into one of the learned professions. I should follow my Father into the Navy after a couple of years at Bradfield, a school which was then gaining a high reputation under Dr. Grey. Did I ever express my wish to go into the Navy? If so, I have totally forgotten the occasion, though probably when I was very small I had declared that I should follow in my Father's footsteps. At any rate when my school-days came it was simply assumed that I should find my career in the Navy and I have no doubt at all that both parents fondly imagined that I was keenly anxious to do so. It is almost impossible, after nearly seventy years, to describe my own feelings at that time with accuracy, but the attempt must be made. I was very shy, very reserved, and very reticent. I envied my fellows who were bound for Eton or Winchester for I looked forward to the experience of a public school; the thought of the Navy was so distant a prospect that I hardly considered it; characteristically I put it out of my mind or, ostrich-like, buried my head in the sand. I was living in the present and took little or no thought for the future. Then the blow fell. In 1902 the Selborne scheme for naval training was announced. My parents were overjoyed and assumed that I should be also. I should be able to start my naval career three years earlier than had been expected, the expense and difficulties of a public school would be spared. All in fact was very right in the world. Nowadays, in a world of psychologists and psychiatrists my inclinations and potentialities would, doubtless, have been discovered and exposed; a properly fed computer would, I believe, have brought out the answer that I was to go to Oxford but the computer was still unthought of. This of course was the moment when I should have spoken but I kept silent and allowed events to take their course, which they did swiftly. A Navy class was hastily formed at Evelyns for some three or four of us; my Father got a nomination for me from the Admiralty in January and in June I faced a board of selectors at the Admiralty. I came away with no tale of a bright remark made to impress the board but suffered a terrible feeling of embarrassment when I was told to go out after the interview and saw three doors before me. Luckily I chose the right one. Some sort of qualifying examination followed and in due course I received my orders to join at Osborne in September. I was twelve and a half years old.

III

OSBORNE AND DARTMOUTH

The old know what they want,
The young are sad and bewildered.

LOGAN PEARSALL SMITH

AT the turn of the century the Navy was still in the 'spit and
polish' era. Appearances were everything, gunnery and
torpedo work were as much neglected as the study of war plans
and naval strategy. Only a small band including Percy Scott,[1]
centred round 'Jacky' Fisher, then C.-in-C. Mediterranean,
pressed ardently for reform. Fisher resigned his post as C.-in-C.
Mediterranean, where he was a full admiral, to replace a rear-
admiral at Whitehall as Second Sea Lord in 1902. He was
C.-in-C. Portsmouth in 1903 and First Sea Lord in 1904, an
appointment which he held until January 1910. Nowadays few
would deny that in those years a great constructive revolution
was carried out, and that in a service rendered by its traditions
one of the most conservative in the world. It is strange that this
revolution, which saved the country in the 1914 war, has had to
wait for more than fifty years for an adequate and definitive
history, and that it should have been left to an American
historian holding a Chair in Hawaii, and later in California to
supply the essential book.[2] The reforms began with personnel
reforms, the most important of which was the Selborne[3]
scheme announced in 1902. The crux of the scheme was a
system of common entry and training for all executive officers,
engineers, and marines. These were to be trained at the newly
established Royal Naval Colleges of Osborne and Dartmouth
(two years at each) and in the following four to five years as
cadets, midshipmen, and sub-lieutenants first in a training
ship and then in ships of the Fleet. Behind all the reforms lay

[1] Captain, later Admiral Sir Percy Scott (1853–1924).
[2] *From the Dreadnought to Scapa Flow*, by A.J. Marder.
[3] The second Earl of Selborne (1859–1942), First Lord of the Admiralty 1900–5.

the mechanization of the Navy. The new-style cadets were to spend about one-third of their time at the Naval colleges in theoretical and practical engineering. Ewing, the newly appointed Director of Naval Education, had held professorships at Tokyo, Dundee, and Cambridge and was a dedicated and gifted engineer. His new scheme of education, which applied to the entire Navy, had as its primary objective to make every man in H.M. ships a stoker and a mechanic.

This was indeed an educational experiment of great importance. It owed much to Selborne, much more to Ewing,[4] but the driving force throughout was that of Fisher. And what a driving force! A decision to build a college at Osborne was taken in December 1902; the first spade was put into the ground in March 1903; the buildings were opened by His Majesty the King on 4 August; the first-term cadets, seventy-five of them, joined on 15 September. Had Fisher not had himself made C.-in-C. at Portsmouth it could never have been done. All this is a matter of history and need not be elaborated, but it seems necessary to explain what the prospect was for the first term of seventy-five cadets—the first term at Osborne, and two years later the first term at Dartmouth. In one sense we were pioneers, in another the guinea-pigs of a great experiment. How, then, did Osborne look through the eyes of a guinea-pig? Certainly much was expected of us. The Captain, Rosslyn Wemyss,[5] wrote in the first number of the *Osborne Magazine* (December 1903):

These last three months have been the beginning of the new naval officer, and on the foundation of this term will rest the structure of tradition for the new Navy. . . . It is impossible to impress too strongly on the cadets how much depends upon them . . . *they* it is who will give it its tone for years to come and create the traditions which will be handed down to future generations.

Truly a formidable task to entrust to boys of such tender years. Our average age was 12 years 7 months; height 4′ 10½″; weight 5 stone 9 lb; chest measurement 25⅓″.

We, the guinea-pigs, were of course only dimly conscious of

[4] Sir Alfred Ewing (1855–1935), Director of Naval Education 1903–16, then Principal and Vice-Chancellor, Edinburgh University, 1916–29.
[5] Later Lord Wester Wemyss and Admiral of the Fleet (1864–1933), first Captain of Osborne, 1903–5, replaced Jellicoe as First Sea Lord 1917.

all these great matters. It was enough to try to realize that we were not only schoolboys but also budding naval officers, for we could not fail to see that we were of interest to a great many important people. Educational theorists and practitioners as well as naval officers were constantly visiting us and we were inspected many times in the term. An official inspection by Jacky Fisher was followed by a private visit from King Edward VII and then by a visit from the Prince and Princess of Wales. We were even transported *en masse* to Portsmouth to be a guard of honour for the visiting King of Italy, and a special committee from the U.S.A. came and 'dissected' Osborne to the most minute detail. Few guinea-pigs can have been so carefully and constantly scrutinized by the researchers as were we! It was also apparent to us that Osborne was unlike an ordinary school because our daily lives were ordered and controlled by naval officers and only our studies entrusted to the care of the masters. This division of authority, but for the fact that the staff was hand picked, might well have caused trouble, and there was, I think, at the beginning a tendency on the part of the officers to regard the masters as rather second-class citizens, or 'schoolies' as the old naval instructors had sometimes been termed, but the awkwardness, if awkwardness it was, soon died away both at Osborne and Dartmouth. Still in 1903 there was no doubt that the cadets looked up to the officers as being finer and much more magnificent than the masters. My own feelings were mixed. To me the officers seemed to be god-like beings for whom I felt immense admiration—but it was admiration and not envy. Instinctively I was much more drawn towards the masters because they came from those desirable places where my hopes were fixed—Oxford and Cambridge—and because they, or some of them, were chiefly interested in those subjects to which my mind was attuned. At the start the post of a master cannot have been wholly satisfactory, for much of the reward of a schoolmaster's life comes from his interest in and care for his pupils, quite apart from his teaching in class. The masters must have missed this part of their normal activities, the more so because they were better equipped than the officers for this task. After all a naval officer must have found it strange to be put in charge of twelve-year-old schoolboys. In my first term the Captain, seeing me alone, told me to walk with him across the playing fields. I was filled with apprehension, which grew when I realized that he was taking the opportunity to give me advice which would be useful to me throughout my life. 'Never lend money to your friends' was his first admonition. This left me cold, for I had no money and by then not very many friends. His next pronouncement was more helpful: 'When you are in a company of people let others talk and only intervene when you know as much about the subject as they do.' I was twelve and a half and he was already a great man (later in 1917 to succeed Jellicoe as First Sea Lord) so for the rest of the walk the conversation was one-sided. Yet it was good advice and I have often felt indebted to him for it, though it was only long afterwards that I realized that he had been practising his technique of training the young on me.

It would not be true to say that I was unhappy during my two years at Osborne. There were good and firm friends; there were games, and still better those few hours which could be spared for the study of 'History and English'; the strict discipline and the use of every available minute for one activity or another suited me; best of all there were the holidays (even though we had to call them leave) which were times of undiluted pleasure. But over all there hung a cloud, at the beginning no bigger than a man's hand, which was to grow till it obscured my whole sky. It was simply my conviction that I had embarked on the wrong career and that a mechanized Navy was not the place for me. I saw the danger but how could I escape it?

In September 1905 our term,[6] now reduced to about sixty-three, was transferred to Dartmouth, where once more we were to start a new college and help to form its traditions. The conditions, however, were different from those in 1903, for there was much more continuity. With us to Dartmouth went three officers and eleven masters, including Ashford,

---

[6] The record of this first term under the new scheme was remarkable. Though thirteen died in or before the First War six reached Flag rank as Admirals, one became an Air Marshal, another an Air Vice-Marshal. Between them they amassed thirty-nine decorations which included ten D.S.O.s and eight D.S.C.s. A reunion luncheon was held in September 1973 to celebrate the seventieth year of our joining at Osborne, and this was attended by six of the nine survivors. Celebrations of fifty or even sixty years are common, but one of a seventy-year span must be unusual, if not unique.

the headmaster. In addition we inherited the playing grounds and shore establishments of the old *Britannia* and took in a term of cadets entered under the old scheme. They, of course, had not been at Osborne but they were older than we were and would go to sea a year before us. Four of us (or was it six, I have forgotten) had orders as cadet captains to join a day early, and I felt some trepidation when I learned that I was to be cadet captain to the old entry term. That was a prospect which gave me no pleasure. I joined, therefore, in a state of depression, full of anxieties, doubts, and forebodings. A walk round the grounds afforded a gleam of light for we chanced on the racket-courts half-way down the hill between the college and the Sand-quay workshops. There is no forgetting the thrill which the sight of those courts gave me. My happiest hours at Dartmouth were spent in those courts, and rackets gave me much more than temporary pleasure. The necessity for quick decision, the need to take risks, the very pace of the game, the need for con-centration, and the need to forget the watchers in the gallery above all combined to build up my morale and to bring me to trust to myself rather than to others. In different circumstances cricket might have done it for me too, but cricket at Dart-mouth did not then hold the position which it should have. Rugby football was very much the Navy game, but cricket was hardly more important than boat sailing, boxing, and gym-nastics. Furthermore, since in theory we played as 'the Ship' many of the sides in the summer were composed of officers and masters together with a few cadets. It was difficult to get a 'cadets only' eleven together as a team or to feel that one had a real responsibility to do so. There was an ominous sentence in a schedule of education drawn up by Fisher, Ewing, and Ashford[7] before the colleges were opened: 'Cricket, football, and other games will be taught, not merely left to the boys to pick up.'

At Dartmouth the pace was greater and the pressure more severe than at Osborne. As Hughes puts it in his *The R.N.C. Dartmouth*, 'There can be little doubt that in the early days of Osborne (and Dartmouth) cadets were hustled too much. The limited time allowed for saying their prayers and brushing their

---

[7] Sir Cyril Ernest Ashford (1867–1951), Headmaster of Osborne to 1905, of Dartmouth 1905–27.

teeth (almost by numbers) made for neither godliness nor clean-liness. Everything was done at the double, whether there was need for haste or not.' Inevitably those subjects which attracted me least assumed more and more importance. If in the time-table a quarter of the available hours are given to engineering in the workshops, if many hours must be devoted to drill and physical exercises, if many more go to science and applied mathematics, and if navigation and seamanship have also to be studied, it stands to reason that little time is left for literary and humane studies.

Yet on this subject I must be fair. The teaching in history and English and in languages was always excellent and in some cases brilliant—nor was it the intention of the architects of the New Scheme to confine us to technical subjects. The truth is that Fisher wanted to have the best of both worlds—to have young officers liberally educated and also trained to a high standard in technical matters—and he very nearly brought it off. Much though I rebelled (in secret) I believe that he was right, for he foresaw the inevitable war, and always insisted that the Navy must be trained for war and ready for war at a moment's notice. For that contingency early training was a necessity and the interest of individuals was of no consequence compared with the national need. Whether entry at twelve and a half and a strictly naval training was the best method of turning out officers with initiative is another question. Probably the plan of introducing an extra public-school entry, as Churchill did in 1912, at seventeen was the best solution. The public-school boys brought in fresh blood and were an incentive to those who had entered earlier.

What of my cloud? Alas! it grew with each succeeding term. Physically I was a late developer, small and not strong, and I found the pressure almost overwhelming. In early days at Osborne I had usually been about third in the weekly mark list, but I passed out sixth. At Dartmouth I could only keep my place by very, perhaps excessive, hard work. I felt that I was slipping and knew that when the time came to go to sea I should probably slip further. Steadily I became more and more convinced that I must, somehow, change my profession. During my last summer term I so far screwed up my courage as to tell my parents something, but not enough, of my difficulties. The result might have been expected. They thought that my troubles were temporary, they knew that I had done my best and that the loss of a few places was of no great moment; when I went to sea I would surely find compensation in new scenes and fresh tasks; in any case I must try out life in the training cruiser and take no hasty or rash decision. To one master at Dartmouth I had also opened my mind. The Revd. E. H. Arkwright had been one of the original band of masters at Osborne and had come on to Dartmouth as second master to Ashford. A born school-master he had observed my progress and my anxieties, although he was not my tutor, and he sensed some of my shortcomings as well as my capabilities.

Once in the summer of 1907 he took me out sailing in his dinghy on the river and after a time handed over the helm to me. 'Ought I to go about now?' I asked as we neared the shore.

'You are in charge,' he replied, and at the end of the day a terse comment: 'Sometimes one must decide things for oneself.' He was a sound counsellor. In one letter he wrote to me: 'After all, we possess one thing in common, the gorgeous (quel adjectif, mon Dieu!) power of reticence, and it binds, if I may say so, tighter than speech.' In the course of the summer he had a talk with my Mother, but for the time being my fate seemed sealed; I must go to H.M.S. *Cumberland* for the two terms' cruise as a sea-going cadet.

IV

THE NAVY

The Royal Navy of England hath ever been its greatest defence and ornament; it is its ancient and natural strength; the floating bulwark of the island.

SIR WILLIAM BLACKSTONE

THOSE two terms are, in my mind, a medley of blurred recollections. Learning to lash a hammock with the correct seven turns; diving (much against my inclination) from the quarter-deck; playing hockey on the parade ground at Port Mahon where the Spanish Horse artillery and Mounted Mule battery provided a considerable hazard if one strayed too far; reading Kipling in the few spare moments late at night, and realizing that the water was indeed black because it was so deep; best of all the first sight of the Bay of Syracuse, where history seemed to come alive; Malta and Algiers and Gibraltar, Vesuvius and Pompeii and Vigo. In the days of package tours almost everyone finds the way to the Mediterranean, but sixty years ago only the wealthy could expect to go there, and we were lucky to see so much of the world in two short cruises. Did my parents hope, or perhaps expect, that this good fortune would make me change my mind?

It was not so, for the desire to escape became steadily stronger. One of my term mates, Chris Arnold-Forster,[1] was in the same predicament as myself, though his portion was perhaps even less happy than mine, for his father had been Secretary of the Admiralty, and representative of the Admiralty under Selborne and had been actively engaged in pushing through the new scheme. He became later Secretary of State for War. For Chris to withdraw was even more difficult than for me. At Gibraltar at the beginning of our second cruise, we talked over the position and from there I wrote the decisive letter. In fact

[1] Cmdr. Hugh Christopher Arnold-Forster (1890–1965), Assistant Director of Naval Intelligence 1942–5.

I asked my Father if he would withdraw me—under any conditions which he might wish to impose. Under the prevailing conditions no midshipman could retire—he could only be withdrawn by his parents. I wrote also to other relatives and to Arkwright. The answers, when they came, almost brought me to surrender. 'I cannot tell you,' my Father wrote in his opening sentence, 'what grief your letter gave to your Mother and myself.' They had both, he continued, thought that my distaste for some things in naval life had passed, and they had 'rejoiced' over my cheerful letters during the first cruise. Nor had I said anything when on leave at Christmas to disabuse him of this belief. He spoke of the prestige of the Service, of the honour of belonging to it, and even so far broke through his habitual reticence as to mention the troubles and inconveniences which he had to contend with in his own youth. I must struggle through as he had. There was, too, the clinching argument: 'I cannot afford to start you afresh in another profession, and if I were in a position to do so I am sure that in after life you would regret having changed, and would blame me for having allowed you to do so.' My Mother took the same view: 'We are trying to persuade you to stick to your post, not from a selfish motive at all, nor to save ourselves the disappointment— though I confess it would be a very bitter one to us both—but really because we believe in years to come you will look back upon it as a wise decision.' My brother, who understood my feelings better than anyone else, thought that I was justified in trying to change my profession but thought too that, in the family circumstances, it would be impossible for me to do so. Even Arkwright could give me little comfort. He would not chill my ambition, but it was a moral question as to whether he could advise anyone to oppose his father; he would, however, go to see my Mother and talk it over with her.

That was my blackest hour and almost I surrendered, but not quite. I like to think that my motives were not wholly based on obstinacy or selfishness or upon my realization of any inadequacies as a naval officer, but rather on the conviction that I had some talents which could be useful in the appropriate sphere. Most of all the strong but irrational desire to get to Oxford urged me on. Once I had broken silence the dam was breached and I poured out all my doubts and wishes. My letters, fortunately, have perished but I still have a little bundle of the replies which have one common feature. At no time did anyone blame or reprove me—each one was only anxious to do what was best for me—and gradually my Mother began to come round. At the end of February she wrote: 'We will have a good talk "over a pipe", as Father says, when you come home . . . I am so thankful that we are not a divided family. . . .' In short it was agreed that I should, at least, be allowed to put my case when the second cruise ended. The cruise ended in mid-April and we had our final examination. Passing-out lists depended on the results of the examinations at the end of our Dartmouth time and at the end of the cruises, and eight of us scored three 'ones'. I was seventh, with a first prize for English and for Scripture Knowledge (my term mates must have been an ungodly bunch).

I cannot remember how I contrived to win over my parents during my leave, but somehow the miracle was performed. I must go to sea as a midshipman and they hoped still that I would change my mind; if I did not my Father would go to the Admiralty in July, and ask that I should be withdrawn. One hidden reef remained. Would the Admiralty agree to waive the repayment of the moneys which they had spent on me? If they did not agree it would be impossible for me to be withdrawn. In the event my Father called at the Admiralty in mid-July and sent in the application on the next day. After an agonizing wait notification of my release came on 1 September. Meantime I joined *Britannia* in the Channel Fleet. She was one of the King Edward VII class, the last of the pre-Dreadnought battleships.

The life of a 'snotty' in 1908 was not a bed of roses, and the outlook was in some ways ominous for me since, as the first term trained under the new scheme, we were exposed to criticism on every side. A majority of officers both senior and junior thought that the 'new scheme' cadets had been pampered, and that it was even more necessary than heretofore for 'junior snotties to be shaken'. This attitude towards the new scheme persisted for a long time. One of my term mates wrote to me in 1912:

I am still doddering along as an underpaid and overworked sub. I've been in destroyers ever since I was promoted, and like it as much as it is possible to like anything in the service. The Commodore, Arbuthnot, is the deuce of a 'nut' and once upon a time the terror of every snotty he met—he doesn't give us much rest and is terribly down on New Scheme subs. but he is quite straight and doesn't bully one. I've got an awful drunken little stiff of a skipper, who I fight with every day, but as he sleeps for 14 hours out of his twenty-four, he doesn't worry me too much.

Charles Morgan,[2] the author, who entered Osborne three years after me, recounted his experiences in *The Gunroom*, published in 1919. This work, which was mainly autobiographical, gave a lurid account of gunroom life in the years before the First War. Here is one of the more attractive characters, a captain, speaking.

Give them boys, as fine human material as is to be found in the world, and for four and a half years they educate them magnificently. Then, before they are eighteen, when their minds are in a most impressionable stage, these boys are sent to sea. They are subjected to persecution; they are flogged continually for no specific wrong-doing; they are deprived of all opportunity for solitude or thought; they are put in a crowded mess where they are cut off from intimate association with men older than themselves, from women of their own kind, from art and culture, from trees and birds, from all legitimate amusement.

Morgan himself was 'rescued' from the Navy by Chris Arnold-Forster, who appears in the book under the name of Hartington. I believe that Charles Morgan greatly exaggerated the persecution which he underwent, but I cannot but agree with some of his other criticisms. Everyone was forced into a mould; there was a discipline of iron, and a requirement of absolute efficiency, which pardoned no faults and forgot no weaknesses. I am clear, too, that we were overworked. To run a duty boat, and to keep watches, together with all the multifarious duties of a midshipman at the same time that work had to be done in preparation for his next examination was too great a strain for boys of seventeen, even if they were supposed to have reached a premature manhood.

We, however, were fortunate for we carried no senior snotties on board, and therefore escaped all that persecution which is

---

[2] Charles Morgan (1894–1958) entered the Navy as a cadet in 1907, served in Atlantic and China 1911–13 and throughout the 1914–18 war.

described in *The Gunroom.* On board most ships at the time
'Little Benjamin, our Ruler', a stout but whippy stick, was
in almost daily use, but it was not so with us, for our sub was a
civilized and humane person. I was beaten only once—for leaving the compass uncovered when at sea—and I cannot remember how many cuts I received. I was convinced that I had not
been responsible for the alleged crime, but it never occurred to
me to question the justice or propriety of the sentence. Someone
had blundered and someone must be punished. Nor did a singularly painful experience make me an opponent of corporal
punishment; it might indeed be damaging to the morals of
certain of the more sensitive—it was doubtless beneficial to the
majority. I did feel, though, that I hated the thought of having
to inflict the punishment myself.

For the rest, my four months in the gunroom has left a
medley of confused memories, most of them connected with
my own inefficiency. In the early morning, sent to bring the
beef on board I almost carried away my mast and had to pull
in to the shore instead. For this my shore leave was stopped for
a month—a punishment which made little difference to me as I
was quickly taught how the signature of the officer responsible
for signing leave chits could be forged. Though all knowledge
is worth having, this particular skill has not been used by me in
later years. Again I remember searching aimlessly and unsuccessfully for a torpedo lost in Lulworth Cove and, more vividly,
being towed back by the steam pinnace when I had hopelessly
miscalculated the set of the tide in Cowes Bay—a humiliating
experience. There was, however, one pleasing interlude. Before
we joined *Britannia* we had reached the final of the Fleet golf
competition, and orders came that the gunroom was to supply
two players for the final on one of the Weymouth courses. *The
Times* reported the match, under the heading 'The Channel
Fleet', as follows:

The final round for the Challenge Cup in the inter-ship competition
was decided . . . on the morning of the day of leaving Portland.
H.M.S. *Britannia* won by ½ point, H.M.S. *Hibernia* being the 'runner-
up'. While at Christiania, Lord Charles Beresford presented the cup
to the winning team . . . Engineer-Commander Hart, Rev. Hewet-
son, Lieut. Henderson, Capt. Morgan, Lieut. Hamilton, Midshipman Tennant, Midshipman Masterman, and Surgeon Braithwaite.

I played atrociously, but fortunately my opponent was equally incompetent, so that a halved match was a fair result. How many cuts I should have received had I lost it is not now possible to guess, but I think that they would have been many, for the Navy demanded success and had no pardon for failure.

In the middle of the summer the Fleet went to Norway and Denmark for the summer cruise. This I can reconstruct with tolerable accuracy, for all junior officers afloat were required to keep a daily journal. How in the cramped space and turmoil of the gunroom we contrived to keep this daily record both accurately and neatly I cannot comprehend; perhaps the fact that the journal had to be initialled by the Captain at stated intervals and that it carried marks at the annual examination in Seamanship and Pilotage may have had something to do with the work which we put into it. Track charts had to be inserted for all voyages.

The movements of the Fleet always excited interest. At Dover the Fleet had been visited by the French President; at Christiania ships were manned and dressed and salutes of twenty-one guns were fired for the King and Queen of Norway. Later on when the Fleet was in Aalbeck Bight there was a less welcome visitor. I entered in my journal:

At 7.30 the *Hohenzollern*, flying the royal standard of Germany, and attended by the cruiser *Stettin* and a despatch vessel, appeared from the southward. As she approached the fleet royal salutes of 21 guns were fired by all ships. The *Hohenzollern* and her escort steamed through this, ships being manned and dressed. Three cheers were given as she passed each ship. She then turned and, steaming back again, shaped course to the northward.

I wonder if the cheers were whole-hearted. At the end of the cruise a week was spent in manoeuvres. The plan of the manoeuvres was outlined both to the ship's company and to the officers, and I made a summary of it in my journal. The details are now of no importance, but one fact stands out. The Blue Fleet commanded by Lord Charles Beresford was based on Norway and was expecting an attack from the Red Fleet coming from the west. The C.-in-C. had expected that the two halves of the Red Fleet would join by way of the straits between the Orkneys and Shetlands and had therefore taken the Fleet northward. At the same time the Straits of Dover was watched by the *Duke of Edinburgh*. In the event wireless communication broke down and the C.-in-C. withdrew the Blue Fleet to its base on the western coast of Norway. Is there a hint here that 'communications' were to be the weak link in time of war?

My captain was utterly unable to understand my wish to withdraw. 'How', he asked me, 'could I possibly prefer a sedentary life to a life in the Royal Navy?' But he played the game and I left carrying a chit which certified that I had served as midshipman under his command from 4 May to 10 September 1908 and that I had conducted myself 'with sobriety and in every way satisfactorily'. So ended my naval career—almost to a day five years after it had begun. I was seventeen years and eight months old.

This moment, as I left the Navy, seems the right time to take what is now called a cold hard look at myself. I should not have been a good naval officer. In the first place I shunned responsibility. One of the more percipient of my term mates at Osborne gave me, for a time, the nickname of 'Timid'—and never have I hated any nickname more, because it contained an element of truth. He did not, I believe, suggest that I had less than the normal supply of courage but only that I would hesitate between two opinions and, in the end, tend to take the more cautious line of action. That was sadly, but quite certainly, true. 'Safety first' is no bad motto for a motorist but it is ill-suited to a naval officer. In wartime my inability to translate thought into immediate and effective action might have been an even greater handicap, for, as Bertrand Russell put it, victory in war comes to those who have the most certainty about things in which doubt is the only rational attitude. Furthermore experience had already shown me that I was attracted, from the naval point of view, by the wrong things. I revelled in the old things and rejected the new; at Malta, for example, I would find far less interest in the Fleet lying in the Grand Harbour than in the records of the Knights, or the stories of the great siege. For a mechanized modern Navy I was temperamentally and intellectually unfitted.

Yet there is something to be said on the other side. It is true that I should not have been a good naval officer; it is also true that I should not have been a bad one. My judgement was good,

I was (then) industrious with a compulsive need to complete any task which I undertook. Early in life I had experienced the need for discipline and realized (as few do nowadays) that no system of education is a sound system without it. I had learned how to work and how to obey. I had, too, during my five years of training acquired a great admiration for the Navy—an admiration which I have never lost and which had grown steadily the more clearly I recognized that such talents as I had were better adapted to some other career. So I believe (though who can judge himself?) that I should not have been a *bad* naval officer, and that, given good leadership, I might have been at least up to the average—but that was not enough.

Since that time a good deal of responsibility has come my way and I no longer dislike or reject it with the old vehemence. Perhaps it is a criticism of the 'early entry' that we were cast into a mould too soon and that this stifled initiative. In my case this explanation does not appear to be valid. Caution, the desire to do the right thing, the tendency to hesitate between opinions, excessive reticence, all those things would have cramped me in my career, and even now I am not wholly free from them. Goethe's words were for me painfully true. 'Thought is easy, action is difficult, to translate thought into action is the hardest thing of all'—but it is the essential qualification for the naval officer.

V

GETTING TO OXFORD

If you are determined to get it you will find a way.

MAZZINI

ELEVEN days after I stepped ashore at Portsmouth I was at
work with a crammer in Westgate. There was, indeed, no
time to waste. It had been agreed that I was to have my chance
of going to Oxford but I could only do so if I could win a
scholarship there; otherwise the plan was financially impossible.
My chances in the cold light of reason were far from rosy. I
knew a good deal about ships and guns, about engine rooms and
boilers, about navigation and the mathematics which lay
behind that science—but very little else. But I must try for a
scholarship in history, for that was the only subject which
offered me any hope of success. In addition I must, by the end
of the year, pass Responsions, an examination which in those
days meant Greek as well as Latin. Of the latter I had a good
grounding at Evelyns, but the former I had only just started
and I had, of course, abandoned both at the age of twelve. In
spite of this daunting prospect I felt a sense of freedom—and
oddly enough, of confidence; for the first time I was to spend all
my working hours on subjects which I had always wished to
study. I do not doubt that the elements of science, and especially
a scientific method of thinking, should be taught to all, but
sometimes when I have read or heard the bitter complaints of
the scientifically minded that they are condemned to the useless
study of the classics or other literary studies I have been tempted
to enlarge upon the unease, sometimes verging on despair and
bitter frustration, into which one would-be humanist, whose
bent was literary, faced the demands of a scientific curriculum.

Once more fortune was with me. P.B. Allen, who taught me
at Westgate, was a devoted and single-minded teacher and had
the additional and rare gift of understanding his own limitations.

He gave me his time unstintedly and sent me also to another coach in the town, P. E. Roberts. Paul Roberts, after a brilliant Oxford career, and a few years as secretary to Sir William Hunter to assist in the writing of the *History of India*, had been stricken by illness and ordered to live in the Isle of Thanet. Once a week I went to him and learned how an essay should be written; those who were his pupils later at Oxford will know that I could have had no better tutor. But for him (and without lowering my debt to Allen) I should, I think, never have won my scholarship. That was the thought in my mind when, in 1947, Paul Roberts as Vice-Provost admitted me as Provost of Worcester in the College Chapel.

My terms at Westgate were happy ones—much happier than those of my fellow-pupils, who were struggling for pass examinations or for an Army entrance. Toughened by the Navy I used to bathe before breakfast every day until and including 5 November, when a light powdering of snow on the edge of the sands warned me that it was time to desist. I grew physically as well as mentally and the hours of so-called work were in fact hours of recreation. In April of 1909 I was to make my first attempt at Oxford.

It seems strange that I had only visited Oxford once before in my life at the turn of the century. Of that visit I have an oddly clear recollection, and this is a true recollection and not a 'recovered memory' as many recollections are. The stray letter which has been preserved, a note in a diary or in a book of some other person will recall the fact, but that is only a re-covered memory, consciously brought back to life. When I was a preparatory-school boy we used usually to go to the seaside— such was the phrase used then—for the month of August, but occasionally we stayed at home at Heathcroft. When we were at home it was part of our routine to bicycle over to Wellington College and bathe of a morning in the outdoor swimming-bath there. That was considered a great pleasure and so—sometimes—it was. But not always. Adults could swim and dive so much better than a skinny little ten-year-old that a good hot sun alone could make the exercise really agreeable. Even so the Wellington bath was preferable to the bathes which we had when at the seaside. There we had to use those dark and gloomy bathing-machines which an aged horse

would draw into the sea—and after a long interval bring us back
to land. In the interval we should have made the descent from
the machine into the cold and hostile sea, clad in those full-
length bathing-suits, which seemed always to be clammy even
when they were supposedly dry. And in the machine the same
inappropriate advertisement always met the eye:

> If you want a good cigar that's not too mild or full
> Try the happy medium—the Flor de Dindigul.

Surely the Wellington bath was the happier choice! Among
those who bathed at Wellington was a preparatory-school
master who spent his holidays in our village, and he it was who
invited my brother and myself over to Oxford. In Jack Slessor's
book of reminiscences,[1] I note that the same master introduced
him to the pleasures of bathing. The journey to Oxford, in
1901 or 1902, was an expedition that required some planning.
We would bicycle to Blackwater station and proceed by the old
S.E. & C.R. railway to Reading—there we would change
stations and travel by G.W.R. to Oxford. Not a difficult
journey but one that had to be treated seriously—for the two
lines seemed unable to synchronize their movements, and even
if they tried to do so their efforts were not often effective since
the old S.E. & C.R. had a well-deserved reputation for un-
punctuality. Would it be enough to allow one hour and a half's
margin of safety at Reading? Probably, but by no means
certainly. We set off and duly arrived at Oxford, but that was
not the starting-point of a conducted tour. We did not visit
Christ Church and Magdalen, the Bodleian or the Divinity
Schools, or indeed any of the famous sights. I think that we
must have walked from the station to Folly Bridge, but memory
is hazy. All that I recall with clarity is that we were at some time
rowing a boat along one of the streams between Folly Bridge
and Hinksey; that we ate our sandwiches and drank what was
then known as 'fizzy lemonade'; that we bathed in the stream;
that we caught our train at Reading and finally bicycled home
late at night from Blackwater. How curious are the tricks of
memory! I can still feel the texture and atmosphere of the third-
class railway carriage on the return journey, yet no single
memory of Oxford itself remains from that day's visit. No

[1] Marshal of the Royal Air Force Sir John Slessor, *These remain* (1969).

dreaming spires, no impressive buildings, no fluttering gowns—
nothing stayed in the mind except a third-class railway carriage
and a rather uncomfortable bathe in a secluded stream. I am
hard put to it to explain why I never made another visit to
Oxford until 1909. In the years that passed I thought more and
more of Oxford; I read about it; I watched the result of Oxford
and Cambridge matches with all the fervour of a partisan; I
cherished the belief that somehow and somewhen I should find
my way to Oxford—but I did not see the city again until
April 1909 when I entered for my first scholarship examination.

The examination was held in Merton Hall and was for
scholarships at Merton, University, and Brasenose Colleges. I
came up the night before the examination commenced (for I
was to stay with an old friend of my Father's, a retired colonel)
and called at my brother's rooms in the cottages at Trinity.
These were the first Oxford rooms which I saw. For the first
two days my hopes were high, but they were soon rudely
dashed. The examination was controlled by Arthur Johnson,[2]
Fellow and Chaplain of All Souls, who at that time taught at a
large number of Oxford colleges. In appearance he was a
sixteenth- or early seventeenth-century type, his tastes were those
of a country gentleman, combined with those of a nineteenth-
century cleric. Had he lived fifty years later than he did he
would have perished in the High, across which he wandered
without any concern for the oncoming traffic. 'I am thinking
what I shall say in my lecture as I cross from All Souls, and I
am remembering what I forgot to say as I return.' My own recollection of his lectures is that they were concerned with some
elaborate family disputes with regard to property, but his
History of the Small Landowner was a minor classic, and his
Europe in the 16th Century was a model textbook. I can see, in
retrospect, that my entry for the examination was almost
an impertinence; how could I after two terms at a crammer
compete with scholars from the schools? None the less I, and
a good many others, did not deserve the treatment which we
received. On the morning of the last day Arthur Johnson
announced that some of the candidates need not trouble to

---

[2] The Revd. Arthur Henry Johnson, probably most widely known for his long-
lived textbook, *The Age of the Enlightened Despot*.

write the papers that remained and a list of about a quarter or a third of those present was read out. Like the rich young man we 'went away sorrowful'. I have always thought that our exclusion was an act of cruelty which could not be excused; we should at least have been allowed to write the papers even if our performance in the earlier papers had ruled us out for serious consideration for a scholarship, and I question whether the time which the examiners had had was sufficient to warrant so drastic an execution. I cannot deny that I felt some *Schadenfreude* a few years later when I read the records in the Schools of the chosen scholars. Their performance was abysmal.

Beyond a transient attendance at his lectures I did not meet Arthur Johnson again until 1919 when I was a lecturer at Christ Church and acting for the first time as an examiner. By then colleges offering scholarships in classics and history were divided into three groups, arranged on the sacred principle of equipollence (a Balliol word!). Each group included eight or nine colleges. At the first examiners' meeting Arthur Johnson and I were appointed to set the paper on European history. The paper covered a long period and candidates could confine themselves to the shorter period which they had studied. There were usually about eighteen or twenty questions. Arthur Johnson issued his orders: 'Write out your questions and bring them round to my rooms at All Souls at four o'clock on Friday.' I was young enough to take an inordinate amount of trouble over my task and I flattered myself that I had constructed some good and not too stereotyped questions—so I entered All Souls on the Friday in complacent mood. 'Do you want tea?' asked Arthur Johnson. I was clearly expected to say that the trouble was unnecessary but he had chosen the hour of four and I was thirsty, so I said, 'Thank you, yes.' 'Then I suppose I must get some' was the somewhat grudging reply. The tea fetched, our work began. 'Read me your questions and we will see how they fit in with mine.' I read them out and A.J. made some objections to all except three, which he declared acceptable. 'Now', he said, 'I will read you mine; let me know if you have any criticisms to make.' He then read out some thirty-two or thirty-three questions, most of which seemed to me to have done duty many times before, but my confidence was shaken and I did not venture to suggest any deletions.

'Good,' he said, 'we will insert your questions in the appropriate places, and then the paper is finished.'

In a state of some perturbation I hurried round to Arthur Hassall, who was my chief at Christ Church, to ask his advice. I told him that I knew that the other examiners would reject the swollen paper out of hand and that I did not mind, but that I did object to being held responsible for such a monstrous production. 'Don't worry,' he said, 'but give me his draft paper and show me which are your questions.' I gave him the paper and he marked three large red crosses upon it. The next chapter in the tale was written at the meeting in Merton S.C.R. when all the draft papers were presented. When we arrived at 'European History' Arthur Hassall went at once into action. 'This is a ridiculous paper,' he said, 'there are only three decent questions in it.' 'And which are they?' was Arthur Johnson's unwise response. Guided by his red crosses A.H. read out my three questions, and Arthur Johnson was not amused. 'Don't sit there snarling at me like a tiger but if you don't like the paper go away and write a better one.' Anyone less like a tiger than Arthur Hassall it is impossible to imagine but he was well able to handle the situation. 'Of course I will,' he replied, 'I'll take Masterman with me and we'll draft a good paper in a quarter of an hour.' That, in fact, is exactly what we did, and I could not help feeling that my second clash with Arthur Johnson over scholarships in Merton had amply avenged me for my earlier disaster.

I must return to 1909. Worcester, examining by itself, advertised a history scholarship in June, and for this I entered my name. I suppose that a student of form would have offered long odds against me and, in retrospect, I am amazed at my own quiet, though unacknowledged, confidence. For this un-reasoned optimism I had one excuse. My coach, P.B. Allen, was himself a Worcester man and the walls of his room in which I worked carried a number of college groups—cricket elevens, the Lovelace Club, and so forth. Moreover, Roberts also had been a scholar of Worcester, and in some curious way I felt the sense of belonging to the College before ever I had set foot in it.

I stayed, as on the previous occasion, with my old colonel and joined in the morning the throng of candidates waiting to go into the Hall. Many of the faces of my competitors were familiar, unpleasantly familiar, for most of them had survived for the last day at Merton; but in spite of this, the start of the examination was an unforgettable and exhilarating moment. Merton Hall had impressed, or perhaps oppressed, me with its almost threatening antiquity, but Worcester Hall gave me at once the feeling that I belonged to the College. This sense of belonging to any institution or society or body of men is one of the felt needs of many men in many different spheres; it gives strength to the school and to the regiment, to the trade union, and even to the political club. *Esprit de corps*, it has been said, is the enemy of patriotism, and this is partly true, for it is often impossible to feel the same close attachment to a large body, whereas the small unit attracts at once loyalty and affection. Worcester Hall, with its panelling and its magnificent fireplace designed by Burgess, together with its light and lofty ceiling which was the work of Wyatt, was especially adapted to draw the newcomer to itself. I fell in love with the Hall at that moment, and the hope of being in time a member of the College, of which the Hall was the hub and centre, became almost overwhelming. More than fifty years later the so-called restoration of the Hall was, for me, the saddest of all episodes in the College history.

'Wars', said Clausewitz, 'are won by fighting and by the bloody outcome of battle.' Scholarships are not won by wishful thinking but by writing papers of which the examiners approve. Something of the papers I remember, but not a great deal. My essay was very short, but it seemed to me to be good, though everyone else was apparently trying to impress by quantity. There was an uneasy moment when I discovered, to my surprise and alarm, that I was expected to attempt a Greek as well as a Latin Unseen. I had by that time acquired enough Latin to make some sense, though with pain and grief, of an ordinary and not too difficult piece of Latin prose, but my Greek was at the most rudimentary stage. I knew the small letters but was still uncertain of the capitals. Still the effort had to be made, for no examinee should ever refuse to play under the examiners' rules—besides some Greek words awoke echoes of their English derivatives. I came to the conclusion that I was translating the account of some desperate struggle, but whether it was a fierce debate or a sea-fight or perhaps a fire I could not with certainty determine. Most of the candidates handed in their unseens long before the allotted time was up, I worked on with feverish zeal until the last available moment. My paper must have been a curiosity—a post-impressionist or even an abstract picture of the scene which was—no doubt—depicted in the original with crystal clearness in impeccable Greek.

There was a meeting on one of the evenings when the dons moved restlessly among the candidates and drew them into conversation. One candidate who had filled his mind with a recently published work by Durning Lawrence, like the *Ancient Mariner* seized upon each don in turn to dilate on the importance of the Baconian theory. He did not make the impression which he desired. There was also a viva, conducted somewhat informally by Hadow[3] and Marriott.[4] I cannot remember what Hadow asked me and I never came under his influence for he left to become Principal of Armstrong College that autumn, but I always felt proud that he had been one of my examiners. Many of his letters are preserved in the College Library and among them I found a letter to his mother. 'Most of the week', he wrote, 'has been taken up with scholarships. We have made a fairly good election—very miscellaneous but I think there are some wits among them.' The word 'miscellaneous' was well chosen. Marriott, then engaged on his *Second Chambers*, characteristically talked to me of legislative procedure. In my ignorance I did not know that bills could be originated in the Lords, but the form of the questions (for Marriott was a compulsive lecturer) showed me that they could be and I was able to adapt my answers to the situation.

On the last evening of my stay Lys, who was then Bursar and Classical Tutor, asked me to walk with him round the garden. With extreme care and delicacy he explored the situation. It seemed that the College would like to have me among its members; should I be coming up if I was not awarded the scholarship or exhibition? He could not, of course, speak for the examiners—he could not be sure that I should win anything. I was compelled to reply that I could not come to Oxford without a scholarship and that even the exhibition, being of less

---

[3] Sir Henry Hadow (1859–1937), later Vice-Chancellor of Sheffield University.
[4] Sir John Marriott (1859–1945), Secretary, Oxford University extension delegacy, 1895–1920, successively M.P. for Oxford 1917–22 and York 1923–9.

value, would not make my entry possible. I should have to try again elsewhere in the coming year. With even greater delicacy he discussed rooms. Scholars, he said, ought to have a priority in choice of rooms but for personal or private reasons they often preferred cheaper and quieter rooms to the better sets. The mention of scholars in this context gave me encouragement and I replied that my naval training had made me immune from noise and turmoil but the cheaper the rooms were the better suited they would be for me. Indeed for one who had recently lived in a gunroom and slung his hammock in a crowded chest-flat the cheapest rooms appeared palatial in both size and comfort.

My election was posted next day and letters came to me from Daniel and Lys. This was a curious correspondence, for Daniel, the Provost, was succeeded by Lys, and I, in turn succeeded Lys. Both letters were kind and congratulatory, but both reminded me that residence and emoluments depended upon my passing Responsions in September. Both, by implication at least, voiced some dubiety about my success—as well, if they had read my Greek Unseen, they might! Other letters followed, one of them from Arkwright. 'Jacky Fisher was delighted at your success. I saw his letter to Ashford! But he dare not boast of it, he says. So I thought.' Using the old cliché 'without undue modesty' I regard the scholarship examining at Worcester in June of 1909 as a model exercise. When selecting scholars examiners are looking for those who show most promise for the future. Achievement gives a rough guide to what may be expected but, often enough, the inexperienced examiner lays too much stress upon it. Of course the examiner must be fair, but let him beware of an excess of fairness. If he awards scholarships on a strict measurement of marks obtained he is all too likely to find himself electing a series of good second-class men. He should trust his own judgement and be prepared to recognize any signs of real merit or any spark of real intelligence. To this topic—which to me is an entrancing one—I must return later. I spent August with Roberts and his sister at a house they rented at Canterbury, and prepared myself for Responsions. Has anyone ever had more pleasure from the first four books of the *Aeneid* and the *Alcestis* and *Medea* of Euripides? I doubt it. I passed Responsions in September and so, at long last, the way to Oxford was clear.

VI

WORCESTER COLLEGE IN 1909

So, last in order, first in my regard,
Dear Worcester! . . .
DEAN BURGON

I N October 1909 I came up as a scholar to Worcester. What
of the College then? It would be both courteous and correct
to start with the dons. I open the *Calendar* for 1910 (the first
calendar in which my name appeared, for it included those
who had come up in Michaelmas Term 1909); the dons had a
character of permanence which undergraduates did not possess.
As at most Oxford colleges of that date the teaching staff was
small, even when compared with the small number of undergraduates. This fact is partly explicable when it is remembered
that classical Greats was considered of supreme importance
and that other Schools could expect only the minimal share of
Fellowships. Theology, medicine, mathematics, and law were
reasonably respectable, and each of these subjects might expect
the odd Fellowship, but scientific Fellows were almost unknown,
there was no modern language Fellow at any college till after
the war and even modern history could, as a rule, only expect a
lectureship.

Daniel was my Provost, and for him I retain a lasting affection and respect. When I hear the words 'Provost of Worcester',
it is of him that I think first of all. At that time he was seventy-
three and he seemed to us a venerable figure, belonging to the
past rather than to the present. This, in a way, was true for he
represented the old, beautiful, scholarly, clerical, and comparatively leisured Oxford. In appearance he was magnificent;
making his inspections as Clerk of the Market, clad in his D.D.
scarlet robes he was a memorable sight. His great beard, once
golden, was, when I first saw him, almost entirely white, but
this only enhanced the majesty of his appearance; his complexion was bright and sanguine and his stance upright. He

was a fine man, with something of the appearance of a Viking chief, and yet we felt that he was gentle and understanding. His portrait by Furse, finished by Sargent, is as good a portrait as there is in Oxford; it hung until 1967 on the south wall of Hall opposite the High Table. Perhaps some future generation may return it to that, its proper place. Daniel had held many offices in College and University—Tutor, Bursar, Dean, and Proctor: his friends had been scholars and men of letters, ecclesiastics and painters, poets and men of learning. His press was famous, and added to the reputation of the College. Many appreciations of men are lacking in sensitivity but this is not true of those published in *The Daniel Press* (1921), a book printed on the Daniel Press in the Bodleian, which contained memories and recollections of some of his friends. Perhaps of them all Sir Walter Raleigh [1] comes nearest to the truth when he speaks of 'a character that was not so much a character as an atmosphere'. Certainly he had created an atmosphere at Worcester, an atmosphere of culture and humanity, of humour—or perhaps rather gaiety, and appreciation of the things of the mind. As a young don he had been chiefly responsible for the redecoration and beautifying of the Hall and the Chapel, and in the latter his sometimes whimsical fancy finds full scope. His portrait, as a Viking chief, together with those of other fellows, appears in a fresco on the north wall; birds and insects and flowers are depicted on every wall; the prophet Daniel sprawls in the lunette over the altar; some of the words of the Te Deum, curiously and artificially divided, encircle the chapel, words so contrived that the single word 'God' appears alone behind the Provost's seat; curious animals and monsters form the end portions of the pews. Daniel was not the architect nor yet the 'internal decorator', but the whole building, a thing of colour and light and fantasy, breathes his spirit and his magic. If at the time when I came up he had lost some of his youthful spirit no one thought the worse of him for that. Giving out notices in Chapel he once said—or so it was reported—'Next week Wednesday and Friday will be on Wednesday and Friday.' We all knew what he meant. His reputation and that of his family brought many friends and many of the scholarly

[1] First holder of the Professorship of English Literature at Oxford, 1904, and Merton Professor of English Literature from 1914.

and artistic to the College. It was, I think, in my second or third year, that he brought his close friend Robert Bridges[2] to read a paper to the 'Lovelace Club'—the chief of the Worcester literary clubs. The paper was to be on 'Prosody', and for some days we tried feverishly to learn something of the subject in order that we might make intelligent comments and ask reasonably informed questions of the poet. But the paper was in a sense no paper. Instead Robert Bridges read to us his own verse written in hexameters—pausing occasionally to add a comment. 'My brother,' he said, 'beautiful words, Virgil could have done nothing better than that.' The paper ended; we made our halting comments and asked our clumsy questions; throughout the Provost slumbered quietly in his chair. Then the two friends rose to leave us. 'How did you like my paper?' asked Bridges. The Provost was equal to the occasion. 'I did not hear it very well,' he said, 'I'm getting a little deaf.' 'Never mind,' said Bridges, 'we'll go back to your Lodgings and I'll read it to you again.'

The atmosphere which Daniel created—perhaps unknow- ingly—was one of culture and humanity and friendliness; it was fostered by his family. Mrs. Daniel was a skilful painter and an able helper in all the work of the press; an artist in her own right, she was also the kindest of women, the most sensible of the feelings of others. There were two daughters, Rachel and Ruth, who were apostrophized by the President of Magdalen in a poem, printed by the Daniel Press.

> Mistress Rachel, Mistress Ruth
> Dancing down the ways of youth.

Rachel's first birthday—in 1881—was the occasion for the finest production of the Daniel Press—*The Garland of Rachel*— which was a collection of poems by seventeen contributors. The names of those who contributed included those of Austin Dobson, Andrew Lang, John Addington Symonds, Robert Bridges, Lewis Carroll, Edmund Gosse, Francis Bourdillon, W. E. Henley, Frederick Locker-Lampson, and Margaret L. Woods. What a commentary on the range and standard of Daniel friendships! Rachel had married before I came up, but Ruth, the younger sister, was still living with her parents. I say

[2] Poet Laureate 1913–30.

'still' for her life might easily have taken a different course. She was engaged to Compton Mackenzie in 1903; the engagement was broken off in 1905. There is a long and touching account of this in Compton Mackenzie's *Life and Times, Octave III*; of this no one could complain, but Worcester men of my generation—or such of them who survived the First War—did resent the fact that Compton Mackenzie wrote a novel which described this engagement and also gave a vivid and easily recognizable picture of Daniel and Mrs. Daniel as well as of Ruth. *Guy and Pauline* is a good and indeed beautifully written work of fiction, but Worcester men could never like or approve it.

In 1909 Ruth Daniel had recovered all her gaiety and charm, and no one could readily observe that, in the old phrase, her heart had been broken. She had, to quote Walter Raleigh once more, 'some of the same magic [as her parents] a kind of fairy pleasure and goodwill, which makes the day brighter'. With undergraduates, especially the shy and embarrassed, she was perfection. The Daniels kept open house, and it was customary for us to go to the Lodgings for tea on a Sunday at least once a term. On one occasion a very shy freshman, entering the drawing-room, could see only one unoccupied chair, towards which he made his blundering way. 'Oh, no,' called out Ruth, 'you can't sit there, that's the dog's seat. Come and sit on the floor by me and make yourself comfortable.' A few minutes later Lord Curzon, the Chancellor of the University, came into the room, and made for the same seat. 'Oh, Lord Curzon,' said Ruth, 'you mustn't sit there; that's the dog's seat—besides I've just turned an undergraduate out of it.' The Chancellor was less amused than the rest of the company.

I turn to the *Calendar* for 1910 and read the list of the Fellows. There were eight of them, but of these four were not concerned with teaching work in the College. The Senior Fellow was the Revd. George Stott, who had taken his B.A. in 1837, and must therefore have been at least ninety-two years of age—I never saw him. The Vice-Provost was T. W. Jackson, who was sixty-nine; he was ill and retired in the following year. Him, also, I cannot recall. The third was William Odling, the Waynflete Professor of Chemistry, aged about seventy-five, the fourth Pottinger, who had once been Law Tutor and was, in 1909,

Librarian. Him I came to know fairly well, for in my second year I took on the office of sub-librarian, for which I received a salary of, I think, £20 a year; my duties were to attend to the Library for an hour in the morning and enter the names of those who took out books. Pottinger was a remarkable man, but when first I knew him he was already eighty-five. He found the stairs leading up to the Library somewhat irksome, and morning after morning I suffered from a premonition that he would expire on the Library floor. In his youth he had had distinction as a lawyer and had been counsel for Jowett in his heresy case. In the Library the pamphlet collection was his special pride—and it was indeed valuable and interesting. Cyril Wilkinson, whom I succeeded as sub-librarian had warned me of some of Pottinger's peculiarities. One of them was to take in a very large number of parish magazines—which he directed should all be catalogued and placed on the shelves. Since the inside portion of these works was always the same it seemed to us best to disembowel each of them and retain only the outer sheet; this we did, but our work, which certainly helped to keep the problem of shelf space under control, was concealed from the Librarian. Pottinger was a curious man. We believed that he had lost all or most of his money in an abortive attempt to produce champagne in Somerset. There is a picture of him in stained glass in one of the Library windows; he is pictured in his ancient great coat, already green when I knew it, which had survived from the campaign in the Crimea. He stands feeding swans on the College lake, a venerable but out-moded figure— in a way somewhat pathetic, a link with a past which was already fading.

There were, then, only four Fellows who were concerned in the teaching in the College, Gerrans, Lys, Lee, and Cunning-ham. Gerrans was a remarkable man with a great dome-like head set on a sturdy and substantial body. He was in the early fifties and played a considerable part in University as well as College life. He was not only a member of Hebdomadal Council but also, as the *Calendar* shows, a Delegate or Curator of in-numerable University bodies. His subject was mathematics. I was his pupil for a month. Of Gerrans I saw little after this early encounter but he was always well disposed towards me and I regarded him with respect, tempered with awe.

Lys, the second of the teaching Fellows, played a much greater part in my life and became a friend as well as a pedagogue. His whole life was devoted to the College for he had come up as a scholar in 1882 and with the exception of eighteen months remained there till 1946. He was a dedicated man, but whereas Daniel had devoted himself to Worcester men Lys was concerned chiefly with the College itself—its buildings, its finances, its gardens, its lake, its trees and flowers and birds. Daniel had greeted Arthur Landon, a collateral descendant of Provost Landon, with the words 'the same old name in the same old place'. Lys thought more of the life of the College than of individuals. When I came up it was true, I think, to say that freshmen thought little of Lys; in their second year they began to respect his unwearying devotion; in their third year they realized how much they owed to him and came to respect and appreciate his work. He had become Bursar in 1903, when the finances were at a low ebb and when the property had been somewhat neglected and he set himself to the long task of restoration. The College tenants were quick to note the change. Daniel as Bursar had been generous and compassionate to the tenants, as two silver bowls presented to him by them bore witness; Gerrans was competent and just, but uninspired; as undergraduates we thought it almost a duty to destroy any of the hideous furniture which he had introduced; Lys was a crusader, determined to restore the College fortunes. As one tenant put it, 'There was Dr. Daniel, and he was a gentleman; and then Gerrans and he was a business man; but now its that there Lice.' Lys was indeed, the model Bursar. A plaque in the south wall of the Lodgings in 1968 well describes him:

This stairway was built in 1968
in memory of the Reverend
Francis John Lys
1863–1947
Scholar, Fellow, Provost
of this College
Vice-Chancellor of the University
1932–1935
ΟΙΚΟΝΟΜΟΣ ΠΙΣΤΟΣ ΚΑΙ ΦΡΟΝΙΜΟΣ

Indeed the College was seldom if ever out of his mind. Once Milburn, who had recently become Chaplain and Fellow, preached in the College Chapel, and was flattered to note that the Provost seemed to be following his sermon with absorbed attention. It was always an agreeable custom at Worcester for the Fellows to walk in procession to the Lodgings after the service, and Milburn was, not unnaturally, expecting that some word of commendation on his sermon would fall from the Provost's lips. Lys spoke, but not the expected words. 'I have been thinking all this evening, Milburn,' he said, 'whether we ought to have continuous or intermittent flushing in the New Building.' One of Lys's merits was that he was incapable of seeking for easy popularity. He thought only of the good of the College, and never paused even to think of what effect his words or actions might have on individuals. As a consequence many thought him arid and sarcastic; they could not have been more wrong, but their error was easy to explain for his mind never strayed from the work in hand. Walking in the Provost's paddock towards the end of his time as Provost he gazed at the fruit trees which he had planted, and—as though thinking aloud—remarked to me, 'I always pray that my successor will be a pomologist.' Fortunately for me that particular qualification was not considered essential by the Fellows of Worcester. His first wife was a great contrast to him. Slim, elegant, and exotic in appearance, she might well have served as the model for any one of the pre-Raphaelite painters, and to her charm she added the gifts of great intelligence and of artistic appreciation. She had gained a high class in Honour Moderation and rumour had it that Jacky Lys had married her quickly lest she should get a better class than his in Greats. With all these gifts she lived tensely on her nerves and was unable to restrain her horror of bores and boredom. She liked to have the young about her, and made no secret of her lack of interest in the pompous or the elderly. On one occasion at a dinner-party in the Lodgings she had placed an undergraduate next to her in spite of the presence of several senior members. 'How do you like this dinner service?' she said, with a view to learning something of the undergraduate's powers of artistic appreciation. 'Oh, I think it's beautiful, Mrs. Lys.' 'Do you? I have told the Provost several times that it's ugly and quite unworthy of the Lodgings. Now watch the Provost at the other end of the table.' She then picked up a plate and threw it against the closed window, where plate and window-pane shattered together into fragments. Lys maintained his calm, but a sad little, 'Oh, my dear', was heard to issue from his lips. Once, towards the end of her life, I was talking to her in the drawing-room between tea and dinner, when to my surprise a servant came in carrying a soup tureen, together with a large cup. From the tureen Mrs. Lys ladled herself a quantity of black coffee, and laughed off my suggestion that she was indulging a bad habit. 'We have a dinner-party for tonight, and one or two heads of houses as guests. I am only making sure that I don't go to sleep— they are so insufferably boring.' I have moved on too far, but I recall that in my undergraduate days she was a kind and colour-ful person, who raised the heart and the eyebrows in about equal measure. Lys remarried and the charm and affability of his second wife made her the ideal consort for the Head of a college. Lys himself succeeded Daniel as Provost in 1919, and was Vice-Chancellor from 1932 to 1935. This was the crown of his career, and gave him immense satisfaction. Like many others he came to the office rather too late for he would, I believe, have been a great Vice-Chancellor ten years earlier. As things were he was highly competent and effective—and much given to hospitality for the first two years, but was a tired man in the third year of his office.

The Law Tutor was R. W. Lee, Bobby Lee, as we then called him. He, too, was a character, and he exercised considerable influence on his pupils. I think of him now as a small, compact figure, well but soberly dressed, with the clipped speech of the lawyer, and a fairly sarcastic yet kindly manner. When I asked his scout about him some years later he gave the unexpected reply, 'Mr. Lee? Oh, he put on a clean silk shirt every day.' I do not believe that this was true, but on such small things do reputations rest. Bobby Lee's publications were not extensive, but he published a History of the Papacy (of which I still have a copy) written in Latin hexameters—one line or two to every Pope. Years after he visited Rome and was given an audience by the Pope who referred in flattering terms to this work. He wrote a similar work on the Archbishops of Canterbury. After a spell in Canada Lee returned to the Chair of Roman-Dutch Law in Oxford—a Chair which he held until 1956.

'Jock' Cunningham was the fourth of the Fellows who were

engaged in teaching; his subject was ancient history and he was also Dean. A shy man, with a rather large face, and an awkward and somewhat ungainly walk and manner, he was yet in a curious way the most sympathetic of all our senior members. A perceptive man too. One evening he passed me in the Quad and remarked, 'You read the lesson in Chapel tonight with a great deal of feeling and very well, Masterman'. How did he guess that that especial piece of praise was precious to me, for I had been lucky enough to have read the thirteenth chapter of Ecclesiastes that day and had indeed devoted a great deal of time to preparing it. Jock Cunningham succeeded Pottinger as Librarian in 1911. Alas! he died in 1918. An armorial window in the Library rightly records that he died prematurely, but that he had accomplished much in a short space of time.

Besides the teaching Fellows the College had two teachers; one for theology, whom I did not know, and one for modern history, J.A.R. Marriott. From my second term onward Marriott was my tutor and played a great part in my life, and I was and am deeply in his debt. These facts and the fact that outside the College he was indisputably the most important and distinguished of our dons must excuse the length of my account of him. To say that Marriott was a remarkable man would be an extreme example of meiosis. He was unique. Up to the end of his life he maintained that he should be described as a 'politician', but to that word he did not give the generally accepted definition. To him a politician was one who had 'espoused the state', who in one capacity or another sought to serve it. To teach and to write history was to be a politician as much as it was to sit in Parliament at Westminster. In his own case, though he was a Parliamentary candidate in 1886, he did not achieve his ambition to be a member of Parliament until 1917, when he was elected for the City of Oxford. He lost this seat in 1922, but sat as member for York from 1923 to 1929. Had he been a younger man he would most certainly have attained high office for he had all the qualifications for success at Westminster—qualities more adapted to that place than to the quieter stage of a university. He would maintain, however, that in the years between his degree and his entry to Parliament he was actively and always engaged in politics.

As a full-time tutor at Worcester, at one time he taught nearly a quarter of those in the College who were reading for a final honours school, but this was a very small part of his work. In 1895 he succeeded Michael Sadler as Secretary to the University Extension Delegacy (University Delegacy for the Extension of Teaching), a post which he held until 1919. This entailed not only the administration of a large and complex organization but also the delivery of lectures in all parts of the country from Lancashire to the Isle of Wight and from Bournemouth to Tunbridge Wells. In the course of the forty years prior to the outbreak of war in 1939 he reckoned to have given 10,000 lectures. Incredible but it was true! 10,000 lectures, an average of a lecture a day for five days a week kept up for forty years. Even after his retirement, and when in the late seventies, he was still giving forty to fifty lectures in every year. But that was not all. When he had reached his eightieth year he had published, as he wrote in his autobiography, 'Some forty volumes—scholarly in scope', and in addition was one of the most prolific contributors to the reviews—especially the *Quarterly*, the *Fortnightly*, and the *Nineteenth Century*. At that period the reviews had, to a great extent, supplanted the pulpit as an organ for influencing and forming public opinion and Marriott's articles were among the most influential. His works, too, were important and valuable, especially those connected with political science and constitutional history. His *English Political Institutions* (later incorporated in the *Mechanism of the Modern State*), for example, is in my judgement the best short book ever written on the subject; his *Re-making of Modern Europe* (1909) went into its twenty-first edition in 1933 and was thereafter incorporated in his *History of Modern Europe*. 'Remarkable' is a hopeless and inadequate word to use to describe such a record and such an output. What would a modern researcher say if asked to produce forty volumes, deliver 10,000 lectures, and hold a full-time teaching assignment at the same time? The mind, as Wodehouse would say, boggles.

When I became Marriott's pupil much of all this lay in the future and the rest was hidden from our eyes; to us he was simply the History Tutor. Was he a good tutor? For me the answer must be an emphatic, 'Yes'. His own enthusiasm for historical studies was infectious, he knew the value of occasional praise and his comments were always to the point. On one occasion early in my association with him I had taken unusual pains in writing an essay on the French wars of religion. Laboriously I explained how I would treat the subject, how divide it, and how finally bring it into review. Marriott listened carefully and then pronounced judgement: 'Too much scaffolding left up.' Perhaps for some men he would not have been an ideal tutor, but for me he was excellent. I liked and admired him and accordingly I surrendered completely to his direction.

Since those days I have often pondered on his character and career. He was, of course, as with his immense energy and phenomenal output he had to be, always in a rush. Clad in a long overcoat he would teach or lecture in Worcester and then mount his bicycle with a huge brown leather bag suspended on the handle-bars and ride to the Examination Schools to lecture there. When he arrived he would pull his gown out of the bag and start to lecture while he was still putting it on. His appearance was leonine, his manner when lecturing (and he was always lecturing) didactic—and at times almost hectoring. Yet no one, in my opinion, could state a case or expound a view with greater force or more clarity. His mind, I believe, was not strikingly original, but it was capacious and an instrument of extreme efficiency, and so he prevailed by means, less of persuasion than of irresistible force. Like most of us he was a man of contradictions, and he had the faults of his qualities. In the first place he was egocentric. His autobiography *Memoirs of Fourscore Years* is full of interesting tales and facts, but it is marred, for me at least, by the over-emphasis which is laid on the good opinions by others on his work. One whole page, for instance, is filled by press-cuttings of a eulogistic type about his *Second Chambers*. It was because of this, I think, that he was not properly appreciated in Oxford. Many of the historians fought shy of him because he was thought to be both hectoring and superficial (an accusation patently untrue), others because he seemed to them more a journalist and a politician than a man of learning (a criticism for which there was some ground). That he was lacking in sensitivity and tact in his dealings with others is unfortunately true. Once, when he had to leave a tutors' meeting before the business was ended he strode from the room and turned out all the lights as he left. 'That', said Lys drily, 'signifies the state of mental darkness in which we are cast by

the absence of our colleague.' On one occasion I went down to
the Examination Schools for the first lecture of his course. 'At
the end of this lecture,' he began, 'each of you will buy a synopsis of the course; it will cost sixpence and I shall not give change
to anyone. If you have not a sixpence on you, you must borrow
from a friend.' Well and good; and we all lined up (it was a
well-attended lecture) to buy our copies of the synopsis from
the pile which lay on the lecturer's desk. As he handed out each
copy Marriott tore off the outer sheet and flung it on the floor,
which was soon smothered in paper. Not unnaturally some of us
picked up the discarded sheets; on them was printed the title
and the information that they were Oxford Extension Lectures
—underneath were the words 'Price—Twopence'. I have my
decapitated copy still. Perhaps this egocentricity and lack of
sensitivity partly explains why he was not made a Fellow until
1913, although he was the most distinguished and perhaps the
most able member of the teaching staff of the College. He was,
which some did not realize, a devout and practising Christian
with large and generous thoughts, and he left a large fortune
to establish the Marriott Trust to assist the sons of the clergy
in the Oxford diocese. Yet on small things he was parsimonious
and even miserly. It was said that this more than anything else
lost him the Oxford election of 1922. He used, it was alleged, to
stop his taxi some few yards short of his house in order to keep
within the two-mile limit from Oxford station. At one of the
last meetings of his supporters he demanded in his customary
style questions and criticisms of his conduct of the campaign.
'What else could I possibly do to ensure success? Tell me.'
There was silence. 'Come, come, I welcome criticism; is there
any possible action in which I have failed; any task left undone?' Then a little old lady at the back piped up: 'They do
say, sir, that you never give more than twopence to a porter at
the station.'

But these are minor blemishes. In all, what a man and what
a career! His years in Parliament show quite clearly that he
might have risen to almost any height had his active political
career started earlier. Alas that he was not born into the television age, for on television he would have been superb.
Thousands, too, must have cause to thank him for an introduction to the value of University teaching. For me he remains

'my tutor' and I cannot forget or minimize the debt which I owe to him.

The other permanent part of the College was the body of College servants. The Head Porter was Joe Jennings, heavily built, lethargic in manner, but probably competent. His main interest in 1909 was football and he played a not inconspicuous part in football administration, especially in that of the newly formed A.F.A. The scouts were a notable breed, many of them dedicated men—dedicated, that is, to the College which they served. And service was no light task. Laying coal fires in College rooms at 7 a.m., they seldom turned for home until about 9 at night—and there was no let up on Sundays. In 1909 they were, in my recollection, a remarkable set of men. My own scout Hollis had been a soldier, and had every merit, except that of self-expression. He had charged with the Lancers at Omdurman, but when questioned was unable to remember anything about that memorable day. It had just been another day's work in his military life. When I returned as Provost in 1947 he was still acting as servant to the Dean, but he was crippled with arthritis and could move with the utmost difficulty. I used to wonder how he could drag himself up the steep staircase to the Dean's room—but he did. More notable was Wyatt, who figures in the Diary of Willie Elmhirst—a diary to which I must refer later on. Wyatt was, in all ways, the ideal of what a senior college servant should have been. Years after, in 1951, I read an account of him in the *Reader's Digest*, under the heading of 'The most unforgettable character I've met'. The writer was a Rhodes Scholar, J. S. Childers, and the article is a gem of a character study. Wyatt looked after his 'young gentlemen' like an anxious parent. When examinations were pending, books and dictionaries were laid ostentatiously on the breakfast table; when Childers bought a bottle of absinthe back from Paris, Wyatt was full of reproof, 'Asking your pardon, sir, but isn't absinthe a dangerous drink?', and then a few days later, after remarking that Oscar Wilde had drunk himself to death, 'I understand it's habit-forming, sir.' Later in the day when Childers returned to his room his dictionary was open at the page where the definition of 'absinthe' appeared: 'A green alcoholic liquor . . . its use causes nervous derangement.' Two days later the bottle of absinthe was withdrawn. When a

glove, left on the spikes on the wall of the College as its owner
was climbing in, fell into the hands of the Dean, Wyatt hastened
to the rescue. 'I have destroyed the incriminating companion
glove, sir. I did it with pleasure, for it was a gaudy and unworthy garment.' Shades of Jeeves! He had the highest regard
for Oxford, and sent his son to Jesus, though it would have
been easier to send him to Cambridge. But no. 'Cambridge, sir,
is a boisterous place.'[3] Wyatt was a fine all-round athlete, and
especially successful as a cricketer. Sometimes in the Long
Vacation he joined a touring side, partly composed of Worcester
men; then and then only did the gap which he insisted upon
between the College servant and members of the College disappear. Another stalwart was Drake, who later in life became
even more distinguished than Wyatt. In 1909 he was Common
Room man, but he soon became butler, a post which he retained till his retirement in 1946. After that he lived near by
for the next ten years. In the Buttery he ruled over an unofficial
club for undergraduates where good manners were taught.
Naturally I knew him even better towards the end of his life
than in my undergraduate days. At that time I thought of him
chiefly as a cricketer, for our College servants fielded a notable
side which made a practice of winning the inter-collegiate
Servants Cup. In 1925 it is recorded that the competition had
been played seventeen times, and that the Worcester College
Servants had won nine times and been in twelve finals. Moreover Drake, Wyatt, and Johnson (the Chef) had played in all
twelve finals. And what a trio—Wyatt, tall, a little stiff, distinguished in appearance as in manner; Johnson of middle
size, sturdy, and amiable; Drake, small, almost dapper, rubi-
cund, and jolly. Drake was almost fanatically devoted to the
College and loved every stick and stone. When I returned as
Provost he told me that the College had never looked so beautiful as when he joined it as a boy of fourteen in 1881. I asked
him why it seemed so specially lovely just then, and he opined
that the explanation was that the hatchment of Provost Cotton
hung over the entrance gates. I begged him to be content with
the recollection and not to wish to see another Provost die in

---

[3] One is reminded of a story of Raymond Asquith's. He visited Cambridge and
on his return to Balliol was asked by his scout, 'What sort of a place is it, sir?
Something in the Keble line?'

office—even for the sake of artistic satisfaction. After his retirement he wrote a few short notes of his experiences. The last sections give a vivid account of Worcester as it was in the eighties:

My duty in Hall as a junior servant was to wait on the Freshmen.
If we got 17 or 18 in October it was thought the College had done
well. There were always a few who had been turned down by some
other college, but most of them declared they were glad they had
come to Worcester. They were admitted to College by a short
entrance examination. I don't remember anyone failing in this,
even if they had to be sent down later on. They saw Oxford life as
it was then, made many friends, learnt how to carry their wine, how
to carve, and meet other men's sisters and many engagements began
in this way.

In the city Drake was almost as well known as in Worcester.
Roberts told me once, as Bursar, he was making some consider-
able purchases in a furniture store. The assistants were rather
lethargic, but suddenly everyone seemed to spring to life and
Roberts heard a murmur from the other end of the room,
'Worcester is here', as Drake appeared through the door.

Outside servants included Rogers, the groundsman—the
doyen of Oxford groundsmen. He had been appointed when the
College ground was at Cowley and had been the chief architect
of our present ground. He was responsible in an unauthorized
capacity for many grounds outside our own, including Agar's
Plough at Eton. An excellent umpire, he seemed to me to
resemble an elderly tortoise who would protrude his head
with unfailing justice to declare my fate at the wicket. Like all
good groundsmen he was not always easy to deal with. As
Wilkinson put it: 'He would find a number of excellent reasons
for not doing or allowing what he would then proceed to allow
or do.'

The gardener who will always be associated with Worcester
was Will Ward, whom I knew better at a later time than in
1909. He always took pleasure in reminding me that he was
my senior in the College, for he had come as a boy in 1904 and
he would point with pride to a Russian oak in the Meadows
which he had helped to plant in the year of my matriculation.
A great gardener, an indefatigable worker, he had a character
which all could admire and a voice (with Oxfordshire accent)
which made speech with him a never-ending pleasure.

Such were the permanent members of the College in 1909. Far more important, as we thought then, were the undergraduates; even though they were birds of passage. For Worcester, we felt instinctively, belonged to us even if our tenure was to be short. And how right we were! The odd picture in my mind is that of an opera. The dons provide the script and the music and the orchestra; the College servants are the dressers and the scene-shifters; but the performance is given by the undergraduates, and the caste changes year by year. A college is a living body, subject to change, sometimes more healthy than at others, but with an ethos all its own, which persists though it may be modified. Perhaps all this was clearer at Worcester than at most colleges, for we were a small body. Those receiving tuition when I came up were, as nearly as I can calculate, about ninety in number—in other words a body small enough for all—except the recluses—to be known by all. In many ways this was a drawback, but the advantages were clear, for in all societies over-great size is apt to crowd out humanity and compassion. Of our number about a third came from the public schools or the more distinguished of the grammar schools; the rest from every kind of educational establishment, including, most fortunately for us, a fair sprinkling of Rhodes Scholars and men from overseas. Into this society a freshman was received with open arms, especially if he could offer anything which might add to College life. Within a couple of days from his arrival the freshman would have been visited by many small parties of senior men, eager to find out if the newcomer could be enlisted into the ranks of the musicians or the rowing fraternity; the literary set or the athletes, the religious enthusiasts or the O.T.C., the scholars or the playboys (though that word was then unknown). Yet all these sets joined forces and cross-fertilized each other. All my life I have heard the bitter complaints of those who think that colleges are the preserves of the privileged, and that those outside the charmed circle are mercilessly excluded. The elementary fact seems to be forgotten—that those who choose or select the members are seeking always to get the best that they can—come from where they may. At a time when the best education in the country was provided in the public schools it stood to reason that a college was glad to have a large public-school entry. As time moves on and those outside the public schools are better taught the proportion changes. It is equality of opportunity that should be aimed at—not an artificial plan to include a higher proportion of one particular class or one particular stratum of society. There are few satisfactions in life superior to that of belonging to a society or a fellowship; the thing which opens the door is a common interest. At Worcester there was no painful interval of probation; a man who was prepared to participate was welcomed to the fraternity almost before he could realize his good fortune. Rose-tinted spectacles? Perhaps, but that is my recollection. The men whom I first met in October 1909 I can only mention here. Three Wilkinsons, Harold (or Billy) Morgan, Jock Cumberlege, Bertram Long, Landon, and Gallwey who delighted us with their singing, Reggie Thatcher the organ scholar, Whittall, Hardy, and a dozen more. Of those who influenced my mind I cannot forget a Rhodes scholar, Carroll Wilson—lawyer and bibliophile who became the great authority on Verdant Green. When I reread their names I feel that the undergraduate age is of all periods in life the best for the making of lasting friendships.

What sort of life did we live? No period in my life is harder to describe than this—and for a special reason. How can I be sure that I am really recapturing my memories of that time? Am I not transferring back the sensation of a later period, and fondly imagining that my thoughts more than half a century later were really those which came to me whilst I was an undergraduate? For example I am firmly convinced that the gardens at Worcester and especially the walk past the cottages to the cricket ground made a greater impression on me than any other scene. From the quadrangle through the tunnel—popularly supposed to be the entry used by Alice to Wonderland—into the gardens, past the best of all herbaceous borders, along the lake, peopled by gay and sometimes exotic birds, into the cricket ground, with its smell of newly cut grass and the sounds of the lawn-mower or the crack of bat upon ball. Only a couple of hundred yards but a feast of sights and sound which brought one always not only the expectation of instant happiness but also serenity of mind and a belief in the rightness and the security of life. But did I feel this at the time? Be that as it may I must

do my best to describe our life in Worcester in my first undergraduate year.

First of all I am sure that Worcester, more than any other
college, was self-sufficient, almost insular in its life. The University meant little, almost nothing to us, for Worcester was enough
of itself. We did not visit other colleges much, except for lectures
and, except in a few cases, we did not belong to University
institutions such as the Union, the O.U.D.S., or the clubs.
With a peculiar, unjustified, and parochial pride we were fond
of saying that our own clubs provided better speaking and more
enjoyment than did the Union, and that our play-reading and
acting club, the Buskins, was quite as good as the O.U.D.S.
That great and gifted athlete, Geoffrey Foster, who had gone
down shortly before I went up, was held to have been of less
value to the College than he should have been because he was
always engaged in playing games for the University! I, myself,
never had a blue for any game in Oxford though I think that I
might have won one or two had I been at a larger or more
fashionable college. None the less we were inordinately proud
if any of our number did succeed in making some mark in
University affairs. A curious contradiction, which can be explained, I think, by the false pride of the poor relation. Of the
social clubs in Oxford most of us had hardly heard. Billy
Morgan was our solitary representative of Vincent's when I
came up—and he had gone down when in my third year I was
elected, and I think that very few of my Worcester contemporaries were members of the Grid. We were better represented
at the Union and in the O.U.D.S.

A very important factor in bringing us together was the
geographical layout of the College. Were I designing a college
or a hall of residence I should make it my first consideration to
arrange that the Lodge was so placed as to communicate
easily and directly with the centres of activity within the college.
Everyone has to go to the Lodge, to get letters, to read notices,
even only to get out of the college; it is impossible to avoid
meeting other men there, even if one wished to do so. You may
build common rooms and create societies, but a recluse or even
a shy man may well avoid them and continue in his lonely way;
he cannot avoid, try as he may, the chance encounters within
or outside the Lodge—he will, literally, run into his fellow-

men there, and personal propinquity leads inevitably to easier communication. At Worcester the Lodge itself was small but the main and short, but broad, passage outside it opened out into the wide cloister and loggia—a perfect ambulatory. Here is the real centre of the College, and here, I think, the main source of its sense of unity. How different from Christ Church, which had three entrances and no natural meeting place! Both the Hall and the Chapel open directly onto the loggia, and the entrance to the Library is in the entrance passage immediately opposite to the Lodge. Furthermore the J.C.R. (in those days) was at the north corner of the loggia, and the Buttery down the steps which led from the loggia at the southern end. Everything seemed designed to bring the College together; it was impossible even to leave the College (except for those who climbed it after dark) without entering the loggia and passing by the Lodge. 'Communication', that most difficult (and most modern) of arts, did not have to be artificially created; it was inevitable. To add to our blessings the College garden with its lake marched with the College cricket ground. In a word we were a self-contained unit, sufficient for ourselves. Why should we bother ourselves by straying into less favoured colleges when we had at hand and within our own walls all that was needed for living the good life?

The dominant note in undergraduate life derived from this insularity, or self-sufficiency, or even aloofness. The more cut off from the University and other colleges Worcester was, the more were Worcester men brought into contact with each other and, as a result, the more they tended to participate and to take their part in every College activity. I think that I always knew this, but I did not fully realize all the implications until much later in my life. In 1968 a diary kept by an undergraduate who came up in Michaelmas Term 1911 and kept through his freshman's year, came into my hands. He was Willie Elmhirst, and the diary had been preserved by his brother—L. K. Elmhirst of Dartington Hall. When I read it for the first time I had the unique experience of reliving a whole year of my youth for it gave a day-to-day record of what was my third year at Worcester. The predominant note in the diary is one of zest and enthusiasm; in every part of College life he played his eager part, indeed the scope and variety of his interests and activities is staggering.

And that, if my recollection is accurate, was true of very many Worcester men of my day. In all these activities I took part—except that I did not join our dining club—the Kingsley. This I have always regretted, but I felt obliged to decline on the score of expense, though I did not give that reason in my letter. At that time one had a curious inhibition against pleading poverty. An error, but it was part of our code of behaviour. 'Nihil Vigorniense a me alienum puto' might have been our motto.

Here once more the question of 'size' obtrudes itself. We could all have two years in College, and some could have three. I could never understand the thinking behind the policy of some Cambridge colleges of sending out their freshmen and keeping senior men in College. How much better to insist that each man should start in College and stay there for his first two years. National need and government prompting have since then forced most colleges to expand beyond their optimum size and national needs must be met. But surely every effort should be made—if the college system is to continue to confer its benefits—to keep numbers down to a size which its rooms, and offices and administrative arrangements can cope? The lifeboat after the wreck can take on board a number of extra bodies, but if aid is given to too many the boat will eventually sink.

VII

OXFORD BEFORE THE FIRST WAR

Best trust the happy moments. What they gave
Makes man less fearful of the certain grave
And gives his work compassion and new eyes,
The days that make us happy make us wise.

JOHN MASEFIELD

ONCE more, what sort of a life was it that we lived?
Memories crowd one upon another; one can only select,
almost at random, and try however imperfectly to generalize.
It may seem odd, or even perverse, to a modern reader who
has been brought up on the fallacious theory that Oxford was
the home of idle aristocrats if I turn first to the work of a scholar,
for work was, for the majority, the centre as well as the background of our lives. In a modern house, electrically heated, it is
not uncommon to rely on background heating with radiators
or under-floor heating, and to reinforce this with electric fires,
which give brightness as well as warmth over short periods. It
was like that with our work and studies. The bright moments
which fix themselves in the memory, belong to our extra-
curricular activities—but the background, the permanent,
was what is, perhaps inadequately, described as 'work'. In
the richer and more fashionable colleges I should surmise that
the number of the idle was greater than with us—but even at
Christ Church or Magdalen there were many men whose first
need was to secure a degree, as well as many who worked for
enjoyment as part of their university life. Many, it is true,
worked for a pass degree—whereas nowadays only those aiming
at honours have any chance of securing a place—but is that all
gain?

Work then did form the background of our lives, even for
those who tried to cut that work down to a minimum. For a
scholar, like myself, there was an added incentive; I had to

make good and justify my position—and for this I must fall as well as I might into a working routine. The mornings were usually divided between lectures and reading, and in the winter, the two hours between tea and dinner were a good working time when it was considered right and proper to sport one's oak to maintain privacy. After dinner, on many but not all nights, we worked also. But we did not advertise the amount of our work; for some obscure reason it was considered good form to pretend that we worked little or hardly at all. An eminent bishop, once my colleague at Christ Church, told me that there were two principles which should be observed at Oxford. The first that 'no gentleman works after dinner'. And the second? I asked. The second is that 'no gentleman works after lunch'. The bishop was a learned man and had achieved two first classes, so I surmise that he had not conformed to his principles. Very, very few first classes were won without industry and hard work.

So much for the background heating, what of the electric fires? It was an active life. Most of us rowed or played games in the afternoon, and sometimes, since the College was small, one could row and play a game on the same day. The height of luxury was reached in the winter afternoons. There were no bathrooms, so we fetched boiling water in large tin cans from a tap by the kitchen and filled our tin baths which we put in front of our sitting-room fire. Lying in a tin bath, in front of a coal fire, drinking tea, and eating well-buttered crumpets is an experience which few can have today. Normally we had a good breakfast, but lunch nearly always consisted of a commons of bread and cheese and marmalade and this we took in each other's rooms, as dinner was the only meal in Hall. I suppose that our standard of living was determined by our income, and I believe that mine was about the average. My scholarship was worth £80 and my parents gave me another £100. To this I added about £20 from my sub-librarianship or from a summer tutorship, so that my annual income was normally about £200. Of course I had a home to go to in the vacations but the £200 had to cover everything else—fees and battels, clothes, journeys, and the (not inconsiderable) expenses of many games. It was sufficient, but it did not leave enough margin for waste and riotous living.

The main difference from the practice of today came from the use of leisure in the evenings. It is sometimes forgotten how recent is the provision of modern amenities. We had no radio, no television, no cinemas, and in consequence we had to provide our own amusement and our own methods of relaxation. There was of course the theatre but most of us would only go to that about twice a term—partly because we had other things to do and partly because of the expense. I simply cannot understand why the three performances which I remember best are Galsworthy's *The Silver Box* (or *Strife*), the Bensons in *The Taming of the Shrew*, and a superb piece of acting in *The Speckled Band*. I must have seen many greater plays and better actors but it is those three which stay in the mind. There was also a sort of music hall—the East Oxford—but that was only visited on Saturday nights by those who wished to create a disturbance and tempt the notice of the Proctors. There were concerts too, but I was not musical, though I would occasionally go to a Balliol concert on a Sunday night. Yet our evenings were by no means dull. Worcester probably had more literary clubs per head of the population than any other college; besides that few evenings passed without some of us collecting together in the rooms of those who had pianos and singing the songs which most knew. There were hours during which the playing of instruments of music was not allowed but I think that the rules were often broken. I could not sing (at least not in tune) but I enjoyed the companionship. When there was no music and no club meeting there still remained the unending talk, the debate, the discussion. That, if universities are to retain their appeal, must always be the essential feature of university life. What did we talk about, what did we discuss? I suppose that I could say 'everything under the sun' and leave it at that, but perhaps it is worth while trying to recall what topics attracted us most. On the whole religion was less discussed than might have been expected in an Oxford which was still predominantly clerical. Probably those who were seriously concerned with religious problems were more attracted to University than to College societies. So far as religious observance was concerned we were still living in the past, but our practice was liberal when compared with that of some other colleges. There was compulsory chapel and we were obliged to attend one service, Matins or

Evensong, on Sundays and four services in each week. We had, however, the great privilege of counting attendance at the evening service (at 6 or 6.30) on week-days as 'a chapel', a privilege most welcome especially in the winter. If four 'chapels' were not kept the delinquent would be summoned by the Dean and occasionally fined. At some colleges the quota was fixed, not by the week, but by the term, during which forty chapels had to be kept. 'I am', said one friend after about a third of the term had passed, 'now dormy thirty-nine down.'

Politics held us more and provoked more discussion. Liberalism caught me up—perhaps this is not so strange as might at first sight appear. More than any other doctrine the theory of free trade had completely captured my intelligence. I had, too, absorbed and accepted the Whig interpretation of history. Moreover the Liberal spokesmen of the day—especially Asquith and Grey—commanded my allegiance, and I was an avid reader of John Morley. Today it is forgotten how much influence his works had on my generation. The two books which influenced me most were quite different from each other: J.S. Mill's *Political Economy* and J.R. Seeley's *Growth of British Policy*. Lloyd-George did not command the same respect, for the taint of being a 'pro-Boer' still clung to him. Yet in spite of the fact that it was a time of political turmoil I do not think that we felt so much personally involved in politics as do the undergraduates of today. As for University politics they interested me not at all.

There was, naturally, a certain amount of bawdy talk as there must be when the young are together, and we discussed sex and sexual problems. But unless my recollection is quite wrong there was much less talk of sex than there is nowadays. Possibly a kind of unconscious Victorianism restrained us. Some men, it is true, were known as 'womanizers' and had little credit; for the most part there was a sort of unwritten but wholly indefensible convention that the society of women—of our own kind or of other—should be kept for the vacations. Curiously homosexuality was little discussed—'curiously' because the Oscar Wilde period was only a few years behind us. Of literature and books we talked unceasingly—and of course about personalities and our own affairs. I am sure our talk was of the kind that always prevails at a university, covering every subject and the solid basis, as I believe, of a sound university life.

The absence of outside amusements and amenities in the College threw us back upon ourselves and was a cause not only of much singing and continuous meetings and discussions but also a good deal of youthful and harmless—or nearly harmless— horseplay. It was not unusual for the Dean to be drawn from his room about midnight in order that he might quell disturbances, indeed an evening was considered only half completed if he was allowed to sleep in peace. Of such revels the leading light in my first year was Harold (or Billy as we then called him) Morgan—I was seldom engaged and was at best a camp-follower. One night, as one of many who seemed to include the greater part of the College, I followed him into Worcester Place where Ruskin College was then lodged. The rumour, no doubt quite erroneous, had spread that students at Ruskin had purloined the eggs of the Provost. The street was crowded with shouting and missile-hurling undergraduates when the Ruskin defenders opened their upper windows and poured hot—or perhaps boiling—water on the throng. 'So that is how the medieval fortress was defended' said my companion. On another occasion I stood guarding a ladder below the Dean's bedroom. Billy climbed up with the purpose of sewing up the legs of the Dean's pyjamas. The project failed—Billy climbed down the ladder with the disgusted comment: 'He wears a night dress.'

On one occasion only did I play a leading role—a responsible role, even if not a glamorous one. I have told this tale before, but since it was almost my only excursion into unlawful enterprises I shall tell it again. Billy Morgan had run foul of Marriott for some reason which I have forgotten and decided to settle his score by blowing up my Tutor in his rooms. He came to me and invited my co-operation, which as a flattered junior man I was very ready to give. He then explained his plan. 'You read your essay to Marriott after dinner,' he said, 'and on the next occasion you must make it long and interesting so that his attention is riveted. I, meantime, shall affix my bomb to the outside of his shuttered window. When it explodes you must hurry Marriott down to the Fellows' Garden to see what traces there are of the miscreant. You will not find any.' Marriott's room had a window which looked out over the Fellows' Garden, and, since the levels on the two sides of the buildings were different it was only about five feet above the ground. The beauty of the plan was that Billy would not go to the garden at all, but would be lowered by a rope from an upper window in order to affix the bomb and time fuse. When that was done he would be hoisted into safety.

The essay was certainly long, and full of contentious remarks, and I read it as loudly as I could. The wooden shutters of the window were closed, the curtains drawn, and Marriott carried out his usual routine of boiling a saucepan of milk (a practice of his which caused me irrational irritation) beside his armchair. Very faintly I heard muffled sounds which I rightly connected with the fixing in position of the bomb, followed by silence which indicated that Billy had been hoisted into safety. My own sensations were mixed; partly the keenest hope for the success of the plot, mingled with the anxiety of the goat, tethered to attract the tiger. Then came the explosion! This was before the days of world wars and we didn't know much about explosives, but Billy was a man who did not do things by halves or leave anything to chance. The wooden shutters and the curtains were blown into the room, the saucepan of hot milk was splashed all over the floor, the room was smothered in dust and smoke. Marriott reacted in a manner which I had not expected, though it was entirely in accordance with his character. 'I might have been killed,' he exclaimed, 'they don't know how valuable I am.' I urged him to run down to the garden to search for the malefactor, and there we were soon joined by the Head Porter and by the Law Tutor, Bobby Lee, who had rooms on the same staircase. He seemed to me to show only modified pleasure when he learned that the History Tutor was alive and apparently unharmed, but applied his legal brain to solving the mystery of the outrage. Without success, for Billy had taken every precaution. After placing the bomb he had climbed out of College, and then knocked in about an hour later, thus giving himself a perfect alibi. ('I almost believed that he was not involved when I saw the Gate Bill,' said Truslove, the Dean, long afterwards.) In the morning Billy wrote a message from the J.C.R. Committee to the Dean expressing horror at the explosion and offering to turn all the energies of the J.C.R. into an attempt to discover the perpetrator of what he called 'this dastardly outrage'.

Soon after the end of the war I was dining at Worcester and walked up the hall by the side of Billy Morgan who had returned to Oxford to command the O.T.C. Marriott was just in front of us. 'Did he ever find out who it was?' Billy whispered. 'I think not,' I replied, and we placed ourselves one on each side of Marriott. I am pretty sure that he never did, for the story did not die. About twenty years after the incident had happened I was dining at All Souls where Bobby Lee, then Professor of Roman-Dutch Law, began to narrate his account of it, with some pardonable embellishments. 'Then', he said, 'I saw a pale and hysterical little scholar cowering behind the smoke in a corner of the room.' 'Steady,' I said, 'I was that scholar, but you did not arrive until we were already in the garden looking for footprints.'

Did we drink much? The question is always asked and receives many a different answer. It is probably true that each age tends to exaggerate the drinking habits of its predecessors. With the best will in the world I cannot be sure. A good deal of beer was drunk and a good deal of port on special occasions, but very little sherry. On the whole I incline to think that we drank less as a regular habit and more on special occasions, such as bump suppers, twenty-firsters, and the like. It so happened that Einstein's stay in Christ Church coincided with some spirited correspondence in *The Times* on the heavy drinking at the Universities. Einstein was incensed, and was even ready to write to *The Times* to defend the reputation of Christ Church for sobriety. He had, he said, never seen an inebriated undergraduate. I was tempted to encourage him to write, but I am glad that I refrained. Someone who held the opposite view to him might have discovered that, except on special occasions, he always retired to bed at 9.30. In the matter of drinking I believe that the moderns have a great advantage over us. The increase in travel had made the young, as well as the old, acquainted with the wines of the Continent, and a wine-drinking country is, on the whole, a happy country. If you are one of a party and enjoying yourself in a wine-drinking country the world is with you; not so if spirits only are drunk, or even beer.

Days spent in study and in games—in discussion and in action —it was a strenuous and rewarding life. Sundays made a break, since the Victorian tradition of the day of rest was still, by the majority, observed. The days of the tall hat were over but we dutifully put on a bowler and paid a duty call on married dons and on friends in North Oxford. The week-end habit had not taken root among us. I went home for the Coronation celebrations in 1911, otherwise I did not leave Oxford in term-time. About dress we were very conventional—there was the accepted attire for all occasions and it caused great embarrassment if the conventions were ignored. In the summer a straw hat was the accepted headgear and—for a year or two at least—it was considered a great *faux pas* to wear a hat with a smooth instead of a serrated brim. By the same token there was a brief fashion to wear a cloth cap with a commoner's gown. On one occasion, wishing to be in the swim, I had discarded my scholar's gown and borrowed a gown from a commoner friend. I met Cunningham in the Lodge. 'I did not know, Masterman,' he remarked with his gentle smile, 'that we had deprived you of your scholarship.'

In point of fact we surely lay too much stress on this matter of undergraduate dress. Over the last hundred years male dress has changed very little, as a study of college groups will show beyond possibility of denial. Mr. Gladstone visited Oxford and spent a week at All Souls in 1890. His hosts, with dubious propriety, noted down the sayings and remarks which he made, even those which he made at breakfast. And what stirred him most? Not the authorship of Homer or the state of the Irish church but the lamentable dress and appearance of the undergraduates. Things had been far better when he had been President of the Union sixty years earlier. Some of his contemporaries, 'young men at Christ Church', made a point of promenading the High in the most careful attire. Some of them kept a supply of breeches which they used only for this purpose, and in which they never sat down lest creases should appear. And now, in 1890, he had seen a man in shorts in the High! 'Shorts in the High'—it was surely too much, even for a very modern world. It is a human and understandable weakness on the part of the elderly to rail at the dress of the present day but I question whether our plaints are justified, though I confess to an irrational dislike of long hair and a rational distaste for dirty trousers.

Such, as I remember it, was life at Worcester when I matriculated. How would it compare with the life of an undergraduate today? It is tiresome to repeat in different words something which one has once written so I draw instead on my 'Introduction' to Willie Elmhirst's *Freshman's Diary*. Were we, as insurgent youth is apt to think, just a set of idle layabouts, intent on pleasure, careless of the well-being of any except those in our own class? Surely not. On one point I would wish to be as clear as I can be. To praise the past it is not necessary to denigrate the present. In every generation there are idle men and industrious men, sad men and happy men, traditionalists and reformers, the distinguished and the obscure. A comparison which seeks to prove that one generation of undergraduates is better or more deserving than another seems to me to be futile, for, if we keep our minds fixed on the normal and disregard the eccentric and the revolutionaries, we must come to the conclusion that though there are differences the similarities are far more striking and far more important. In every Oxford generation there is the same eager and questing discussion, the same wish to enjoy and to profit from the experience which is offered, the same criticism of existing conditions. The majority of every body of freshmen when they come up in Michaelmas Term feel, and rightly, that with them

> The world's great age begins anew,
> The golden years return!

Yet there is one great difference. We of the older generation lived in a 'carefree' age; not so the undergraduate of today. The wars and disasters of the last half-century have, inevitably, shaken the confidence of the young, not only in the wisdom of their elders, but also in their own future, and so the undergraduate of today is chary of embarking on a career which does not offer some sort of security, and his present is clouded by too much planning for an uncertain future. We, on the other hand, lived in the present and for the present. Perhaps we were unconsciously selfish, perhaps we were self-centred, perhaps we were complacent, and perhaps it is true that the undergraduate of today has a better developed social conscience and that he extends his sympathy and often his aid, to a much wider circle. But there is something to be said on the other side. 'Carefree' we were, but that word does not connote idleness. My own recollections tell me that the things of the mind were not neglected in the Worcester of my undergraduate days and that there were many who worked and studied as zealously as their successors do today—even though they contrived to play as well as to work. This was, by any reckoning, a sane and balanced life.

I return to myself. How did I fit in to this new and exciting life? In the first place there was no disappointment and no disenchantment. Oxford was all that I had hoped for and seemed to offer unlimited opportunity and unalloyed satisfaction. I got off, it is true, on the wrong foot. My object was to start work on history as soon as possible, but there was another hurdle barring the way. Before starting in the Final School it was necessary first to pass the First Public Examination which, except for those seeking honours, meant Pass Moderations. But here was a difficulty. Pass Moderations included Greek and Latin translations as well as Latin prose and I doubted whether I could muster enough Greek and Latin expertise in the time at my disposal. It then occurred to me that I might use the knowledge which I had painfully acquired in the Navy to take Honour Mathematical Moderations—though I did not at first realize that this would entail three terms' work. Accordingly I went to Gerrans, who accepted me as a pupil, and for him I worked for three or four weeks. He summoned me to his rooms in John Street at 8 o'clock on a late October morning. I sat in front of him at his desk. 'Do you see my pencil anywhere?', he began, 'I have been looking for it all the morning.' This, I think, must have been a gambit often used before, but it did not fill me with enthusiasm—the more so as I realized the great gulf between Oxford mathematics and that branch of the subject which I had studied before. At the end of three weeks I realized the mistake which I had made, but I also observed a means of escape. The Law Preliminary Examination was held in the ninth week of term, and for it no Greek was required. There was unseen translation in Latin and French, the elements of Roman Law to be studied in Gaius, the constitutional history of England, and a French set book—*La Cité antique*. It seemed a gentlemanly kind of escape route and I had nearly five weeks to do the work. Gerrans, understandably, was ready enough to release me and remained friendly to me for the rest of my career, Bobby Lee gave me a brief talk on Gaius, and a friendly scholar in his second year helped me with some Latin unseens. In the event all went well though I went to sleep during an early paper and had to be roused by a kindly invigilator.

In my second term (Hilary Term 1910) I was able to start on my real work with Marriott, and to tie up some loose ends. Those who took the Law Preliminary had also to take what was known as an 'additional subject in Responsions'. This was A. de Tocqueville, *L'Ancien Régime et la révolution*, and no book in my experience has ever fulfilled its function better as a text-book for examination. A style well suited to the historian, a sufficient supply of facts, plenty of ideas which invite observation. It is sometimes discarded for a time but always returns. Presumably Paley's *Evidence of Christianity* performed a similar function at Cambridge, for it was a set book there for a hundred years. A rhyming section was apparently constructed to assist the less gifted, and passages from this were quoted in *The Times* when the centenary year arrived. A few lines (I hope that I quote them correctly) stick in my mind:

> The disciples then, goes on old Paley
> Continued in the Temple daily
> Washed in the Blood and free from sin
> Showed the good state that they were in.

Besides the additional subject it was also necessary to pass Divinity Moderations or 'Divvers' at any time before the Final School, and it seemed sensible to get it out of the way early. Candidates were examined in two of the Gospels in Greek and in the Acts of the Apostles in English, and scholars were fined by the College if they failed. It was usual to cram desperately for a few days, but I was taking no chances. I was fortunate in two ways—the Provost always set an Essay in the New Year on some biblical topic and in 1910 he gave the 'Journeys of St. Paul' as his topic. The prize was of the value of £5 and that was a considerable attraction. I also had the advantage of seeing Ronnie Knox's game, based on snakes and ladders, by which commoners were taught St. Paul's journeys. It was cunningly constructed, and the squares covered by the shipwreck sent the unfortunate back the whole way to the start. Divvers was a cause of much ribaldry and some blasphemy. (A large white sheet on which was written: 'Divinity Stakes. Names and weights of the Apostles', accompanied us to the schools.) But it was not a very serious examination or an effective method of advancing the Christian faith. At the end of my second term I had surmounted the early obstacles, and could devote myself without interuption to the History School; best of all there was to be no further examination for more than two years.

For my first summer term and first Long Vacation I eased up a good deal; probably nature was demanding a brief rest. Nor would the events of that time lend themselves to fine writing. How often do we read the magnificent and reckless descriptions of obstreperous youth? How often the struggles of the poor but determined scholar overcoming all his difficulties by strenuous endeavour and proud parsimony? But how seldom the lives of the normal and the middle-class—the centre-of-the-road men, pursuing their conventional way, undisturbed by excesses or eccentricities of those around them? Such a one was I.

By the beginning of my third year I began to take more part in Oxford life outside the College and to make friends in other colleges. This change was due chiefly to games and athletics. In the Long Vacation playing cricket and lawn tennis such friendships were easily made, and many of them were lasting. The same was true of the track at Iffley Road. I had gone down there at the beginning of my third year to take part in our College sports, and in order to win—or lose—a small bet about the height which I could jump. The habit once formed gave me enjoyment and in the Hilary Term I won the high jump against Cambridge at Queen's Club. It was no startling per-formance, but also by no means contemptible; 5′ 8″ does not sound much, but I had to contend with a heavy track and a puddle of water which almost, but not quite, spoiled my run in. The *Morning Post* saw reason to comment on my 'springy foot and straightforward unsophisticated jumps'. Even in those far-off days we had our heroes; the most notable was the then President of the O.U.A.C.—G.R.L. Anderson. No one who saw him hurdling could fail to perceive that here was grace and beauty allied with supreme self-control and power. We all confidently expected that he would win the 120 yards hurdles at the

Olympic Games in 1912. Alas—a tragic fall robbed him of that
honour. Yet his record was outstanding. After first classes in
Honour Moderations and Greats he went into Cammell Lairds
at Birkenhead. There he had digs with another Trinity friend,
Arthur Hills—and I stayed for a night or two with them in
1913, and saw their long day of strenuous work. In spite of this
Twiggy Anderson returned to Oxford to win an All Souls
Fellowship at the end of that year. Another stalwart was
A.N.S. Jackson, a famous miler, who not only won the 1,500
metres in the Olympic Games at Stockholm but was also
awarded three bars to his D.S.O. during the war. Our weight-
putter was E.P. Hubble,[1] an astronomer of very great distinction.
On the Cambridge side was Philip Noel-Baker.[2] It is unlikely
that the University sports will see again two rival Presidents of
the stature of Anderson and Baker.

Before that—at the beginning of my third year—I had passed
through something of a crisis. I knew that I must get a first class
if I was to follow the course which I wished; I was obsessed by
my old failing of seeking safety first; should I not be wise to
postpone my Schools for a year 'to make certain'. In retrospect
I am sure that the overriding motive was to prolong an existence
which gave me unalloyed pleasure, but I had something of a
case for postponement. My special subject—the Civil War—
was to be included for the last time in 1912, after which it was
to be superseded by the Revolution of 1688. I had spent some
time in the Long Vacation on the Civil War but I was not
satisfied with the progress which I had made. The new subject
seemed to give me a great opportunity, for I could continue it
with an attempt to win a University prize—the subject of the
Stanhope Prize Essay for 1913 was announced as 'Thomas
Osborne Earl of Danby and Duke of Leeds'. To win a University
prize would give me just that qualification which I should need
if I was to pursue a University career. Rather to my surprise
the College agreed to my proposal and this enabled me to
enjoy as well as to profit from my last two years. For my third
year I went into digs in St Michael's Street with my brother
from Trinity (who took Greats that year) and for my fourth

[1] Edwin Powell Hubble (1859–1953), American Rhodes Scholar at Queen's
College; Astronomer, Mount Wilson Observatory, from 1919.
[2] Nobel Peace Prize 1959, held ministerial offices 1945–51.

1910

1889

✻ and an Anglo-fop of the first water.

year I stayed in the same rooms with Jock Cumberlege[3] and G.T. Pearson, another Worcester friend, as my companions.

In those years my working habits changed. In the early years I had attended a good many lectures, some of which were rewarding. A.L. Smith, whose description of the slave state had caused a coloured man to faint in Balliol Hall, lectured on Aristotle's *Politics*. Ernest Barker, who filled St. John's Hall with his lectures on Anglo-Saxon and Norman history, had a magnificent Lancashire accent. On one occasion speaking of local differences in the country he said, 'I myself, when I first came to Oxford, had something of a Lancashire accent.' The whole Hall burst into cheers. Grant Robertson at All Souls and Marriott himself were the most histrionic and had, I suppose, made the most careful study of the art of lecturing. Others were good, though less showy—Wakeling, Lennard (who had just started his teaching), and Arthur Johnson. Vinogradoff I could not properly enjoy for he suffered from an imperfect command of English. My attendance at his lectures soon ceased; my notebook bears the legend, 'In vino veritas', and then a blank.

In my later years I went to fewer lectures but I always attended Firth's classes and seminars. With regard to my own reading my habits changed. I soon came to the conclusion (and I have expounded this doctrine ever since) that, though there are no rules for genius, the normal man engaged in intellectual pursuits cannot read with profit for more than about six hours a day. Probably practical work in the laboratory or the hospital can make the working day of a scientist or medical student a good deal longer, but I am sure that a six-hours average is about the maximum for an 'arts' student. How often has a tutor listened to the boast of a pupil that he has worked an eight-hours day, and known that in fact he has only sat in front of his books for that length of time and done a great deal less than one of his fellows who has worked at top pressure for half that time! In the summer terms of my last two years I changed my routine. We dined early and I could generally count on starting the working period by 8 or 8.30. From then on I would work

[3] G.F.J. Cumberlege, D.S.O., M.C., Publisher to the University of Oxford 1945–56.

steadily till about 1 or 2 with a coffee break about midnight. That meant a late breakfast but it did leave me free to spend the daylight hours playing cricket or lawn tennis—or even on the river. A wet day (and we did even then have some wet days) would give me the chance of making up any lost hours. On such days I would habitually ensconce myself in the Radcliffe Camera where the atmosphere was conducive to serious study. The peculiar smell of that building is with me still. Our Worcester Library was then a library and not a reading room and the undergraduates' Reading Room was an unsatisfactory place to work in. For a large part of my fourth year I concentrated my efforts on the Stanhope. Worcester was peculiarly rich in the pamphlet literature of the seventeenth century and I spent many hours, or rather many long days, in studying them— both for my essay and for my special subject in the Schools. Indeed I put so much into the essay that I came to think— subconsciously—that I must win the prize. Towards the end of the year I would surreptitiously study the notice boards on my way to the Bodleian to see whether my success had been posted. Vain hope! On one morning I read the notice which told me that the prize was not mine. The winner turned out to be A. Browning, scholar of Balliol. The subject must have captivated him as it did me for he spent much of his life on it, and published in 1951 when Professor of History at Glasgow University his final three volumes on Danby. It was a blow to fail in this enterprise, but Firth consoled me. He told me that my essay had been good and that I had used the pamphlet literature very well, but that I ought to have visited both the Public Record Office and the British Museum, instead of confining myself to Bodley and to Worcester Library. Also I had not dealt adequately with the later part of Danby's life. None the less he urged me to continue with historical research in the seventeenth century. His criticisms were just, his interest encouraging. Later on I learned that the entry had been an unusually strong one and had attracted many more competitors than usual for an essay prize; among my companions in failure was Goronwy Edwards, later Professor of History in London.

The extra year, even though it had been due in the first instance to my inclination to procrastinate and to my selfish wish to prolong a very happy existence, was not without its uses. It had given me the itch to write and it awakened a keen desire to undertake historical research. In addition it had given me time to prepare for the Schools without the need of feverish last-minute cramming. An examination which lasts for six full days with two three-hour papers each day is a severe test of stamina and character as well as of knowledge, but I found it almost enjoyable. We were lucky to have perfect weather and so I was able to have a couple of hours tennis each evening to refresh me for the next day's toil. My viva was less formidable than I had expected. It was started by Hodgkin, who was examining for the first time, and he began by questioning me about my special subject—the Revolution of 1688. On this I felt considerable confidence. Apart from my own work I had attended Firth's seminar, as also had Hodgkin. As he, however, had only been able to attend occasionally, whilst I had not missed any session, I felt, justifiably, that I knew more about it than he did. He approved of my first two answers, but after my third answer said, 'No, I don't think so.' The Chairman, C. R. L. Fletcher, then intervened. 'But I do', he said. 'What Mr. Masterman means is this.' He then delivered a short speech, and asked me if that had been a correct interpretation of my answer. It cannot be wondered at that I expressed agreement with him. After that I was in smooth water and had little difficulty in satisfying the Chairman, when he took over the interrogation himself. Fletcher, no doubt, behaved with the utmost impropriety and had no reason at all to snub Hodgkin, but I could but feel grateful to him. His action at my viva was in character, for he was a man of strong, almost fierce, views, loyal, generous, stimulating but unconventional and outspoken and careless of the opinion of others.

The examination was held in June but the results were not published until the first week of August and it was the practice to leave a small sum with the Clerk of the Schools so that he might send a telegram to the candidate. I was playing in a two-day match at Radley against the Radley Rangers, and my telegram arrived at lunch-time on the second day. I had made 0 on the first day, but the ball looked very large in the afternoon of the second and I scored 78. How long did that take me? As the years recede the time becomes shorter and shorter, but I am at least sure that I never batted with more complete confidence. Then at the end of the day I mounted my bicycle, with my cricket bag balanced on the handlebars, and rode back in the warm still evening air to Oxford—a very happy man.

VIII

APPOINTMENT AT CHRIST CHURCH

Today the heirs of Wolsey's great foundation, visibly secular and
superbly young, possess the place where the Black Monks of Canterbury dwelt and pay their shy and intermittent homage to the old
ideals of study and of prayer.

C. E. MALLET

THERE was now no doubt in my mind about the career
which lay, as I hoped before me. My ambition was to
write, to carry on with the study of history, above all to remain
in some capacity or other in Oxford. The best of all rewards
would be a Fellowship—beyond that my most sanguine
aspirations did not reach. But Fellowships were very hard to
come by. In my own College Lys was a lecturer for eleven years
before he became a Fellow, and Marriott for nearly thirty.
Pottinger, to give an earlier example, had had an even more
lengthy wait before he was elected to his Fellowship. An
obituary notice in the College *Report* for 1910–11 tells the story:
'He took a First Class in 1847 and was a candidate for more than
one Fellowship; but the Oxford of those days had no room for
an enthusiastic adherent of the school of Cobden, and he
presently withdrew from a competition the inutility of which
was not obscurely hinted to him.' He did not become a Fellow
till 1883. The prospect of having my own inadequacy 'not
obscurely hinted at' was not alluring and it seemed clear to
me that I could only hope for an appointment after a fairly
long novitiate. I planned, therefore, to take a B.Litt. if I could
support myself by giving some private tuition and I determined,
if I secured my First Class, to try for a Fellowship at All Souls.

In point of fact neither of these projects became necessary.
Trinity had advertised a lectureship, leading to a Fellowship, in
the summer and much to my surprise Raper, then Vice-
President, asked—or rather instructed—me to enter my name.

Raper was a strange man, a maker of Presidents though never President himself. I had got to know him when my brother was at Trinity and used sometimes to dine with him there. 'On medical advice I am not allowed to drink wine unless it is watered' he said one evening as he filled his glass with port. A scout stood beside him with a glass of water and a toothpick on a silver salver. Raper dipped the tooth pick in the glass and then allowed a couple of drops from it to fall into his port. I pointed out that the election at Trinity was to be made before the results of Schools could be announced and it would be un-pardonable *hubris* on my part to enter the competition—but Raper insisted and I gave way. I thought at the time that I was ill advised but in retrospect I believe that he did me a good turn. Once I had entered for an appointment of this kind it was known in Oxford that I was, so to speak, eligible for considera-tion if occasion arose. All my life I have been singularly fortunate in that appointments have been offered me and that I have not been compelled to solicit support or to plead for consideration. So it was in 1913. Christ Church proposed to appoint a lecturer with the prospect of a studentship after a year and I was asked to put in my name. In this case I felt no reluctance, for the choice would not be made until after the Schools results had been published and candidates would, I understood, be inter-viewed at the beginning of Michaelmas Term.

In October the Dean invited me to stay with him at the Deanery for a long week-end in order that I might be inter-viewed by the Selection Committee. There he exercised on me that compulsive charm which in personal relations made him irresistible. I dined alone with him on my arrival, waited on by his butler whose saturnine visage seemed to justify the under-graduate legend that he was a reprieved criminal saved by the compassion and support of the Dean. Tommy Strong ate and drank more quickly than anyone I have ever met; he probably regarded both eating and drinking as an interruption to thought and conversation. I had time to take one or two spoonsful of soup and to answer one question when the Dean had finished his soup—upon which the butler removed both plates, one nearly full and the other empty, and hurried us on to the next course. Another night I dined for the first time in Christ Church Hall—an evening made memorable by the spectacle of

Charles Fisher,[1] who had injured a leg, being carried by under-graduates into Hall in the old sedan chair which was kept below the Hall staircase. The interview came on the following day. The Dean sat at one end of the table, I at the other. Hassall and Charles Fisher were on one side, Blunt and Anderson on the other. No doubt the members of the Committee expected the Dean to subject me to a searching interrogation whilst they sat back and listened, but Tommy Strong was not a man to waste time. After all, I had been his guest for a couple of days and he had no doubt found out all that he wanted to know. He asked me, therefore, only one question: 'Mr. Masterman, are you a candidate for this lectureship?'; I replied, 'Yes'. 'Would any of you like to ask Mr. Masterman any questions?' There was a long and embarrassed pause, for no one was ready to begin. At length Blunt pulled himself together and said, 'Mr. Masterman are you married?' I replied, 'No'. Anderson then tried to come to the rescue: 'Aye, but hae ye perhaps any entanglement?' The rich Aberdonian impressed the 'tang' on my mind like a branding iron. A little shaken, I again replied, 'No'. There was another long pause ended by Charles Fisher. 'Mr. Masterman,' he said, 'what do you do in the afternoons?' This I felt was a loaded question; I had played a good deal of cricket with Charles and had in fact spent a week with him on a Free Foresters' tour only a couple of months previously. After brief deliberation I said, 'It depends on the weather.' Hassall, whom I knew to be anxious to elect me, seemed to be enjoying himself and asked no question. So there the interview ended. In Tom Quad I began to wonder whether one 'Yes', two 'Noes', and one 'dependence on the weather' could have given the Com-mittee a fair measure of my intelligence. I need not have worried. By the time that I was interviewed the other candidates had been eliminated or had withdrawn and I had no competi-tion to face.

At the end of the week I went to Christ Church again in order to arrange for the immediate future. I still thought of competing for a Fellowship at All Souls, but already in August Feiling had warned me of the dangers. If successful at All Souls I should have to promise not to accept a Fellowship at any other college for seven years; he therefore advised me to consider the

[1] Student at Christ Church, and Censor, killed at the Battle of Jutland.

Christ Church offer with care. If only a lectureship was offered I should compete at All Souls but if a lectureship was offered together with the promise of a studentship at the end of the probationary period then I should certainly not try for any other post. Tommy Strong was much more decisive and I learned from him then something of the pride and prestige of the House. In effect he forbade me to enter. Christ Church, he said, had chosen me and would not allow any other college to have the opportunity of criticizing the wisdom of their choice. A lecturer of Christ Church was not to be examined by any lesser place. Furthermore if by any unlikely chance I were elected my loyalties would be divided and that was wholly unacceptable to him. Feiling, who had himself been a Fellow of All Souls when elected to Christ Church had, I knew, suffered to some extent from this double attachment and Strong's opinion left me with no option—even if I had not been in agreement with him. Meantime I was told that I was to go for a year to Germany both because a change from Oxford was desirable and because I clearly needed some time to prepare myself for teaching.

The few weeks before my departure for Germany at the beginning of November were singularly happy ones, for the autumn of 1913 had brought much good fortune to the family. My parents had celebrated their silver wedding in September; in October both my brother and myself would be ourselves in our chosen professions. Christopher, my elder brother, was more worthy of congratulation in this than was I, for he had had a hard row to hoe. Immediately after taking Greats in 1912 he had entered for the Civil Service examination and had gained a place for appointment in Rhodesia, only to receive a shattering blow by failure to pass the medical examination. With great pertinacity and courage he determined to try a second time and went to a crammer in London for his preparation. In 1913 he passed into the I.C.S. and received an appointment in Madras but the medical barrier still had to be surmounted; only after an agonizing delay and the intervention of a specialist was a grudging acceptance agreed by the official doctors. That was the beginning of thirty-four years of service in India. So there we were—both self-supporting and both started in our careers. For myself all seemed set fair; in front of me there seemed to be a life of terms and vacations in orderly sequence, a life of learning and of sport, further off and vaguely the expectation of marriage and a family; no overweening ambitions but solid and satisfying and within my grasp. The war was to alter all that.

IX

GERMANY 1913–1914

The Englishman has a gentleman's agreement with providence to
see error and change his ways five minutes before midnight strikes;
the German has a gentleman's agreement with the devil to see his
mistakes five minutes after midnight.

KURT HAHN *quoting* DELBRÜCK

BRIEF visits while still in the Navy had done little to alter the
feeling of novelty which must strike everyone who makes his
first journey abroad. There were no passports or visas and no
time-wasting on tiresome form-filling; one took a ticket in London
and went to Berlin. The crossing to Flushing by night was rough
and a Dutch pastor, who shared a cabin with me, spent a good
deal of the night on his knees in prayer. Then came the long
journey across the north-German plain during which I was
impressed by that distinctive crockery which seemed to be an
emblem of international travel and invited comparison with
the grubby meals then served on English trains. On the platform of the Friedrichstrasse Bahnhof I explained in English that
I knew no German and could not, therefore, find my way un-
assisted to a hotel. It is nearly always true that competent
persons like to exhibit their competence and their superiority
to the helpless. In a few moments I was surrounded by eager
volunteers, one of whom placed me in a taxi, recommended a
suitable hotel, and gave me, in perfect English, the fullest
instructions with regard to the fare which I should pay to the
driver and the questions which I should ask at the hotel before
I booked my room. On the next morning I went down to
Lichterfelde in the suburbs and reported myself to Tilly's cramming establishment there. Here I must explain that, owing to
my lack of German, I could not go at once to a university so I
had arranged to start my 'German year' by attending this
institution. At that time Tilly had a considerable reputation
and his clientele included officers preparing for interpreter-

ships, medical students, academics like myself, undergraduates, and some schoolboys who were preparing to go to a university. It was a strange place where discipline was rigid and life austere. The younger pupils lived in the house, the older in lodgings in the neighbourhood, and I was lucky to share digs with a major in the Greys whom I found a congenial companion. The only difference between the older pupils and those under twenty-one was that the former were excused P.T. before breakfast. All had to conform to the inflexible rule that no language was ever to be used except German. A pupil who asked his neighbour in English to pass the mustard to him might well be threatened with expulsion. We were not even allowed to read anything in English. Classes were held throughout the morning, most of them taken by members of the Tilly family. In the afternoons schoolmasters from the neighbourhood appeared to take us, each separately, for conversational walks. The theory was that we should talk, think, and live entirely in German and cut ourselves off altogether from English. This rule I could not implicitly obey, for my interest in what was happening at home was too strong. My newspapers were carefully selected; the weekly edition of *The Times* gave me the main news, the *Field* kept me up to date with sport in England and the *Nation*, which in the main represented my own political point of view at that time, made sure that I did not lose touch.

The teaching at Tilly's was no doubt efficient but it was not suitable for me because it was based on phonetics. I have, as I then discovered, practically no aural memory at all whilst my visual memory is—or was—good. A word can be repeated to me half a dozen times and I have still no recollection of it, or of its meaning, until I have seen it written or in print. Unlike Macaulay's housemaid, I could never learn to chatter in a foreign tongue with an easy use of a small vocabulary; in consequence the direct method of language teaching, and still more, phonetics, were of little use to me. My most vivid memory of Tilly's is a class held by one of the daughters—a child of about twelve with two flaxen pigtails—in which we chanted German songs and ballads in unison to the accompaniment of a gramophone. I stood between a man who had just sat (unsuccessfully) for an All Souls Fellowship and a doctor who was already the holder of two medical degrees.

Es zogen drei Burschen wohl über den Rhein,
Bei einer Frau Wirtin da kehrten sie ein.

So we chanted, led by the gramophone, and patiently bore the
unflattering comments of our instructress. I stayed only a few
weeks at Tilly's and then transferred myself to the flat of one of
the schoolmasters with whom I had taken my afternoon walks.
He lived in the working-class part of Berlin and his newly
married wife had previously been a school-teacher also. Both
took trouble to help me and I begun to make some progress but
I cannot pretend that that Christmas was a festive season for
me. Both Herr and Frau Thies departed for Hamburg to spend
Christmas with their parents, leaving me alone in the flat
which was, fortunately, most efficiently heated. I learned the
simple technique of wrapping briquettes in newspapers before
feeding them into the stove—but exercise of any kind was difficult since Berlin was under a deep carpet of snow.

All in all I felt that my first two months had been a marking
time and a preparation rather than a part of my experience.
There had been, however, one interlude which taught me something of another side of German life. Soon after I arrived in
Berlin I had received a welcoming card from Armin Stein, a
former Rhodes Scholar at Worcester, who was doing his national
service as an *Einjähriger* at Rathenow with the *Zietenhussaren*.
He pressed me to spend the next week-end with him and promised the attraction of 'races on Sunday'. I accepted and travelled down by train to Rathenow on the late afternoon of a
Saturday. Of the promised races I can remember nothing at
all—but the Saturday evening festivities are unforgettable.
The Zieten Hussars were one of the crack cavalry regiments of
the German Imperial Army and the officers certainly lived up
to the regimental reputation. Throughout the evening we drank
great quantities of that Bismarckian beverage which was
compounded of stout and champagne in equal parts. It seemed
imperative to me that I should last the course without disaster
and I felt some pride when I managed to get to bed without
assistance. Sleep was profound, but waking had the character of
nightmare. My head seemed scarcely to have touched the pillow
when I felt, with horrid apprehension, the touch of cold metal
across my jugular vein. I compelled myself to remain absolutely

still and forced myself slowly to open my eyes. Bending over
me was an *Unteroffizier* with a square Teutonic face and an
immense moustache, in his hand a long and evil-looking cut-
throat razor. Slowly, with great relief, I realized that he, whom
I had thought an assassin, was only the barber and that he had
lathered and started operations before I had woken up. To be
shaved in bed was doubtless common form for the Zieten Hussars
but it was a luxury which had not previously come my way.

By about the middle of February I had acquired enough
German to be able to take part in ordinary social intercourse
and I moved on to my next port of call. This was at Cassel,
where a German friend of Dorothy Williams (the daughter of
my Oxford colonel) lived with her husband. He was a school-
teacher, but on a higher social and educational level than
Thies; at his flat I begun to enjoy many of the amenities which
I had lacked in Berlin. Cassel was an attractive place; the
Rembrandts in the picture gallery were superb; the theatre put
on a succession of plays by Ibsen, Chekov, and Shaw. I saw
Pygmalion there almost as soon as (or perhaps before) it was
produced in London. My hosts, too, had many friends, especially Eitel, who was a landscape painter and carpet designer. In
short I began to enjoy myself and to take some benefit from my
stay abroad. In the Easter vac. Geoffrey Baskerville, a Keble
don, came out with two Keble undergraduates and together we
spent an agreeable holiday in the South—visiting among other
places, Hohenzollern and Hohenstaufen, Schaffhausen, Stutt-
gart, and Bregenz. Then in April I moved on to Freiburg im
Breisgau, and was matriculated in the University there for the
summer semester.

The term at Freiburg was the main purpose of my 'German
year', for I was expected to learn something of German methods
and German university teaching. Advice had been showered
upon me in Oxford as to the best way of profiting from my
'German year' but no one had given the same advice. John
Murray, most unexpectedly, had urged me to run boldly into
debt rather than to miss any chance of experience. Others had
urged travel to as many parts as possible, but all, except perhaps
Hassall, were unanimous in their respect for German methods
and German learning. The respect for learning was well
founded but admiration for German methods was probably

exaggerated. I had had little opportunity of following John
Murray's advice in the first few months when visits to Potsdam
and Dresden had been my only relief from the monotony of
Berlin, but I fully intended to make good my omissions in the
summer. Hampered by difficulties of speech one is only three
parts alive, but by the time that I went to Freiburg I was pro-
ficient enough in German to take my full part in University
life in that enchanted city. North Germany had been harsh
and unwelcoming, the warm and friendly South cast a magic
spell on me. It was there that I saw the last of the old Germany
and the last of the old German University life. Much, though
not all, of the Oxford charm was there. True, there was no close-
knit college life, and no tutorial system but there was the same
gregarious and friendly companionship of undergraduates—at
the *Stammtisch* which I frequented with four friends at mid-
day or over a *Maibowle* in the evening at this or the other
hostelry. And then the town itself! Little rivulets flowing, or
dancing, down many of the streets, lilac flourishing on the
walls of the houses. Two occasions in particular stand out in
memory. One was with a student *Korps* or *Burschenschaft* to
which I was once taken, where for a whole night we celebrated
the coming of the May. We drank and sang the traditional
songs 'Du wunderschöner Monat Mai', 'Der Mai ist gckommen',
and the rest, and drank toasts and made speeches to one another
until the dawn came, when we all went out into the open air
to greet the coming of May. With hindsight how tragic it all
seems! The other occasion was the break which we had at
Whitsun, when I undertook a week's walk in the Black Forest
with Jock Houstoun-Boswall.[1] The names of all the villages are
forgotten, but not the singing and laughter of the *Wandervögel*
as we met them on their walks or in the inns at night, nor yet
the local wines, of which every valley had its own, nor yet
again the Feldberg on which there was still a trace of snow, or
the Titisee all bathed in sunshine. That summer was indeed
the last of the old Germany and I am glad to have seen it.
Froude knew it all when he wrote of the middle ages, 'And now
it is all gone—like an unsubstantial pageant faded. Only in
the silent figures sleeping on their tombs and perhaps in the

[1] A personal friend, sometime secretary to Sir Archibald Weigall, Governor of
South Australia 1920–2.

sound of church bells could he hear the faint echo of a vanished world'. To Freiburg I have never returned—nor would I wish to—better to keep one's memories.

Another great joy in that summer was given me by the opportunity of playing games once more. Lawn tennis was a major sport and the tennis club the centre of social life. Once again I learned the immense advantage which games give to the player in forming friendships and getting to know his fellows. In mid-July we had our tournament and I managed to win both the open and the University singles with the majestic titles 'Meisterschaft von Freiburg' and 'Akademische Meisterschaft'. Looking at some old press-cuttings I see that I lost one set in each five-set final, but that the real crisis had come in the semifinal of the open singles in which I had, contrary to expectations and aided by a favourable shower of rain, just got home against the former champion of the club. It speaks volumes for the German sportsmanship of those days that my success did not seem to annoy or irritate either the members of the club or the local reporters. All seemed to have been friendly to me though a Mr. was always inserted before my name to point to my foreign origin.

On the more serious side Freiburg came up to expectation. I was befriended by Eitel, a *Privatdozent* and the brother of my Cassel acquaintance—and I had introductions from Oxford to some of the professors. Freiburg had had for some time a high reputation for its medical school and arts subjects were rapidly gaining ground also. My first call was on Wolfgang Michael,[2] the historian of early eighteenth-century English history who gave me much help and encouragement. My first lunch with him showed me a picture of German family life. There seemed to be innumerable daughters and when at the conclusion of the meal we all rose and gravely shook hands with each other, murmuring 'Gesegnete Mahlzeit', I wondered whether I was being given a gentle hint that it was time for me to take my leave. It was not so, for Michael was prepared to discuss Robert Walpole and kindred topics as long as the most demanding student could wish. The leading historian at Freiburg, however, was not Michael but Meinecke, at that time perhaps the best-known and most influential of German modern historians.

[2] Author of *Englische Geschichte im achtzehnten Jahrhundert*.

German historians had played their part in the accomplishment of German unity and their political influence was therefore greater than that of their English contemporaries. Meinecke's interests were much in the sphere of political thought and his *Weltbürgerthum und Nationalstaat* was an important and influential work. It was, therefore, considered a high honour to be allowed to take part in his seminar, to which on the strength of my Oxford introductions I was admitted. Further I was allowed to attend as an observer and not expected to do any share of the work. The seminar was on Bismarck and my privileged position soon almost brought me to disaster. On one afternoon some matter of constitutional history suggested a comparison with British procedure. 'Ah,' said Meinecke, 'we will ask Herr Masterman about that.' Alas! The afternoon was hot and Herr Masterman was asleep. I thought that this accident would lead me into disrepute but the reverse was the case. 'Who', said the students, 'is this foreigner who is so eminent that he is admitted to a seminar from which most of us are excluded, and allowed to go to sleep there without reproof, let alone expulsion?'

The lectures at Freiburg were for the most part good and usually more lively than those at Oxford. One professor who lectured on German literature to a very large and noisy audience excited scenes of enthusiasm and applause. Sometimes at the end of his hour there was almost a riot, for he would continue long after the prescribed time had elapsed. The audience was then divided into two parties; one cheered him on, the other, using the continental method of expressing dissent, shuffled their feet until he was almost inaudible. Of examinations I did not learn much but I believe that they were taken with much seriousness. There was one precipice near the town which was the traditional spot for academic suicides. Medical students had an escape route; if they failed, so friends told me, they could become dentists.

So the summer passed. At the beginning of July I was joined by Timothy Eden,[3] who had been sent out to me by Hassall to do some reading for the History School which he was to take later on from Christ Church. At the end of the month

[3] Sir Timothy Eden (1893–1963), painter and author, elder brother of Anthony Eden, Lord Avon.

Jock Balfour[4] came out also. I planned an agreeable August—
some travel in the South, perhaps a couple of tennis tournaments, some reading of contemporary German literature for
which up to then I had found little time. But the war came.

[4] Sir John Balfour, later Ambassador to Spain 1951–4.

X

RUHLEBEN

That it may please Thee . . . to show Thy
pity upon all prisoners and captives.

THE LITANY

However could you have let yourself be caught in
Germany? You have studied modern history, you must
have known that war was imminent, in Heaven's name why
didn't you get away? Was it folly or pride or just incompetence? Such questions have pursued me for fifty-odd years and
demand an answer. In the first place very few people in England
believed in the imminence of war and fewer still thought that
they would be involved, even if the country was a belligerent.
If England was at war would she not fight in the old traditional
way, subsidizing continental allies and sending a professional
army to assist them, while the Navy swept the seas and pro-
tected our island fortress? The campaign of Lord Roberts for
compulsory service and all his warnings had left me, as well as
many others, cold. We had all read Norman Angell's *The
Great Illusion* and thought that the inutility of war had been
demonstrated beyond the possibility of rebuttal and we sneered
at the doctrine that peace could only be secured by preparation for war. 'If you wish for peace, prepare for peace', we
argued in our superior way. In fact I and others had a more than
average share of that supposed moral and intellectual superiority which is, now as then, the curse of British Liberals.

In Germany I had my warnings. In Berlin in the early days
I used—on occasion—to go to the Cathedral, not for spiritual
refreshment but in order to improve my German by listening
to the sermon. On one Sunday I arrived very late and was not
edified by the sermon which was a fulsome tribute to the blessings of monarchy. The explanation came at the end of the
service; royalty was present in force. As the royal party left the

Cathedral to go the palace opposite, the Kaiser received a very lukewarm reception but the Crown Prince an enthusiastic one. I asked a German friend for the meaning of this and received the reply, 'Our Kaiser is believed to be in favour of peace, whilst the Crown Prince is all for war.' My second warning came at Freiburg during a festival evening of songs and toasts. A fellow-student, who had drunk deep, proposing my health declared that, though the cannon of our two countries would probably be thundering against each other in a few months' time, he still held me in high regard. I replied that I thought the idea of war a chimera and reciprocated his good wishes. The third and clearest warning came when the Archduke was assassinated at Sarajevo and it came from one well qualified to judge. Michael was a trained historian and also a Jew, with a Jew's instinct, born of centuries of persecution and adversity, for the coming of catastrophe. 'This means war,' he said to me. 'You should leave for England at once.' Thinking him a scare-monger I paid no heed and in a few days the danger seemed to be forgotten. From England, naturally enough, came no warning or suggestion of return. Jock Balfour, who for family reasons must have been as well advised as anyone, did not arrive in Germany from England till 29 July. Other countries arranged things better. After the war had begun there was much speculation about the policy of Japan. In one issue of a Berlin newspaper (I think the *Berliner Tageblatt* or the *B.Z. am Mittag*) I read a leading article with its heavily printed headline on the front page, 'Ein tüchtiges kleines Volk'. Alas for the hopes of editors! Within a week Japan had entered the war against Germany and a new headline appeared: 'Eine Rasse von gelben Affen'. But unlike the British the Japanese had not waited to be rounded up. Warned by some oriental system of bush telegraph the Japanese in Germany had, during that week, mysteriously melted away.

Had I decided to get out in the days immediately preceding Great Britain's entry into the war that would probably have proved impossible. On 31 July Timothy Eden decided that he would make for Switzerland on the way for home, and Jock and I accompanied him to the station—only to be told that no civilians could travel owing to the German mobilization. After this rebuff we had a council of war and discussed whether an

attempt should be made to journey north and try to get out
through Holland or the Baltic. In my own case there was no
question. It must be remembered that in 1914 the mass internment of enemy civilians was a thing unthought of; at the worst
we should be stranded in a hostile country for a month or two
until our exchange was arranged. Moreover, a German friend
who was a minor Government official, informed me that there
were orders given that, should Great Britain come into the war,
all British subjects were immediately to be evacuated to Switzerland. About the journey to the north he was equally decisive—
travel that way would be impossible. So I should stay in Freiburg where I was known and where no sort of harm could
come to me. I have no doubt that my friend was sincere, but
he was wholly in error. Minor officials everywhere have an insa-
tiable desire to let their friends know that they are fully informed about and trusted with the plans of their superiors.
Often they are not. Here I return to our council of war in which
other Freiburg residents participated. There were over a
hundred British in Freiburg—but only one passport, which
was the property of Jock Balfour. All of us were agreed that a
journey north would be an act of folly, but one of our number
thought that it should be tried. This was Ronald Squirl (afterwards famous as Ronald Squire the actor) whose widowed
mother lived in Freiburg. I had played a good deal of tennis
with him in the preceding weeks and knew how worried he
was at our situation. He was engaged to be married in August
(to Martin Harvey's daughter) and felt that he must make an
attempt to get to England, even if the journey was only a hopeless gesture. Someone suggested that his chances might be improved if he armed himself with Jock's passport although no
two men could be less alike. Jock has always believed that I was
the instigator of this plan—or crime—and he may well be right
though I thought for a long time that the offer was an act of
spontaneous chivalry and daring on his part. Perhaps we should
share the credit or the blame. In the event Ronald took the
passport, and *mirabile dictu* it brought him in safety to England.

So I remained in Freiburg. The blow fell on 5 August when
I found a note from my landlady, 'Ich ersuche sie in Anbe-
tracht des Krieges mit England mein Haus bis heute Nachmit-
tag 3 Uhr zu verlassen. Frau Lohmüller.' I have little recollec-

tion of the last few days at Freiburg, except for one scene in which Eitel acted the part of a friend to me. Seeing me sitting alone in the hotel dining-room, he invited me to join him at his table since Englishmen were not popular at that moment. He was in uniform and on his way to the front. Very soon after 5 August all the English colony was rounded up and transferred to hotels in Baden-Baden. Here we lived a strange, dream-like life, following the course of the war as best we could in the German papers—waiting for news of an expected exchange. The sensation was one of watching a theatre performance from a box—but the box door was locked. The exchange negotiations, however, did not prosper and at the end of October an ultimatum was published, stating that unless all German civilians were released by 5 November every Englishman in Germany would be interned. And so it was. On 6 November we were rounded up in our hotels and taken by train to Rastatt, where we spent, I think, four nights in an unpleasant and rather dirty gaol. Then on 10 November we were taken by train to Berlin and lodged in Plötzensee prison. The journey lasted about thirty hours, and we were not very popular travellers. In particular Timothy Eden's monocle seemed to rouse the onlookers to fury. Plötzensee was much better appointed than Rastatt—after all it was in the capital and catered for more notable criminals than Rastatt could entertain—but Russian prisoners had preceded us there and the bed-bugs were many. Most of us were glad enough to leave for the unknown on 28 November. The unknown was Ruhleben and there I was to spend almost exactly four years.

Ruhleben has gathered round itself a considerable body of literature. Books, articles in reviews and journals, Government white papers, newspaper comments—not to speak of an almost complete collection of camp productions preserved in the library of the Harvard University Law School. The greater part of these writings is ephemeral, but one book stands out, written by J. Davidson Ketchum and published in 1965. Ketchum was Professor of Psychology in the University of Toronto and had been interned at Ruhleben when he was twenty-one. It is a substantial book, the fruit of many years of study and thought, and founded on the letters, diaries, and cards of fellow-prisoners. As he did not, unfortunately, live to finish the book, the last year of our captivity is imperfectly recorded, but the first three years, especially the first six months, are surveyed by a perceptive and unprejudiced mind and give a record which needs no further elaboration. I must, therefore, guard myself from the attempt to retell the history of the camp, but some brief account is necessary as a background to my own personal experiences.

First of all it must be stated without circumlocution that, if the four-year period is treated as a whole, we were well treated by the Germans, but that this statement does not apply to the first four or five months. These were a dour experience, when discomforts and hardships were undergone. The camp was sited on the Ruhleben race-course and the prisoners were quartered in the stables, which were at once renamed 'Barracks'. The ten stables were substantial buildings; through each ran a cement corridor, on which opened twenty-seven horse-boxes and two stable-boys' rooms which were inhabited by the German guards. The upper storeys were partitioned into two haylofts, reached by external stairways. These lofts were so low that a man could only stand upright in the middle of the building. There was an eleventh barrack—of wood—and numerous other buildings were erected as time went on. Each barrack had to accommodate over 300 men, and the overcrowding was excessive. In the lofts the straw mattresses touched one another, and those who had a place in a horse-box considered themselves extremely fortunate—although there were six men in each box. Though the compound was brightly lighted by arc-lamps the barracks (for so I must call them) themselves were hardly lighted at all; there were two electric bulbs in the corridor and two in each loft, but the boxes had no light at all. The only washing facilities for over 300 men were two taps for cold water, one at each end of the corridor. These conditions, though severe, were not intolerable but it has to be remembered that we had no other resting-place—in our box or loft we slept, fed, and lived. The food provided was inadequate. A contractor had undertaken to feed us for 66 Pf. a day, but it was soon revealed that the greater part of this sum stayed in his own pockets. The menu was not appetizing; breakfast consisted of dry bread and acorn coffee, the midday meal was soup, in which the advertised meat was seldom to be found, the evening meal a piece of blood sausage with skilly or cocoa. The bread ration was soon cut down to one-fifth of a loaf a day. In the early days extra food could sometimes be obtained at a canteen, but many of the prisoners were hungry men during that winter. The Souvenir Album of the Ruhleben Exhibition in 1919 thus summarizes the situation:

The British endured the malevolence of the Prussian junker with its injustice, the shouting and mechanical ineptitude of the guards, the want of beds, the absence of due heating, lighting, sanitary arrangements, the absence of proper nourishment, the total lack of hospital arrangements, the floods in the yard, the want of news, the nowhere to sit and nothing to sit on.

The compound itself in which the barracks stood was a sea of mud in wet weather, and a storm of dust when dry. In front of the grandstands there was, however, an open broad promenade and there we walked in order to keep warm so long as light lasted. Personally I was lucky; not only did I get a place in a box quickly but also I was placed in Barrack X, which was adjacent to the latrines—an important advantage in the cold of a Berlin winter. Cold and over-crowding—they are the abiding impressions; I am left with the conviction that my own health was saved by a sleeping-bag which Jock Cumberlege contrived to have sent out to me. Of course the hardships which we underwent were trivial compared to those of combatants, and less than nothing when one thinks of internment camps of a later war, but at the time they excited commiseration, especially for the elderly and for those who had been taken from sanatoria and hospitals.

It is difficult to assess accurately the size of the camp at any one time, for many departed, and many newcomers arrived. In all probably about 7,000 passed through, but the official history records that 4,400 was the largest number present at any one time. They were a wonderful assortment of contrasting types. First of all there were 1,400 seafarers—deck officers, engineers, crews, and fishermen, most of whom had been seized at Hamburg. To them we owed much, for their derisive laughter could quell the noisy orders of the guards even though it often landed them in the cells, and their absolute assurance of ultimate victory coupled with supreme contempt for all things German did much to raise camp morale. The next

largest class was business men, about 1,000 of them, ranging
from directors of companies to junior clerks; after them professional men and academics, of whom there were, surprisingly,
over 700; next trainers and jockeys from the Berlin race-courses,
and golf and football professionals; workmen, amongst whom
the skilled predominated over the semi- and unskilled; finally
some 'various', men of any kind of occupation or of none. Truly,
all sorts and conditions of men!

With the coming of spring everything changed. Up to then
everything had been on a temporary basis, for everyone
expected that the exchange negotiations would be brought to a
satisfactory conclusion. It was not a question of whether we
should be exchanged, but only of when and on what conditions.
In fact the matter was difficult, for the Germans demanded 'all
for all', and the British 'man for man'. As there were 26,000
German civilians in England and only 4,000–5,000 English in
Germany the deadlock persisted throughout the war. On 4
March it was announced that the negotiations had broken
down and in consequence the Ruhlebenites had to adjust their
minds to a long stay. The second factor in causing the remarkable change which came over the camp was that by March
parcels from England began to come through in a steady stream.
It is hardly an exaggeration to say that for the rest of the war we
were fed from home, through the Red Cross, whilst the Germans
only contributed a token ration to us. The third factor in bringing about the change was the acquisition of one-half of the race-
course for a recreation ground. This did not belong to the
German Government but was rented from the Rennbahn
Company. On it we were able in time to play every kind of
game and it changed the whole character of the life of the
camp.

The change from a motley collection of prisoners herded into
a camp to an active and integrated society was both rapid and
memorable, and it was brought about by the prisoners themselves. In effect the prisoners took over the camp from their
captors and ran it in their own way. To this the Germans
contributed. Graf Schwerin, the septuagenarian Commandant
was a humane man, who openly declared that civilians should
never have been interned at all, and who, on one occasion,
offered his resignation rather than impose a ban on smoking.

Baron Taube, the Camp Officer, though of uncertain temper and limited intelligence, was susceptible to flattery and could be managed. The guards, too, truculent at first, soon came to see on which side their bread was buttered. If they had trouble in their barracks the trouble disturbed the officers as well. The Graf was said to have remarked on one occasion that his 250 soldiers were a greater burden than his 4,000 prisoners. If a soldier did run foul of the officers the punishment was severe—he would be sent to the front. How much better to stay comfortably at Ruhleben and drive a thriving trade with the prisoners in English newspapers and similar luxuries which could be bought in Berlin! In the summer these facts were tacitly acknowledged; in September the guards were removed from the barracks, and all effective control handed over to the prisoners and their officials. Occasionally, of course, the Germans intervened and imposed mass punishments—as for example when two rank buttons were removed from the cap of an *Unteroffizier* or when some skilful seaman cut the halyards and thus prevented the hoisting of the flag on the Kaiser's birthday.

It was a German-reared internee who best described the activity of 1915: 'You English seem to set to work as if you were founding a new colony.' That was exactly what was done. A few facts will support this argument. A year or so after the camp had been established there was a 'civil service' of about 200 men; a police force commanded by a golf professional; a most efficient parcel service and post office; kitchen, canteen, and hot water services—all taken over from the Germans; fatigue parties and cleaners. A convalescent barracks, equipped from British funds, supplied the deficiencies of the German medical staff; games were organized and great barrack competition aroused; the theatre flourished—in all 128 different productions in those years—concerts were frequent and of high standard—exhibitions of art and of handicrafts. All these things were made possible by the steady demands made for space, demands assisted by the American Embassy.

Among all these things education was the chief feature of the camp. It became a university and a school combined. Already in December 1914 some of the academics, led by a group of Cambridge scientists, had formed the so-called Arts and Science

Union which provided open-air lectures in many subjects as soon as the weather permitted these to be given on one of the grandstands. Among them was James Chadwick[1] who lectured on radio-activity. The Arts and Science Union lacked organization and was in time swallowed up by the Camp School. The school was organized by A. C. Ford[2] and became the most important part of the camp. Apart from lectures, circles were formed for those interested in many different subjects and in them papers were read and discussed. The classes, however, were of course the major undertaking. By 1917 the school prospectus shows that there were seventeen departments and 247 teachers, many of whom had been trained in the camp itself. The year was divided into terms and vacations and all the pupils were registered. In the later days examinations were taken in the camp—from the London Chamber of Commerce and the Royal Society of Arts as well as for matriculation at London University. That such examinations could be held in the camp is a commentary on cultural relations between states, even in time of war.

Two distinct pictures of Ruhleben are retained in my memory —and they are very different from each other. One is of a prison camp and covers three or four months; the other is of a civilized and active society, fully and purposefully engaged, which lasted for three and a half years. It was in fact a great social experiment, the building of a society. Apart from lecturing and running the History Circle I spent much time, as most prisoners do, in studying languages. The greatest pleasure came from Italian, partly because that language and way of life seemed then to be the antithesis of all things German but also because the Italian department was controlled by Matthew Prichard, who was by any standard the most remarkable and in some ways the most influential man in the camp. Holding a post at the Museum of Fine Arts in Boston, he was an authority on Byzantine art, on Matisse, and on the philosophy of Bergson and had, in addition, the qualities of a later-day prophet who attracted to himself the more cultivated and better-educated

[1] Sir James Chadwick, Master of Gonville and Caius College, Cambridge, 1948–58, Nobel Prizeman.
[2] Arthur Clow Ford, O.B.E., External Registrar of University of London 1936–46, and Secretary to Universities' Council for Adult Education 1947–50.

young. The Italian Circle showed great and sustained activity and even published its own paper, *Messaggere*, in which among the literary articles could be found accounts of Ruhleben football by a football professional and musical criticisms by an operatic tenor who had appeared in many of the European opera houses. For the rest I was active in the games of all kinds which we arranged on the race-course and was, for a short time, captain of my barrack.

Outstanding incidents were few, and are of little interest now, but a visit from Roger Casement is worthy of record. We did not know who the visitor was—but only that the military authorities were calling up Irishmen to be interviewed by him. The indignation of one of them, later editor of the *Irish Times*, was typical of the reception of Casement's suggestion that Irishmen should join him against the English. Only in the barrack reserved for coloured prisoners did a certain number declare that they were really Irishmen and as such glad to leave the camp. They were not accepted, and Casement left the camp, apparently disillusioned. After a day or two, however, three Irish divinity students, quiet and reserved men, who had talked to Casement, very unobtrusively left the camp. But Casement can have had little profit from them; one became a Catholic priest—the other two volunteered for military service in the British Army.

XI

END OF RUHLEBEN AND RETURN TO ENGLAND

Stone walls do not a prison make
Nor iron bars a cage.

RICHARD LOVELACE

IN the long years of waiting there were some attempts at escape, but all but very few ended in failure. Why were there not more? In the first winter an exchange of all prisoners had been expected almost daily and after that the rumours that new exchange negotiations were under way were frequent and eagerly believed. It was also believed—perhaps the Germans propagated the myth—that anyone who attempted to escape would forfeit his right to be exchanged. Nor were the hopes of release unfounded. In England there was a steady stream of protest against the internment of civilians; speeches in Parliament, white papers, letters to *The Times*. As late as February 1917 a mass demonstration was held at the Kingsway Hall to demand the release of British civilian prisoners. The Bishop of London was in the chair and the first resolution was moved by Lord Charles Beresford, who with naval directness declared that the removal of the 26,000 Germans interned in England would be of immense advantage to the country quite apart from the recovery of 4,000 Britishers. The release of those over forty-five was actually agreed in December 1916 but only a very few left before the arrangements broke down. In June 1917 an Anglo-German conference opened at The Hague and decided in August that the forty-five-ers would definitely be released, together with 400 others whose health was suffering, who would be sent to Holland. Vain hopes! It was not until January 1918 that the agreement was acted upon and that 350 men left the camp.

It was as late as that that I first thought seriously myself of attempting escape. W.F. Mackenzie, a very able business man with knowledge both of Germany and of Holland, was in touch with a Dutch smuggling organization who had already had some success in getting prisoners from other camps out of Germany by the railway. Mackenzie was released to Holland in January 1918 and offered to try to arrange a passage for me. An agent of the Dutch firm contrived to visit me in Ruhleben and told me that in a week or two I should get a message giving me a date and rendezvous in Berlin. It would be up to me to get out of the camp—but this could be done by bribery of a sentry. Nothing happened and not until after the war had ended did I learn that the agent had tried once too often and had been captured and presumably shot. Other plans had to be made.

When the summer came a fellow-prisoner, Barney Saunders, approached me and discussed a joint attempt at escape. At first I was not very keen, and stressed the difficulties in our way, but I was stung by one remark of his: 'I think it is a duty to try to get out to do our bit; we are far too comfortable here'. That was decisive and I agreed to join him. My escape attempt was not sparked off by an overpowering wish for liberty, still less by dislike of or impatience with camp life. I knew quite well that I could last out the rest of the war in security and without discomfort. Nor can I plead very lofty motives of patriotism. 'Noblesse oblige' sounds well, but often, as in my case, it disguised a much less worthy motive. That was, quite simply, that I felt I had to do what would be considered the right or decent thing to do.

Once engaged I made the best plans that I could. I knew myself well enough to be sure that I could not make a successful trek across Germany even if I could get hold of the requisite maps, provisions, a compass, and so forth; on the practical details I should break down. On the other hand I was confident that I could keep my head and bluff my way along once I was outside the camp, and certain considerations confirmed me in this belief. Money was available, and many can be bribed in the fourth year of a war; my German was passable and though I could not expect to be taken for a German, I could probably use the Dutch which I had learned in the camp to pass myself off as a Dutchman. Most of all I traded on my conviction that, after the long years of war, German security measures and the production of passes and permits would have largely fallen into desuetude. So the plan evolved. Once out of the camp we would travel boldly by public transport to within twenty or thirty miles from the frontier. After that Saunders would be in command and I should follow his lead.

The method of getting out of the camp was carefully thought out and worked perfectly. The road to Berlin ran immediately outside the front of the camp and past the main gate. Outside the road was the railway line from Spandau to Berlin, and on this line came the trucks bringing the parcels for 4,000 men. When a parcels train arrived, usually about once a fortnight, a fatigue party of prisoners took out a very large open cart or truck which was hauled by two ropes—with seven or eight men on each rope. The guard room was immediately alongside the main gate and before this was opened those on the ropes were counted by two of the German guards. This counting was never very expertly done because the men concerned took pleasure in tormenting the guards. On the day in question, 3 August, the counting was even more disorderly than usual. Most of those on the ropes were seafarers and all played their part magnificently. A splendid fight broke out, which rapidly became a riot. The guard turned out and succeeded at last in restoring some sort of order so that the men could be counted again. Eventually they were, but by that time Barney Saunders and I had replaced two others on the ropes and two parcels of clothes (our going-away kit) had been thrown into the cart. The gates were opened and out we went. Inside the trucks the food parcels were piled up to the roof; some men got inside and passed them out to others who put them in the cart, so that when a truck was half emptied there was a clearing in the middle of the truck about the size of an old-fashioned bathing machine. Into one of these Saunders and I had our package of clothes passed up and there we changed rapidly from our clogs and corduroys into ordinary civilian kit. We then dropped out of the truck on the far side from the camp and walked down the line towards Berlin. The guards throughout had stood by the cart and we were, therefore, concealed from them by the trucks themselves.

After a couple of hundred yards we recrossed the railway line and rejoined the road. Here when we were less than a quarter of a mile from the camp disaster threatened, for we saw,

walking towards the camp, a newly joined officer. This was
the son of Graf Schwerin, the Camp Commandant, who had
just been appointed as an A.D.C. to his father. I realized at
once that he could not yet be acquainted with the life of the
camp but that he would probably know that some of the
prisoners—especially those who were *deutschgesinnt*—were sometimes sent into Berlin for business or legal matters. Would he
know that they were always sent under guard? Probably not. I
told Saunders not to attempt evasion but to take off his hat and
bow formally to the Count. The bluff worked; the Count
seemed to hesitate, but then returned our greeting with a
salute and walked on.

We reached Berlin, I suppose, about ten or eleven in the
morning and with a long day before us—for it would clearly
be rash to take a train until the evening. We parked ourselves
for the day at an address given us in the camp, a brothel of about
middle-class standard. We were well received—not for ourselves
or for our money but because we were able to give 'Madame'
two cakes of soap—a luxury beyond price in the Germany of
1918. But it was a *very* long day.

In the evening we walked to the Lehrter Bahnhof where I
made a long and careful study of the conditions of travel. I did
not know with any certainty whether travellers had to produce a
passport or *Polizei Ausweis* or some such document but, as I
expected, all formalities were swept aside in the evening rush
hour. Unfortunately in the course of the day I had discovered
that my companion's German was execrable—he had only to
open his mouth to proclaim himself an Englishman—so I was
compelled to tell him in all circumstances to remain dumb and
to indicate by signs that he was stone-deaf if anyone addressed
him. I then, when the crowd was most dense, advanced to the
ticket office and bought two tickets to a place (I have forgotten
the name) not far distant from the frontier. As the train came in
the crowd was dense; we made, as arranged, for different
carriages but it was hard enough to get a place, as previous
occupants protested that there was no more room. I had to take
the offensive and to roar with an accompaniment of oaths that
I had paid for my ticket and had as much right as anyone to
travel (which was not true!). The overcrowding did not last
long, for at every station numerous passengers got out, until at

length I was left with only one fellow-passenger in my carriage—
and he a high-ranking German officer. He was tiresome because
he tried repeatedly to engage me in conversation and I had to
feign sleep for the greater part of the night. My last recollection
of him is that he insisted on waking me up to point out to me
the Minden monument in the early morning. When we arrived
at Löhne the train stopped and everyone had to get out. I was
not seriously perturbed, for Löhne is only, as the crow flies,
about fifty miles from the Dutch frontier, and I was confident
that I could find a local train or other public transport to take
us at least twenty or thirty miles nearer our goal. First, however, as I explained to Saunders who had rejoined me, we must
walk in a confident way into the town and wait for the evening
to make our next journey. But on the platform of Löhne
station misfortune befell us. Apart from soldiers there were
some ugly-looking civilians on the platform, one of whom produced a revolver and accused us of being escaping British
officers. It was useless to protest that we were innocent Dutch-
men (one deaf); escape was impossible and we were taken
under armed guard to gaol in Hanover. In fact, fate had dealt a
cruel blow. The date of our escape had synchronized with the
mass escape from Holzminden and the country was alive with
military and police searching for the tunnellers. But for that
unfortunate clash of dates I am still obstinately convinced
(though probably wrongly) that we should have got through
to Holland. A number of escapes fail because of the long trek
across country, because of exhaustion or lack of provisions.
Starting fresh with only twenty-odd miles to go and with time to
observe the frontier our chances must have been at the least fair.

Loyalty to the Hanoverian dynasty had propagated in
England the legend that the best and purest German was
spoken in Hanover, but that was not my experience. Among
the prisons that I have known Hanover takes a low place.
The wearing of convicts' clothes is bad for morale and the room
which I occupied for the first night had walls covered with the
scrawled curses and lamentations of French prisoners—
apparently expecting or condemned to death. They were not
pretty reading. After that came seven days of solitary confinement. The rules for this punishment were strict; the cell was
darkened by a curtain over the window, the food was bread

and water, and the mattress was removed from the bed. After the first few days, however, my gaolers relented (whether officially or not I cannot tell) and gave me a mattress and, I think, some soup or coffee. Exercise for about twenty minutes was taken in a small yard by squads of prisoners—each walking with about half a dozen paces between one and the next. A guard stood at each end of the yard. I learned on my first day's exercise what the practice was. As we reached the point furthest away from a guard the prisoner next behind me moved quickly up and spoke—there was just time for one question and an answer on each round: 'What are you here for? Is it murder?' I indicated that it was not. Rape, theft, assault with violence were all tried, and my reply that I was a political prisoner received no credence. Sadly my questioner gave up his probe and dropped back on each round for a word with the prisoner next behind him. Saunders I did not see—he must have come out with some other squad.

When the seven days were over Saunders and I were reunited and recovered our own clothes. Though I was in poor shape my companion seemed to have taken it all in his stride and his cheerful optimism soon restored my morale. We were sent by train to Berlin in the company of two guards, both of whom were friendly. We arrived in the evening and were taken to a large room in some barracks or prison—a room large and empty, save for a few unfortunates on the floor and a large trestle table down the centre. I began to settle down on the floor, but one of the friendly guards advised me not to. 'Lie down on the table,' he said, 'you'll soon see why.' Soon I did. The room was used to take in all the riff-raff of Berlin arrested in the streets after nightfall. Before morning we had almost a full house, which Dickens better than anyone else could have described, and I was glad enough to have my reserved place. In the morning we were moved to the Stadtvogtei to await further orders.

At least since the days of Jeremy Bentham most prisons are much alike, both in structure and routine, but at the Stadtvogtei I sensed that German discipline was beginning to break down. We were allowed for short periods to walk on the iron passages outside our cells and talk to one another, and several of those to whom I spoke proved to be soldiers who for one reason or

other had been sent back from the front. They made no secret
of the fact that they were glad of this reprieve and one told me,
without contradiction from his fellows, that Germany was
'kaput'. This was welcome information but I was still concerned
about our own fate, for we expected to be sent to one of the
punishment camps, of which we had heard some gloomy reports.
From this we were saved by Kurt Hahn, who contrived to visit
me and insisted that I should petition to be sent back to Ruhleben instead of going to a prison camp. No one understood the
German mentality better than Kurt, and he had always put
forward the view that—after a war—a country would be judged
by the world very much in accordance with the treatment that
had been meted out to prisoners. You must stress, he said, the
good treatment which you have had in the camp, and the fact
that you have been assisted in your work by professors in the
University of Berlin. You can add that you have assisted in
many ways in the running of the camp and that you hope to
continue this work. You can add that you attempted escape out
of a sense of duty—in order to assist your country. That argument will be understood. So far I saw nothing to object to but
the final sentence in the letter which Kurt dictated to me gave
me pause. In it I gave my word of honour that I would not
attempt another escape. It is true that a second attempt would
in the circumstances be doomed to failure from the start and
that the war was clearly near its end but I knew that the promise
was unworthy. If I had tried to escape (as I said) from a sense
of duty it was certainly my duty to try again if opportunity
offered. I gave way and signed the letter to the *Königliche
Kommandantur* in Berlin. Within a few days Saunders and I were
sent back to the camp.

The last few months in Ruhleben passed as the earlier ones
had done. In my view the most meritorious thing about the
prisoners—now reduced to less than 3,000—was that they kept
up their spirits and all their activities to the end. The day came
when the revolutionaries lined up the officers in the compound
and tore off the epaulettes from their shoulders, whilst we
watched like neutral observers at a football match. After that
we could, for the first time, leave the camp almost without
hindrance, and watch the course of events in Berlin. There,
whatever may have been the case elsewhere, the revolution

was strangely orderly. Once in the Tiergarten, there was a splutter of machine-gun fire and the crowd scattered, but even then, so strong was the engrained habit of discipline, that hardly a German disobeyed the notices which forbade them to step on the grass. 'Verboten' was still 'Verboten' even in November of 1918. At long last the trains provided for us arrived. So to Stralsund, and Hull, Catterick, and home.

XII

CHRIST CHURCH AFTER THE FIRST WAR

In the august procession of Colleges, Christ Church leads the way.

W. TUCKWELL

AFTER five years of absence my home-coming should have been a time of great relief and happiness and so, in some sense, it was. To see my Mother again, unchanged and to me faultless, was of itself almost enough to wipe out the memories of the long years of imprisonment—but she was alone, for my Father had died in 1916 and my brother, who had been allowed to join the Indian Cavalry in 1917, was in Egypt or Palestine awaiting, as he thought, his return to India. But my state of mind, as I recall it, was neither happy nor composed. Indeed for some weeks I was in a state bordering on depression. Imprisonment works in different ways on those who undergo it. Many brood and go over, time after time, their own experiences and their own thoughts. In my case I shrank from the thought that I must take up the teaching of men returning from the war. All my friends and contemporaries had played their part and contributed to the victory; many had died, all had fought, whereas I had spent four years out of danger and in comparative comfort. My predominant feeling was one of shame. I had played no part in the greatest struggle in our national history. Of course this attitude of mind was, on all rational grounds, ridiculous, but reason in such matters plays a small part compared to emotion. If only I had escaped in time to join up or even if I had not given my parole to desist from further attempts to escape! Then, I felt, I could have held my head up and felt in some sense justified. As things were I felt ashamed.

From this rather morbid state of introspection I was saved by Tommy Strong. As soon as I arrived at Christ Church he encouraged me to talk and, rather hesitatingly, I exposed to him all my doubts and misgivings, and showed him a copy of the letter which, at Kurt Hahn's dictation, I had written to secure my return to Ruhleben. The Dean said without circumlocution that he saw nothing blameworthy at all in the letter and then, with infinite tact, proceeded to explain to me that my preoccupation with my own affairs and my own state of mind was quite unworthy of me. I do not remember that he made any overt criticism at all but in his own almost miraculous way he conveyed to me the conviction that I had no moral right to brood over my own shortcomings when I should have been throwing all my energies into doing the job for which I had been appointed.

Nor was there, in fact, any time to spare for self-examination. Those who remember Hilary Term of 1919 will need no reminder of the speed and determination with which Oxford resumed its peacetime life. A tutor with half a dozen pupils in the first week of term was probably teaching, or trying to teach, twenty or twenty-five a fortnight later. It was not that we had any high-flown ideas about a country for heroes to live in but only that we were determined (often subconsciously) that what was good in pre-war Oxford should be handed on to the new generation. We were not preoccupied with theory or techniques of teaching but only with practical problems and day-to-day tasks. The immediate post-war generation which came up in 1919 and 1920 has been sadly underestimated by its censorious successors. In fact those years were a period of active endeavour and strenuous determination both to make up for the lost years (for so we deemed them) and to push forward into the future. In one sense we were all liberals then! Nor has sufficient credit been given to the wide and healthy tolerance of the returning warriors which enabled them to continue and coalesce easily and amicably with the younger men who came directly from the schools. Into this exciting world I plunged with enthusiasm; in less than a term I felt as though I had been at the House all my life. For the rest of the University I took little thought; Christ Church by itself was enough; in particular my colleagues in the Senior Common Room were the foundation of my new world.

The *Calendar* for 1920, the first in which my name appeared as a Student (I had been a lecturer since 1913) brings each colleague of that time vividly to mind. Charles Fisher, the dominant figure before the war, had been killed at Jutland. The eldest, Baynes, elected in 1873, was Secretary to the Governing Body and wrote to us always in a peculiar violet ink. He usually prefaced his remarks in the Governing Body on any topic with the words, 'In days gone by we used . . .'. Next came Arthur Hassall, my chief, and senior History Tutor, who had brought me to the House. A small and lively man, full of gaiety and goodwill, he had done more than anyone else to create good relations between the Senior Common Room and the undergraduates. At Governing Body meetings he would often leave his place and stand beside the fire—his only contribution to the debate being a cry of 'Divide, divide' when the discussion seemed to be lasting too long. Of University business he was critical, if not contemptuous, and he advised me to shun it when I could. 'Pair with two people and then vote twice' was a characteristic piece of advice. He was full of ingenious strategems such as that shown in his treatment of the Crown Prince of Siam—later King Rama VI. The Prince's countrymen expected him to return to them with some distinguished degree, but this was plainly impossible. Hassall gave him, at the beginning of term, an essay to write on a most unlikely subject—the War of the Polish Succession, and on that same subject the unfortunate Prince continued to write as week succeeded week. Eventually a letter was sent to Siam to say that the Prince had shown so much talent for historical research that it had been decided that he should write a book rather than take a degree. A slim volume of about forty pages was printed at Oxford in 1901 and numerous copies were exported to Siam. In the preface the future king expresses the hope that his book may be of use not only to members of the University who are reading for the History 'School' but also to all who are interested in eighteenth-century European affairs. The assistance rendered to the learned author by Arthur Hassall is graciously and suitably recognized. I wonder how many copies of the work survive.

Next in order was Blunt, our senior philosopher; almost blind, he used to lecture without notes and with the door of the room open. It seemed to the hearer that some sentences would never end, or at least never reach a grammatically correct conclusion,

but they always did. 'No one', as he once said to me, 'who has
attended my lectures for Greats and lasted to the end of them
has ever failed to get a first class—unless, of course, he ended in
a madhouse.' We all deferred much to his judgement, but the
Canons feared his acid comments and penetrating criticisms of
them—he referred to them as the 'debenture holders' and they
shuddered. Blunt's knowledge of practical affairs and of finance
was respected by us all, even by the undergraduates. Ten years
later Willie Kent-Hughes [1] wrote to me from Australia: '. . . If
old Blunt is still meandering around the meadows, please tell
him from me that I have lived to remember his final words to
me on our Arbitration Court system, namely, "Well, my boy,
your Arbitration Court may be a fine thing on a rising market.
When you have tested it on a falling market, come and have
another chat to me." I wish I could.'

The Senior Censor, who had attained to that office as a result
of the war, was Sidney Owen, or 'Young Owen' as my seniors
called him, because his father had also been a Student of
Christ Church. No one better deserved the appellation of a
'character' than he; for he combined a remarkable appearance
with idiosyncrasies and remarkable views delivered in a high-
pitched voice on a variety of subjects, and an undisguised
devotion to the pleasures of the table. His round and sanguine
face was surmounted by beautiful soft white hair; he walked
with a curious flat-footed shuffle which carried him along at an
unexpected pace. His arrival at the House was the outcome of a
misunderstanding. During the Long Vacation one of the
Canons called on the Dean and told him that a terrible mistake
had been made. What was it? 'Mr. Dean, we have elected to a
lectureship a man who has never been baptized!' Consternation prevailed, for Michaelmas Term was approaching when
the new lecturer (then studying in Germany) should have taken
up his appointment. 'Old' Owen came to the rescue. 'I have', he
said, 'a likely son who has just been appointed a lecturer in
classics at Liverpool.' 'Wire to him at once', said the Dean,
'and tell him that he is appointed at Christ Church.' History
does not relate anything of the feelings of the authorities at
Liverpool—still less whether anyone was bold enough to suggest
that the peccant scholar in Germany (who afterwards held a

[1] Sir Wilfrid Kent-Hughes, Australian Minister for Interior and Works 1951–6.

high place in another Oxford college) might be advised to undergo an adult baptism. When Old Owen died his son showed a true measure of piety. He decided that he must commemorate his father when engaged in the two activities which give him the most pleasure—golf and drinking port. For the space of a year, therefore, he played his golf in a black skull-cap and drank no port at all. The stock of Madeira in the cellar was, however, reduced almost to vanishing point. It was his custom to have terminal dinners with an old friend at another college—turn and turn about. The friend married and retired to North Oxford where, after a time, he invited Owen to dine with him. The old feasts were to be resumed. Alas, the dinner was not a great success, for a sudden silence allowed every guest to hear Owen saying to his hostess, 'I suppose that in North Oxford you dine in the middle of the day.' In the vacations it was his practice to go away for golf to one of the seaside courses on the south coast; on one occasion at Bournemouth after lunching on an over-large hot lobster he was attacked by a violent bleeding at the nose and was stretched out by the side of the second green. His venerable appearance and snow-white hair dabbled in blood excited the compassion of golfers near by but no one could find a remedy until his caddy, a boy of resource, thrust his putter down the back of his neck. It was a notable picture which might attract a Victorian artist—'Science coming to the rescue of scholarship'. For Owen in his own way was a good scholar though he had the misfortune to run foul of Housman who was a better scholar and who fell almost savagely on Owen's writings about Juvenal.

If Owen could be called a character, the Law Tutor, Carter, could certainly make the same claim. He combined with a brilliant intellect and the keenest legal judgement a sardonic wit and supreme egotism. He is the only man of whom I put knowingly a rather unkind but not unfair portrait in a work of fiction. He appears as Sir Smedley Patteringham in *Fate Cannot Harm Me*, and it says much for Carter's sense of humour that he was pleased rather than annoyed by the portrait. The principles which governed Sir Smedley's life were originally three—'Self not service'; 'Live and let die'; and 'The best is good enough for me'. To these he added a fourth, 'Anything to give pain', but this one was not applicable to

Carter, who cared little about the pain given to others and very much about the pleasure given to himself. A hedonist, he extracted all the pleasure which he could from every trivial hour. The strictest instructions were given to his scout to call him each morning at eight so that he might have the pleasure of going to sleep again whilst others worked. 'A cold and rainy morning, sir, the Dean and Censors look very miserable and are coughing; the papers say that the Bishop of Downshire died last night.' With a sigh of contentment Carter would resume his rest. He was a supremely idle man. It fell to my lot as Censor to inquire, at the Dean's request, into the work which Carter was actually doing in order that decision might be taken about the extension of his studentship. The inquiry soon revealed that it would be impossible to justify the extension. When freshmen arrived in October eager to start the study of the law, Carter would address them and vehemently recommend that they should read some other school; those who persisted were sent away and told to 'browse generally in the field of law' and not to return until the beginning of the following term. His textbook on contracts was a marvel of compression and he was a gifted lecturer, but his course seldom lasted through the term. If attendance decreased, Carter would blandly declare that his hearers seemed to be losing interest in the subject. 'I share this lack of enthusiasm,' he would say, 'and the course will be discontinued from today.' After I had reluctantly reported to the Dean that it would be hardly possible to renew his studentship and this judgement had been transmitted to Carter, he accepted the verdict with aplomb. 'I do not mind leaving now,' he said, 'but the thought of idleness is abhorrent to me.' He then suggested that he should spend the intervening year before his retirement as a sabbatical year—'to refresh himself for further labours'. He retired to Chambers in Albany where he had a magnificent collection of silver, and there I dined with him alone to celebrate his eightieth birthday. It was wartime and rations were scarce—but not for Carter. After sherry we sat down to an enormous dish of lobster Neuberg and a bottle of champagne. I thought, naturally enough, that this was our dinner but it was not. A partridge for each of us followed and then a vast apple dumpling with another half-bottle. After port and cigars Carter announced that, since the occasion was a special one we must not neglect his green Chartreuse. For a man of eighty he certainly did himself well. In Albany he was looked after by a housekeeper whom he referred to always as 'the Christian woman', because she alone had been proof against his occasional outbursts of bad language. I remember, too, in my youth a notice in the caddy-master's room at a golf club in West Cornwall which proclaimed that no caddy under the age of fifteen was to be allowed to carry for Dr. Carter because of his language.

It is easy to represent Carter as something of a bad influence, but that is not the whole story. I believe that he had a great legal brain, had he only used it, and certainly he was a master of the spoken word. His conversation was a perennial—and sometimes unholy—joy. As a companion in the evenings he was without a rival and I believe that every single member of Common Room regretted his departure. Certainly I did—the virtuous are not always better company than their erring brothers.

In charge of ancient history was Jock Anderson. Dark, thin, with an immense black moustache and a strong Aberdonian accent, he gave at first the impression of dourness, but this was quickly removed by his engaging smile. For some inexplicable reason he had more personal charm than any of my colleagues. Later he was elected (rather against his will, for he loved the House) to the Camden Professorship of Ancient History which took him from us to Brasenose. Jock was a generous-hearted as well as a generous-minded man, but he retained the minor inhibitions of his youth and early domicile. Playing golf with Frank Taylor at a course in France they found themselves faced with a drive over a very rough ravine. Jock waggled his club long and anxiously with the expected result. The lost ball had already done good service but the search continued for a long, long time before Jock could be induced to abandon hope and bring out another ball from his bag. In the afternoon the players reached the same tee and Jock's wagglings of his driver seemed to be unending. At the last moment he stopped, picked up his ball, said, 'I'll gie ye this hole', and walked on to the next tee.

The Steward, who in other colleges would have been called the Domestic Bursar, was A. K. Slessor, a retired major who had once been an Exhibitioner of the House. A man of strong views often forcefully expressed, he was also a man of natural courtesy and with the ability to act as the most gracious of hosts. His great moment came in 1924, when the old stables and the old choir school were to be removed. The Governing Body had agreed to build on this site an arcade of shops and offices, which would have brought in a considerable revenue, but when the old buildings were pulled down and the south front of Christ Church Hall and the adjacent buildings revealed, Slessor went into battle. He had some fine photographs taken of the south front and had them published in *The Times* with an article publicly protesting against the vandalism which was contemplated. Murmurs arose that he should be removed from his office but his case was won, and the plans for rebuilding abandoned. The war-memorial garden and that majestic view of Christ Church as the incoming traveller crosses Folly Bridge are Slessor's enduring monument. The financial sacrifice made by Christ Church ought to have been remembered during the controversy about the Meadow Road.

Osler, Regius Professor of Medicine and, as such, a Student of Christ Church, died in the autumn of 1919, but even the few months when I knew him were enough to show me that he was one of the greatest of men. Nearly forty years later at Johns Hopkins University at Baltimore, when looking at his portrait by J. S. Sargent, I ventured to murmur that I had once been his colleague—and that alone gave me a higher reputation than I had ever enjoyed before. I recall his cheerful advice that I should drink more (though not necessarily alcohol): 'Take twice as much as you make' (which seemed to me an unrealizable ideal), and an admonition to take snuff whenever possible to avoid colds. Our other Regius Professor, Gilbert Murray, Professor of Greek, apart from his great literary eminence and his academic fame, was the leader of the Liberal Party in the University. It was a misfortune that we saw little of him in Christ Church—probably his vegetarian and teetotal habits made Common Room uncongenial for him. Even to Osler and Murray the next of our body was not in any way inferior, for he was Jackie Beazley—who was later to become the greatest archaeologist of the time with a world-wide reputation for his work on Greek vases. In 1919 he was a young tutor, already a genius (Tommy Hutchinson always called him by that name) with charm and gaiety and knowledge lightly borne. As a companion he was incomparable. He never loved to spin the ostentatious continuity—his fancy always strayed like a butterfly from one thought to another—or rather like a bee, sucking honey from every flower. I met him once hurrying in cap and gown towards the Ashmolean and was told that he was about to lecture. 'What,' I said, 'at half-past two on a summer afternoon?' 'Why, yes,' he replied, 'I like to lecture then; it keeps the rotters away.' Yet he was by no means critical of sport and spoke to me often of it. Once in his company watching a great batsman I apologized for using the word 'beautiful' about a stroke which he had just made. 'No, no,' said Beazley, 'beautiful is the right word, and you do well to use it. Here, as with my vases, is true aesthetic beauty.' He had a passion for prize-fighting and its history and loved to talk of this and kindred subjects, but he had not himself participated in similar activities. I cannot forget his account which he gave me of an athletic triumph at Christ's Hospital, where he was at school. 'I was,' he said, 'Senior Grecian, and as such it was right that I should hold some athletic office; accordingly I was made captain of the 2nd XV. We had an away match, to which we travelled by train. I liked most of the members of the 1st XV very much but the 2nd XV were a dull lot, so I travelled in a different compartment from the rest of the side and read one of the plays of Euripides. The time arrived when I realized that we had passed the station where I should have got out. I caught a train back, changed, and walked on to the ground. We were leading by a few points and five minutes of the game remained to be played. I did not make any physical contact with anyone on the other side, but I was able to lead the cheers at the conclusion of the game. On our return journey Euripides was again a better companion than my team-mates.' In the Governing Body Beazley spoke seldom and shortly, but on one occasion he was moved to real eloquence. We were discussing the loan of a picture to some exhibition abroad—I think that it was the Piero della Francesca, a frail picture painted on a panel—and it seemed that permission would be given when suddenly Beazley burst into a torrent of words. He described the opening of an exhibition, the unpacking of the exhibits, the careful hanging and meticulous control of every detail. Then came the change—the end of the exhibition and now everything was chaos—half-fitted crates, pictures carelessly stacked against the walls, litter everywhere, dirty paper and packing everywhere scattered and blowing around, a scene of desolation and disorder. Shelley's *Ode to the West Wind* was brought into play:

> Thou from whose unseen presence the leaves dead
> Are driven, like ghosts from an enchanter fleeing,
> Yellow, and black, and pale, and hectic red,
> Pestilence—stricken multitudes!

When Beazley ended no hand was raised to permit the loan of our picture.

After Beazley came John Murray, but of him we saw little, for he was M.P. for West Leeds and taught only at week-ends. Soon too he was to move on to become Vice-Chancellor of the University of the South-west at Exeter. He had a wonderful power of extracting knowledge from the written word. One candidate to whom we hesitated to award a scholarship was pronounced by John Murray, after reading his papers and without seeing the candidate, to have been underfed; he would certainly develop with the more generous fare provided in Oxford. The verdict turned out to be true.

Dundas, who returned from Burma early in 1919, lived to become the best-known and most honoured of all Christ Church tutors; *D. Portrait of a don*, written by Roger Venables, describes him with an accuracy which makes further description unnecessary. If the history of Oxford in the first half of the twentieth century is written in detail Dundas might well stand as the type of tutor who devoted his life to his pupils without any other competing activity.

Hutchinson, the Treasurer, was of a different type from all the rest, for his life was much concerned with matters outside the College. Devoted to field sports of all kinds he was especially addicted to hunting and was Secretary of the Heythrop Hunt. After taking a first class from Magdalen in the Schools he had worked for the Duchy of Cornwall and he brought to Christ Church a breath of the outside world and a keen intelligence allied with business acumen and financial flair. In all matters connected with the Estates his word was law and he gave me my first lesson in behaviour at the Governing Body. 'Always', he said, 'support the Dean.' Tommy's language was of a different order from that of the rest; he would refer to the Master of Pembroke, with whom at that time we had some dealings over property, as 'the cove over the road'.

Chaundy, the Mathematical Tutor, was considered at that time to be so far to the left as to be almost a revolutionary. He came from an old Oxford family and was addicted to Morris dancing and Labour politics. In fact he was the most kind-hearted of men, a brilliant teacher, and a modest and retiring man. Of Feiling, my colleague and close associate for nearly a quarter of a century, I must speak later when I discuss the History School. Lastly on the list was Rawlinson, the Classical Student and Tutor in Theology. One of the authors of *Foundations*, he had fluttered the ecclesiastical dovecotes and some of the Canons viewed him with wary eye. He was to become in time Bishop of Derby and his friends always wondered that he did not rise even higher in the hierarchy. It was rumoured that, as a bishop, he did not feel that any subject had been adequately discussed until his own view had been stated.

Almost at once the body was further strengthened by appointments which were, to my knowledge, almost all the personal choice of the Dean. Heaton for Medicine, Russell for Chemistry, and John Barrington-Ward for Classical Honour Moderations were followed by Lindemann, Frank Taylor, and Roy Harrod. It would be difficult to think of—or even to invent—a society to which a young man would have been more glad and proud to belong. All were men of intellectual distinction, gifted in many and various ways, but from my point of view they had one quality in common. One and all they gave me welcome and friendship; what more could I have asked?

XIII

LIFE AT CHRIST CHURCH, ESPECIALLY THE CENSORSHIP

(A Vancouver journalist:) I went to Oxford, I guess your tutorial
system there is the nearest thing to the teaching methods of Jesus
Christ that exists to-day.

R. FURSE, Aucuparius

I N the 1920s, what a place Christ Church was—magnificent
yet friendly, regal yet tolerant. Before the First War and to
a lesser extent between the two wars, differences between colleges were sharply defined and each college cultivated its own
ethos. Of recent years these differences have sensibly diminished,
and there is a tendency (not entirely to be approved) towards
equality and uniformity. I recall one undergraduate in the early
twenties—a social and rather flamboyant figure who told me on
inquiry that he was at 'Wadham-Oh'. 'Why', I asked, 'this
strange answer?' 'Oh,' he said, 'friends in London always
expect me to be at Magdalen or the House, and when I say
that I am at Wadham they always say "Oh!"—so now I save
them time by saying that I am at "Wadham-Oh".' Both
the colleges to which I have the honour and privilege to belong
were then—as now—proud places—and rightly so—but their
pride took very different forms. Worcester, as I have tried to
show in an earlier chapter, prided itself on its unity, its independence of the University, and its gracious way of living; it was
not rich or ostentatious or even very distinguished, but it was
self-sufficient and happy, and no one who has read Burgon's
poem on it could fail to recognize the magnetic charm which it
exercised over its members. Christ Church was proud in a very
different way, and paid no heed whatever to the criticism of the
vulgar world. Years later, at a Gaudy, I tried to put into words
what Christ Church really was at that time, basing myself
upon a phrase used by Churchill who, when speaking at a
previous Gaudy, had declared that the essence of the House
was 'Freedom and Continuity'.

'What does Christ Church stand for? If we trusted to what in the jargon of today is called our public image of half a century ago we might believe that Christ Church was filled entirely with men of one type—wealthy and prejudiced aristocrats, with a contemptuous disdain for those outside their own circle, men addicted to pleasure and field sports, and, above all, incurably idle. The truth was, and is, quite different. There is *no* pervading Christ Church type. The glory of Christ Church lies in its diversity. If I tried to find a formula I could only say that it seems to me that we achieved unity (or perhaps I mean harmony) without uniformity and certainly without regimentation. It is right, I am sure, that every college should have its own particular nature and its own customs and it may well be what some historians call a "good thing" that in some colleges there should be a more all-pervading college spirit, an exaggerated *esprit de corps*. Here at the House I think that we prided ourselves that men could pursue their own particular line of life and pursue it in their own way. Indeed there was a sort of lofty indifference to the doings of other men and other colleges. Christ Church was large enough and great enough to let each go his own way and develop his own interests. There was room for artists and athletes and aesthetes—even eccentrics —as well as for scholars and scientists and future statesmen. I think that our right hand did not worry over-much about what our left hand was doing. Diversity—that was the keynote.' After all, of my two colleges, the first was almost the smallest and the second the largest in Oxford. Nothing has ever shaken my belief that Worcester exerts a charm and fascination which no other college can match; nothing again has ever made me doubt for a moment that Christ Church is incomparably the greatest of all Oxford colleges. A colleague of mine once accepted a post at Cambridge; 'Do you not feel', he was asked, 'that your loyalties are now divided?' 'No,' he replied, 'my loyalties are not divided —they are multiplied.' So it was with me.

There was another great difference between the two, of which I was, at the time, oblivious. At Worcester life could be in some sort parochial, but it was impossible to be long at Christ Church without making contact with the greater world outside Oxford. It is often said that great influence was exercised by the week-ends of All Souls, but I believe that much more influence

on the country was—over the years—exercised by Christ
Church. The reason for this is clear. Arthur Hassall was fond of
relating an incident which occurred when Theodore Roosevelt,
the President of the U.S.A., visited Oxford. He was, as many
are, somewhat bored by the conducted tour to which he was
subjected, for academic matters were not his major interest,
but when he entered the Senior Common Room at Christ
Church everything changed. 'On this wall', said Arthur
Hassall, 'are our Governors-General and Viceroys of India and
on that wall our Christ Church Prime Ministers.' 'What?' said
Roosevelt. 'All these from this one little college!' After that
everything connected with the House was of interest to him.
Every year after the Encaenia the Honorands, the recipients of
honorary degrees from the University, were guests at the
Christ Church Gaudy; every sovereign since Tudor times had
visited the Deanery; in modern times there must have been few
men prominent in Church or State who had not at one time or
another been entertained in Christ Church. In a word the
House was linked with the Establishment, and it would have
been impossible to be for long a Student without coming into
contact with the greater world without. Certainly for me it
opened out wider horizons. And we never forgot for long that
we were a royal foundation. In a speech at one dinner Sir J.J.
Thomson, at that time Master of Trinity College, Cambridge,
delighted us with the words: 'King Henry VIII when he
founded Christ Church, sternly repressed his natural inclination to found a woman's college.' Christ Church had a great
and proper conceit of itself. At one Censors' dinner an old
member who had been invited as a guest and who had acquired
reputation by his speeches and activities in Parliament, spoke
too long and with too much regard for his own performances
at Westminster. At length after he had referred more than once
to what he had said 'in the House', an irate Student rose in his
place and reproved him. He had the affectation of omitting his
'aitches', a not uncommon habit at that time, and his words
were short and to the point. 'You should know, sir,' he said,
'that in this place the 'Ouse means 'ere.' When speaking of
Christ Church Barrington-Ward was prone to use the phrase
'our noble selves'.
    Christ Church was both officially and in fact a 'peculiar

place', and this because the Cathedral was within its walls and because for three hundred years it had been governed by the Dean and Canons alone. The Students who would of course have been called Fellows at other colleges had little or no power, and their position was inferior to that of the Fellows of much less important colleges; essentially they were little more than salaried teachers, though they could, and did, expect to be promoted in time to a Canonry or to some other ecclesiastical preferment. Only the Dean and Chapter together with noblemen could, up to 1858, sit at the High Table in Hall. The crisis came in the middle of the nineteenth century and the new Christ Church dates from the Christ Church Oxford Act of 1867.[1] The demands of the Students were three: that the conditions of the Students should be raised in all respects to the level of Fellows of Colleges; that the Dean and Chapter should be given either fixed stipends or a due allowance of the Estates; that all accounts should be properly inspected. All these demands were met by the Act and to us nowadays it seems self-evident that they were just and necessary, but at the time the changes were not easily made. Some had argued for the severance of the Ecclesiastical from the Collegiate establishment; others had looked upon any change as an act of expropriation of the Church. One Canon declared that he 'would not degrade Christ Church to the level of a College'. It speaks volumes for the good sense and humanity of all concerned that the changes were carried out with comparatively little friction. By the time that I was elected the Governing Body was composed of Dean, Canons, and Students, and the Students were obviously in complete control. The Dean had the difficult task of acting at the same time as Head of a College and Dean of a Cathedral Chapter. Proceedings were usually harmonious, yet many of my older colleagues could well remember the older generation who had wrought the changes, and traces of the old controversies still remained. Dodgson (Lewis Carroll) at times seemed still to be the presiding genius of the Common Room. That differences were not more in evidence was, in the first instance, due to Dean Strong himself. He, above the rest, stands out in my memories of the immediate post-war years.

His was an extraordinary mixture of qualities; friendliness

[1] See E. G. W. Bill and J. F. A. Mason, *Christ Church and Reform 1850–1867* (1970).

and compassion disguised under a cloak of intense shyness; a phenomenal memory for persons and faces; a knowledge of music which had made it possible for him to remain at Christ Church, had he so wished, as organist instead of lecturer; an outstanding ability to conduct business and to hasten decision; wit and humour which bubbled up at the most unexpected moments. When he left in 1920 he wrote with his own hand a letter to every member of the House, senior and junior, and no two letters were alike. Yet many years later, when he resigned as Bishop of Oxford, he allowed a silver salver which the Common Room had given him in 1920 and which was inscribed with the names of all his colleagues to be put into the sale at Cuddesdon. 'It was an ugly piece of silver' was his comment. Percival, who was then the Steward, had to make a hasty journey to buy in the salver; where it now is I do not know. I believe that he numbered Chateaubriand among his forebears, and perhaps this, coupled with his north-country ancestry, explains in part the many contradictions of his character. As Vice-Chancellor in wartime he was remarkably successful; the *Christ Church Record* helps to explain.

[Early in the war] a sudden call was made for motor-cycle dispatch riders for France. The register of motor licences was locked in the Proctors' box and the Proctors were away; without hesitation, Strong had the box broken open, and the men were secured in time; Sir Charles Portal was one. One can think of Vice-Chancellors whose reactions would have been more constitutional, and slower.

Bishop successively of Ripon and Oxford, Strong was never again, I think, so entirely well fitted to his tasks as he had been at Christ Church. 'I forget sometimes,' he once told me; 'I was preaching in a distant Yorkshire village and using an old sermon. The phrase slipped out before I realized what I was saying. It was this: "If you turn to your Homers, you will find . . .". But no harm was done—my congregation believed that I was referring to their pigeons and my reputation was enhanced.'

As I have said, Christ Church was both an Oxford college and a Cathedral chapter. This unique status resulted in a peculiarity in the way it was governed. The Dean had a full job in his clerical capacity and in consequence the control of the College fell, almost of necessity, into other hands, and Christ Church was in fact run and controlled by the two Censors, whose duties were all-embracing. They were, of course, appointed by the Dean, but this was in fact only a convention—for they were in practice chosen by their predecessors—the ex-Censors. Perhaps it would be true to say that the Collegiate side of Christ Church was in the hands of a triumvirate, the Dean and the two Censors, and of them the Senior Censor was often the most influential. Apart from having a powerful influence on the Governing Body the Censors allotted rooms, acted as Secretary to the Tuition Fund, superintended attendance at chapel or roll-call, presented for degrees, acted as Senior Tutor and—most important of all—controlled admissions. They were also the disciplinary officers. In a word the Censors ran Christ Church, and their influence—especially that of the Senior Censor—was as great as that of the Dean himself. One of them was always 'in course' —the senior for the first half of term, the junior for the second. Owen had carried on for the greater part of the war years, but he was, not unnaturally, coming to the end of his tether and not fully equipped to deal with the post-war rush. Timothy Eden, who was concerned to see that his brother Anthony[2] should come to the House, wrote me a letter full of foreboding. He had visited Oxford and found the Dean charming but 'non-committal', whilst Owen was 'completely gaga' and unable to appreciate the situation. I must, Timothy urged, make strenuous efforts to ensure Anthony's acceptance. I did.

All this changed when Dundas returned at the beginning of 1919. He became Junior Censor to Owen, rapidly transformed chaos into order, and inaugurated a new and beneficent spirit into the censorship. In December 1919 Owen retired—Dundas became Senior and I Junior Censor. This was the beginning of six happy years in office—four as junior to Robin Dundas, and two as senior with Frank Taylor as my colleague. Happy but strenuous. I remember no occasion when the Censors were at odds with one another, or at variance with the Dean, but of course my memory may be at fault. Memory is like a selective weed-killer which destroys the weeds but leaves the good grass to flourish—that at any rate is my experience.

Robin Dundas set a very high standard; he knew—and

2 Later Lord Avon, Prime Minister 1955-7.

prided himself on the knowledge—every undergraduate, whether they were his pupils or not, and managed somehow to entertain them all in turn in his rooms. In my case the whole set-up and the multifarious duties of the Censors made it inevitable that relations between them and the undergraduates should be close, friendly, and continuous. The tutorial system, the best and most fruitful of all Oxford traditions, which binds together pupil and teacher in a way that no other relationship can, was, in the case of the Censors, enlarged to embrace the whole College. The Censor's day started with morning roll-call at eight—followed by morning prayers in the Cathedral. This was a chore but it had compensations. Roll-calls were a comparatively modern innovation. In the past compulsory morning chapel (so many a week) had been the universally accepted rule at all colleges, though the purpose was often rather practical than religious. It was necessary to get the men out of bed so that the scouts could do their rooms. At times efforts were made to encourage attendance at chapel; when I was Senior Censor Dean White called a small committee for this purpose—himself, Rawlinson, the Clerical Student, and myself. Various remedies were prepared—most of them resisted by Rawlinson and myself, but eventually we agreed that the Dean might have a hymn on one morning of the week—i.e. on Mondays—provided that at least ten undergraduates were present. I think that the Dean did not play quite fair, for he exerted his personal influence to persuade about a dozen men to attend on the next Monday. In the aisle was placed a harmonium, used for choir practice, and vulgarly called 'the Eunuch', with the organ scholar sitting before it. The Dean gave out the number of a hymn and the Eunuch, after a big pause, played an introductory tune, unknown to us all. The Dean, using words seldom heard in the Cathedral, said, 'I'm sorry, I mean number so-and-so', and cheerfully the Eunuch played one of the best-known hymn tunes. On the following Monday a large congregation appeared, to savour this new entertainment—but alas!—it was a Saint's Day and on Saints' Days surplices had to be worn and Holy Communion was celebrated. So the would-be singers were turned away and the plan for 'a hymn on Monday' abandoned.

On the very first occasion on which I took roll-call the full splendour of the Christ Church portraits burst upon me. I had seen them many times before but never in so good a light and never with time properly to appreciate them. The morning light poured in and the masterpieces of Reynolds and Gainsborough, Romney and Lawrence and the rest were seen as I had never seen them before. Stories of these pictures abounded; here, for example, was Penn, the only portrait in armour of them all; here was Millais's Gladstone, looking like the representation of Victorian certitude; here a magnificent Reynolds of Markham which recalled another portrait of the same sitter by the same artist which hung in the Common Room dining-room. This was a much smaller picture which had been discovered by the Regius Professor of Ecclesiastical History in a scout's pantry where the canvas had been used to wrap up a pair of football boots. How it came there no one could say. Two less important pictures hung at the end of the Hall. Dodgson, strangely and unnaturally pallid, owing to the use of some inferior pigment, and an insipid portrait of Rosebery. How was this magnificent collection of portraits assembled? Quite simply it was a Christ Church practice in 'days gone by' to send its more distinguished sons a letter praising their achievements. The early part of these letters no doubt varied but the conclusion was always the same. It was a request that the recipient would 'enable the Dean and Chapter to place his portrait in the Hall'. Many swallowed the bait and employed the best artists of the day, but Rosebery behaved differently. Christ Church, he replied, would probably wish to have a portrait of him as he was in his undergraduate days, and he therefore presented a portrait of himself as a very young man. This, since he had been sent down for running his horse in the Derby and attending the meeting, was both a courteous and subtly reproving gesture. Here too was Speaker Abbot looking as he must have looked on that famous night when his casting vote on the motion for the impeachment of Dundas deprived the younger Pitt of his chief supporter; here too the brilliant blue coat of Louis Devisme which seemed to many the most attractive picture in the collection. To me it seemed that the whole history of eighteenth- and nineteenth-century England unrolled itself in Christ Church Hall, whilst I watched undergraduates signing their names in haste to escape missing chapel. The addition in 1922

was also an exciting picture—Orpen's portrait of Tommy
Strong. There had been a strong movement to employ Augustus
John but some of the Canons and some of the tutors were dis-
trustful of him since it was proposed that he should bring a
caravan to the Meadow and it was thought that there might be
more wives than one in the party. In the event the commission
was given to Orpen, whose picture is, to my mind, a masterpiece. At the time it was thought to be a blunder that Owen,
who was in charge of the arrangements, had confused length
with breadth and that the picture therefore looked ill among its
companions. The annual report cautiously stated that it was 'a
striking picture, though its light-coloured background hardly
harmonises with its setting'. Tommy Strong himself complained
that Orpen failed on several occasions to turn up for the sittings.
His excuse was that he was engaged at the same time in painting
Landru, the French murderer, and that, whilst the Dean could
afford to wait, Landru certainly could not. What has happened
to the Landru portrait, and was it ever finished? I do not know,
but James Gunn[3] told me long afterwards that he knew of it,
though he was ignorant of its fate. Surely it might have been a
masterpiece! It may seem too much of a digression to write of
the Christ Church pictures, but I believe that possession of
artistic treasures of this kind plays a much greater part in the
life of a college than is generally supposed. They act as a rein-
forcement of tradition, an encouragement of taste, and a con-
firmation of faith in the future. Christ Church was in this respect
peculiarly fortunate. Apart from the collection of portraits and
generous benefactions, notably those of General Guise and Fox-
Strangways, we had in the Library a fine collection especially
strong in Italian primitives and including the superb collection
of Italian drawings. In the Common Room among the engrav-
ings and more modern portraits were three pictures, given by an
old member—Garrick by Pine, a landscape with cattle attributed to Cuyp, and the portrait of an old lady by Franz Hals.
When in the thirties I became for a short time Curator of
pictures I relied much on Horace Buttery, that best of restorers,
who succeeded in finding the original of our 'Cuyp' which had
once been in the Cowper collection. Our picture is almost
certainly by Van Strij. Tommy Hutchinson was delighted at

[3] Sir James Gunn, R.A., portrait painter (1893–1964).

this attribution, for in his view the cow in the foreground was not from the purely agricultural standpoint a desirable animal ('A cow's body should have the shape of a brick'), and great artists should choose the best for their models. The Hals was a priceless possession; looking back I wonder how any Curator of Common Room could have slept quietly at nights if he considered its vulnerability—a small picture, hanging unguarded in a room where an active thief would have had little difficulty in breaking in. Yet it remained in the Common Room a joy and refreshment to us all until 1969 when it was removed to the new picture gallery. Even then there were loud lamentations at its loss. Only since 1964 have the Christ Church drawings received proper care and attention under the control of Jim Byam Shaw, and the pictures from him and the Curator.

In another matter Buttery proved himself a skilful and successful helper. A portrait in the Library, of a gentleman, had been listed in the Borenius catalogues as 'Tintoretto—School of'. Buttery succeeded in establishing its authenticity and Borenius, in a long appreciative letter to *The Times*, accepted that it was indeed by Tintoretto and that it would 'henceforth claim a more distinguished rank in the collection to which it belongs'. My own contribution to the artistic side of our life was small, but it gave me satisfaction. As Curator of pictures I succeeded against some opposition from reactionaries in having the pictures in Hall lighted. Nowadays it seems almost incredible that this should not have been considered essential, but at the time it was thought by some to be a dangerous innovation.

To the duties of the Censor I must now return. Presentation for degrees was not an onerous duty though I disliked it because it involved presenting in Latin, and I was always afraid of forgetting my words. ('Don't worry,' said Hassall, 'I always used to recite a sentence or two from Stubbs's *Charters*; that did just as well as the correct formula.') Sometimes special cases were amusing. I took up Sam Morison, the recently elected Harmsworth Professor of American History, to be matriculated in the Divinity Schools. We lunched first and lunched well and then walked across the High for the ceremony. Sam was clad in the curious three-quarter-length gown of a research student and was smoking a long and opulent cigar. As we walked through Bodleian quadrangle I saw the Vice-Chancellor appearing from the opposite direction and begged Sam to abandon his cigar. He stubbed it out on the wall of the Divinity School, with the sad comment 'and it was drawing so beautifully'.

Sam himself, as others of our importations, was a breath of fresh air in our community, for he combined a strong belief in tradition with the open-mindedness of the New World. Early in his time at Christ Church he was walking round the meadow with Mrs. Rawlinson—'We ought', he said, 'to be more friendly here and use each other's first names; mine is Sam, what is yours?' 'Mildred' was the reply. At the same moment they both realized that the popular press at the time was full of the attempt to mate two Polar bears at the Zoo, who bore the names of Sam and Mildred. When he left England Sam wrote in the *Spectator*, under the title 'My time of wine and roses', one of the most perceptive accounts of Oxford in the twenties.

Another censorial duty was the allocation of rooms. This was not in itself of major importance but it was worth while to take some trouble to ensure that men were put on staircases where they would find congenial company and also that their private wishes should be consulted so far as was possible. A strict rule was observed that no freshman should see his rooms before he arrived—otherwise requests for changes might have become a nuisance. I broke the rule once, but this exceptional case made me determined never to do so again. I was harried almost beyond endurance by a mother who wished to put especially valuable curtains in her son's rooms, and I agreed eventually to show her the rooms on the strict understanding that no plea to change them would be considered. The rooms were in Old Library and the sunshine poured in as we entered. 'What a perfect room—far better than I could have hoped for, and what a lovely great cupboard for his clothes!' 'That, Madam,' I said, 'is not a cupboard—it is the bedroom.' On another occasion I put a freshman into a set of rooms immediately below the Censor's rooms in Peckwater. He was Herbert Ford, a relative of Henry Ford, a notable footballer and a man of strong common sense, and much liked by his contemporaries. Perhaps I was a little naughty (to use the vulgar expression) to put him in rooms which had been vacated by a noted aesthete. His predecessor had decorated the rooms in a strange and *outré* manner; the ceiling was black, and the walls black and gold.

After a week or two I asked Ford how he liked his rooms. 'Very much, they're very comfortable.' 'Do you find anything odd about them?' 'No, why should I?' 'Well, they are rather out of the ordinary, don't you think?' He thought for a while and then said, 'Well, yes. There doesn't seem anywhere to hang up your pants.'

In the years immediately after the war there were many cases of men who wished to change their schools or who were uncertain whether they should take the shortened course which was conditionally allowed or stay for their full time. These were discussed at the weekly tutors' meetings and the view of the Censors was not uncommonly the decisive factor. A letter from Anthony Eden in 1921 might be taken as an example. 'I feel', he wrote 'that I must write and thank you for the efforts you so kindly made to postpone my examination ... perhaps an extra year has saved me from a bad crash this summer in my schools.' In the event he was awarded a first class in Persian in the following year.

Admissions were a much more important matter—indeed for any college it is of overwhelming importance. If the right men are picked the college will prosper—if not, not. How should a year's entry be chosen? With scholars and exhibitioners no problem arises; they win their places through competitive examination and no favouritism or personal fancy enters in. Yet even in the case of scholars examiners have to remember that they are looking for promise as well as for advancement and that examiners can err. In one scholarship examination at Harrow three candidates, who afterwards became famous, were not elected. They were F.E. Smith, Leo Amery, and Ramsay—later Master of Magdalene College, Cambridge. It is understandable that F.E.'s scholarship may have been rough and that Amery may have been better adapted to some other subject, but if pure scholarship was the only criterion, how was it possible for the examiners to miss Ramsay—one of the most accomplished scholars of his generation? The manner in which this notorious example of examining incompetence became known was this. Discussing examinations F.E. quoted the first few lines of the Latin Unseen—Ramsay immediately recited the rest of the passage. At the age of eighteen the written examination is not of itself the perfect and complete test. Still no doubt

the scholar does gain his due reward. The choice of commoners
is more difficult. Our methods in the 1920s may have been
rough and ready but I think that they were generally effective.
Of course every candidate had to show, from his record and from
an entrance examination, that he was qualified to come to a
university, but we did not necessarily accept someone who had
better marks than his rivals.

At Christ Church then, as at other colleges, the Entrance
Examination itself may have been something of a façade but the
sifting and selection of candidates was not. It is necessary, too,
to explode the always recurring misapprehension that men were
chosen for reasons of social acceptability or because they belonged to a particular class. Every Admissions Tutor is moved
by the desire to secure the best men that he can for his college,
irrespective of their origin; he is looking for merit, but not necessarily only for merit as displayed in written examinations. We
used to sit on a committee with the Dean in the chair for the
purpose of interviews, and all the tutors took a lively interest
in those men who were likely to be allotted to them, but the last
word was (though this was not admitted) in the hands of the
Censors. We had, of course, many letters and documents—
not all helpful. One parent wrote to inquire what sort of testi-
monial to character would best serve his son's interest—should it
be written by a near relative or by his schoolmaster or by the
police? After I had cautiously replied that we liked to have
testimonials from those who really knew the man concerned, I
received a business-like document from a Chief Constable. An
American, whose social ambitions outran his intellectual qualifications, tried to impress me by writing that he belonged to
'the bloodiest club at Harvard'. Another anxious and aristocratic parent wished his son to read agriculture; in the course of
a lengthy letter he contrived to spell—or mis-spell—the word
agriculture in six different ways. Dean White, who did not
relish these interviews, although he conducted them with great
courtesy and sympathy for the victims, once took a candidate
through his school career and through his proposals to work
at Oxford. 'And after that in the future life?' asked the Dean.
The reply which closed the interview was unexpected—'I hope
to go to Heaven, sir'. On the whole I do not think that committees are the best agents for settling admissions. Too often

the views of members cancel each other out, and the final result is a series of compromises; men of reasonable ability with fair examination marks who are really of mediocre ability are taken to the exclusion of those whose future is more risky but of greater possibilities. To my mind this matter of selection is of prime importance and not only in academic life; I must return to it in a later chapter.

I have left to last the most important part of the Censors' duties—the disciplinary control. It was a long-established belief that the work of deans in colleges and of Censors in the House was difficult and that undergraduates could only be controlled by a mixture of tact and punishments. As in industry, it was thought to be a matter of 'Them and us' rather than of 'all on the same side'. Gloomy tales were handed down to us—of Univ. in 1880 when, as a result of a clash with disciplinary authority, the whole college, with a few exceptions, was rusticated for the last few weeks of term. Nearer home we heard frightening accounts of the great Blenheim riot of 1892, which had developed into a dispute of almost national concern. The walls of Tom Quad were plastered with immense daubs of paint calling down damnation on the Dean and blessings upon the Duke of Marlborough and the House was, for a time, in a state of almost open revolt. Pictures which used to hang in the Steward's office portrayed the scene of these outrages. Probably the root cause of the trouble was that the Senior Censor had been too long in office and was out of touch with the opinions of the undergraduates.

The reality in 1920 was wholly different and the plain fact is that there was no disciplinary difficulty whatever. That at least is the impression left on my mind. My naval upbringing had left me with an engrained belief in authority and it simply did not enter my head that there would be any remonstrance if I felt it necessary to assert authority. I had too a foretaste of my task when I was for a short time a barrack captain in Ruhleben. In that capacity I had no sanction whatever but that really presented no problem, for most men are reasonable if fairly dealt with. I had, too, a year as Pro-proctor for Trinity in the year 1920–1. Reggie Weaver[4] had asked me to act, since his college was short of suitable candidates for the office. Frightened

[4] J.R.H. Weaver, President of Trinity College, 1938–54.

only of the ceremonies because of my lack of Latinity, I accepted on the strict understanding that I should take no degree days but should compensate by doing an extra share of parading the streets at night time. Weaver kept strictly to the bargain, but I repaid him ill since I collected fewer fines than any previous Pro-proctor. In those days the Proctors took the weekends themselves and the Pro-proctors the other five days. I was not idle but really the state of the University did not demand any sort of crusade against bad behaviour. Most of us thought that the rules which forbade drinking in public houses and which demanded the wearing of gowns after dark were already outmoded, but a slow approach usually well advertised, and the use of a blind eye, especially where older men were concerned, made the maintenance of a decent level of order easy to maintain without any loss of prestige or face for the Proctors. The fact indeed was that the Proctors defended the undergraduates and saved them from the ordinary courts. On one occasion only I went to the Vice-Chancellor's court to hear the case of a Christ Church undergraduate who had been accused of creating a disturbance at an inn at Binsey. On a hot summer's day he had tried to get a glass of beer, only to be told that he was a few minutes too late. He protested and struck the proprietor a blow in the face; the wife tried to get between them and also, accidentally, received a blow. The barman was even less successful and took a punch on the nose. The court scene, with Stallybrass of B.N.C. sitting as Assessor, would have made a good television picture. It was important for the undergraduate that the proceedings should be in the Vice-Chancellor's court because his father controlled newspapers in America and publicity in the Press would have been, to say the least, unfortunate. I had put in a note defending the character of the accused and declared that he was of a mild and inoffensive disposition, but unfortunately he was also a well-known oarsman and a boxing blue. The first witness, the proprietor, produced an ugly object—his battered set of false teeth new, as he alleged, that day and now useless. The wife, when her turn came, held up a twisted piece of wire, which represented all that was left of her pair of spectacles, also purchased that forenoon. The barman outdid them both; he had bought a new suit that very same day and the suit, as all could observe, was now nothing but a pile of bloodstained garments. The coincidence of all their contemporary purchases seemed to stretch credulity rather far but the case did not bode well for my undergraduate. However, as I must suppose, negotiations had been going on behind the scenes and an offer, I think, of £20 turned the woebegone faces of the victims into smiling rejoicing. I seemed to hear the innkeeper murmuring that the undergraduate could return at any time and have the same entertainment for the same price. In 1922 I narrowly escaped being further concerned with University discipline when the turn of Christ Church came round to elect a Proctor. Fortunately Chaundy was senior to me and a judicious tea-party which I gave for Mrs. Chaundy was sufficient to convince her that Chaundy ought to accept (which at first he had been unwilling to do). He left his mark on the proctorship by introducing a system of green lights for undergraduate cars—for the car question was beginning to form a considerable part of the Proctors' work.

Discipline, then, was no problem at Christ Church in my years as Censor. Minor disturbances there were, but they were of small importance. A Bullingdon dinner, for example, might be followed by a riotous mob in Peckwater and this caused difficulty with men who came from other colleges and had found their way in. The Christ Church men could be dealt with easily and without animosity. The same is true of bump suppers. After the father of a pupil had visited me and showed me that he had lost an eye from a firework at a bump supper I felt an almost obsessional distrust of fireworks, just as I had of wanton destruction. One vivid memory of the end of a bump supper remains. Sometime after midnight when the revels were coming to an end an intoxicated undergraduate found the door of the J.C.R. locked. The door had two panels of frosted glass and the undergraduate kicked one of them violently and cut his leg to pieces. A rough tourniquet was tied and his leg was held up, whilst he lay on his back. I hurried to the Lodge and telephoned to two or three doctors, finally securing the one who lived closest to us. Meantime the faithful friend of the victim had arrived, and incensed by the treatment the victim had received attacked the second panel of the door with the inevitable result. He too was laid on his back and his leg held up in the air.

The doctor arrived but turned out to be almost stone-deaf; it was not possible to explain to him how two men should be lying side by side with their legs in the air and both covered in blood. No matter—he was efficient in his task and no great harm was done.

Christ Church was, presumably, much the same as other colleges. An undeserved source of satisfaction to me came when Phelps of Oriel wrote to complain of rowdyism in the House and ventured to give me some hints on the maintenance of discipline. On the night when his letter arrived the undergraduates of Oriel burned down a wooden cabstand which stood in Oriel Square and to which they objected; my answer to the letter was therefore a polite rejection of his proferred advice.

In the University the best-known incident was the alleged attempts to poison the Vice-Chancellor (Farnell) with a box of chocolates. This affair certainly had its ludicrous side, for the Vice-Chancellor called into consultation Professor Soddy, who had no doubt that a criminal attempt had been made. As Dr. Lee's Professor Soddy was attached to Exeter but he was also a member of Common Room at Christ Church. A Nobel prize-winner and a great chemist, he was also a great quarreller and at Christ Church he found a worthy opponent in Headlam, the Regius Professor of Divinity. To our huge delight the two indulged in a controversy in the columns of *The Times*. Soddy was an eminent scientist, Headlam an equally eminent theologian, but the controversy was concerned with economics, a subject about which neither of them had much claim to pontificate. Surreptitious attempts to induce them to dine on the same night and to place them side by side unfortunately came to nothing.

The rights and wrongs of the case of the poisoned chocolates are now of no special interest but the affair gave me an opportunity of learning something about the Vice-Chancellor's character. Farnell was a strange mixture; a distinguished scholar and writer and personally an endearing man, he was almost, as his autobiography shows, overwhelmingly naïve and wonderfully prolix. Firmly convinced that the University was threatened by a subversive spirit among the young which it was his mission to suppress, he decided to rally support and invited the disciplinary officers of all the colleges to dine with him and discuss the situation. After a most agreeable dinner we adjourned to the Vice-Chancellor's study where he stood in front of the mantelpiece and talked with spirit and enthusiasm about sailing ships and Greek myths. One of the deans seized the opportunity of a pause in the lecture (for such in fact it was) to suggest that we ought to discuss the problem which had been the cause of, or excuse for, the dinner. 'Ah, yes,' said Farnell, 'we must indeed.' He then embarked on a long account of the condition of the University. Another dean interrupted him. 'I'm sorry, Mr. Vice-Chancellor, but I must go; I've forgotten my key and I can't get into my college after midnight.' We all got up and made our excuses. Farnell's words on our departure were characteristic. 'Thank you, gentlemen; I've thoroughly enjoyed the evening and the discussion of our problem has been most helpful to me.' So far as I recollect no one except himself had contributed a single sentence to the discussion.

Looking back on my years as Censor I feel that discipline in a college at that time really presented no problem whatever—provided only that certain principles were observed. In the first place there must be *clarity*; everyone knew that provided they were reasonable they would be treated with tolerance, but that if they broke known rules (and there were few of these) they would have to pay the penalty. I treasure a letter from a Rhodes Scholar written forty years later in which he thanked me for saving him from disaster. After speaking of his 'nocturnal depredations' he continues:

Doubtless you have forgotten them after forty years, but they included forging the Dean's signature to get out of Peck Gate after hours, scuttling back into Tom Gate at 19.99[5] minutes after midnight and an hour later stealing and unintentionally demolishing the Archdeacon's tricycle in an ill-advised attempt to ride that ancient vehicle down the ten steps leading to the Meadow Buildings. Except for your humane intervention . . . the careers of Lovitt and Smith might have ended ingloriously in rustication or worse. Shielded by the strong arms of Masterman and Dundas, we were merely gated for a few weeks. This afforded us a much needed chance to cram (with no help from the seemingly derisive Don Carter) for seconds in Jurisprudence 1922.

[5] Tom Gate is kept open until twenty minutes after midnight for Christ Church keeps the correct time for Oxford and not Greenwich Mean Time.

It must be clear, too, what measures or rules were serious and what were not. Excessive noise might be tiresome, but, as a wise predecessor in office told me, 'If Peckwater is quiet you may be sure that the men are gambling or engaged in other vices.' Drugs, at that time, were not a serious menace. The second great principle is always to avoid sarcasm. Men who will accept any straightforward reproof will harbour ill feeling for a very long time if they are sneered at or treated sarcastically. Words which seem harmless to the speaker can wound bitterly. Once in my early days as Censor I learned the truth of all this. Some damage had been caused and a good deal of breakage and I needed to fix the fines for reparation on the culprits. One of them, an excellent man, was something of a sea lawyer and I felt sure that he would have constructed an alibi or some other excuse for himself and so indeed he had. After lengthy explanations I expressed doubts about his story and he countered by saying, 'But you are doubting my word and practi-cally calling me a liar.' According to all the rules of the game I should have withdrawn immediately, but I was out of temper and replied, 'That is about the size of it.' I realized immediately that I had gone much too far and should have to apologize, but there was no need. A slow smile passed over his face as he said, 'And you wouldn't be so far wrong either.'

Much later in my life I saw time and again how much sarcasm and innuendo are resented and how seldom they are effective; on the other hand the direct question or straight-forward comment seldom hurts. In particular I recall a con-ference attended in about equal parts by shop stewards and middle management. At one session a lawyer lectured on the legal aspects of trade-union disputes. To me he seemed, in the current phrase, to fall over backwards to understand and justify the position of the shop steward, but as the subsequent dis-cussion showed, his audience did not trust a word that he had said. All the time they were suspicious that he, a lawyer, was leading them up the garden path. At a later session there was a lecture by John Garnett of the Industrial Society, who pulled none of his punches and criticized both management and unions with knowledge and with force. In his case the reception was utterly different. Everyone wanted to join in the discussion— no one resented for a moment the criticism of himself or his friends, for everyone realized that there was no deception and no attempt to evade or side-step the issues involved.

Since the normal time for being a Censor was four or five years the control of Christ Church was in the hands of comparatively young men and this was a priceless advantage, responsible I believe for the thoroughly sound relationship of dons and undergraduates. All in all the early twenties were a happy time and I still feel amazed at the false picture which has been painted of them. To judge from accounts which one reads and the memoirs which are published, the University was peopled by two groups—of 'hearties' and 'aesthetes'—and a large proportion of the men had come up only to have a good time. Nothing could be more untrue. Of course there were some who had come for rest and restoration after four years of war—and why not? They did more good than harm. But by far the greater number came because they keenly wished to come and to get the benefits, and the qualifications, for civil life which the University could give. The picture of those times is blurred, and the memoirs of those times are not always helpful because too often our picture of past times in Oxford (as elsewhere) is taken from the memoirs of the brilliant and the unusual, or painted in the glaring colours of the satirist, striving for literary effect. Members of a small group or clique form a hopelessly exaggerated view of the importance of their own coterie and the normal man's life and activities are forgotten. Curiously enough the best *aperçu* of life in the early twenties is to be found in an article in the *Oxford Magazine* for 2 June 1967, written by Vernon Fork, a name which thinly disguised that of the then Master of Pembroke. It is in the form of a letter written by an imaginary civil servant recalling his Oxford life in the early twenties and is entitled 'Dull but True'. It described with truth and clarity the life of the ordinary or normal man—and therefore that of the great majority. Dull? I do not think so, but the last sentence is true enough, 'No publisher would look at it for a moment.' What is forgotten is the splendid work done by the returning 'warriors', whose influence was almost always for the good, and who, with the utmost patience, put up with some rules and regulations which must have seemed somewhat puerile to them. They made intercourse between teachers and taught a pleasure and a privilege and convinced me that a gap between school and university was, when possible, an advantage. It is tempting to pause and write about many of that generation of undergraduates, for they taught us much in manners and human relations. I confine myself to one story. Dining one night as a guest of Victor Cazalet[6] at the Cranston which housed a number of our senior undergraduates, I found that the company was all male with the exception of Lady Keeble.[7] After dinner Victor asked her to recite to us; she agreed without demur, but selected an inappropriate subject and recited to us a supposedly humorous tale about someone who had been knocked over by a railway train. Without any hesitation Victor showed his incomparable social flair. 'Lillah,' he said, 'you couldn't possibly know, but how could we applaud? One of our undergraduates was killed on the line a few evenings ago.' She responded at once—'Let me recite again'—and gave us the *Golden Journey to Samarkand*, more beautifully delivered and spoken than I could have imagined possible.

[6] Lt.-Col. Victor Cazalet (1896–1943), M.P. for Chippenham from 1924, political liaison officer to General Sikorski from 1940.

[7] Lillah McCarthy (Lady Keeble) (1875–1960), distinguished actress.

XIV

TEACHING AT CHRIST CHURCH AND THE SCHOOL OF MODERN HISTORY

History on her rightful throne and by the side of her eloquence and war.

W.S. LANDOR

THE administrative work of the Censorship, important though it was, was still only a *parergon*—my main work was that of a history tutor, for this was the post to which I had been appointed. For thirty years the teaching of modern history was the central feature and the prevailing interest of my life. Something, then, must be written about modern-history teaching at Oxford, and its development.

It is difficult nowadays to realize how completely the School of Literae Humaniores—Lit. Hum. or Greats as it was called—dominated the intellectual life of Oxford in the closing years of the last century, almost to the exclusion of other disciplines. Here I am not speaking of the place taken by science—that is a different subject—but only of the place of Greats among the humane studies. At the turn of the century every Head of a House had read Greats, as had the great majority of Fellows of Colleges; of the scholarships and exhibitions offered the great majority were allotted to classics. Furthermore those Fellows who professed other subjects, for example law or history, had for the most part begun their careers by reading Greats before passing over to another subject. It is not too much to say that a man who had not read Greats was considered to be a second-class academic, and this belief persisted to a late date. It used to give Robin Dundas, my close friend and colleague as Censor, a peculiar (and frequent) pleasure to remind me that he had opposed my election to the House on the ground that I had not had the great experience of reading Lit. Hum. Some time in the late twenties or early thirties when I was a member

of the Appointments Committee I was asked to give a preliminary interview to a few candidates for appointment to
a firm which manufactured stockings. I glanced at a letter
written to the Committee by the firm. 'We do not ask for any
special knowledge or qualifications,' it said, 'but only that the
candidate should have taken a first class in Greats, since we
understand that that school monopolises all the good brains
in Oxford.'

Greats, in fact, was held to be the perfect training for the
mind. Classical Moderations, dealing with the literature of
Greece and Rome, was followed by the Final School which
combined ancient history with philosophy and thus gave the
student a full and rounded knowledge of the ancient world.
How could the study of modern history, or economics, or
politics, be undertaken without loss of objectivity and without
bringing in propaganda and prejudice? To the purist any suggestion of functional advantage from study was anathema; the
mind should be trained without reference to any mundane
task or office which might later fall to the lot of the student. A
man who had attained to a high class in Greats was fitted to
tackle any intellectual task and could rapidly absorb the knowledge needed for any practical task as well. Much of this,
strange though it appears to some of us now, was true. Greats
did produce the men who were competent not only to fill the
learned professions but also to govern and control the country
and the Empire. History or law or modern languages or
English was often taken as a second school and those who taught
such subjects faced the accusation that their pupils were men of
lesser worth. Had not the History School been established to
give an easy option to the sons of the landed gentry? Was not
the Law School a functional or professional affair (which it
most strikingly never was)? Was not the English School—in
Tommy Strong's phrase—'made for school-marms'?

About the turn of the century all this changed. By the time
that I went up to Oxford the History School was the largest
school in the University and a high class in it carried as much—
or almost as much—prestige as the equivalent class in Greats.
A few men of great ability had built it up and established its
high reputation—A. L. Smith, Arthur Johnson, Edward
Armstrong, Richard Lodge, and C. R. L. Fletcher spring at

once to the mind. The story of this period of growth can, by coincidence, be read in ten pages of the *DNB 1931–40*—for those pages contain the obituary notices of Firth, H.A.L. Fisher, and C.R.L. Fletcher. Within the school itself, in spite of its obvious success, controversy raged, for there were two contrasting views about its curriculum and its purpose. In 1904 Firth delivered his inaugural lecture as Regius Professor, and this sparked off the controversy. The lecture was an impressive statement of the science and art of the historian but it was also a criticism of the Oxford History School and its methods. Firth thought that the school was being swamped by men of inferior mental calibre, and that it did not 'train men capable of adding to knowledge' and did not produce historians. By inference he suggested that the Oxford tutors were working on the wrong lines. Twenty-four tutors published a refutation and criticism of the Professor's lecture, to which Firth replied in a further pamphlet. The argument was clear-cut. The tutors maintained that the aim of the school was not the production of historians but that 'it aimed at the educational ideals of a humane and liberal education through the medium of history and the other allied subjects, for which the University as a place of education exists'. The majority of the candidates 'are in Oxford primarily to be educated and they study the school for that object'. In a word the stage was set for a struggle between the professorial and the tutorial points of view—the former advocating a specialist education, the latter a general education which should fit man for any liberal pursuit, and not only for the life of the historian. Behind the immediate issue lay the respective importance of teaching and research.

There is no doubt that, at the time, victory did not lie with the Professor—a result due in large measure to the manner in which the teaching of modern history in Oxford was controlled. The controlling body was not a faculty but the so-called Modern History Association. This Association began informally in 1869 when the tutors of three colleges opened their lectures to one another's pupils without payment of fee. The Association, entirely unofficial and without recognition from the University, controlled history teaching for many years and came to include all the tutors and lecturers of the colleges. It concerned itself with all matters connected with the subject—the arrangement of lectures, the admission of women to lectures without fee (or chaperones!), the foundation of the Maitland Library, and so forth. From 1908 onwards there were in fact two associations, the 'larger' and the 'inner'. The latter was open only to college tutors, the former included also Professors, Readers, and lecturers. A dinner was held terminally but members of the larger association could only attend that held in Trinity Term, whereas members of the inner association could attend all three. The Faculty of Modern History was established in February 1913 and naturally much business was transferred to it, but the influence of the inner association remained very great. In 1932 and 1937 Powicke, the Regius Professor, came to it to discuss his ideas for the reorganization of the school, but these two friendly and instructive meetings did not result in any significant change. From 1930 to 1937 I acted as Secretary (the only officer) of the Association and was thus able to estimate with some accuracy the extent of its influence.

In the controversy itself I took no active part and had little or no influence. I was a disciple and admirer of Firth, whom I thought to be the greatest of our Oxford historians, but in this particular matter I was wholly on the side of the college tutors. It seemed to me that a great part of Firth's plan was applicable to advanced historical work and not to a first-degree school; there are no short cuts to learning and advanced work needs its foundation of preliminary study. Moreover the contribution made by the college tutors to historical studies was underestimated and compared favourably with that of the professors. An unhappy phrase used by Vinogradoff in a letter to the *Morning Post* about college lecturers 'some of whom can hardly claim more than college notoriety' gave offence and did not help the professorial cause. It is only necessary to read the list of the members of the inner association to realize the injustice of the implied criticism. Yet though I took no part in the controversy it certainly affected my career. When I had been appointed to my lectureship at Christ Church in 1913 I had had no doubt at all about my future career. I should teach to the best of my ability and at the same time pursue my own historical studies; that I should write and become a historian seemed in the natural order of things and I did not consider any other course. Events changed all that. To five years in

Germany had been added six years of Censorship in which time had been given to administration which might have been devoted to research. In 1926 I was already thirty-five and had written nothing whatever. On the other hand I had gained much experience in teaching and felt more and more the satisfaction which teaching can give. Clearly I was ear-marked as a college tutor and nothing more.

The work of a tutor was a demanding one—especially in the years immediately after the war—for he was expected to teach a good many subjects and periods and to keep up with these, and to write his lectures entailed a great deal of reading. This effort no tutor worth his salt would grudge, even though research suffered. Undoubtedly some had to teach too much—of Atkinson, by far the best of military historians of my experience, it was sometimes said that in Heaven he would be found teaching angels in pairs. Personally I thought little about theory and confined myself to practice. It was my job to teach the Christ Church historians and with matters outside Christ Church I had little concern. Before the war the Modern History School at Christ Church had had, I think, no special intellectual repute. It was regarded as a sound education for the average man and a good training ground for men in public life, but certainly not as a specially suitable nursery for scholars and historians. Between the two great wars it grew and flourished amazingly. At the beginning our team consisted of Hassall, Feiling, and myself, but Hassall belonged to the old school and kept a certain number of the men exclusively for himself, whilst Keith Feiling and I shared the rest, arranging from term to term to which of us they should go. Even so some had to be 'farmed out' as the expression went and it soon became clear that more permanent help would be needed. My two seniors had very different views about our functions. Hassall wrote to me when I was in Germany in the spring of 1914: 'I think that we shall do fairly well in the schools tho' my colleague Feiling is rather *too kind* to the Historians who tend to look too much to *us* and not to depend on themselves. But I hope to correct this in time for it damages a possible 1st class man.' More than fifty years later Keith Feiling, writing about the different types of men whom we taught, sounded a very different note: 'I feel we got some of both worlds by setting out to teach history *thoroughly*; we did not just blither over a pipe or allow that anyone was a self-teaching genius.' Perhaps there is something to be said for both views, for the tutorial system is founded on the belief that men should be treated as individuals and the sauce for the goose is by no means always the best sauce for the gander. Hassall retired in 1924 and thereafter Feiling was in sole command. Roy Harrod joined us for a couple of years before transferring to the newly established school of P.P.E. and thereafter we had Ernest Jacob, Nowell Myres, Patrick Gordon-Walker, Colin Dillwyn, and Michael Maclagan in our team for shorter or longer periods. In 1938 when I left for a sabbatical year my place was filled by R. St. C. Talboys, newly retired from Wellington, who was in some respects the most gifted teacher I have known. He stayed on throughout the war. When in 1946 Keith Feiling became Chichele Professor and I was appointed Provost of Worcester, the Christ Church historians were left in the safe hands of Nowell Myres, Steven Watson, and Hugh Trevor-Roper. There was, therefore, always a team of tutors and the results fully justified the number of tutors engaged. In the early days the majority of all first classes went to Balliol and New College, but by the time of the Second War Christ Church had forged ahead and had secured—since 1919—more firsts in the History School than any other college.

It should not be thought that classes are an end in themselves for they are really only labels. The important thing is the discipline of the school and this is valuable to all who undergo it, and not only to those who excel. There is a fascinating letter of Walter Raleigh's in which—as an examiner in the English school—he pleads that two candidates, a man and a woman, should not both be sacrificed by being awarded first classes. 'The age of Chivalry is dead,' he wrote, 'but a father who is a bore isn't the canker in a family that a mother who is a bore is.' Possibly his rather perverse view can be explained by the fact that Raleigh himself had been placed in the second class at Cambridge. When all is said and done the number of firsts which are won does give a rough guide to the vitality and efficiency of the teaching.

Could it be said, then, that the Christ Church History School satisfied the demands both of those who argued that a university course should be only a training of the mind and also of those who wished to see it as a preparation for life in the world of affairs? I am sure that it could, for the list of those distinguished men who graduated through the Christ Church History School is staggering. On the professional side (if the phrase is allowable) Firth himself would surely have felt satisfied. Some fifteen held teaching Fellowships at Oxford—half a dozen held Chairs at Oxford or elsewhere, and among them were numbered men as prominent as A. L. Rowse, Hugh Trevor-Roper, Michael Howard, and Alastair Buchan. On the other side, if it may be so described—that of public service—the record is equally striking. Among those engaged in politics were Osbert Peake (Lord Ingleby), Derick Heathcoat Amory (Lord Amory), Alec Douglas-Home, Alan Lennox-Boyd (Lord Boyd of Merton), Derek Walker-Smith, Ralph Assheton (Lord Clitheroe), Edward Boyle (Lord Boyle), Patrick Gordon-Walker. Overseas could be added Wilfrid Kent-Hughes, Commonwealth Minister for Interior and Works in Australia, and Dias Bandaranaike, Prime Minister of Ceylon. Civil servants and diplomatists abounded—Roger Makins (Lord Sherfield), Ambassador at Washington; K. P. S. Menon (one of our earliest, cleverest and most agreeable pupils), Indian Ambassador in Moscow; Dick White, head successively of M.I.5 and M.I.6; Denis Greenhill, Permanent Under-Secretary at the Foreign Office. There were also two bishops—Cyril Easthaugh of Peterborough and Trevor Huddleston of Masasi and Stepney; a Judge of the High Court (Seymour Karminski); a Lord Mayor of London (Denys Lowson), and a Lord Mayor of Oxford (Michael Maclagan). Among writers besides the professional historians were Lord David Cecil and Lord Birkenhead; among industrialists, business men, and bankers were Jim Pitman, Cecil King, Roger Makins (Lord Sherfield), and William Goodenough. A hostile critic might well argue that such men as these would have risen to the top whatever subjects they had studied and whatever university they had attended. That is probably true, but it does not invalidate my claim that the Christ Church History School provided a splendid training ground both for scholars and for men of affairs. Christ Church could claim that it was, on many counts, the leading college in the University and that, in one department of life at least, it had out-Jowetted Jowett.

The Christ Church History School was in a very real sense the creation of Keith Feiling, whose inspiration made it what it was. Not only was he a gifted teacher but also a practitioner skilled in writing and research. There is no doubt whatever that men thus qualified make the best University tutors, for research and teaching cross-fertilize one another. My own role was of necessity a humbler one, but my deficiencies were disguised by the expert knowledge not only of Keith but of Ernest Jacob and Nowell Myres. I was simply a tutor, without the added qualification of the researcher. The danger for people like myself lies in the fact that, lacking the inspiration of personal intellectual adventure, they may well become lethargic and stereotyped in their teaching and cynical in their approach to their pupils. 'There he goes to give his same old lecture, without a hair on his head or a hope in his heart' was the description of one Oxford don of my time. Cruttwell, whose speech was usually abrasive, often applied to tutors like myself his favourite word 'a hack', and others would dismiss us as crammers. But that is not the whole story. To me there has always seemed to be a close analogy with the medical profession. The Professors and Readers and University lecturers are the specialists—the ordinary run of college tutors are the G.P.s—and both have their uses. Nor do I shy at the word 'crammer', a word, as it has been said, coined by those who cannot teach, to describe those who can. My contribution to the school was far less than that of Feiling, but it was not negligible. Keith himself, most generous of men, wrote to me long after our teaching association had ended and after I had sent him a record of the school: '. . . but your system and staff work and knowledge of men was the greater contribution, you know.' Pride is one of the deadly sins but, sin or not, I plead guilty to it whenever I ponder over Christ Church History School between the two wars.

XV

CRICKET

I think you'd ask a bloke to put his bloody marriage off for a game
of cricket.

Hugh de Selincourt: The Cricket Match

G AMES have played so great a part in my life that I must
devote a chapter, or even two, to them and, since the
twenties were the years in which I played most, this seems the
most appropriate place. But there are difficulties. To write
about one's own sporting successes is to fall between the Scylla
of conceit and the Charybdis of false and fatuous modesty.
And not only that. All my life I have heard the parrot-like
criticism of games-players—'Why do they waste so much time
which could be spent on more worthwhile activities? Why is
credit or even honour given to those who excel in such trivial
things?' A games-player is, in such discussions, permanently
on the defensive.

Perhaps the best line of defence is to attack; I will therefore
state my own view without circumlocution. To my mind the
value of games has not been exaggerated—indeed rather the
reverse. I do *not* think that in schools and universities we pay
too much attention to athletic success; I believe that games help
the development of character and assist the growth of scholarship. In a word I am a whole-hearted supporter of those who
believe that men should develop as what used to be called 'all-
rounders'. What are the grounds for this belief?

Almost every educational theorist has argued that games and
athletics have played in the past too great a role in schools and
universities, but most teaching practitioners would agree (even
if they would not admit it) that academic and athletic success
usually advance together. If one flourishes so does the other. At
Oxford in the twenties critics spent much time in deriding
Brasenose as a college where only athletes were considered and

where intellectual progress counted for little. In the sixties even
more opprobrium was heaped on St. Edmund Hall, by then
one of the largest colleges, though fifty years before it had been
only a Hall and of no special reputation. Let us look at the facts.
Once a year in *Oxford* appear college notes in which each college describes the events and the successes of the year. Most
colleges record new appointments and honours together with a
record of first classes and prizes and some mention of blues won
by undergraduates. In 1969[1] most of the colleges were able to
claim three or four blues in various sports, but St. Edmund Hall
has a rather different style in its entry. This runs as follows: 'As
in former years the Hall contributed a substantial number of
Blues to the main University teams playing against Cambridge;
it also won the inter-collegiate cups in Cricket, Rugby, Soccer,
Athletics and Tennis.' This if anything is an understatement,
for St. Edmund Hall provided a solid foundation for nearly
every University team in the last half of the sixties, and was for
a time also head of the river. 'And so,' the theoretical student of
sociology might say, 'I suppose that with all this waste of time,
idleness flourished and learning declined.' Far from it. A record
of the Final Schools, known as the Norrington table, analyses
the results and places the colleges in order of academic achievement. In the 1969 list St. Edmund Hall comes tenth out of
twenty-eight colleges. On another system of reckoning the
percentage table, St. Edmund Hall comes out third. When Oriel
was head of the river in 1935 five of the men in the boat got
first classes in their Final Schools.

It is an error to dismiss games as time-wasting. Many other
activities are more detrimental to work than athletic pursuits—
religion, politics, and acting would come high in this category
but all are to be encouraged, provided only that a man knows
how to marshal his preferences and does not attempt too much.
Nowadays protests and demonstrations are the great time-
wasters and lack, in my judgement, any compensating benefit.

A century ago outdoor sports were largely, though not exclusively, the preserve of the well-to-do, but from that time onwards games became more and more important and spread
into wider circles. The golden age of amateur games was the
twenty-five years immediately preceding the First Great War; I

[1] This was written in 1970.

had the good fortune and the privilege to see something of that golden age.

What are the advantages which games give to those who practise them? The old ideal of a healthy mind in a healthy body, the benefit which physical training gives to the character by its discipline, the virtues of loyalty and self-abnegation inculcated by team games, are all ideas which now evoke little but a faintly patronizing tolerance or even contemptuous ridicule. These are platitudes and therefore unworthy of notice. That they are also true is forgotten or ignored and, in any case, they do not explain the fundamental value of games.

The greatest virtue which games have is that they breed a spirit of tolerance—sympathy too and perhaps empathy, but tolerance above all. I know that the case of that great cricketer David Sheppard can be quoted against me, but not even the intolerance of the Bishop of Liverpool can make me doubt the truth of the general proposition. It is not surprising that games should create a tolerant frame of mind, for games-players are practical craftsmen, well aware of the difficulties of their craft. Every cricketer can appreciate the feelings of a nervous batsman or an unlucky fielder. Very different is the case of the non-playing critic in the pavilion, and very different, too, the attitude of mind of the pure intellectual. Intellectual arrogance is a hateful thing, and intolerance is its child.

The second great advantage which comes from games is akin to the first. More than any other activity it enables men to get on terms with one another. 'Communication' has been a favourite word in the sixties—it will no doubt decline in the seventies but it is convenient to use it here and right to assert that no other activity promotes communication both between individuals and between countries than do games. I surmise that music may have the same sort of magic, but lacking (alas!) a true appreciation of music, I cannot tell. I know only that games bring men together to an extent that nothing else in my experience can, and I know, too, that the majority of the friendships which I have made and such understanding as I have acquired of other people and other points of view stem from active participation in games.

That must be my excuse for the egotism which prevails in the rest of this and the following chapter. In an autobiography

I cannot exclude some account of the games which I have played. They are all gone and forgotten now but, because they formed a part of my life and because they brought me into touch with many people whom I should otherwise not have known and because they took me to places which I should otherwise probably never have seen, it would seem wrong to leave them unrecorded.

Cricket was my first and most enduring passion—a word not too strong to describe the feeling of countless schoolboys in my own boyhood for what was then a truly national game. Most boys then followed the futures of their county side with an attention not given to their leaders in Church or State. It was even remarked that the word 'Cobden' was better known as the hero of a famous hat-trick at Lords than as the name of the great protagonist of Free Trade. Once at Oxford I began to take part myself in the cricketer's life. College cricket was great fun and did not, I believe, interfere with work. At Worcester we were allowed two away matches—played in my third year against Radley and East Gloucestershire at Cheltenham—for the rest our fixture list was mainly against other colleges. Here there was an admirable system in which two-day matches were played, starting at 2 p.m. and finishing at 6.30 each day. The best cricket of all came with the Long Vacation—village cricket when at home, country-house cricket, and matches of the so-called wandering clubs—i.e. those clubs which had no ground of their own.

Of country-house cricket much has been written and certainly it was at its peak in the years immediately before 1914. In a fascinating account of Edwardian England Mr. J.B. Priestley has described the life of the great country houses of those days and has stressed the magnificence, the opulence, and the objectionable luxury. True enough, but not the whole story. If my recollection is correct there was a widely held belief that life at the great mansions where Edward VII was entertained was rather bad form and that some of his wealthy associates were not the most desirable companions for the monarch. On the other hand nothing could have been more pleasant than cricket played at the less advertised but surely more agreeable country houses. I have given a picture of it which is, I think, not over-coloured in *Fate Cannot Harm Me*. At one match in the Midlands some five or six of our side were put up at a near-by house, where we arrived after the first day's play just before dinner. (It was a two-day match.) One of the party was Sir Timothy O'Brien, once declared by W. G. to be his first choice as an opening batsman, who had stayed in the house many times before. Our hostess met us at the door with the news that George, her husband, was confined to his room with gout and that Tim must take the head of the table. When the butler brought him the first bottle of champagne to taste Tim gave it the most serious attention and then waved it away. At that time I had seldom, if ever, tasted champagne except at weddings and bump suppers or similar feasts, and I felt that there had been a disaster. 'How awful for you', I said to Tim after dinner, 'to have to say that that bottle was corked.' 'Corked?' was the reply. 'Never tasted a better bottle in my life, but the butler here is an old friend of mine.' Later in the evening Tim showed another side of his generous character. About half a dozen of us were playing some gambling card-game, fashionable at the time, and I, being unwilling to risk a coup, not unnaturally lost steadily and became seriously alarmed that I should not be able to pay my debt. Tim was the only considerable winner but two young ladies had both made enough to make themselves happy. The end of the game came. 'No one has won anything worth talking about,' said Tim. 'We can't bother to add up all these figures', and he tore up all the score sheets before the ladies could make their protests. I have no doubt at all that he had observed my anxiety. Country-house cricket was terribly damaged, and in many cases destroyed, by the First War, but it survived in a few chosen places of which Arundel was the chief. The Duke of Norfolk's weeks there must have taught a younger generation something of what pre-war cricket had been.

Club cricket, on the other hand, was as vigorous and as pleasant after the war as it had been before, and in it I took my enthusiastic part. The best of all the wandering clubs to my mind was the Free Foresters—the best because we always insisted that members should qualify both as really competent players and as persons with whom we should all wish to play. When I first joined the committee the club was under the benevolent despotism of Eustace Mordaunt, who presided over our annual meeting for the election of members. We used to settle at the beginning of the meeting how many votes would be needed to secure election. On one occasion a candidate was thought by some of us to be unsuitable, though he was a very good player. We did not vote him in, but there was some embarrassment because his proposer and seconder were both old and highly respected members of the club and we were unwilling to offend them. 'Leave it to me', said Eustace. He wrote to the proposer, an old friend, and said that the committee had felt that the candidate was rather too young for election. The hint was not taken, and in the following year the proposal was made again, but on this occasion Eustace's letter had the desired effect. He wrote with regret to say that the committee considered that the candidate was rather too old to be elected. I hope that I put back into the Free Foresters something to compensate for all that I had had from the club—for I was on the committee for thirty-one years and the record shows that I proposed or seconded 177 candidates.

The oldest and perhaps the most famous of the wandering clubs was I Zingari, but, though I was on the committee for many years, I never felt for it quite the same affection which I did for the Foresters. I Z. had not moved with the times and retained, I thought, too much of Victorian tradition, together with more than a suspicion of aristocratic snobbery. 'He's not quite I Z.' was an expression which did not criticize a man's cricket but did suggest a social inferiority. Our committee used to meet for luncheon at Lord Dartmouth's house in Belgrave Square, and there was a touch of the burlesque about the proceedings, when we solemnly sang the I Z. song before proceeding to business—a proceeding only saved from absurdity by the presence and voice of Kennerley Rumford.[2] I have an almost nightmarish recollection of one meeting when a distant cousin of the oldest member of the committee was turned down, upon which his sponsor black-balled every other candidate. Things have changed since then, and the club, under the enthusiastic and beneficent governorship of Charles Cobham,[3] has regained all its old prestige and panache. Oxford itself

[2] Kennerley Rumford (1870–1957), singer husband of Clara Butt.
[3] Lord Cobham, Governor-General of New Zealand, 1957–62. Lord-Lieut. of Worcestershire, and Lord Steward of the Royal Household.

provided a fine choice of clubs, and to the Authentics I owed my introduction to club cricket. The origin of the club was strange for, though membership was confined to members of the University, the founder Everard Britten-Holmes had himself not been at Oxford. He gave to the club an extraordinary care and devotion and I have preserved a four-page letter which he wrote to me when I was managing a 'Tics match for him for the first time. He could not come to the match, which was at Sandhurst, himself but I was given notes on every player on my side, details of trains, instructions for paying an umpire, all interspersed with admonitions to uphold the good name of the club. The end of the letter was characteristic. 'I am off on Northern Tour Sunday and down running Western. My funeral will be about the 9th August. Don't come. Have a bottle of the "*boy*" and drink to the 'Tics in future. Yrs. ever, Britten.'

Harlequin cricket was the best of all. I had not been a Harlequin as an undergraduate but was elected after the war and played consistently for the club until the Second War came. Our matches were few in number but they were good and the sides invariably strong—as they needed to be, especially for the military tour in July. In this tour we played four two-day matches, against the R.E. at Chatham, R.A. at Woolwich, Aldershot Command at Aldershot, and R.M. usually at Deal. In 1926 we were so strong that the side could bat in any order. In the first match our expected No. 1 batsman turned up late and Colin McIver at No. 11 was put in his place. Colin made 100, and it was at once agreed that whoever went in last on the tour must go in first on another occasion. All four of the 'No. 11s' made a century in one of the four matches. Looking back I feel sure that it was because Colin McIver ran the tour that I felt these Harlequin matches to have been the best and most enjoyable that I ever played, for Colin was the gayest, the happiest, and the most generous of all my cricketing friends. To be a Harlequin was felt in the Oxford cricket world to be a high distinction and at times those who played would refuse an invitation to play for a first-class county if they had previously agreed to play for the Harlequins. Douglas Jardine, the most punctilious of men, came on one occasion to excuse himself because he had been invited to play for the Gentlemen. 'But', he said, 'I shall only accept after I have found another Harlequin to take my place.'

In 1922 the Oxfordshire County side was revived and I had two good seasons with it in the Minor Counties' competition. My most vivid memory then is of the three Hartley brothers, Oxfordshire farmers and sportsmen of the best vintage, who formed the backbone of our county hockey side as well as of the Cricket XI. Dick, the eldest, was said by W. G. Grace to have been about the best bat outside first-class cricket, Ernest captained the English Hockey XI, and Frank played in the English Amateur Soccer XI on the same day. We also had Charlie Walters, who had been centre-half for Tottenham Hotspur when they won the cup, and who became the doyen of Oxfordshire cricketers. I sometimes wish that I had played longer for the county, but the claims of club cricket, and of lawn tennis, made it difficult to spare the time.

My first foreign tour outside the country came in 1923, when I went to Canada with the Free Foresters under the leadership of Major E. G. Wynyard. Canadian cricket was not very strong, though in Bob Wookey they had a left-handed bowler of the very highest class, and I do not remember that we lost a match, though memory is dim and I may be mistaken. What remains clear in memory is the beauty of the St. Lawrence in late September and the activities of Hart Hall at Toronto—the most successful attempt, inspired by Vincent Massey, to transfer a true university atmosphere to a university in the Dominions. On our side Bob Fowler, hero of the most exciting of all Eton and Harrow matches and the keenest cricketer that I ever knew, was outstanding. He always kept in his pocket a cricket ball which he would spin whenever he had a spare moment with the result that he had developed a muscle of the middle finger of his right hand which was almost as large as a small potato. On the field and off he was irrepressible. At one Kiwani dinner where we suffered the discomfort of community singing before, after, and during every course, he leaped to his feet with the words, '*I* shall now sing "The Wearing of the Green".' It was fascinating to observe how tenaciously Canadians then clung to their links with the Mother Country. I sat at lunch one day with an old man who questioned me relentlessly about the streets and sights of London, only to remark at the end,

'I've never been to England myself.' In an effort to change the conversation I asked if he still played cricket himself. Though I realized that his age made the answer inevitable his reply was not quite what I had expected. 'No, sir, I gave up cricket when they allowed overarm bowling—it has spoilt the game.'

Many other tours followed. In Portugal with the Cryptics I first sampled the hospitality of the famous Factory Club at Oporto, where one was reminded at the same time of the Peninsular War and of pre-1914 Senior Common Rooms at Oxford. After a lavish dinner we adjourned to another room for dessert and three glasses stood beside each plate. 'You are now', said my host, 'going to drink the three greatest ports in the world.' What years were they? 1870, 1878, 1884, 1887?—I cannot now remember. 'You must drink them in this order', he said, and arranged the glasses in a row. My neighbour on the other side then intervened. 'Nonsense,' he said, 'your host is a heretic; you must drink these wines in the order of their age.' So saying he rearranged the glasses and started a fierce altercation with my host. To this day I have no idea as to the order in which I drank the 'three greatest ports in the world', but each one of them was nectar. Twice in the Easter vacation I went to Egypt with sides led by Hubert Martineau—tours where the quality of the cricket was equalled by the pleasure of seeing something of that fabulous country. The treasures of Tutankhamen's tomb had recently reached Cairo and Sukhara was being excavated, but neither of those sights was as impressive as it was to stand on the top of the Great Pyramid at the evening hour of prayer.

My last cricket tour was also my longest, for I was fortunate enough to be invited for the M.C.C. tour of Canada in 1937. We had a competent side, about equal, I should judge, to a good University XI, and were very well captained by George Newman. In 1921 the Free Foresters had played only in eastern Canada, but in 1937 we went across to the west, playing at Winnipeg and Calgary on the way. If there is a more beautiful ground than those at Vancouver—on the mainland and on the island—I do not know it—and I doubt if there is. Canadian cricket had improved greatly and we lost one match against All-Canada; but, alas, the cream of Canadian cricketers lost their lives in the Second War and I doubt whether the improvement has been maintained. I was the veteran of the party and my bowling was not needed, but aided by a good few not-out innings I contrived to come second in the batting averages, and as I also held a good many catches in the slips I could feel that I had pulled my weight. I was never a first-class cricketer and never pretended to be, but I have had the great good fortune to play many different kinds of cricket of varying standard and in many places and to have enjoyed them all to the full.

XVI

OTHER GAMES

He spoke more and more of himself. The 'I's succeeded one another like telegraph poles flashing past when viewed from a fast-moving train.

ANON.

O NE handicap to my cricket came from the competing claims of lawn tennis, for every year in the twenties I was torn between the two. In March of 1919 I wrote a long article for *The Times* on sport at Oxford after the war, entitled 'A great revival'. The title was well merited, for rowing, football, and athletics had sprung to life with startling rapidity, but had I waited till the summer I could have added the story of the even more startling renaissance of cricket and lawn tennis. In the last named I was specially involved, for no old blue had returned and we had to start from scratch. A completely new side had to be trained, and the outcome of our efforts was a victory over Cambridge in June. The Cambridge captain, Newton Thompson, later Chief Justice of South Africa, wrote me a generous letter of congratulation. 'I want to congratulate you on your VI which you trained to victory over us. . . . It must be a matter of great congratulation to you that you got together from nothing a side which beat a Cambridge VI, which I consider quite as good as our sides of '12 and '13.' For the first time I tasted the pleasure of the training, that is of vicarious triumph.

In 1919 I played in my first Wimbledon and I was beaten in the first round by R. V. Thomas, a good player who won the doubles that year with O'Hara Wood. I was far from disgraced, for the match went to five sets and the last was lost 9–7. The match lasted for four hours. After that I played for the next five years, missed four years, and then returned to play in 1929,

'30, and '31. There was a temptation to abandon cricket and aim at the highest distinction at lawn tennis—a temptation especially strong in 1920. In that year I got through two rounds and then lost in straight sets to C.S. Garland (who, like Thomas in 1919, won the doubles in partnership with R.N. Williams), but had done well enough to be picked for England against both Scotland and Ireland. The Scottish match we won but at Dublin things went wrong. Two of our side, including A.E. Beamish, our best player, dropped out through injury at the last moment and the substitutes found were not up to standard. We lost the match but something was rescued from the wreck by W.A. Ingram and myself, for we won all our three doubles matches. Dublin in 1920 was in a troubled condition and we were told on arrival that, though our visit was welcome, we must be prepared for 'incidents' since someone had been shot just outside the Fitzwilliam Club in the previous week. We were instructed to lie down at once if there was any shooting. During one keenly contested double, in which fortunately I was not playing, there was a sudden report and all four players dropped to the ground. But the report was in fact caused by a ginger-beer bottle which exploded in the heat. Had I succumbed to the temptation to try to go further in the tennis world I should, I feel sure, have regretted it. It would have compelled me to give up cricket in the summer and to have trained and played tennis in the winter. Furthermore success would have been unlikely, for Wimbledon always started on the Monday after full term ended, so that my first single of the year was always played there. Besides I was twenty-eight when I first played tennis in the highest class—too old to hope for much improvement. As things were I could enjoy Wimbledon in a carefree and amateur way and still achieve a reasonable measure of success.

In 1921 I lost a centre-court match to B.I.C. Norton. For the first two sets I was consistently foot-faulted at one end and lost both at 6–4. I won a long third set at 12–10, but had not much left for the fourth set. I reflected ruefully that only a foot-fault, called very late, had prevented me from taking the third set at 6–4. Norton went on to win the final, but was beaten in the challenge round by Tilden although he twice had a point for the match. In 1922 Jacques Brugnon (another doubles champion!) beat me—once more in the fifth set. In 1923 after getting through three rounds I lost to D.M. Evans in a long match, which gave Tom Webster the material for an amusing cartoon. Once again the fifth set went to 9–7. The truth was that I had not the opportunity to get fit enough for five-set singles. J.A. Parke, as famous a Rugby player as he was as a tennis player, once told me that he found a five-set single was a much greater physical strain than a Rugby international. I played my last Wimbledon single in 1930, when I really entered by mistake for I had intended only to play in the doubles. My opponent, P.D.B. Spence, who was or had been champion of South Africa, beat me by three sets to one, but all the sets, of which I won the third, went to 6–4. In doubles through the years I had plenty of fun. With W.A. Ingram as my partner I got through three rounds in 1923, and again won three times, partnered by C.H. Kingsley in 1924 before being beaten by a very good American pair in R.N. Williams and W.M. Washburn. The best fun of all came in 1930 when Victor Cazalet and I drew the first seeded pair, J.A. Doeg and G.M. Lott. We lost in straight sets, 8–6, 13–11, 7–5, but we had service to win in each of the sets. Doeg was better known in America than over here. An article in the *New York Times* (3 August 1950) made a careful survey of all the great players between the two wars and decided that Tilden was the best of all and Doeg the best server. I should not quarrel with either verdict, for it seemed to me that Tilden had more variety and command of strokes than any other player of that time, and that Doeg—by virtue of being left-handed—was more difficult to cope with than others of equal power.

In tennis, as in cricket, it was not always the highest class which provided the most enjoyment. In those amateur days tournaments round the country, especially on the south coast and in the West Country, matched for pleasure and entertainment the many parties on private courts. In term time the best of all were at Lord Birkenhead's house at Charlton, whither I first went in 1919. F.E. had become Lord Chancellor at the beginning of that year, and was accustomed to spend most week-ends at Charlton, only some twenty miles from Oxford. As an undergraduate he had been a noted athlete, unlucky to have missed his blue for Rugby football. To the end of his life his language about the University officials who had left

12. St. Vincent Term. Osborne 1903. Dartmouth 1905. H.M.S. Cumberland 1907

13. Coaling ship. H.M.S. *Britannia* 1908

17. England v. Ireland, Birmingham, 1925

18. M.C.C. touring side in Canada, 1937

him out of the side was a lesson in opprobrium. In the later
forties his physical energy was remarkable (he once bared his
muscular forearm to explain to me his success at the Bar).
When we arrived at lunch-time he would already have ridden
or played a round of golf and after lunch tennis went on without
interruption till dinner-time. As a player he lacked mobility
but at the net he was lethal and his comments on his opponents
were worth a few extra points. I used to reckon that, partnered
by him, we could be pretty sure of beating the Varsity third pair
but would probably go down before the first pair. Good though
the tennis was the evening talks were even better; his was, I
am convinced, the most powerful mind with which I have ever
been brought into contact. To strangers he could be formidable,
or even rude if he so wished, and he could enjoy the confusion
of others, particularly if his sense of humour was aroused. On
one occasion a new incumbent of a neighbouring living came
to make a formal call and was received by F.E. in his study,
where the bookshelves were filled by books on Napoleon
and his times. I can still hear F.E.'s chuckle of delight as he
recounted the reverend gentleman's opening gambit. 'Ah,
Napoleon, I perceive. Now I call that a very able man.' One
characteristic of F.E.'s outweighed all others and that was his
loyalty to his friends. Once you were his friend, so you remained.
One would go over from Oxford for the day and be greeted as
though one was the one person he most wished to see. All very
well, a cynic might suggest, he wants to make sure of a good
four for tennis. Not at all. One would go again a little later to
find the house full of cabinet ministers and suchlike folk, but
F.E. would still treat one as the guest he most gladly welcomed.
Could any trait be more endearing in a great man? I never
think of him without affection, or without admiration for his
great qualities. It is, I believe, one of the tragedies of our history
that he died so young, and one of the great 'Ifs' of our time—
to think what might have happened had he lived longer.
Winston Churchill's battle to alert the country to its danger
might have had a very different measure of success had F.E.
been alive to fight by his side.

Another memory. Chartwell was also a place where much
tennis was played, for Mrs. Winston Churchill, as she then was,
was herself a good and keen player. A week spent there gave

me a vivid side-light on Winston's character. At the time
he was, so to speak, in the political wilderness, but was actively
engaged on his life of Marlborough. One evening late in the
week Clemmie[1] upbraided him because he had paid no attention to a party of Boy Scouts who had been encamped in the
grounds for more than a week. 'I've invited them to come up
this evening after dinner,' she continued, 'and they will sing
you their Scouts' songs.' Winston was a little peevish and protested vigorously but he had to give way. After dinner the
Scouts duly appeared and, sitting on the floor at one end of the
dining-room, sang their songs to us. When they left Winston
sprang into action. It was disgraceful, he complained, that
Scouts should have such a poor repertory of songs, but he would
put all that to rights. He would himself compose a song-book
for the use of Scouts. Everyone in the party was put under
orders to assist, by writing to his relatives for older collections
or by going to London to search the shops for earlier works.
Then everything was to go to Winston. For the time everything was to be put on one side. 'Action this day', which was
later to mean so much, was even then his watchword. The song-
book did not materialize, but the picture of a man of almost
fanatical energy remained in my mind.

In the winter hockey, golf, and squash took the place of the
summer games. The peculiar attraction of hockey was that of
all games it was the most firmly and consistently amateur. It did
not attract crowds but only players and competitions, and cups
were sternly forbidden. At Oxford where 'cuppers' between the
colleges were important to encourage the game the Hockey
Association looked with grave disfavour on our operations, and
indeed the existence of the College Cup competition was in
direct contravention of the rules. We saved the situation by an
elaborate legal argument in which we maintained that the
colleges played in the competition *not* for the possession of the
cup but only for the right to have the name of the college inscribed on a plaque upon the plinth. It was a thin argument but
it prevailed. In the twenties the game flourished chiefly because
of the clientele which supported it. Without the prestige of
cricket or football and without the social cachet of lawn tennis
and golf it still attracted a splendid body of supporters, nearly

[1] Mrs. (later Lady) Winston Churchill.

all of whom were players and not just spectators. It flourished among city workers, at the universities, and in the services, which had discovered that it could often be played all over the world and in places where other games were not to be had. The schools, too, began to take it up as a change and relief from too much compulsory football.

Personally I was supremely lucky in that I could, at Oxford, get as many games as I wished either for the College, or for one of the many clubs, or for the county. In the vacation I played for a time for Hampstead and wish that I could have played more for that fine and sporting club—but naturally a London club side could not always find room for someone who could not play regularly. Divisional trials was the next step and then divisional matches for the South. It was interesting to observe how pace and skill improved with each successive step. S. H. Shoveller, the great centre-forward with whom I played several times at the end of his career, once told me that the best hockey he ever played was for England against Ireland in 1912. My own recollection is that I never knew a side to play so well as did one of our South sides against the West. We scored, I think, nine goals but the West goal-keeper played so brilliantly that his place in the English side was assured. That day everything seemed to go right; the sensation was akin to that experienced (if I may trust the word of others) by oarsmen in an eight when every oar is in perfect harmony. In 1925 I was selected for the English side and had three good matches, but 1926 was unlucky for me. I was playing well and looking forward to the international matches when, just at the end of Hilary term, I fell ill. Frank Taylor, my Junior Censor, summoned a doctor, who diagnosed my complaint as measles. My study was approached through my dining-room and I was allowed to interview undergraduates through the open door. So far as I know no one contracted measles through me, but the arrangement strikes me now as somewhat haphazard. Perhaps the explanation can be found in the fact that Frank had summoned a physician who had the highest reputation as a gynaecologist but who was not quite so well thought of in other branches of his profession. I played once again for England in 1927 but that was a poor consolation for the loss of 1926.

Hockey made a great contribution to better relations between countries and in this matter the Oxford University Occasionals were in the forefront. In 1923 we undertook a prolonged tour, starting with three or four matches in Paris and going on to Vienna and Budapest. The French matches were enthusiastically received and for years afterwards the Occasionals in Paris seemed to be playing on their home grounds. That was to have been expected, but the goodwill and friendliness in Austria and Hungary surprised me. At Vienna where we attracted a crowd of about 2,000 we could only draw a splendid game. The city itself had not, of course, recovered its pre-war brilliance but there was evidence that games might play a great part in breaking down national animosities. During our stay we were taken to watch a match which I should have thought hardly possible at that date, a match between Austria and Italy. We were told that the crowd was 40,000 but I think that this was a fantastic exaggeration. Be that as it may the game was firmly controlled by a Dutch referee and ended happily in a draw. At Schönbrunn I was reminded of past glories when a gardener was showing us the view of the palace from one of the outlying pavilions. On a hockey tour clothes are not a first consideration and no doubt some of us were somewhat shabby, but I confessed to a feeling of shame when the gardener, after a prolonged look at my trousers, remarked sadly. 'I *have* shown this view to two Emperors and three Kings on the same day.' At Budapest the hockey was less advanced, but our reception was equally cordial and Admiral Horthy, the Regent, honoured the game with his presence. I believe that this tour was the first of any length after the war and I am sure that it did a great deal of good.

Many other tours followed, in France, Belgium, Germany, and Spain. Some games I remember, some are totally forgotten. Only once can I recall an unpleasant incident. The Occasionals had played in the Barcelona festival tournament in 1931. It had been a pleasant and well-arranged tournament, and we had no hesitation in agreeing to the proposal that we should play an extra match in the country on the day after the festival. This was to be at Tarrasa and we expected a friendly holiday game, but how wrong we were! Hockey, it appeared, was the favoured game of the place, rivalling the lure of the bull-fight. There was a large, noisy, and hostile crowd; the ground was hard and stony

and the pavilion a small wooden hut, which looked difficult
to defend and easy to plunder. We took the elementary precaution of handing our money and valuables to the one member
of our party who was not playing. The game was a battle and
caused me to commit (I think for the only time in my life) a
savage and deliberate foul. On two occasions when, as centre
forward, I got away with some hope of scoring one of the
Tarrasa inside forwards sent me sprawling by hooking my hind
foot with his stick. At the next bully which fell to him to take I
pushed our own inside forward away and took the bully myself,
for I had noted that the enemy had a heavily bandaged thumb.
Instead of striking his stick three times as the rules demanded
I aimed the third stroke—and it was no light one—on his
bandaged thumb. All hell broke loose, and the position looked
ugly but luckily we had a stout-hearted French umpire who
persuaded the crowd to let the game continue. Fortunately we
lost the game, but even so we had to form into a solid phalanx
to struggle to the pavilion, whence we watched with anxiety
the cautious approach of our camp-follower from the other side
of the ground. Mercifully his precious burden had not been
noticed and he reached us in safety. I was not surprised a few
years later when I read that the communist revolt originated in
Tarrasa.

The Occasionals felt, after many tours, that they must do
something to return continental hospitality and the club, in
alliance with the Cambridge Wanderers, arranged a hockey
festival in Oxford in 1933, to which sides were invited from
many countries. For various reasons the Spaniards, the Dutch,
and the Swiss could not come but we had sides from Belgium,
France, and Germany. The official dinner presented me, as
Chairman, with something of a problem, for I knew that each
country wanted to speak before the others. Before dinner and
after several drinks I persuaded the rival captains to spin a
coin to decide their order—I then told them that unfortunately
the English were bad linguists and that, as we were keenly
anxious to hear what they had to say, we hoped and expected
that they would speak in English. For my part, lest there should
seem to be any discourtesy, I should speak both in French and
German. I did not tell them of the careful coaching that I had
had from the Modern Language Tutor at Christ Church. The

plan worked and must have reduced the length of the speeches to an acceptable length.

It was difficult in that atmosphere to believe that a second war was pending. I have kept one short letter typed on thick black-edged paper, which reads as follows:

Hannover. 21.1.36.

Dear Sir,

With great regret we have heard of the death of His Majesty King George V.

We wish to let you know that we feel with you because we are your friends.

Yours very sincerely,
Deutsche Hockey Club
Hannover.

W. F. Fiedler

More revealing was the remark made to me previously at Oxford by the captain of the Köln club, whom I asked if he was a Nazi. 'No,' he replied, 'I am not, but in a month or so I shall be, for Hitler is coming to speak to us and no one can resist him.'

Hockey was my main winter recreation, but I found time for squash and golf as well. For an academic or a business man squash was invaluable for it provided the maximum of exercise in the minimum of time, but among games it was a late starter. The first Oxford and Cambridge match was played in 1925 and most of the courts were built in the twenties and thirties. I played two or three times in the Amateur Championship but without any success—a cause of no surprise, since a hurried rush from Oxford to play in a strange court at an unfamiliar time of day was no proper preparation for a serious match. But I had great pleasure from games at Oxford as well as from club matches in London—on the few occasions when I could get away to play them. Golf was a wholly different proposition. All my life it has been for me a holiday game—a relaxation and a relief from more strenuous and more competitive games. When one considers what it has now become it is hard to realize that in my youth it was both an amateur and a rather aristocratic game. I started as a boy with the old gutty ball—and very hard and unfriendly that ball was if it was not struck cleanly. At

Oxford golf gained immensely in reputation and prestige in the Wethered–Tolley period just after the First War, but they and their contemporaries were strictly amateurs able to play for fun with as much zest as they should in championship golf. I enjoyed many happy games with them both and learned much from them. Playing at Swinley Forest in a four-ball (a form of the game which I usually dislike) with Roger Wethered against Cyril Tolley and Lord Charles Hope we came to a short hole where the other three all found the green with their tee-shots, whilst my tee-shot finished ingloriously in thick heather a good fifty yards short of the green. As we walked forward I stooped to pick up my ball, but was sternly forbidden to do so by my partner. Obediently I took out my niblick and by good fortune reached the green. The three great men putted from about five or six yards and all, giving the hole a chance, were four or five feet past it. My putt from about the same distance went into the hole. Then the denouement. My partner and both our opponents missed their short putts.

Fortunately I was never good enough at golf to suffer all the agonies and frustrations which the game can bring, and so I have been able to enjoy it as a relaxation and refreshment. That, however, does not mean that I played it less keenly or more care-lessly. So-called rag games of any kind are anathema to me. Gathorne Girdlestone, the great surgeon, with whom I played much, seemed to me to have the root of the matter in him. 'When you have a critical putt to hole it is the most important thing in the world; after you have missed it nothing could matter less.' So he told me once and after his retirement he wrote to me to suggest that we should play regularly, 'just you and I, proper fierce happy singles, lots of fun and friendship and the rigour of the game'.

I kept up most of my games until the outbreak of the Second War, and I confess that a newspaper cutting in January 1936 still gives me pleasure.

Few men can have played three different games in first-class com-pany within a week . . . yet J. C. Masterman can claim that distinc-tion during the past seven days. Last Tuesday he played in the South of England squash championship; over the week end he was active on Rye golf course playing for the President's Putter; yesterday he scored two goals against the Cambridge hockey team.

The writer could have added that I celebrated my forty-fifth birthday during that same week.

To have played so long makes it almost inevitable that I should often, and not always intentionally, find myself comparing the past with the present, and wondering where the advantage lies. For the present generation the great and overwhelming advantage which they have over their predecessors is the variety of choice which is offered to them and the greater opportunities of taking part. Here I think not only of games but also of other outdoor sports and activities, sailing and surf-riding, ski-ing and rock-climbing—all out of the reach of most of us sixty years ago, when games for most meant cricket and football alone. But it is not all gain. I am sure that in the conditions of today it is right that the distinction between the amateur and the professional should disappear, but it is all the more important that the old amateur spirit should remain. When games are too highly developed and too much managed they tend to become gladiatorial shows or business ventures.

As to the relative skills of the past and the present I have a clear view. The champion at any time was just as good as he had to be; had he been born fifty years later than he was he would have been a champion. If, for example, Brookes or Tilden played as they did in their prime they would clearly be beaten by Smith or Nastase playing as they do today. But had either of the first two been contemporary with the others, who could foretell the result of a match? And in cricket. No one will persuade me that the great ones of the past would not be the equals of the giants of today. In 1906, in his fifty-eighth year, W. G. Grace played against Cambridge and made 64 and 44 not out in his two innings. Keeping wicket was A. D. Imlay and it was he who told me that he took only three balls left alone by Grace on the off-side. The champion played them all—for practice if nothing else—and the Cambridge bowlers were no slouches!

It is really an idle pursuit to attempt to compare the players of today with those of sixty years ago, but I can count myself lucky to have lived at a time when amateur sport flourished. It may be that, dwelling in the past, I underestimate the skill and expertise of modern players—but of one thing I am sure. The more games that we play, and the more we play with other countries, no matter what their politics may be, the better it will be for us and for the world. It was a dictum of A. L. Smith's that athletics were the great solvent of social barriers in England; if the self-righteous theorists of today could be restrained games could also be a prime force in breaking down barriers between nations.

XVII

OXFORD LIFE BETWEEN THE WARS

There must be a sense, as well, of belonging to something old, and honourable, and beneficent, a sense of being possessed as well as possessing.

L. E. JONES: *An Edwardian Youth*

WHEN I turn back my mind to the twenties the picture is all of Christ Church. In fact I was wholly content; satisfied with my life, happy because I had the job I desired, confident after a very short time that I could discharge it competently and without any disturbing ambitions which might entail change, difficult decisions, or possible troubles. There was much complacency in this, something of idleness, something of a failure to assess correctly the priorities in any scheme of life. It has been said that a bachelor lives like a king and dies like a dog. The truth of the first part of that saying was abundantly clear to me in the twenties.

From matters which did not immediately concern Christ Church or University sport I cut myself resolutely adrift, an abstention which applied particularly to politics, either on the University or national level. The syllabus of the Modern History School stopped short some fifty years before the date at which it was being studied since it was the conviction of those who governed it that present-day events could not be studied objectively or in a scholarly and unprejudiced manner. With this view I was in agreement. Thirty or forty years before my teaching life began, religious beliefs had often bedevilled historical writing, and I remember something of a shock when my own tutor had written off Mary Queen of Scots as 'a shameless adulteress' and dissuaded me from delving into the authenticity of the Casket letters. Furthermore I felt instinctively that a teacher of history lost something of authority if he became an active politician, and I preferred to remain an independent observer rather than a participant in the field of politics. In later days when the universities have been caught up in national controversies and when studies have been enlarged to include the issues and controversies of the day such an attitude of mind would be difficult and perhaps impossible to maintain but I do not think that it was wrong.

In so far as I adhered to any political party I could call myself a Liberal, but I was never what can be described as a 'paid-up member' of any party. Once, and once only, I allowed myself to jump on a band-wagon and add my signature to those of many others on a letter sent from Oxford to the professors and members of the universities in Germany and Austria, advocating the restoration of friendly intercourse. It comes almost as a surprise to me today to read my name in that company, for the letter was signed by all the most liberal of the Oxford dons—by those who were considered to form the left wing of our society; Ernest Barker, G.H. Hardy, Lindsay, Gilbert Murray, and J.L. Stocks among them. But though I regarded myself as a Liberal (perhaps deservedly) my natural instincts were always conservative and with age my conservatism—or rather my innate respect for the Establishment—has steadily grown.

However much I confined myself to Christ Church it was not possible entirely to ignore the impact of the world outside, as for example when a Dean was to be chosen at Christ Church or a Chancellor elected by the University. Tommy Strong became Bishop of Ripon in 1920 and my seniors were full of anxiety about his successor—an anxiety which bordered on panic when it was rumoured that Lloyd George, then Prime Minister, was inclined to choose Temple, then Bishop of Manchester, as our Dean. The Christ Church elders regarded Temple as a revolutionary whose advent would be a disaster. In this they were grossly unfair but there was substance in the objection that Temple would regard Christ Church as a stepping-stone to greater things and would be only a temporary holder of the office. Unfortunately it appeared to us juniors that our seniors, though ready enough with criticism, had no constructive proposal to make. The dilemma was resolved by Lord Birkenhead who dined at Christ Church and listened to the prevailing complaints. 'Leave it to me,' he said. 'Henry Julian White was a colleague of mine at Merton and he will be just the man you need.' F.E. was as good as his word, but found to his surprise that Lloyd George was firmly determined to appoint Temple. It was only after a protracted struggle that F.E. succeeded in his mission. In a very real sense F.E. had appointed a Dean of Christ Church and in this he did us a great service, for White was a thoroughly good Dean and the House flourished under him. He has been called a snob and accused of subservience to the great but the accusation is ill-founded. It is true that he treated the great and famous with extreme deference, but it is also true that he adopted the same attitude towards any obscure scholar for whose learning and character he felt respect. He was in fact a man of great personal humility from which he could be roused only by some open or suspected criticism of Christ Church. He was in no way a great Dean but he was a good and lovable man and that, perhaps, was better than any claim to greatness. Moreover, his moral courage was unquestioned. Once persuaded that any course was right nothing could deter him from pursuing it however much his shyness and humility urged him in the contrary direction. Two incidents remind me of this.

In the Cathedral a concordat had been made between Strong and the Censors that the preacher on Sunday should not prolong his sermon after the clock had struck the hour because long sermons tended to keep undergraduates away from divine service. Shortly after Dean White's arrival Headlam, then Regius Professor of Divinity, continued his sermon for a considerable time after the clock had struck and I, as Censor, delated him to the Dean. Nothing could have been more distasteful to White than any criticism of Headlam, for the latter was not only a fierce controversialist but had been a senior colleague of White's in London. But the Dean knew his duty and administered the reproof, which, though couched in amiable terms, was taken in ill part. 'I shall not feel myself bound by any such absurd convention,' said Headlam—and left us wondering what would occur when next he preached. A term or two later we had our answer. Headlam preached extempore and was in full spate when the clock struck the hour. Always a man of hot temper he paused and glared from the pulpit first at the Dean and then at the Censors. He then repeated the last sentence which he had spoken. There, however, the sermon ended. He was very angry—so angry indeed that he could not remember what he wished to say. He repeated the last sentence once more and then resigned the struggle leaving his sermon unfinished. After that the concordat was not again challenged.

The other incident occurred at Collections, when the men came up in turn before the Dean and Students to hear the reports on their term's work. One man had behaved badly during the term and the Dean, reading his report, worked himself into a state of moral indignation. 'Sir,' he said, 'you have dragged the name of Christ Church in the dirt.' Unfortunately the miscreant bore a name which occurred elsewhere in the list and I was obliged to pluck the Dean's sleeve and whisper to him that he was addressing a dim, blameless, and wholly virtuous scholar. Reparation was hastily made, but what, we wondered, would happen when the real culprit appeared an hour or so later? A dozen tutors sitting round the table waited with undisguised curiosity for the event. It must have needed considerable moral courage on the Dean's part, but he did not flinch when the time came. 'Sir,' he said, 'you have dragged the name of Christ Church in the dirt.'

The appointment of Dean White was the first occasion on which I learned something of Crown appointments. It is one of those appointments which can cause the most difficulty because of the dual nature of the responsibilities which the holder carries. Some think of the post as primarily an ecclesiastical one, whilst others look on it as the headship of the greatest of Oxford colleges. When Dean White died during the Long Vacation of 1934 Baldwin, who was Prime Minister, with characteristic common sense—but perhaps with a measure of insensitivity—sent a message that he wished to know the opinion of the Students and, since he supposed that most of us would attend the funeral, suggested that we should hold a meeting after the service and the interment were over. The meeting was held in the S.C.R. smoking room where only three names were seriously discussed, though no one of them was a member of the House. (I doubt whether this had ever happened before.) We discussed Williams, the Headmaster of Winchester, Alington, who had recently ceased to be Headmaster of Eton, and Homes Dudden, the Master of Pembroke, whose appointment as Dean had already been declared as almost certain by one enterprising journal. By a large majority we opted for Williams and in due course he was appointed.

My own belief was that we had gained a splendid Dean, and that in fact he was, but he was taken away in 1938 to become successively Bishop of Durham and Winchester so that he had small opportunity of making a lasting impression on Christ Church. Williams had offered me the post of Second Master under him at Winchester in 1925 and I looked on him as a friend as well as a great man. He had outstanding intellectual gifts, a fine voice, and a splendid and virile appearance, especially when he was striding across the quad. No one was more easy of access and no one could give wiser or more helpful advice. He had, however, as all or nearly all have, his Achilles heel. He was a poor preacher and for the life of me I cannot understand why this was so. The sermon would begin with every promise of good things to come and yet in some curious way it would peter out. On his first appearance in the Cathedral as Dean a serious gaffe was narrowly avoided. It was customary for the first lesson to be read by a Student, the second by a Canon, and on this occasion it was only at the last moment that I discovered that the lesson appointed was the second chapter of Ezekiel, in which the prophet is at his most vituperative in his denunciation of the children of Israel. The phrase thrice repeated that they were 'a rebellious house' would hardly have been a happy augury for the new Dean! The lesson was hastily changed.

When Williams left in 1938 I was absent in India and had no part in the choice of his successor, but once more that choice was a most happy one, suggested in the first place, I believe, by Gilbert Ryle. John Lowe, who had been a Canadian Rhodes Scholar, was in my opinion one of the truly great Deans. The greater the challenge offered to him the better did he respond to it. When he became Vice-Chancellor—unexpectedly and prematurely—he mastered the difficulties of that position with conspicuous success. Although the war manifestly clouded his early years as Dean he discharged the duties of that office, both academic and ecclesiastical (as the *Oxford Magazine* wrote), as conscientiously and with as much or greater ability as or than any one of his predecessors. Yet he too had his Achilles heel, and this has caused his reputation as a man to suffer. In a single sentence he had no small talk whatever. As a consequence he was thought to be austere and taciturn, when in fact he was only shy and reserved. He was also direct and sometimes too downright in speech to make for easy and familiar intercourse. His first appearance as Dean at High Table was on a Sunday and the company was naturally both numerous and largely clerical. In Common Room after dinner conversation did not flow with its accustomed ease. The Dean finally ended an unusually long pause with the remark, delivered with his slight but clearly recognizable Canadian accent, 'Would any gentleman like a game of cards?' He did not refrain from decisive judgements. An old member of the House, resident in Oxford, had been elected a member of Common Room, less because of his social acceptability than because he was expected to be a benefactor—an expectation which was not in the event realized. Some members who thought him a bore and grumbled at his too frequent visits were answered that his benefaction would in time repay them. John Lowe joined in the discussion with a single devastating remark: 'The worst of benefactors is that they're no manner of use until they're dead.'

Not only Christ Church but all Oxford owed a great debt to Dean Lowe, but I think that his lack of ease in social relations led to an underestimation of his qualities and his achievements. When he resigned, owing to the breakdown of his health I had left Christ Church for a good many years, so that I knew nothing of the negotiations about his successor, but I cannot think that there was any controversy or difficulty. Cuthbert Simpson, like John Lowe, was a Canadian and had been my pupil in the early twenties. Whatever the view may have been in Whitehall he would certainly have been the choice of Canons, Students, and undergraduates and he became, deservedly, the best loved of all Deans of Christ Church. Of his successor it would not be proper for me to speak, but I think it is safe to say that he stood head and shoulders above all others who could have been appointed and that anxiety was felt not about the choice but only about his willingness to undertake the task. What then of Crown appointments? A succession of Deans— Strong, White, Williams, Lowe, Simpson, and Chadwick— make a list of men who would adorn any high position in Church or State. I do not think that any democratic method of selection could have produced better results. Much later in my life it fell to me to be concerned in other Regius appointments in the University and I came to believe that such appointments were, on balance, more satisfactory than those brought about by the more usual method of electoral boards. Perhaps I am defending an anachronism and no doubt my judgement is based on insufficient evidence and is founded on experience and not on rational grounds. Nevertheless I think that it was true in the past whatever may be the case in the future.

Perhaps the election of a Chancellor in 1925 had some in-fluence in forming this opinion. Curzon had been Chancellor of the University for nineteen years and Milner, his successor, did not live to assume office. Joey Wells, the Vice-Chancellor, called a meeting of resident M.A.s to sound out opinion. The meeting, which was held in Wadham Hall, became towards the end almost riotous in consequence of the conduct of those junior dons, of whom I was one, who were sitting at the back of the Hall. The first name to be put forward formally was that of Asquith, Lord Oxford and Asquith as he had just become. He was proposed by Fisher who had recently returned to us as Warden of New College and who had not correctly assessed the temper of the meeting. His speech was long and full of reminiscence and provoked dissent which became more and more audible. When at length he started a new period with the words, 'Once when I was walking on the Embankment with Asquith . . .', the Vice-Chancellor intervened. 'Mr. Warden, we have many names to consider—I must ask you to conclude your remarks.' Something like a cheer broke out at the back of the Hall. The President of Magdalen, Sir Herbert Warren, followed. 'How', he asked, 'could there be any doubt?' The Prince of Wales, a member of his college, was surely the obvious and inevitable choice. He went on to describe the virtues of his nominee, but he did not leave the matter there. 'It is possible', he said, 'that H.R.H. may feel it his duty to decline our offer, in which case we ought to turn to another member of my college—Lord Crawford.' By this time we at the back had heard enough of Magdalen and noise and the scraping of feet drowned Warren's concluding remarks. A third Head of a House, Blakiston of Trinity, then addressed us on behalf of the Arch-bishop of Canterbury. I think that the experience of previous

speakers may have unsettled him; certainly his speech was unfortunately phrased. He was concerned to assure us that the
Archbishop would adopt no narrow ecclesiastical attitude but
he succeeded in saying (or so it seemed to us) that no one was
less of a Christian than the Archbishop. He, too, had to sit down
amid a noisy and hilarious tumult. The Vice-Chancellor can
have gained little from the meeting but most of us went away
convinced that either Asquith or Grey would be chosen. I was,
myself, an out-and-out supporter of Asquith, whose candidature
was warmly and actively supported by F. E. But it was not to be.
Late in the day Cave was nominated in opposition to Asquith
and was eventually elected by 987 votes to 441. I thought, and
still think, that this vote was contrary to right and reason.
Cave was no doubt a good and honest man but his claims to be
Chancellor compared to those of Asquith were negligible. The
result could only be attributed to clerical prejudice, for in those
days it was the clerics, and not the laymen, who kept their names
on the books and thereby acquired the right to vote. Later in
the year I met Asquith—of all unlikely places—behind the
Pavilion at Lord's. I hardly knew him but I could not refrain
from telling him how strongly I felt about his defeat. He made
no effort to conceal his disappointment but he added a revealing
comment: 'I find consolation', he said, 'when I read the list of
my supporters in Oxford, for it seems that nearly all who count
in the University were on my side.' This was true. Much later
in my life I was involved in another battle about the Chancellorship but any account of that must be postponed till the
appropriate time comes to tell it.

The extent to which I was buried in Christ Church and
Oxford affairs to the exclusion of other interests was brought
into clear relief by the outbreak of the general strike in 1926.
Very wrongly I did not apply my mind to the rights and wrongs
of the dispute but simply accepted the prevailing view that the
Government was in the right and that everything possible must
be done to defeat the strikers. In the first days my time was spent
in making arrangements for Christ Church undergraduates to
leave for those places where they could help the national effort;
for the last few days I went to Southampton to work in the
docks. My stint there was short for the strike collapsed quickly
but I recall one strange incident. We were unloading cases from

the hold of a ship—some of the party were below in the hold, some on deck, some on the quayside, and others working the electric crane and grab which transferred the cases from the ship to the quay. The control of the last-named over their piece of machinery was hesitant and imperfect and at one horrifying moment they released the jaws of the grab when the net containing half-a-dozen large cases was poised over the open hatches of the hold. The whole consignment crashed into the hold and I hurried along the deck to estimate the extent of the disaster. As I peered over the edge I thought for a brief moment that the hold was filled with bloody and mutilated bodies. I was mistaken—the contents of the cases had been Heinz's tomatoes and tomato sauce.

XVIII

OTHER ACTIVITIES UP TO 1938

'Ne supra crepidam sutor iudicaret.'
The cobbler should not judge above his last.
PLINY

IN many ways my life during the thirties passed much in the same way as that in the twenties, but there was a gradual but not insignificant change. Without any conscious effort on my part and rather against my will I was slowly drawn out from my secure but limited sphere of activity and constrained to take part in a wider field. So far as Oxford was concerned I can date the change from 1932 when I started a three-year spell as examiner in the final school of Modern History. Examination at Oxford in any of the great final schools is a formidable task. The work starts very early in the year, or even earlier, with the setting of papers and the intensive study of some subjects on which one must oneself give the first mark. In early June the papers are written—the marking of them and viva voce examinations continue uninterruptedly until the end of July or even until the first day of August. In my year as Chairman (1934) there were 270 candidates—nearly all of whom wrote eleven three-hour papers—and five examiners, assisted in a few special cases by assessors. Truth compels the admission that I had put off examining as long as I decently could, for June and July offered all the pleasures of cricket and lawn tennis, but by 1932 I could postpone the task no longer. It was a duty owed to one's pupils to see and understand an examination which could have a decisive influence on their lives.

Though I grumbled at the task I enjoyed it and profited from it and became a convinced supporter of the views that the viva should be an integral part of the examination. The objections to the viva are well known and I need not repeat them, but the advantages of the system as we operated it in the thirties are less well understood. A young and inexperienced examiner is fortified in his judgement when a candidate at a viva confirms the impression which has been made by his papers, and this, which occurs in the great majority of cases, strengthens the confidence of the examiner in making decisions. The viva was only used to help the candidate, for no one, at least at that time, was moved down a class as a result of it. Contrary to the common belief we, the examiners, were not hostile inquisitors but men searching for merit. In borderline cases a candidate might be asked questions to give him the opportunity of filling in some yawning gap which had shown in his papers; in other cases, when for example one of us thought better of a candidate than the rest, the 'prisoner's friend' would seek by adroit questioning to show the merit of the candidate and convince his colleagues that the higher class could be awarded. In a word the viva was used by us to include and not to exclude, to raise and not to depress.

Of course much of the work of those two summer months was drudgery, but the drudgery was relieved by many unexpected and happy occasions when a sudden flash of intelligence or humour lighted up the scene. One candidate—alas, a certain failure—who tried at least to conform to the wishes of the examiners and who was mindful of the rubric which demanded that geographical knowledge should be shown by the drawing of a sketch map in one paper or another was faced with a question about the centres of trade and industry in England in Tudor times. He drew a map of England, which resembled an obese carrot, and marked a large circle—roughly in the right place—to represent London. What else could he add? He must have thought deeply, but without success, for the final product showed only one other much smaller circle in the north, with the legend attached 'Filey (where I live)'. From an Indian candidate I derived a great deal of pleasure, partly because of his quaintly oriental use of English ('Europe weak as chicken before Louis XIV'), partly because his vivid blue turban (he was, I suppose, a Sikh) relieved the hideous monotony of innumerable mortar-boards. His viva occurred on the last day of the examination and did not go well. When rather fiercely dealt with by one examiner he became more and more dispirited and alarmed and clearly resigned himself to defeat. He had been on the margin between a second and a third and the viva did not help him, but we managed in the end to place him above the dividing line. The list was to be posted that afternoon and a small crowd of candidates surrounded the notice board, among them the Indian, no longer with his blue turban but with a yellow turban in its place. He had one look at the list, saw his name in the second class and dashed away from the Schools. Ten minutes later he reappeared with the blue turban again on his head. One of my colleagues supplied the appropriate quotation, 'Our hands and scarves were saffron-dyed by reason of despair.'

Of all vivas the most critical are those which determine whether a candidate can fairly be raised from a marginal position to the first class. In my second year as an examiner one candidate whose papers had been much re-read and about whom there was a division of opinion was expected to settle the question by his performance at his viva. Personally I thought him deserving of a first and I was horrified when three of my colleagues in turn failed to get any adequate response from him. It seemed as though his mind simply would not work. After nearly an hour I passed a note to the Chairman and asked that the victim should be dismissed and asked to return after lunch. A whispered reply informed me that I was proposing an act of sheer cruelty, but that, none the less, my request should be granted. In the luncheon interval I committed an act of impropriety for which, however, I had no regrets. On my way to my College I called in on the candidate and found him in exactly the situation which I had expected. He was seated in his room with a glass of water and a plate of untasted bread and cheese before him, feverishly studying a pile of notebooks. I told him that he was a fool and that only boldness could save him. 'Had he any money?' 'Yes.' 'Was he a teetotaller?' 'No.' 'Then throw away all those notes and your bread and cheese, go to the Mitre and have a good lunch with half a bottle of wine.' When he returned in the afternoon he certainly looked a changed man and I should like to be able to record that his second viva was a dazzling success, but in sober fact my intervention proved to have been unnecessary. During the interval some of my colleagues had reconsidered the case and the last note in my mark-book reads thus: 'Told to return after lunch, but agreed then not to torment him further.' I hope that his first was a help to him—at least he ended his career as a Headmaster.

The viva which I remember best of all was the last held in my year as Chairman. We had had a record number of candidates and all of us were glad to have reached the end of a long trail. Our secretary, Stephen Lee of Magdalen, had arranged that we should lunch lavishly at Magdalen whilst the list was prepared and then return to sign and post it. The last candidate was a possible, or perhaps a probable, first and personally I felt confident that the viva would quickly decide the issue in his favour, but the board was only four strong since, because the candidate was a Magdalen man, Stephen Lee could not take part. To my distress he failed lamentably with the first examiner who questioned him and was even worse with the second. Feeling sure that I could bring out his quality I then took over myself only to fail more dismally, if that were possible, than my predecessors. It seemed that there was no escape from the necessity of attaching the label of a second to him but I determined on a last effort. The board was composed of dedicated, assiduous and fair-minded men and I knew that I could appeal to them with certainty of support. I therefore proposed that we should forgo our lunch at Magdalen, have beer and sandwiches sent to the Schools, take off our coats, and spend an hour re-reading the more important papers, with the proviso that each examiner should take papers which he had not previously marked. The outcome, as might have been expected, was that marks changed hardly at all, and so I was compelled to take a vote. The first examiner said that he must adhere to his vote to award a second; the next said that he thought that the last re-reading had slightly improved the position and he would, with some doubts, vote for a first; the third said that with the greatest regret he must vote for a second; I gave my vote for a first. Had the man not come from Magdalen there would have been no difficulty but as things were I had to give a casting vote. Then and then only could we ask Stephen Lee to rejoin us and ask him whether we had been right or wrong. Stephen had no doubt whatever that we had been right, and was unable to understand how the man, who was indubitably first class, could have given such a lamentable performance at his viva. The subsequent very distinguished career of the candidate upheld his judgement—and ours.

Final School examining led me to take more part in University as contrasted with College affairs. In 1935, much against my will, I stood for Hebdomadal Council and was elected to that august body, which I soon found to be as efficient and hard-working as it was time-consuming. Though I took no leading part in University business I learned much about the University and saw something of the work of the Vice-Chancellor and the permanent officials.

The changes which came to me in the thirties were not, how-ever, mainly the result of the internal life and politics of Oxford but were attributable to events outside the University. Apart from the fact that I wrote my first book at that time, I received a number of offers which would have, if accepted, taken me away from Christ Church. Suggestions were made—though without any encouragement from me—that I should go as Headmaster to one or other of the great public schools or alter-natively as Vice-Chancellor to one of the newer universities. I can only suppose that I had acquired some reputation as a teacher and administrator at Christ Church but perhaps the real reason that I was sought after was simply that the First War had cruelly thinned the ranks of my generation and that in consequence it was hard to find men of the right calibre and right age to fill responsible positions. Be that as it may, I was offered during the thirties a good many opportunities of what, in the profession, could be described as promotion. The test case, if I may so describe it, came in the early spring of 1933, when the Headmastership of Eton became vacant. The first approach, from one or other of the Fellows, came to me through Wilkinson, who had been a beak at Eton for a short time before the First War. Would I allow myself to be considered a candi-date for the vacant Headmastership? I think that I knew from the start that I ought not to accept the invitation and that I was better suited to Oxford than to a school however eminent, but I could not bring myself to a downright and immediate refusal, nor could I wholly dismiss from my mind the prospect which was dangled before me—that of a great and honourable posi-tion, a large income, a magnificent house surrounded by beauti-ful things, hallowed and magnified by time and tradition, and the society of humane and intelligent men. All the kingdoms of the world seemed to be spread out before me. It was a great temptation, but a temptation which I knew instinctively should be resisted. My answer, therefore, to Wilkinson's letter which he passed to his correspondent was in some ways a delaying one. I have kept a copy of my letter and shall quote part of it since it represents accurately the state of my mind at that time.

In the ordinary sense of the term I am not a candidate; that is to say I am not eagerly hoping that the choice of the Fellows will fall on me, and I certainly don't want any of my friends to urge my case. I owe everything to Oxford; I am happy in my life there; I believe that I can probably do more useful work there. If I were to go to Eton I should be plunging into a world of which I know very little and undertaking a job of the working of which I am at present profoundly ignorant. The moral responsibility would be great, the life probably lonely and personal happiness doubtful at the best. I think, too, that it is a position which ought to be filled by a married man and by a man who has a strong sense of moral earnestness. I am not the one and I can't feel confident I am the other either! . . . You will not be surprised, then, if I say that I hope that the Fellows will look elsewhere for their next Headmaster. At the same time I want you to know that I regard it as the greatest compliment which I could have received that you, or any one of the Fellows, should have considered me as a possible Headmaster of Eton. It is a position of much greater distinction and importance than any that I have contemplated as at all likely to come my way. I feel this so strongly that I cannot say at this stage that I would in *no* circumstances accept appointment. If, as I imagine to be the case, the Fellows have a number of suitable candidates before them, I should certainly not wish my name to be added to the list. If, on the other hand, there were real difficulty in finding a suitable successor to Alington the position would be changed—in the sense that what now appears as an opportunity (however unlikely to materialise) might then present itself as a duty. In that unlikely contingency I should be prepared to reconsider the matter.

I went on to say that if the contingency did arise I should ask to go to Eton for a few days to see exactly what the Headmastership entailed and that if after that I did accept, I should be held to be at liberty to resign if at any time the Headship of an Oxford College was offered to me.

The next few weeks were for me an agitating time. A number of the Fellows, most of whom I knew already, came to talk to and if possible persuade me. Alington, too, paid me a visit and spoke with freedom and force. I was not, he said, his first or second choice but I was the best available and he thought that I could not, ultimately, resist the pressure to undertake what he considered a duty. There was also an interview with two of the Fellows in the small front room at Brooks's, in which I found it hard to resist the arguments which were put to me. And, of course, the newspapers were something of a trial. Eton is always 'news' and when the appointment of a Headmaster is under discussion the newspapers are filled with shrewd guesses and prognostications. For part of the time the tension was relieved by a lively correspondence with Lionel Smith, who had also been approached. Each of us took some trouble to try to convince the other that he was the man for the job. In spite of all this I became more and more convinced that I ought not to give way and mercifully I prevailed. In May the Provost—M.R. James—wrote to me a most courteous letter, accepting my wish not to be considered.

We have heard from others [he wrote] of the position you hold at Oxford, and, from yourself, of your extreme reluctance to leave it. And, in view of these two great facts, we feel that we really ought not to press you further to allow your name to be considered in connexion with the appointment. We have heard from many sources of the great influence you exercise over our boys at Oxford and of your many acts of kindness to them, and we are grateful and happy to feel that they have so good a friend in you.

Henry Marten, the Vice-Provost, wrote with equal charm and understanding and thanked me for my 'kindness to all of us under our bombardment'.

Eton was fortunate, very fortunate, that things turned out as they did for Alington was succeeded by Claude Elliott. Claude may have lacked some of the glamour and panache of some of his predecessors and towards the end of his career, when he was Provost, some grumbled at his slowness in the conduct of business, but for staunchness and reliability he was unrivalled and I can think of no one who could have led Eton through the gloomy years of the war as well as he did. For myself the whole episode was, in the long run, of great advantage. I never had one moment of regret or any feeling of disappointment. That was a negative gain, but on the positive side I had been obliged to clarify my own mind and had become absolutely sure that I wished to spend my life at Oxford and that the Provostship of my own College was (if it were offered to me) the only position which could take me away from Christ Church. With clarity came also confidence. I was unashamedly flattered by the Eton offer and much more ready than before to accept responsibility. If others thought that I was fit to be Headmaster of Eton I need not be afraid of accepting responsibilities which I had previously shunned. Furthermore the Eton offer acted as a sort of vaccination against the disease of change. When other offers came—as they did—I could refuse them without that painful period of indecision which such offers often cause. One can be churned up when a proposal is made which would alter one's whole life; I was lucky in that I suffered once, and once only, from that experience—luckier still, perhaps, that the outcome was as I wished. Some of my friends were disappointed but I think that the majority were glad. Philip Landon[1] wrote from Trinity a short but pungent card, 'Thank God! Chiefly because of Oxford; but I think also of your own personal happiness and of your friendships. There are things that you would inevitably have lost; now they are safe.'

Once only, and that very soon after the Eton business, did I hesitate about an offer to leave Oxford. John Reith wrote and asked me to come as his second-in-command at the B.B.C. As always he was clear beyond any possibility of misunderstanding. I might have some chance of succeeding him, but he was only a year older than myself; money was unimportant, except that I must have more than the third man in the hierarchy, lest differentials be upset; did I feel that I could work with him, since he was not an easy man to work with? Over this proposition I should not have hesitated had it not been for my Mother's advice. In the Eton matter she had not attempted to dissuade me but she was happy and relieved in mind when she knew that I should remain at Christ Church. It came therefore as a shock to me when she wrote with regard to the B.B.C. that I ought not to throw away such an opportunity without very careful consideration. She thought that I would be equal to the task and that I should have no difficulty in getting on with subordinates and then went on to say: 'For various reasons I think

[1] P.A. Landon, Lecturer in Jurisprudence, Fellow of Trinity College.

a complete change of work might ultimately become more congenial than a Headmastership—the latter being so much like your present job without the pleasures of Oxford life and society.' She ended her letter as I knew she would: 'Anyhow, whatever is the outcome you will know that your old Mother will feel that you have made the right decision and have her blessing.' I was moved by what she said but my decision was really made in advance and I wrote to Reith to say that I could not accept. Apart from other considerations I held the opinion very strongly that such a post should only be filled by someone who had a real sense of mission—and that was not the case with me. So I stayed at Christ Church and was content and there I remained until the Second Great War disrupted the world once more. Before the war began, however, there was a pleasant interlude in my life.

XIX

VISIT TO INDIA

Travel, in the younger sort, is a part of education; in the elder, a part of experience.

BACON

SINCE the beginning of 1919 I had kept every term at Oxford and I therefore felt myself justified in taking a sabbatical year in 1938, and in using this for the purpose of travel. To choose a companion for a long journey such as I contemplated is no easy matter. A few years before, my old friend Donald Glass had decided to go round the world and had decided to take as his companion a brother officer of the First War. All of his friends warned him that the plan would not work because the characters of the two men were really incompatible, but he scorned our advice, saying that he would easily adapt himself to whatever conditions might arise. The event was amusing for everyone except the two travellers and was related to us by a New Zealander who had just returned to England. 'Donald', he said, 'came down to breakfast one morning and addressed his companion with a few but trenchant words, "We are now in New Zealand, half-way round the world; there are two ways back to England and you may choose."' In my case no such difficulty occurred. One of my oldest and most intimate friends was E. L. Francis (Fuzz, as he was always called), who was at that time a master at the Dragon School and a remarkable character. Elected to an exhibition at Oriel, the outbreak of the war had postponed his arrival in Oxford until 1919. During the war he had been severely wounded with facial injuries—so severely in fact that his wound pension was one for total disablement (yet this did not prevent him from organizing the L.D.V. in Oxford at the outbreak of the Second War and subsequently serving in the armed forces)[1]. Fuzz never allowed

[1] In the First World War he was adjutant 3rd Batt. Wiltshire Regt.; in the Second War, adjutant 70th Batt. Royal Berkshire Regt. and later adjutant 17th Infantry Training Centre.

his wounds to cut him off from any of his activities and he had become one of the best-known Oxford figures in the period between the wars. I do not expect that his name is likely to figure in any future histories of Oxford but I am sure that no one did more than he to build up and restore undergraduate life at Oxford after the end of the First War. He was for many years Treasurer of Vincent's and we had shared many short visits to European countries. How fortunate for me that he was able to take a term off from school at the right time! As he could not leave till the end of Michaelmas Term we could not start until the end of December and he was obliged to be back at the beginning of May. Our plan therefore was to go to Ceylon, India, and Burma together; after that I should move on to Singapore and Java, but events were to curtail my own journey.

I saw the East from a privileged position. Charlie Hopetoun and John Hope—twin sons of the Viceroy—had been at Christ Church until 1935 and invited Fuzz and myself to the Viceregal Lodge at Delhi for a week's stay. Two of Lord Halifax's sons had been my pupils and he, as an ex-Viceroy, had arranged for us to stay with Sir Harry Haig, Governor of the Central Provinces, at Lucknow. Games had brought me into contact with some of the Indian princes, and Oxford friends were profuse in their invitations at other places. So it was that I seemed to be observing a great spectacle in a theatre, not from pit or gallery or even stalls but rather from the royal box. Most of those who visit the East for the first time are impressed above all with the contrast between riches and poverty, and it is right that a compassionate man should feel disquiet at and aversion from such glaring inequality and the suffering which accompanies it. But I needs must recall that my conscience troubled me not at all. What impressed me was not this contrast—obvious though it was—but rather the majesty and magnificence of the British Raj and—even more strongly—the immense efficiency and ceaseless work of that small band of Englishmen and Scots who controlled that vast territory. When time has allowed historians to assess past events fairly and objectively, when racialism has ceased to be regarded as the only offence to be castigated, and when the rare instances of exploitation have become insignificant, it will be recognized, I think, that the rule of the British in India is one of the brightest pages in our history. Personally I shall always feel glad that I had the opportunity to see the British Raj whilst it was still in all its glory.

Of British efficiency in India I had early proof. An old cricket friend, Brigadier Willie Clark, then C.R.A. at Poona, had undertaken to provide bearers for us; when we arrived by sea from Ceylon at Madras there were the two bearers patiently waiting on the quay. How they had come from Poona I do not know. At Delhi itself I was at the time most impressed by the majesty of a state dinner and a viceregal ball. At the latter a long talk with James Grigg,[2] who was just completing his examination of Indian finance and who gave me a lurid account of many of the personalities present, made me feel that I was reading unpublished Kipling stories. But two quite minor incidents left a more lasting impression. I had promised to speak on behalf of the Oxford Society at Delhi and had taken a good deal of trouble to prepare my address, a speech which was delivered before a larger audience than I had expected. At the end I invited questions about Oxford. Then came the shock. The questions, almost without exception, were concerned with the famous 'King and Country' motion at the Union, which had taken place four years earlier. At least two of my questioners declared their intention of sending their sons to Cambridge rather than risk the contagion of a disloyal Oxford, and I protested in vain that this Union debate gave no true picture of Oxford opinion. Till that moment I had not realized how deep had been the wound inflicted on national prestige by that unfortunate motion.

The second incident took place later. Fuzz and I had left the Viceregal Lodge and were staying with Maurice Gwyer, who was then Chief Justice of India and also Chancellor of Delhi University. I was sitting with Maurice one evening in his study when a Professor from the University was announced, and I naturally got up to leave them alone for their talk. Both, however, begged me to stay as they were to discuss University matters and accordingly remain I did. I did not pay very much attention to the conversation in its early stages but I soon gathered that the Professor was advocating some considerable changes, including changes of personnel, in one department of

[2] Sir James Grigg (1890–1964), Secretary of State for War 1942–5.

the University, and that time and again he was insisting that
he was not personally involved, was speaking in an unprejudiced
and objective way and had no interest to declare. No doubt he
protested too much. Maurice listened in silence until the long
discourse ended. Then he gave a long searching look at the
Professor and spoke: 'Can you lay your hand on your heart and
tell me that you do not hope to gain personal advantage from
all this?' The Professor hesitated but admitted at length that he
could not. 'Very well,' said Maurice, 'let us start again at the
beginning and discuss your proposition with this in mind.' I
wonder how many Englishmen could have dealt with an oriental in quite that manner.

One of the highlights of our tour was a visit to the Jam
Sahib at Jamnagar, where we tasted oriental splendour and
hospitality to the full. Every inmate of the guest palace had his
own Daimler waiting outside in case he should wish to traverse
the few hundred yards to the Jam Sahib's palace. The Jam
Sahib himself had succeeded one of my boyhood's heroes—the
immortal Ranjitsinhji, whose room in his palace had remained a
shrine, guarded day and night by an Arab servant and which
could only be entered after shoes had been taken off. One day
the Jam Sahib showed me over another palace which was kept
as a museum, and which afforded many striking contrasts, for
objects of great artistic value were placed beside innumerable
cocktail cabinets and similar objects redolent of modern
vulgarity. In one room I saw a set of silver stools for the Gadi
made of solid silver and said to be the gift of Catherine the
Great. Above them on the wall was a framed manuscript letter
with a number of signatures below it. This I examined and
found it to be a letter which accompanied the gift of a bat to
Prince Ranjitsinhji from the cabmen of Cambridge who had
taken him so often from his college to Parker's Piece. Judging
by the signatures there must have been a great many cabmen!

One afternoon our host declared at lunch-time that we should
all go out to a hunting-box in order to shoot a panther. An
army of servants preceded us; we dined in comfort and then
walked out to a sort of small stone fortress on one side of a large
clearing, in the middle of which was a platform on which a kid
was tethered. The poor creature had been placed there a day
or two before. 'And what happens if the panther does not come?'

we asked. 'The Jam Sahib will stay at the shooting-box and return here tomorrow.' We sat in complete silence on the first floor of the 'fort' for perhaps a couple of hours, in the middle the Jam Sahib in purple pyjamas with his rifle beside him. We were in darkness but powerful arc lamps lighted up the whole of the clearing; only the bleating of the kid broke the silence. Gradually we became aware that something or some creature was moving quietly in the darkness. Then suddenly all was over. Intently though I was watching I could not see the panther leap across the lighted area such was the speed of its leap. With a single stroke it tore out the throat of the kid and then settled down to enjoy its kill. No shot was fired, for the animal was a female and it was hoped that the mate would come to join her; he, however, must have killed elsewhere in the jungle. The panther, as we watched, seemed to gnaw the body haphazardly, but such was not the case. When the meal was completed and the animal had disappeared we went down to look at the body and to verify the strange piece of information which our host had given us. 'No surgeon', he had said, 'could remove the flesh and leave the entrails with more skill and delicacy than the panther.' After a look at the remains I could believe him.

Even this strange midnight episode did not give me quite so vivid an impression as a visit to the small private zoo. There in a cage was the most horrible, the most fear-provoking animal that I have ever seen. There are still lions in the Kathiawar state and this animal was a tigon—or do I mean liger?—when I saw it I stepped back a couple of paces involuntarily for it was indeed the fiercest of any known species. All the hatred and malevolence of the world were in its eyes and I could not bring myself even to look at it for a second time. The occupant of the adjacent cage would have sympathized with me; it was a fine lion, but a lion lacking his tufted tail. This, on an earlier occasion, had got between the bars which separated the cages and had been immediately bitten off by the tigon.

I played a good many games of golf, lawn tennis, and squash during my Indian holiday, but only one game of cricket—if game it could be called. Fuzz and I were staying at Benares with the Maharaja of Vizianagram who had captained the last Indian side to visit England. The great hall of his palace was remarkable for it was entirely decorated with tiger skins, over eighty in number. The skins lay on the floor, hung from its walls and were spread on settees and sofas. All the tigers had been shot by Vizianagram himself, and nearly all on foot, for he was contemptuous of the safer and easier method of shooting from a machan. Vizianagram insisted that, during our stay, I should have a game of cricket on his ground which was sited alongside the palace. 'This', he said, 'is the only ground in India on which Jardine's side was beaten.' In vain I protested that I had no gear and no practice; Vizzy (as I was instructed to call him) was adamant that I must play on the only ground on which Jardine's side had been defeated. In common politeness I had to give way and supposed that a friendly scratch match would be arranged. Not so. When the day came a net was erected on the square in the middle of the ground and half a dozen of the ground staff were mustered to bowl at me, whilst Vizzy settled down as a spectator on the verandah of the palace. I stipulated that I should bowl for half an hour before my innings and thus have a good look at the matting wicket and at the bowlers. What I saw gave me no sort of confidence for two at least of the bowlers were above medium pace and all were anxious to shine under the eyes of their employer. The time came when it was necessary for me to pad up and have my innings, but by that time I had made my plans. Vizzy was watching broadside on and was consequently unable to observe my movements with any accuracy. Any ball which seemed likely to bowl me (and there were many) found both my legs well and truly in front of the wicket. Many times I must have been caught at the wicket or in the slips but at least my wicket was untouched and I was able to find a wicked enjoyment in my conversation with Vizzy when I returned to the palace. 'That is remarkable, I don't think any of my boys bowled you once.' 'Well, no, but I'm afraid I edged an awful lot and I thought your bowlers very competent.' 'I thought you batted beautifully, and I shall present you with the colours of my touring side.' Thereupon he gave me a tie in the colours of his touring side in England. In such manner do the unprincipled sometimes flourish!

We were in Calcutta about to go to Burma when the news came that Hitler had invaded Czechoslovakia on 15 March. The voyage to Rangoon was therefore a time of acute tension, for the ship had no radio and there was speculation on board as to whether we should find on arrival that war had broken out. The immediate crisis passed, as we discovered on reaching Rangoon on 21 March, but the shadow of impending war was over us from then onwards. After Rangoon we visited Mandalay and Maymyo and steamed up the Irrawaddy to Bhamo. We returned to Rangoon and there made our decision to cut short our travels—Singapore must go—instead we would double back to Bombay and take the first ship home to England. Of course we were right to do so. War by that time was coming nearer and nearer and, even if it were postponed for a time, it was surely certain. We reached England at the beginning of May.

XX

THE SECOND WORLD WAR

I never will believe what I don't like to believe and nothing shall
ever make me.

The Duchess of Omnium in *Phineas Redux*, TROLLOPE

M Y failure to have foreseen the outbreak of the 1914 war
was justifiable; my political blindness in the years preceding the 1939 war was not. Never was my behaviour more ostrich-
like, never did I bury my head more deeply in the sand. Instead of evaluating the consequences of the advent of Hitler
and the German military preparations I preferred to cling to the
view that a second war was unthinkable. With an air of superior
wisdom I would declare that no war was possible whilst the
generation which had known the horrors and the sufferings of
the First War were still in control of affairs in all European
countries. Thirty years on, the case might be altered, but not
now. It was a reasonable and tenable proposition, but it ignored
the fact that Germany was in the hands of men who were not
reasonable and to whom my sapient generalizations simply did
not apply. I had done better to have studied the facts, but there
is no more effective method of disposing of unpleasant facts than
by ignoring them.

Yet I had special opportunities afforded me to judge the
situation and even to do my small part in the effort to prevent
the coming disaster. I had been a witness of all the discussions
in Oxford which followed the notorious 'King and Country'
debate at the Union; I had several German friends amongst
whom Kurt Hahn was pre-eminent; I had visited Bavaria as
late as 1937; above all I could have had from Lindemann, had
I only shown myself receptive of advice, every detail of the
German threats. All these advantages I threw away—or, to be
precise—I shut my eyes to all the warnings which I might have
had.

Lindemann, or the 'Prof' as he was then and always afterwards called, was a close—indeed an intimate—friend, a friend to whom, as in so many other cases, I had become attached as a result of a common interest in games. When he came to Christ Church in 1919 as Dr. Lee's Professor of Experimental Philosophy (a subject which really could have been reduced to the one word Physics) he was a devoted amateur of lawn tennis, and we played together constantly during the twenties, not only in Oxford but also in the vacation. At great houses like Charlton and Blenheim, Eaton Hall and Fairlawne, we had enjoyed many happy games together. Though a Fellow of Wadham, the Prof lived at Christ Church and was for many years a dominant figure in the Senior Common Room. In the early days he was not by any means universally popular, for his wit was caustic and he never spared an opponent. Moreover he was obsessed by the idea that science held an ignominious position in the University and that it was his mission to raise it to its proper place. Consequently many of the older dons regarded him as a dangerous innovator, and shuddered at his attacks upon classical learning and upon the older faculties. None the less his early unpopularity has been grossly exaggerated. In the S.C.R. at Christ Church it is true that many members were afraid of him, but in a curious way they were proud of him at the same time, for he opened windows into the outer world and compelled us to think and talk of subjects outside our own narrow sphere. The Prof has not been kindly dealt with by many writers and commentators but one book at least does him justice. Freddy Birkenhead's life—*The Prof in Two Worlds*—is a model biography, fair, judicious, perceptive, and revealing. It brings out, too, an important truth, that success and recognition in a man's life brings, almost always, an improvement in character. We speak, often, of a man 'mellowing' in later life; the cause in most cases is that he has been recognized and accepted by his fellows and that success, however limited, has made him at peace with himself.

In the thirties the Prof's preoccupation with science at Oxford became less demanding than his devotion to Winston Churchill's campaign against the German threat and his advocating of an improved air defence against the German bombing which he clearly foresaw. It was this clear view of the inevitability of war which caused the Prof to stand as a candidate for Parliament in the University election of 1937. I rank it as one of the great misjudgements of my life that I did not inform myself of these dangers: I was not concerned with political parties; I thought, rightly enough, that the Prof was unsuited to the House of Commons; the official Conservative candidate, Sir Farquhar Buzzard, was a close and valued friend; above everything else I simply ignored the vital issue and remained in my state of complacent disinterest. But in 1938 even I could not ignore the danger any longer. The Runciman mission to Prague (August 1938) brought doubts, but I was, as most of my friends and contemporaries were, a supporter of Chamberlain's efforts to maintain peace. At the time of Munich I hurried to London to enter my application to be put on the list of the Officers' Emergency Reserve—an application which was refused because I was in a Reserved Occupation. My Mother kept a diary in which she noted very briefly her engagements and activities, and in which she hardly ever mentioned public affairs, but there is an entry of 30 September 1938: 'Good news, No War.' The crisis seemed to have passed, I replaced my blinkers and turned my attention to the arrangements for my Indian journey.

When I returned to England in May of 1939 the fate of Europe was again poised upon a knife-edge, but once again it seemed, after the Germans had occupied Czechoslovakia in March, that the crisis had come and gone. Throughout the summer all the usual life went on. One day in early July stands clear in my memory. Victor Cazalet, who had taken a house, Great Swifts, at Cranbrook, had invited the Prime Minister to take a day of rest there with a concert of his favourite music in the afternoon and I was bidden to attend to help in his entertainment. I drove over from Eastbourne, where I was living with my Mother, feeling that I should be of very little help to Victor and hardly likely to be of any interest to Neville Chamberlain, whom I had never before met. When he arrived about mid-day I found him altogether easier and more approachable than I had dared to hope. When Victor told him that I had gone up the Irrawaddy to Bhamo conversation became easy, for he had lived for some months in that very place. A strange chance, surely, that I should return from Bhamo and meet for the first time a Prime Minister who knew that distant place intimately and who could speak of it with almost enthusiastic interest! He seemed distressed when I told him that the Joss House had been burned down at the time of my visit. Within a couple of months Germany had attacked Poland and we were at war.

My own reactions to the war can be explained more easily than they can be justified. For twenty years I had lived under the weight of an inferiority complex, never frankly admitted and never openly expressed but none the less burdensome to me. I could never rid myself of the hateful feeling that I had played no part in the First War and that I had in some way let my country down. For that reason it seemed to me imperative that I should take an active part in the Second War, and I pulled every string that I could to get myself accepted for combatant service. I was forty-eight but I felt, and probably was, as fit as most men of thirty. All this was irrational. Certainly if I had been consulted by some other person of my own age and qualifications I should have given sensible advice—'Do the job you are doing and move to some other job if you are needed there in the national interest, but don't waste the time of others by trying to force yourself into a post for which you are not suitable.' It is fatally easy to give good advice to other people— one's own case one does not consider rationally at all. Needless to say my efforts were unavailing. A colonel at the depot of the Scots Guards gave me the clearest as well as the shortest answer—'If the war is short, we don't want you—if it's long, we may be able to find some use for you.'

So willy-nilly I had to carry on at Oxford, until at a later date, and after repeated applications, the Intelligence Corps did find a niche for me. In all my life I think that memories of the period of the phoney war are the most dim. Filling sandbags and piling them round the Christ Church buildings ('And who's going to ever clean this all up?', as the porter sadly remarked); sitting day after day at the Recruiting Board under the chairmanship of Harold Percival; arranging new examinations— most of them designed by the fertile ingenuity of Gilbert Ryle— so that men could take their degrees in a minimum of time;

teaching those who remained in Oxford—a few half-remembered details of that kind and nothing more. Were we all, perhaps, in something of a dream during the rightly named time of the 'phoney' war? In March of 1940 I had the glad news that my application for the Officers' Emergency Reserve had been accepted and at the beginning of June I was called up to the War Office. In July I received my first assignment—to the so-called Interrogation Course at Swanage. That was a good course, well arranged, well officered, and practically useful to anyone who expected to be employed as an Intelligence Officer. The star performer was Enoch Powell, but I did not get to know him, for he was above my class. Most of my time 'out of school' was spent with Michael Bratby, who had some reputation as a broadcaster and writer on birds, Hardy Amies, who was to become a national figure as a dress designer, and Tom Henn, as competent as a soldier as he was later in his capacity of Senior Tutor of St. Catharine's, Cambridge. Once walking on the cliffs Michael Bratby was explaining to me the differences between various sea-birds when an elderly couple spoke to us. 'You must be Michael Bratby,' the old lady said, 'we recognized your voice from your radio talks.' I had not realized till then the power of the spoken word—a power which was later to be redoubled by television. I enjoyed the course, but the experience did something to humble me, for it was borne in on me that my qualifications for military employment were meagre at the best. A certain natural distaste had led me to neglect German since 1919—I could read it almost as easily as English, but I had totally neglected the spoken language. Had I kept up my German studies I might have been of use, but as things were it was difficult to see how I could best be employed. I realized, too, the harsh truth that my reactions were not as quick and immediate as those of my juniors.

I was sent back to the War Office to work, if I remember rightly, on the German Army and to await an appointment. In a few days the picture changed. My telephone rang: 'The D.P.S. would like to speak to you.' I had not yet learned all the language of initials and my reply was dangerously off-hand. 'Who or what is the D.P.S.?' 'I am the D.P.S., but if you have difficulty in finding me ask for General ——.' Very much shaken I then received orders to go at once to Hobart House (or was it Rex House?). On arrival I was told that my name had been suggested as secretary of a committee, of which General Howard was chairman, which was to examine and report on the evacuations from the area south of the river Somme—i.e. all the evacuations excluding Dunkirk. I was given a folder containing a heavy file of documents and ordered to write a memorandum on them for presentation to General Howard on the following morning. The interview, which I faced with some trepidation, turned out to be wholly successful, for good fortune had given me a master whom it was a pleasure as well as an experience to serve. Our first conversation was brief but decisive. 'What do you say in your memorandum about this proposed inquiry?' 'I think, sir, that it is a mistake to have an inquiry at all; surely we don't want to hold post-mortems at this time?' 'I agree, but Winston has determined to have it, so it must be done.' 'I'm afraid that my lack of knowledge about military matters makes me unsuitable as a Secretary.' 'Military matters, I know all about them. Can you write the King's English?' 'Yes, that is about my only qualification.' 'Good, I appoint you Secretary to the Committee.' Then followed my orders.

The three or four days which followed were among the busiest of my life. First I had to contact the Secretariat of the Bartholomew Committee, which had been engaged on the Dunkirk evacuation, and learn from its members the proposed procedure and the methods employed in getting hold of witnesses and information, and in discovering the names of those concerned in the evacuations into which the Howard Committee was to inquire. That took time, but it came within my previous experience. Much more difficult were the practical steps which had to be taken. We had been given two rooms in the Hotel Victoria, then an annexe of the War Office, but the rooms were bare, and it was my duty to convert them into a working office for the General by the following Monday. The multiplicity of authorities within the War Office defied belief. Telephones must be secured from one section, furniture from another, and from a third someone must be found to install the telephones and actually to move in the furniture. Then there were maps to be ordered from another section, stationery and the like

from yet another, and files, some of them secret, from many
more. Worst of all I had to find office staff, for a clerk and a good
shorthand typist were our minimum requirements. It seemed to
me that in the course of forty-eight hours I visited every department in the Office and in all found myself in competition with
other officers, all demanding similar service. Fortunately for
me Pompey Howard was a Lieutenant-General and I used his
high rank shamelessly to secure what I needed, but even this
was not always sufficient. It was very clear to me that if we
were to take a great deal of oral evidence a really first-class
shorthand writer was essential, but such folk were in great
demand. Faced with this obstacle I made a plan. I changed out
of uniform into mufti and made my way to the room where
an eminent and most efficient lady controlled all the shorthand
typists, and there I appealed to her humanity. 'I am', I said,
'a middle-aged academic; what hope have I in competition
with all these generals and senior officers? You must come to
the rescue of a fellow civilian (I had used the opposite argument
and stressed my General's military importance when I had been
dealing with the furniture), for without a good shorthand typist
this committee is ruined.' My appeal prevailed. 'You shall have
the best girl that I have', was the answer. That eminent lady
appeared to me as an angel from Heaven for she not only promised but fulfilled her promise to the letter. I was lucky, too,
in securing an admirable clerk.

The terms of reference of the Howard Committee were
'to enquire into the lessons to be learned from the evacuations
from the area south of the river Somme after the 10 June
1940, with special reference to the possibility of whether the
evacuation of arms, equipment, vehicles and stores, both of
the fighting formations and on the Lines of Communications, could reasonably have been increased under the existing
circumstances, and to report'. The original members of the
Committee were, besides the General, Brigadier M.H. Dendy
and Colonel F. Thornton, and to them were added in the later
stages Rear-Admiral C.P. Herman-Hodge and W.G. Hynard
from the Ministry of Shipping, in order that the provision of
transport by sea could be investigated. Among these men
Frank Thornton stood out. He was a dedicated soldier who had
suffered the terrible blow of a breakdown in health just at the

time when he would otherwise have been in line for high command, and he became an intimate and cherished friend to me. The report was based on the study of a large number of war diaries, reports, and other documents, and upon the evidence of some fifty witnesses, whom we interviewed; it dealt separately with the evacuations from seven ports, whilst the main report summarized the general conclusions at which the Committee arrived. As our work continued a fairly clear picture emerged and the last sentence in the main report shows what that picture was. 'It was too easily assumed that an evacuation could be regarded as satisfactorily carried out if no personnel were lost, whatever sacrifices of material had to be made. This was a humane, but shortsighted and dangerous point of view.'

As Secretary I, of course, took no part in the interviews, but the General had an agreeable habit of telling me to remain after the end of the session and of asking my opinion of the evidence. On one occasion I felt bound to say that I thought that the withdrawal had been hurried unduly and that if a risk had been taken a good deal of precious arms and equipment could have been saved. 'Hurry,' exclaimed the General. 'Haste! Hurry!—I call it a bloody *sauve qui peut*. Turn that into your King's English that you're so proud of and put it into the report.'

Pompey Howard had one supreme merit for the task in hand in that he always refused to blame junior officers unless he was obliged to do so, whilst he never spared those at the top. 'There was so much telephoning,' he said to me once, 'that I simply cannot tell if we should blame the Secretary of State or the Commander-in-Chief.' Personally I thoroughly enjoyed working under him, the more so because I had a few minor successes. When on one occasion it became necessary for the General and myself to go over to Northern Ireland, though the presence of the rest of the Committee members was not required, I found out that there were three ways of travelling to Belfast. It was possible to go by plane, for the War Office ran a shuttle service, though not on every day of the week. If one went by sea one could go either by way of Stranraer and Larne or by Liverpool and Belfast. The first of these routes was favoured by senior officers because it was quicker and said to be more comfortable. My General was inclined to go by plane or, if this was not possible, by way of Stranraer and Larne but I had been long enough in the Army to realize that the comfort of the A.D.C. was as important as that of the General and I had also observed that the Liverpool route would allow us to breakfast on board before disembarking at Belfast. Moreover, as there would be fewer senior officers I saw the prospect of getting a cabin myself for the night journey. With some difficulty, therefore, I arranged that we should go to Liverpool. It was a bad day that we had chosen. When we got to Euston bombs were falling and there was doubt whether the train could be got away, and when we were half-way across the Irish Sea we could see the red glow in the sky which showed how fiercely Liverpool had suffered that night. But we arrived, and had enjoyed each a single cabin and a good breakfast. It was not until we returned to London a couple of days later that we knew how lucky we had been. The train for the other route which should have left four hours after ours was not able to start at all and the plane, hitting a hill in Wales, also failed to reach its objective. Fortunately there were no casualties. The General paid me a graceful compliment when, after hearing of these misadventures, he remarked that he would not in the future criticize any arrangements which I made for him.

The Howard Report was an honest piece of work and I felt pride in it when it was completed, but it was too outspoken to bring any joy to those in authority and was quickly and firmly suppressed. Somewhere in the dusty archives of the War Office it must lie to be disinterred by some laborious historian in the future. It was also completed without any undue delay—too quickly in fact for my own benefit. Had I kept it alive for a few days longer my appointment as Staff Captain would have been confirmed. As things were I reverted to 2nd Lieutenant, Intelligence Corps, and returned to the War Office. Pompey Howard, I think, over-praised my work as his Secretary and promised to find me a suitable job but his help proved to be unnecessary. I expected to be posted as an I.O. to some part of the country and was in fact summoned by the D.M.I. to be interviewed. I hope that I behaved with military correctness when I entered his room, but General Davidson quickly put me at my ease with his opening gambit—'The last time we met you slanged me like anything on the hockey field.' He did not, however, have to find me a post for within a few days after leaving the Committee I was swept into M.I.5—and there I stayed for nearly five years.

XXI

M.I.5

There are currently two schools of thought about our Intelligence Services. One school is convinced that they are staffed by murderers, powerful double-crossing cynics; the other that the tax-payer is supporting a collection of bumbling, broken-down layabouts.

JOHN BINGHAM: *The Double Agent*

WHEN I entered M.I.5 I knew nothing about it whatever. Once only had I been brought into touch with what we laymen thought of, vaguely, as the 'Secret Service', and that contact was more than twenty years past. When I returned to England in 1918 I was asked to see Captain Mansfield Cumming[1] living, I think, in Whitehall Court to give him news of Kurt Hahn. I was also in touch with Kurt's brother, who was still a prisoner of war at Donnington Hall, whom I had just visited. I went to dine with Mansfield Cumming who was the C.[2] of those days, and found him and his wife alone in their flat. The dinner was most agreeable, but we had only been enjoying it for a short time when a messenger arrived and carried C. off with him. He said that he would only be away for a few minutes but it was a long half-hour before he returned. 'I'm sorry,' he said, 'but I had to see that man. He was one of our agents, who was captured by the Germans and shut up in a fortress. We thought that he had been executed. In fact he has lived a prisoner since 1914 and has heard exactly nothing about the war—indeed I'm not sure that he knew that there had been a war. It took time to tell him something of the history of the last five years.' 'And why', I asked, 'has he come to see you now?' C. smiled. 'He came to ask for another job.'

Knowing nothing of M.I.5 or of the many problems of security I was not too pleased to hear of my posting, but in fact I was supremely fortunate. Not only did I join a body of men of high

[1] Captain Sir Mansfield Cumming, R.N. (1859–1923).
[2] The head of M.I.6 has always been referred to as C.

intelligence and clearly defined purpose, but also I found myself in a job which suited me well. My age no longer counted against me; my lack of technical or professional qualifications was of little or no importance; whilst such ability as I had was given full scope, so that when the long four-year haul was over I could feel that I had contributed something of value to the war effort. There was a further advantage of which I soon became aware. In joining M.I.5 I became one of a team, a team of congenial people who worked together harmoniously and unselfishly, and amongst whom rank counted for little and character for much. It was a hand-picked service and a standing example of wise selection.

When the war began I had envisaged a hard time for myself, and in a sort of way I had, with my memories of my uselessness in the First War, a kind of unconscious wish for trials and discomfort. In the event I enjoyed, although through no effort of my own, a singularly easy and usually comfortable existence. For most of those four years I lived in my Club with occasional days of leave in my rooms at Christ Church. The more anxious time came early, for the Howard Committee kept me in London throughout the Blitz, an experience which cannot easily be forgotten.

Living through great events the individual does not rightly apprehend their significance, and even a quarter of a century later it is not the magnitude of the decisions or even the great actions of the protagonists but rather the small personal incidents which stick fast in the mind. That, at least, is my own experience. I think that I was as frightened as the next man by the bombing, but not more so; it would be fair to record that my behaviour through that period was decently average, perhaps because it did not occur to me that I should myself be a victim. As the attacks continued one became in a curious way inured to the strain, and I am quite sure that I was more frightened and demoralized by the two sudden and unexpected raids in April and May 1941 than by the whole of the 1940 Blitz. In the early period all the best characteristics and many of the idiosyncrasies of the British stood out and made defeat seem impossible.

I lived at first at the United University, and had the good fortune to occupy a bedroom fairly low down on the west side

when a bomb destroyed a part of the top floor of the Club and
caused some casualties. From there I transferred to the Oxford
and Cambridge, which carried many of us through some of the
worst days. I recall the indomitable woman who turned up to
do her cleaning chores in the early morning although her own
house in the East End had been almost totally destroyed in the
preceding night. She did her job and then returned to see what
could be salvaged from the ruins. I recall too one breakfast
when a member had arrived from the country after travelling
through the night. For us the night had been a bad one; many
raids, a great deal of damage, and very little sleep. Everyone
was tired and jaded and each was bracing himself for the exer-
tions of another hard day. In walked the country member, the
picture of rude health, and began to order his breakfast. 'I'll
have some toast . . .' 'I'm sorry, sir, we cannot make any toast
this morning.' 'Then bring me bread instead, and I'll have an
egg and bacon and coffee.' By this time the whole room was
listening and deriving considerable pleasure from the dis-
comfiture of the country member. This, we thought, will teach
him what life in London is like. 'I'm sorry, sir, we can't boil any
milk for coffee, and there is no bacon, but I can get you some
tea, and I think there is an egg.' But the country member had
the last word. When the last of his demands had had to be
refused he glared round the room and spoke. 'This', he said,
'is what comes of having women waiters in the Club.'

From the Oxford and Cambridge I migrated to the Reform,
and there it was my inestimable good fortune to be allowed
to live until the conclusion of the war. The evening there when
the Carlton, next door, was bombed was noteworthy. The Carlton was hit during dinner-time and the Reform itself was soon
on fire, though the fire being efficiently mastered more damage
was done by water than by fire. Once more the national
characteristics of individuals revealed themselves with startling
clarity. When long lines were formed to carry the books from
the library and deposit them in heaps on the floor of the hall
(lest the water should damage them) immediate controversy
arose as to the relative importance of the various books. Which
should be saved first—German pamphlets or British works of
reference? Shortly before midnight, whilst the fire-fighters
were still engaged in the top storey where my bedroom was,

I fell into conversation with an elderly member, who, to my surprise, was reading in the dim light a classical text—and without the aid of glasses. 'It is very tiresome,' he said, 'I have been repulsed from my room, where I should do no harm, for I only want to fetch my slippers. I may add', he said, 'that I am eighty years old, and have a cold bath every morning.' I pointed out that we could hardly interfere with the fire-fighting operation, but he insisted on making another attempt. His obstinacy prevailed and I saw him later reading contentedly and with his feet shod in comfortable-looking slippers. His name was Dr. Moon.

A stroke of rare good fortune came my own way. Will Beveridge, who also lived in the Club, urged me to get hold of a mattress and stake out a claim for a place in the semi-basement, where he had already installed himself. In this semi-basement was a broad passage with bedrooms leading out of it and facing the south front. For about three months my mattress was on the floor next to Beveridge's and in that time I learned from him the secret of the proper use of time. After spending all day at work on his report he would dine—rather late—at the Club and then play bridge so long as anyone wished. A hundred up at billiards, if anyone would play so late, followed and he then retired to rest. His clothes seemed to fall off him and he was in bed and asleep (usually after reciting a few lines of poetry) before I had time even to undress. In the morning the picture was the same. He would shave, have a cold bath, and dress in the shortest space of time imaginable, and when I, starting from the same point of time, arrived in the dining-room I would find that he had completed his breakfast and *The Times* crossword as well. I used to wonder whether I was learning the secret of great men. Was it not possible that they could achieve so much because they wasted no single moment and retained perfect serenity of mind, coupled (I might add in Beveridge's case) with complete belief in the rightness of their own judgement?

After a couple of months Beveridge was given a bedroom, and a little later I had the same good fortune. The assistant secretary came to tell me that the Club hairdresser had died and since he could not in wartime be replaced, the saloon would be given to me as a bedroom. Round the walls hung the photographs of Liberal statesmen of the last fifty years. I could not have believed that they had all been so hirsute, and often wished that the hairdresser could have included at least one statesman after, and not before, he had been operated upon by the barber. Aesthetic considerations apart my room was a perfect asylum— no place in all London could have been safer from the danger of air attack, and it was only a five-minute walk away from my office in St. James's. I lived there till the end of the war.

One other day, a sad one, is also unforgettable. It was a Sunday morning and I was attending a conference in the top storey of Norfolk House under the chairmanship of Sir Findlater Stewart. [3] When the sirens sounded some of us thought that our position was unpleasantly exposed, since the walls of the upper storey were largely composed of glass windows. Findlater Stewart was quite unperturbed, but at length (none too soon, as we thought) he rose from his chair and ordered the conference to adjourn to the basement. Passing along the passage it was impossible not to look out, whatever the danger, and there I saw the approaching V bomb make a curious corkscrew-like descent behind the houses on the other side of the Park. Only later did we learn of the tragic hit upon the Guards' Chapel. I am convinced that the V bomb must have been hit, for in no other way could its descent be explained.

It is almost impossible to think of prolonged happiness in time of war, but I am sure that I had less discomfort and more job satisfaction than anyone else of my acquaintance. In addition the times of relaxation—and there must be some such even in wartime—were genuinely happy. In London itself Rowlie Ebbisham, whom nothing could move into safety in the country, entertained three of his friends to dinner and bridge almost every Thursday evening. Boyd Merriman, the judge, and myself were the most regular of the guests. Then, too, Victor Cazalet, up to the time of his tragic death, entertained royally at the Dorchester. Two evenings there were especially memorable. At one of them, when about sixteen people of both sexes were present, I was perturbed to find that Joad was among the number of those invited. I thought of him, without charity, as

---

[3] Sir Findlater Stewart (1879–1960), Permanent Under-Secretary of State for India 1930–42; wartime head of the Home Defence Executive.

the man who had lured undergraduates into that fated vote
against fighting for King and Country and I asked Victor if I
might sit as far from him as possible. 'Curiously,' said Victor,
'several others have made the same request.' In the event I
sat next to Sir John Anderson (Lord Waverley), who turned a
baleful eye on Joad and spent most of dinner-time expounding
to me Dicey's *Law of the Constitution*, with which work I was
already well acquainted. Joad himself arrived very late, dressed
in hobnailed boots and thick woollen socks to indicate that he
was pursuing farming operations at Hampstead, and soon proceeding to monopolize the conversation, or rather to deliver a
series of lectures to the whole company. But his collapse was
sudden and complete. Unwisely he strayed into some financial
dogmatism and gave Reggie McKenna the opportunity to fall
upon him and demolish his whole argument. I have seldom
seen anyone more completely deflated. When he left, the company was with difficulty restrained from passing a vote of
thanks to McKenna.

The other evening which I mentioned was one when
General de Gaulle dined with Victor. It was at the time
when he was pressing for the second front and anxious to
convert us to his view on that topic. Victor asked him if he
would prefer to talk to us in French after dinner as that would
naturally make his task easier, but de Gaulle firmly refused. 'I
want to make my thoughts clear to you Englishmen,' he said,
'and so I must speak English.' He did so for about a couple of
hours. I have met in my life a good many great men but none
of them bore the stamp of greatness more clearly and unmis-
takably than de Gaulle. From that day onwards, whatever he
might say or do, I could never really think ill of him.

It was not only in London that my wartime life was easier
and more congenial than that of most of my contemporaries.
My Mother, much against her will, had been compelled to leave
her house at Eastbourne, but I was able after a time to find her
asylum with friends in Oxford. Consequently when I had any
leave I could live in Christ Church and see her at the same
time. Moreover, since life in Oxford limped on during the war
I could get a game of cricket or hockey or tennis or golf whenever a day or two's leave became due. Golf presented the most
difficulty because of the shortage of petrol, but in this case I

was saved by the Regius Professor of Medicine, Sir Farquhar
Buzzard. Throughout the war he did the work of two men—
inspecting hospitals, reporting on medical establishments, and
stimulating medical services all over the country. The Regius
Professor holds among his other offices the charge of the alms-
houses at Ewelme, and Ewelme is very close to Huntercombe.
When our week-ends coincided Farkie would observe, 'I think
I am due to inspect Ewelme tomorrow'. The inspection was
duly performed. The route back led naturally through Huntercombe and there we would play a round and forget—for a time
—the war. There was, however, one drawback. By the end of
the week Farkie was a tired man—and well he might be. He was
also a rather careless driver, and the prospect of a forfeited
licence was always in our minds. One day in the middle of
summer the disaster came perilously near. Let the Professor tell
the story. 'I was driving along at a very reasonable pace when
a young woman on a bicycle came charging down a side
lane; hit my car amidships; parted from her bicycle and was
flung into the field beyond. My first thought was that there
would be no golf to-morrow—my second that I was a doctor
of medicine. I took my black bag out of the car and went into
the field to see if life was extinct. There on the grass sat the young
woman, powdering her nose. In apologetic tones she spoke: "I
did ring my bell." That was her defence.' Farquhar Buzzard
was a true friend to me, and especially in the war years. His
portrait by James Gunn, which hangs in Christ Church Hall,
is not, to my way of thinking, a great work of art, but it shows
the man as he was. He sits four-square facing the onlooker—
firm, forthright, perhaps a trifle opiniated, but a rock of a man,
utterly reliable, staunch, stalwart, and loyal.

But what of M.I.5 and the work in it? In one sense the war
came at an awkward moment for M.I.5. Colonel Vernon Kell,
who had founded the department in 1909, was still in command
in 1939 but he was sixty-seven, in poor health, and nearing
retirement. Nor was his organization really equal to the
demands of a second European war. There were good men and
good women in the department but not enough of either, and
there were, too, some who were inefficient. The nettle was
grasped by National Security Executive, a body whose head
was Lord Swinton. Kell resigned in the summer of 1940 and

there was no one in the organization of the right age and experience to succeed him. Brigadier Harker took over temporarily whilst an ex-Indian policeman, Sir David Petrie, was appointed to investigate the working of M.I.5 and to recommend the necessary changes. The investigation led to a reorganization of the department and to a manifest improvement in efficiency, and Petrie himself was appointed Director General. Harker had the good sense to recognize that he was not the man best fitted to hold the top position, but he remained to serve Petrie loyally as his deputy and chief administration officer throughout the war. It thus happened that for almost the whole of my service I had the privilege of serving under David Petrie, than whom no Security Service could, in my opinion, have had a better chief. He was a rock of integrity, the type of Scot whose reliability in all conditions was beyond question, with strong and independent judgement, but ready and willing to delegate and to trust.

He was helped by the fact that, however the former directorate might be criticized, it had assembled a body of remarkably able men. Some of the senior officers were perhaps past their best but the 'middle management' (if one may borrow a phrase from the industrial world) was strong. In particular those with whom I came into closest contact—Guy Liddell, Dick White, and Tom Robertson—combined between them not only knowledge of security and its problems but also a singular flair for making the right decisions in the curious world of espionage and counter-espionage.

Guy Liddell, an accomplished cellist who had been an intimate friend of the Mendelssohn family and a man of infinite diplomatic skill, could hold his own in any company. At first meeting one's heart warmed to him, for he was a cultured man, primed with humour and friendliness. In a way he belied his appearance, for a stranger might well have thought him a gentle and agreeable dilettante—but that was far from the truth. No man was better informed about the details of his profession than he and no one pursued his objective with more firmness and skill. With Dick White, once my pupil at Christ Church, I was naturally on intimate terms already. After leaving Oxford he had spent a year as a Commonwealth Fellow in America and I remember, after his return, a long discussion with him, when he was faced with the choice of teaching history at Wellington or joining Kell in M.I.5. I do not recollect that I tried to influence him in either direction, but his choice of a profession turned out to be of signal benefit to the country. He was destined to be head successively of M.I.5 and M.I.6. My immediate chief was Major (later Colonel) T. A. Robertson, or Tar as we all called him. Tar was in no sense an intellectual but he had certain qualities of a high order. A born leader, gifted with independent judgement, he had above all an extra-ordinary flair in all the intricate operations of his profession. Time and again he would prove to be right in his judgements when others, following their intellectual assessments, proved to be wrong. To work under and with him was a privilege and a happy experience and I think that his decision at the end of the war to leave the service in order to farm was one of the greatest losses which M.I.5 ever suffered.

Such were the professionals, to whom we—the amateurs—were attached. The amateurs, drawn from many sources, did not need to fear comparison with any of the other war-time Government offices. In particular we were strong on the legal side. From the Bar came Barry, Pilcher, Stephenson, and Milmo, all destined for the High Court, together with Jim Hale, Theo Turner, and Cyril Harvey, the last named a brilliant legal scholar with a touch of real genius. He often delighted us with his light verse, a form of art in which he might, had he wished, have rivalled the acknowledged master, A. P. Herbert. Among the solicitors were John Marriott, Christopher Harmer, Martin Furnival-Jones, and Ian Wilson. The academic world contributed Herbert Hart, later Professor of Jurisprudence at Oxford, the business world Bill Luke and Cyril Mills, and from other walks of life came Kenneth Younger, Victor Rothschild, Hugh Astor, and (in some ways the most remarkable of them all) the artist Tommy Harris. Long afterwards I remarked to Dick White that the amount of talent in our office was both remarkable and the cause of our success. His reply surprised me. 'In the national interest,' he said, 'I think that we appro-priated too much talent. The demand for men of ability in other departments was enormous and perhaps we were a bit greedy.' I am inclined to think that the criticism was valid but certainly it was a happy office to work in. Scorn has been poured

on Kell and others for their creation of a service based on personal selection and emphasizing the need of social acceptability,
but to my mind the 'proof of the pudding' came during the
war years and justified Kell to the full.

My life in M.I.5 began with a strange contrast. I started at
Blenheim where some sections were posted in the Palace, and
thither I commuted from my rooms in Christ Church, but after
a few weeks I was transferred to our Headquarters at Worm-
wood Scrubs. Life there is described thus by Cyril Harvey, in a
poem entitled *Scrubbs to Scrubbs*:

> What of the gaol, now cleared of scrubscious youths?
> At once there occupies its cells and towers
> A corps of para-military sleuths
> Whose devious minds divide the working hours
> Between re-numbering their own Divisions
>   And making even more obscure decisions.
>
> How do they work? What means have they to crush
> The serpent head of the detested foe?
> We ask in vain, for Echo answers 'Hush!'
> Such things are not for vulgar folk to know;
> Suffice it that they serve the Commonwealth
> With silent subterfuge and solemn stealth.

At the Scrubbs I felt as though the First War had come again,
for all prisons are much the same, not only in their lay-out
but also in their peculiar atmosphere. My sojourn there was
short, since the whole department was soon transferred to St.
James's. There I spent the rest of the war, living at the Reform
Club only a few hundred yards from the office. At first I was a
lodger but after a short time I was—to my great content—
allowed to become a member, thus incurring a great debt to
one of the most hospitable of clubs. Few people during the war
can have been so fortunate as I in finding, for four years, a
home so convenient, so near to their work, and so frequented
by interesting and friendly people. As to the office, no description of mine could better that of Cyril Harvey in his 'Ballad of
Physical Security'. I have put this in an appendix.

Very soon after entering M.I.5 I was allotted to a section
controlled by Tom Robertson, the task of which was to recruit
and run double agents—a special task outside the main work

of the department and one not envisaged when the war began. It is tempting to write of it at length but I must refrain because, at the end of the war, I wrote a book on *The Double-Cross System in the War of 1939–1945*. The briefest account of our work must therefore suffice.

The main work of the Security Service—as M.I.5 was more accurately called—was, when the war began, to round up all the German agents or spies in this country and so to maintain security by preventing any leakage of information which might be of assistance to the enemy. It was due, I believe, to the ingenuity of Dick White that the double-cross system was developed. He wrote a memorandum in the early days in which he pointed out that spies captured in England could be used, if they could be 'turned round', to send false information to Germany and that this was altogether a better plan than that of their summary execution. Probably he did not realize at the time the extent to which his plan could be developed and how triumphantly successful it would turn out to be.

Double-cross agents have been used since time immemorial but usually for short-time purposes and never, I believe, on the scale to which we developed the plan during the war. In my book I set down the objects of working the double-cross system. They were:

(1) To control the enemy system, or as much of it as we could get our hands on.
(2) To catch spies when they appeared.
(3) To gain knowledge of the personalities and methods of the German Secret Service.
(4) To obtain information about the code and cipher work of the German service.
(5) To get evidence of enemy plans and intentions from the questions asked by them.
(6) To influence enemy plans by the answer sent to the enemy.
(7) To deceive the enemy about our own plans and intentions.

It must be realized that we began with counter-espionage, passed to intelligence, and finally took a part in deception, but it should also be noted that counter-espionage remained of paramount importance, even at the time towards the end of the war when everyone was concerned with strategic deception, to which the double agents by their messages to Germany could make a substantial contribution. The staggering fact is that we did in fact get our hands on all the German agents in England, though it took us a long time to be sure that this was the case. Only when we were satisfied that this main counter-espionage task had been successfully completed could the double agents be used for passing over misinformation and ultimately take part in the great culminating deception of 'Overlord' in June 1944. In retrospect it is clear that we were slower in using the weapon in our hands than we need have been, but extreme caution was justified since an early failure might have wrecked the whole system.

Double agents were of many kinds—men inherited from the pre-war period, men dropped by parachute or sent over by submarine, men who acted for purely ideological reasons, men who wished to make money from the most dangerous of professions, even men who never existed at all, except in the minds of the Germans and ourselves. They communicated with their German masters in various ways—by radio, by secret writing, or by personal meetings. The control of them was a difficult and complex task. It was necessary to organize not only their actual lives but also the 'notional' lives which the Germans supposed them to be living. A single agent, for example, dropped by parachute in England, might need a care officer, a couple of guards, a wireless operator, and a housekeeper for his exclusive use. We had, therefore, on our hands not only intelligence work of importance but also a not inconsiderable task of administration.

My own part in all this was that of a 'back-room boy'. I had only occasional contact with some of the agents and had little say in the construction of their traffic (i.e. the messages which they sent), but I was a Chairman of the Committee (the Twenty Committee, so called because in Roman numerals twenty is represented by a double cross) which brought together the approving authorities, settled and combined the messages of the different agents, and decided how and where the agents were to be used. The first meeting of the Committee I shall not easily forget, for the fighting services as well as various departments all sent senior officers to represent them and I, a very junior officer, had the embarrassing duty of telling the members that I had orders to take the chair and preside over the meeting. It says much for the members of the Committee that this anomalous situation was accepted by all and caused no sort of difficulty—indeed the co-operation of many departments, the absence of red tape or protocol was, in my judgement, the solid basis on which the success of the double-cross system rested. I called the first meeting of the Committee for 16.00 hrs. on 2 January 1941 and made then a small but important decision, to wit that tea and a bun should always be provided for members. How utterly trivial! Nowadays such a decision can only provoke a contemptuous smile, but in the war years the case was otherwise. In days of acute shortage and of rationing the provision of buns was no easy task, yet by hook or crook (and mostly by crook) we never failed to provide them throughout the war years. Was this simple expedient one of the reasons why attendance at the Committee was nearly always a hundred per cent? The Twenty Committee held 226 meetings, the last on 10 May 1945 and only one one occasion was a vote taken; all other decisions were arrived at after discussion and without a vote.

It is tempting to try to assess my own contribution to the whole operation. I had nothing to do with the executive side of the business, since my function was really advisory and of course I had nothing whatever to do with the planning of major deception. For that the double-cross agents acted simply as one of the several channels through which the deception plan was foisted on the Germans. On the other hand I could claim to have worked effectively to harmonize the interests and demands of different services and different departments—or, to put it shortly, to make the machine work. When it is remembered that no message could be sent by the agents which had not been approved by higher authority it will be realized how important co-operation was. Anyone who has lived, if only for a short time, in Government offices or in Government service, who has walked, albeit delicately, in the corridors of power must have realized the immense difficulty of maintaining whole-hearted co-operation between different bodies and different authorities. The British Civil Service was filled by able and efficient men, the fighting services were controlled by men as strong-minded and as dedicated as at any time in our history, yet even so clashes of interest between different departments were far from uncommon and action was often delayed or halted by them. In the nature of things the double-cross system was tangled with many authorities, whilst at the same time our work often demanded quick and critical decision. The work of the Twenty Committee was to harmonize conflicting interests, to carry several departments with us, and to avoid—so far as we could—the delays which too often appeared to paralyse action. No doubt personal relations with men outside the office played an important part. In the early days Walter Monckton at the Ministry of Information was most helpful and Findlater Stewart at the Home Defence Executive was the staunchest and most potent of our supporters. Above all Philip Swinton, when Chairman of Security Executive, maintained us against all criticism and actively assisted all our operations.

At times the whole system was threatened, but somehow we always managed to survive. A crisis came in the summer of 1942 when Philip Swinton left us to take over control in West Africa. He was succeeded by Duff Cooper with whom I had a long interview in July. He did not, I judged, approve of the double-cross system though he visited our office and had the system explained to him. As his Memoirs prove he thought the Twenty Committee superfluous and I think that he contemplated bringing our activities to an end. We survived, but in August of the same year we had to round another awkward corner. The Director of Naval Intelligence (Adm. Godfrey) proposed that the XX system should be placed under the Controlling Officer of Deception and that the Twenty Committee should be dissolved. This proposal was fortunately rejected because it would have ended all our work in counter-espionage and intelligence. The most dangerous moment of all came in the spring of 1944 and showed clearly enough the frailty of our position. An *Abwehr* agent with whom we were in touch, scenting the ultimate defeat of Germany, made suggestions that he should defect to us. That would have been disastrous. Had he defected, the Germans would have known that he could give us information about all their (supposedly invaluable) agents in England, and we should have been compelled to end all their activities, since the

Germans would realize that they had been in fact double agents unless we arrested them and closed them down. The danger was averted but it was a close-run thing and I do not believe that the XX system could have survived had the landings in Normandy been postponed even for a few weeks.

All in all I spent four and a half years in the Security Service. I was a pure specialist, engaged on double-cross work and nothing else. Even other branches in M.I.5 were almost unknown country for me. All the main tasks of a security service, formidable at any time but vital in the war years, were generally outside my ken. For the most part life was a prolonged slog, a life of office work and files, innumerable conferences and discussions, plans and negotiations. But it was a fascinating job and one which compelled me to refuse all proposals that I should be transferred to other work. There were of course 'high spots' of interest and excitement. To listen to one of our wireless operators, imitating after a year of practice the style of one of the agents speaking to the Germans was a thrill; so too was the sight of a large tin container in the office which housed the body of 'Major Martin'—the 'man who never was'; so again was a meeting about midnight with an agent who had just visited his German masters. He was a business man from a neutral country, well trusted by the Germans and—with much more reason—well trusted by us. The Germans proposed to him that, after his good work in England, he should move to America and set up an agency there. At that time the U.S.A. were still neutral. I interviewed him in a hide-out not far from Piccadilly Circus and asked him how the negotiations in Lisbon had gone. When he replied that all had gone well I asked what often turned out to be a key question. 'Did they give you adequate funds?' Payments made often gave a rough guide to the trust reposed in the agent by the Germans. 'Oh, yes, they gave me about £6,000 or £7,000 in American dollars.' 'And where is the money?' 'I think that I left it in my coat at the Savoy when I changed to come round to see you.' My heart sank when I thought of all this money left in a coat thrown aside in a hotel bedroom, but my anxiety was quickly removed. 'No, I'm wrong, I did change it over before I came out—here it is.' Sure enough, American dollars to the value of some £6,000 were handed to me and I well remember that I felt nervous as I walked at midnight through blacked-out London to deposit the notes in the office safe.

Such moments were rare; for the most part my activities were little different from those of a multitude of workers in many departments at Whitehall. When the end of the war came I found myself, owing to my age, in Group 1 for release and on 7 July I was eligible for fifty-six days' release leave with final release on 1 September. In point of fact I stayed on in the office and, at the request of the Director General, David Petrie, and of his deputy Guy Liddell, who was head of B Branch, I wrote the story of the double-cross system during the war years. I completed the book by mid-September; now a quarter of a century later I feel both pride and amazement that I could have written it in so short a time. My efforts in later years to reveal the story by the publication of my book is a saga in itself—but that tale must find its place in a later chapter.

Four and a half years is a long time to spend on one undertaking and I have no doubt that that period of service had a profound effect on my character and my thinking. So far as espionage and security were concerned I had come to the firm conclusion that straightforward espionage was practically valueless in wartime, though in peacetime it might return substantial dividends. Security, on the other hand, difficult to the point of impossibility in peacetime, was comparatively easy in time of war. As to double agents I had learned how, in favourable circumstances, they could be the most powerful of intelligence weapons. But beyond all this I had lived and worked in a different world from that to which I was accustomed. I knew something of Whitehall and of the machinery of Government and of the lives and motives of public men. More and more I realized that the problems which faced them were inevitably in essence human problems and that the human element was, in the end, the decisive factor in that new world just as it was in the University world to which I belonged and to which I should return.

XXII

RETURN TO OXFORD

Real development is not leaving things behind, as on a road, but
drawing life from them as from a root.

G. K. CHESTERTON

WHEN I returned to Christ Church in October 1945 I had
the curious sensation that I was reliving an earlier part
of my life. Another great war had ended and once more Oxford
had to resume her traditional place in the national life. For the
second time it was the duty of us all to restore the best of the
old traditions and the old values and once again the only effective agents for the task were those who returned after a five-
year absence. It is often thought, and said, that the returning
warriors of 1919 were mainly concerned to enjoy life and to have
a good time. This is only true of a minority; the majority felt a
pressing need to hand on to their successors the good things
which they had themselves enjoyed in the past. The prevailing
wish was for restoration and conservation. In 1945 it was again
the returning warriors who set the tone and dominated the
newcomers. In each case the task was performed to admiration
though the debt has never been adequately acknowledged.
There was, however, a subtle difference. The First War had
started with the terrible slaughter of a very high proportion of
the best and ablest of the young; the Second had started with
the phoney war and had developed in such a way that service
at home and even in a civilian capacity had differed little from
service in the armed forces. Moreover, it had lasted longer and
gradually but inevitably the conclusion had been reached by
many that it had been an unnecessary war—unnecessary in the
sense that better leadership could and should have prevented it.
If the military leadership in the First War could be, and was,
criticized, how much more was it certain that criticism after the
Second War should fall upon the politicians? Very few of the

military leaders in World War 2 could be seriously faulted, but very few of the political leaders of the years preceding the war could escape censure. I do not think it is conceivable that an election held at the end of the First War could have overturned a political leader who had been the architect of victory. After the Second War things had altered. At the time the rejection of Winston Churchill appeared as the supreme example of national ingratitude, but such was not, I believe, the case. The motives of those who voted him out of office were grounded on a desire for political advance and did not preclude full recognition of the fact that he had saved the country. Those who came up in 1945 and 1946 were as anxious as their predecessors a quarter of a century earlier to restore the best of what had obtained in the past, but they were also avidly keen to mould the future—they were hungry for politics and saw it as their business to insist that the country should never again be betrayed into a senseless war. From the University point of view both generations had a common advantage—they had had a period—short or long—of national service.

Naturally I viewed the scene from a different angle in 1945 than from that of 1919, when I was myself one of those who returned. There is a wide difference between twenty-eight and fifty-six! Moreover, my own position in the University was about to change, for in September 1946 I was chosen as Provost of my old College, but the election, the summit of my ambition, was clouded by a great personal loss.

In 1946 I learned, as my friend Lys often pointed out to me, that the Olympian Zeus deals out good and ill with impartial hand. I was appointed to the one job of all others which I hoped for and desired, the Provostship of Worcester, yet in the same month my Mother, who had been for so long the centre-point of my life, died in Oxford. She had suffered cruelly from arthritis for some years, but the stroke which killed her was unexpected. Mercifully she lived only a few days after the stroke. My old fault of burying my head in the sand had caught up with me once more. My Mother was eighty-six and yet I had not contemplated moving into the Lodgings without her; when she died all the savour of living in that most lovely of all Oxford houses left me. For more than fifty years she had never failed me and to her I had taken all my problems and difficulties.

Always she had provided guidance, encouragement, and love. She had only one grievance against me in that, contrary to her hopes and wishes, I had not married, but she was much too wise a woman to press or upbraid me about that. For the rest we were in perfect harmony and to her I had always turned in times both good and bad. Her death, as I now realize, made a profound difference to my whole life. Up to then the family had always been the centre-point and 'home' wherever my Mother happened to be. Now all was changed. My brother was Deputy High Commissioner for the U.K. in Madras; my uncles had died one after another; my cousins were scattered over the world. In consequence my job became the pivot on which my life turned and I was based—for the rest of my life— not on a family or a home but upon my friends and my profession. My life, which had been private, became public.

The negotiations which sometimes precede the election of a Head of a House have been described by C.P. Snow in *The Masters*, a book which, whatever may be thought of its taste, is surely a work of art—for, though all one's sympathies are engaged on the side of one candidate, one knows at the end that one would have voted oneself for the other man, however unsympathetic one found him. I hope that no such fierce controversy was raised by my election, which was, I believe, primarily due to Cyril Wilkinson. He had approached me before the war, when it was thought that Lys was about to retire, and he came to me again when the war ended. To his inquiry only one answer was possible. I told him that no post in the world could give me greater satisfaction but that his own claims were patently superior to mine; in no circumstances could I be a candidate if he, who had devoted his life to the College, wished himself to be Provost. His reply was characteristic. 'If I became Provost you would remain at Christ Church, if you became Provost we can both work together at Worcester.' It therefore came about that the College agreed upon my appointment on 27 June and I was formally elected on 30 November. The ceremony of admission took place on 1 January 1947. Whether my election was matter of dispute or whether it was generally acceptable I do not know and should not wish to—for inquiries on such a matter are dangerous. Judging from the kindness with which the Fellows welcomed me I venture to guess that there was no strong opposition, and I know that I had the good wishes of my predecessor.

At Worcester the Provost, as well as all Fellows and Scholars, was admitted in Chapel with traditional formulae in the Latin tongue. Paul Roberts, as Vice-Provost, addressed me in Latin. And here I make a confession. Both as Provost and later as Vice-Chancellor nothing made me feel more nervous and uncomfortable than the necessity of using a Latin formula. In one's own tongue it is easy to correct a slip or conceal temporary forgetfulness of the words required but in a foreign, and especially a classical language, any lapse is liable to be fatal. I used to spend long hours on practising these short Latin speeches and making sure, with the help of the Classical Tutor, that I should not be guilty of false quantities. At the time other and irreverent thoughts passed through my mind, particularly the tale of Dr. Jeune, sometime Master of Pembroke and Vice-Chancellor. One night at a Vice-Chancellarian dinner-party a lady asked him how Heads of Colleges were chosen. Dr. Jeune's reply suggests, either that he was something of a humorist or, and more probably, that he disliked being questioned at his own table. 'Madam,' he said, 'the Fellows of a College meet together and choose the best-looking among their number to be their Head.' The lady was not satisfied. 'Oh, Master, I feel that there must be a mistake somewhere, for I dined with the Provost of Worcester last week.' Dr. Jeune was equal to the occasion. 'Madam,' said he, 'you may have dined with the Provost, but you have not, I think, met the Fellows of Worcester.'

To be Provost of Worcester was the summit of my ambition. I thought then, and I have never had cause to change my mind, that it was the most desirable of all positions. It promised a life of opportunity, lived in an atmosphere of learning and culture, in the company of congenial yet provocative friends, and with all the stimulus that art and pleasing architecture and beautiful gardens can give. From one window I could look into the College quadrangle, from another I could see the College garden, from yet another I could turn my eyes to the College cricket ground. Is it as good a life as it was then? I cannot say. I am not sure whether I pondered much at the time about desiderata for a Head of a college, but I have thought much about it since and am satisfied that, though I fell far short of my ideals, I did on

the whole cling to the main principles which should guide a
Head. Above all the Head of a college must think of his college
first and all the time. To me the thought of a Provost or other
Head living outside and away from his college is an outrage—
which no college should contemplate, much less tolerate. As a
corollary to this a Provost must feel a genuine personal involvement in all the members of the society—senior and junior alike
—and must enter himself, as far as he may, into all their activities and interests. I was myself matriculated by Herbert
Warren, the President of Magdalen, who was generally regarded as a snob, as indeed in a certain way he was, but I
remember talking of him with Lord Chelmsford, at the time
(alas! so sadly short) when he was Warden of All Souls. 'Warren',
he said, 'had a large table in his drawing-room on which in
massive silver frames were displayed the photographs of his most
intimate friends. I was put in that group on the day when I succeeded to the peerage—and removed from it on the day that I
joined the Labour Government. But make no mistake, Warren
was the best President that Magdalen ever had. Who else could
have done so much for Magdalen men?' Jowett, I suppose, had
the same quality, for it was he who made Balliol men an important part of our national life. There have been others equally
memorable, but in every case such men gave themselves heart
and soul to their colleges. When I was appointed I made dili-
gent inquiry and satisfied myself that there was no danger that
I should be immersed in University politics, for, if events followed their normal course, I should not be eligible for the Vice-
Chancellorship until I had reached the age of ninety. That
seemed a fair margin of safety. *Dis aliter visum*; I became Vice-
Chancellor only ten years after my Provostship began. Certainly
my immediate predecessors, Daniel and Lys, had given me a
strong lead, for both of them had spent their lives in furthering
the interests of Worcester and I surmise, though I cannot know
at first hand, that among earlier Provosts, Cotton was of the
same timber. Cotton is included in Burgon's *Twelve Good Men*
as 'the humble Christian' and it may be that he was more concerned with the spiritual than with the material welfare of his
flock, but his devotion to Worcester is indisputable. The story
of him which survives is that of a map of the world which hung in
his study, and on which large areas were painted black.

Undergraduates believed that the black areas denoted the existence of coal, but in fact they indicated those parts of the world where heathen darkness prevailed and into which missionaries had not yet penetrated. Of course devotion to a college does not mean that its Head should divorce himself altogether from other interests—rather the reverse. He needs to be in touch with the outside world, for it is into that world that his men must go and it is his duty to know something of what they will find when they enter it—and even, sometimes, to help them when they get there. But it does mean that his college should always hold the first place in his mind and that nothing should make him cease to give it his first priority.

What did I hope to do myself as Provost? All of us when we embark on a new job dream dreams and see visions. I did not, I think, ever analyse or particularize my own hopes and ambitions but I am clear what those dreams were. Arthur Young says in his *Travels in France*, 'In every bosom whatever, Italy is the second country in the world—of all others, the surest proof that it is the first.' My unexpressed ambition was that every Oxford undergraduate could say 'If I was not where I am I should like to be at Worcester.' A worthy ambition, if only a pipe dream, but how could it be achieved?

Advice in plenty came from my seniors, but I have forgotten most of it, though that of Miles, the Warden of Merton, sticks in the memory. 'Know your statutes,' he told me, 'and know them well; if you do you will always be able to control your Fellows.' Luckily I never found the need of coercing the Fellows by such legalistic methods. Of one thing I was quite certain. In any institution or society the all-important factor is the quality of the men who compose it. Rules and regulations, theoretical aims and policies, laws and customs and conventions are worth nothing in comparison with the human element. Bad men make good institutions bad and good men make bad institutions good. If a college is to prosper it needs a body of good Fellows and still more a body of good undergraduates. Everything else is unimportant compared to this and it was, or it seemed to me, the first duty of the Provost to apply himself to the task of strengthening and developing the personnel of the College. The College, as well as the University, had to re-create itself after the long years of war. In the dark days of 1942

Philip Landon of Trinity had written me a characteristic letter from Cornwall.

There is, perhaps, just too much time left over, during which one has to muse over the sorrows of the world, which have been caused entirely, I think, by Voltaire and Rousseau. The moment the canaille were told by the one that religion is untrue and by the other that they were égal with their superiors, the knell of western civilization had sounded, and the only remarkable thing is that the end has been so long delayed. Thank God I have not been responsible for adding to the population! However, if we survive this war, you and I will fight another great fight for the preservation of the few good things that are left to us.

How far I was fitted to take the lead in this work of reconstruction in Worcester is a question which I am not the best person to answer. Of my limitations I was conscious at the time and am more conscious now. Always I have lived in the present but my eyes have been on the past; the truly creative people also live in the present but their eyes are on the future. None the less a large part of the problem in 1946 was the same as that in 1919— to preserve or reintroduce the best of what had obtained in pre-war days. This was a matter of conservation for which I was better equipped than for any task of innovation or reform. Far more interested in men than in measures and much more concerned with individuals than with ideas or causes, I could apply myself to the human side of things and to the individual interests of the men, letting theories and plans for reform go hang.

XXIII

PROVOST OF WORCESTER

Success should come late in life in order to compensate for the loss of youth.

HAROLD NICOLSON: War Diaries

IN a final analysis the Head of a House makes his own job. He may set himself to build up the financial position of the college and attempt the rather disagreeable task of raising money from benefactors, but such work is probably better handled by financial experts; he may try to exercise a moral leadership or to improve the academic standard of the College, but such things are usually better done by the tutors; he may see himself as a disciplinarian, holding his men on a tight rein, but the Dean can do that as well as, or better than, he. As a general rule he does better to choose men and to influence them rather than to act himself. In the statutes under which I was appointed it was stated that the Provost had 'authority over all the members of the College, and all persons belonging to it' and was to 'superintend the discipline and education of the College, and the management of its property'. He could also, if he wished, take part in the teaching. I think that the key-word is 'superintend'. It is sometimes forgotten that the Head of a House (except at Christ Church) is democratically elected by the Fellows and it is they who decide what the needs of the College are. To what extent the elected Head obtrudes his own views is a matter for his own choice, and there have been cases where Fellows searching for a King Log have succeeded in appointing a King Stork. Sometimes, too, a King Log, once appointed, has proved difficult to dislodge. Immorality was one reason for dismissal, but in many colleges only 'grave immorality' was held by the statutes to be sufficient, though where 'gravity' began is hard to understand. Certainly in many cases holders of the office hung on too long—as for ex-

ample did Magrath, who was Provost of Queen's from 1878
to 1930, when he died 'in harness' at the ripe age of ninety-one.
The highly coloured and no doubt mainly apocryphal story
of the attempt of the Fellows to dislodge him used to be related
with gusto by the Head Porter. The Provost's routine was un-
varied—living in the comfort of the Lodgings he emerged in
the afternoon for a drive in a victoria, he lived mainly on boiled
fish and did not drink, so that there seemed to be no reason
why his quiet and orderly life should not be prolonged indefini-
tely. A deputation of the Fellows visited him and proposed that
the Lodgings should be redecorated at the expense of the College to mark the appreciation of the Fellows for his long
services. The Provost gratefully accepted and was then told
that he must vacate his Lodgings for six months so that the
work could be done. It was generally believed that the Fellows
cherished the sinister design of so interrupting the placid existence of their chief that he would not long survive. The outcome
of their plot, if it was a plot, was very different. 'The Provost',
as the Head Porter told the tale, 'took rooms at the Boar's Hill
Hotel; he dined lavishly at the public table every night; he
challenged the Master of University College to a game of golf
at Frilford, and he ordered a new suit of clothes with *two* pairs of
trousers. The man will never die!' I was myself elected under
statutes which allowed my tenure to be prolonged after the age
of seventy, but I decided from the beginning that I should not
even consider any such prolongation.

In the body of Fellows I was more than fortunate, for all of
them were known to me and all were devoted to Worcester.
The Vice-Provost and Estates Bursar was Paul Roberts, who
had helped to prepare me for my scholarship examination in
1908–9 and who was by general assent one of the best History
Tutors in the University. Next came Cyril Wilkinson, the Dean,
who had been a close friend since my undergraduate days. He,
of all men, had the best claim to be considered an Oxford
'character' at that time and his technique as a Dean was superb.
Stories about him abounded and always he seemed to know
exactly how to deal with a peccant undergraduate. Lord
Nicholas Gordon Lennox, then a freshman, thought it worth
while to try to get leave to have a car, though cars were then
forbidden until a man's second year. Almost any other Dean

would have said at once that he could not make exception
to the rule save in very special circumstances and that the
activity in motor-racing at Goodwood did not come into that
category. Wilkinson too refused, but in his own manner.
'Gordon Lennox,' said he, 'you ought by now to know that
you came to Oxford for the development of your mind and not
for the whisking about of your body.' As Dean he used to address
the assembled freshmen in Hall. On one occasion having subjected them to a careful and unfavourable scrutiny he began his
address with the words, 'It is well to remind ourselves, gentlemen, that first impressions are often erroneous.' Even more
pungent, though equally courteous, was his answer to a peculiar
approach made to him in 1946. Lord Montgomery had, it is
believed, expressed the wish or hinted at the possibility that he
might well fill the position of the Head of a House at Oxford
or Cambridge—provided that the chosen college had a good
garden. This seemed to point to Worcester and an emissary
from the great man came to sound Wilkinson about the project.
The reply was devastating. 'Tell the Field-Marshal that I
should very much like to be a Field-Marshal—but I do not
think that I have the requisite qualifications.'

Apart from two Professorial Fellows there were nine Fellows
engaged in teaching, including Roberts and Wilkinson. Somerset, of sprightly wit, was a historian but his main interest lay in
music; Bryan-Brown the Tutor in Classics who was to become
Public Orator; Milburn the Chaplain, later Dean of Worcester
(the Cathedral not the College!); and then Master of the Temple
Alan Brown, Law Tutor and a future Mayor of Oxford; Asa
Briggs, afterwards Vice-Chancellor of Sussex; Geoffrey Dawes,
physiologist, soon to become Nuffield Director of Medical
Research; and David Mitchell, Tutor in Philosophy. There was
also one lecturer—William Holmes, a biologist. Bursarial duties
were handled by Roberts (Estates) and Milburn (Domestic)
though after a short time Milburn became Senior Bursar and
Alan Brown Domestic Bursar.

Lys had, indeed, chosen his men well, but one weakness
stands out. The humanities were well catered for, but what of
science and mathematics and modern languages? It was
customary to send out undergraduates who studied certain
subjects to tutors in other colleges or to coaches, but that meant

that they forfeited some part of the benefits of the college system. Years later, at the end of my Provostship, the picture was very different. Then there were, excluding the Professorial Fellows, four in number, and a research Fellow, fifteen teaching Fellows, divided between classics, ancient history, modern history, law, theology, physiology, physics, chemistry, economics, philosophy, and modern languages. There were also four lecturers in German, biochemistry, engineering, and politics, and very shortly after his arrival my successor was able to add music and mathematics to the list. The College, in fact, grew to its full stature at the beginning of the sixties. I must admit that the development was not wholly to my liking, for I believed that the optimum number for the College was exceeded when provision had to be made for the teaching in College for so many subjects. The number of tutors must of course correspond to the number of undergraduates and growing numbers created problems of accommodation. To this linked problem of admissions and accommodation I must return later.

More important even than the Fellows were the undergraduates. In 1946 as in 1919 there had been an influx of war veterans as soon as the war ended and, as on the earlier occasion, they were a fine body of men. I may be accused, and often have been, of thinking that all my geese were swans but there was at that time such superfluity of choice that it would have been a misguided governing body at any college which did not fill its places with suitable and worthwhile men. In my earliest days as Provost I received a telephone call from Penzance from the son of a Cornish fisherman (or, to be more exact, the owner of a couple of fishing smacks). The candidate had just completed his service in the R.N.V.R. With regret I told him that all the places for the following term were filled and that there was already a waiting list in case any last-minute cancellations occurred. I was sorry, but there was no hope for him. To my surprise and consternation he stood on my doorstep at 8 o'clock on the following morning, having travelled up during the night. I protested that I had been as clear in my refusal over the telephone as was possible. 'You were absolutely definite,' he replied, 'but you said that there was a waiting-list. I've come to beg you to put me as high on that list as you fairly can.' It's not necessary to describe exactly how I acted; sufficient to say that he was a member of the College in the ensuing term.

Granted this firm foundation, the problem remained to ensure that quality was maintained. In other words, what was to be our policy for admissions—and in this my views had not changed since my days as Censor at Christ Church. I had always rejected the plausible but fallacious argument that all places should be filled by competitive examination. Such a system would, in my view, result in a college filled by men of the same type, many of them respectable mediocrities. Entrants would be judged by their past performances at school, and this would turn the schools into cramming establishments and encourage too early specialization. Our aim at University level should be not to choose only the men who had achieved the best examination results during their school years but also to choose those who were likely to do best—and incidentally contribute most to the College and University—some three or four years later. I saw the problem of selection somewhat after this wise: first anyone would be taken who showed real promise of intellectual distinction—some, though not all, of those would win scholarships. After that we would take many other qualifications into consideration. It was a saying of Aristotle's that a man capable of one virtue was ultimately capable of all; it is also true that a college, like a university, needs diversity of gifts among its members, for it is not merely a factory for producing graduates. So, for example, a man who could play the flute better than anyone else in Wiltshire would have something to lift him out of the ruck and make him worthy of consideration. There had, of course, to be a written examination but this would serve, not as a competitive test, but as a qualifying examination, used to show that the candidate was capable of profiting from the privilege of a University education. Furthermore, a preference should be given to the sons and near relatives of Old Members, as being those who would be the most likely to absorb the spirit of the place and be most loyal to it. 'No man', it has been remarked, 'can serve an institution with a full fidelity of comprehension who has not fed, or fed himself, on its memories.' The decisive argument is simply this: in selection for entry one should look for promise rather than for previous performance. Mistakes will be made, but the dividends which accrue will far more than compensate for them. The alternative is a college spoiled by uniformity and over-populated by decent mediocrities.

Anyone engaged in the operation of selection for a college or university I would urge to read two pamphlets: the first of them was originally published in the *New Yorker* on 10 September 1960 and is an account of the selection process at Yale. A masterpiece of reporting, it describes with verve and humour the long process of selection of candidates for the places at Yale for the preceding year. And what a process! The examinations, the visits to schools, the intelligence tests, the interviews both with candidates and their instructors, the weighing of evidence and comparison of individual records—all are there and all are described before the final choice is made. There is, too, a denouement. In the course of her researches the reporter (a woman) had become interested in one candidate, the son of a friend, but thought that he would be excluded because his examination results were not sufficiently impressive. When the reporter visited the Dean for Admissions for her last interview she found him sending a letter of rejection to another candidate, whilst her own friend had been accepted. 'That friend of yours was admitted,' he said, 'and on not so good a record, or such high examination scores. We just thought he was more of a guy than this lady's son.' Perhaps intelligent favouritism is the keynote of successful selection.

The second pamphlet to which I alluded is an Arthur Mellows Memorial Lecture, given by Sir Ernest Barker in 1951, on the development of education in England during the preceding fifty years, and in it he pleads passionately for 'some little diversity to vary the monotony; some sort of individuality; some respect for personality and some feeling for its varieties'. Sir Ernest was a radical thinker and a leader in progressive ideas in my early days, but, though he had himself come up the hard way and was the product of a working-class family, he was ready to extol the value of diversity in a university and the virtue of hereditary ability. He pleaded for 'the mixture of the intellectual flyer, the youthful adept in examinations, alert but possibly narrow, with the slower starter of a broader range who can bring something from his home and heredity to contribute to the common stock of the school and the University'. And he goes further: 'Ability, I have come to believe, tends to be here-ditary . . . I would also keep places in our Universities for the old and traditional elements to balance and stabilize the new springing talent which is being introduced . . . by State Scholarships to the Universities.'

No doubt the system on which we (I say 'we' for no Head of a house can by any stretch of imagination be regarded as a dic-tator) filled our places at Worcester would be regarded nowa-days as perversely orientated and hopelessly outdated. Egali-tarianism is in command and the permissive society vaunts its victories. None the less I believe that the old system served us well—much better indeed than any scheme of entry governed by a rigid process of examination. Critics who complain—and how bitterly they complain!—that preference is given unfairly to the products of public schools or to the sons and relatives of Old Members, always blind themselves to the fact that the prime objective of every tutor for admissions is to find those men who will be most helpful, not only to themselves but also to the College—from whatever school or home they come and that those who prove themselves most helpful to a college are later most useful to the State.

It is also untrue that we showed that kind of political bias of which we were sometimes accused. It is an advantage, I think, that a Provost (or any Head of a House) should not engage in party politics, whatever his own political views may be. Early in my time as Provost I interviewed a candidate who, holding the rank of captain, had lost a leg at the crossing of the Seine. As we talked and as I listened to some of his comments I sensed that he held left-wing views and said that I supposed that he was a member of the Labour party. 'Labour,' he ex-claimed, 'that feeble pink lot! No, I'm red, I'm a Communist.' This did not (though perhaps it should have) cause me any misgivings, for I felt that the College could absorb men of any political complexion. In the event I was proved right. The man concerned, who had brains and humour as well as strong political views, threw himself into all College activities. His rooms were a centre of discussion and debate and, since the loss of his leg prevented him from playing cricket, he acted as scorer for almost every College match which took place whilst he was up. Twenty-five or so years later he was elected to an important

headmastership and one of the Governors told me about his
interview. The first question put to him was almost a blow
below the belt. 'Would you like to explain to the Board of
Governors why you only achieved a third at Oxford?' His
answer 'was to the effect that, coming from a working-class
family, via the Army, quite unexpectedly to Oxford he rapidly
came to the conclusion that it would be the greatest mistake to
spend his years there sweating blood for a first—that Oxford
had such an enormous amount to offer that the sensible course
would be to savour it to the full and not spend his time with
his nose in books but to be satisfied with a third (he said there
was a fourth, but it was very difficult to attain!)'. My informant
suggested to him that his Provost would probably have approved
of this policy; I am glad to say that he replied that he thought I
probably should have but that I had on many occasions urged
him to do more work.

Admittedly the system which we adopted was paternalistic
and would not commend itself to the educational theorists of
today, but it suited us well. One firm principle was that preference should always be given to those who had completed their
military service over those who had not. I am sure that this was
right. A man coming straight from school might well come up
without any plans for the future, simply because he was following the normal course. A man who had served for two years
came up because he was keen, often desperately keen, to do so.
Those unsuited to a university usually found out during their
period of service that a career without university training was
more congenial and more suitable for them. In my experience
the interruption of study was very seldom harmful and often
positively advantageous. Here I should note what seems to me
the main trouble which has followed the growth of the new
universities. The Robbins Report stated, and rightly, that any
one who was qualified to go to a university should have the
opportunity to do so; it also made it clear that the complications of modern life, especially modern industrial life, imperatively demand an increased supply of graduates. The report,
however, should have added that about half of those qualified
would be better advised *not* to go to a university at all for there
are other paths to success and other spheres of usefulness apart
from those for which graduates are needed. Contrary to the

general belief and judging by the standards of the past, it is easy for anyone with some brains and a little application to qualify, but when all, or nearly all, who qualify do come up, many are profoundly disappointed and waste not only their own time but also the time of others. In addition a tendency seems to be growing to regard those who have not been university trained as second-class citizens—a tendency which is clearly divisive in the country. It is a lamentable and dangerous mistake to think that someone who has been to a university is necessarily superior to someone who has not. How quickly things change! I am glad that my time as Provost was ended before the days of the permissive society, for which I have no sort of sympathy. Perhaps I have lived too long and do not understand modern ways. Be that as it may, I cannot but think that those who support a permissive society mistake the nature and purpose of a university—to which it is essentially a privilege and not a right to go. Basically the difference between 'then and now' is that, whereas in the past men were anxious to live the full life of a university and thought it a privilege to be accepted, they now think that they are received as of right and consider that the State owes them three years of university life. What they owe the State in return is less stressed, for the ordinary or normal man, who in the old days felt that he had a debt to his parents to repay, does not feel the same obligation to the State. The rejection of authority and of experience seems to me foolish and misguided and ends in the total loss of those benefits and advantages which the young might have from their elders. In my youth we were often told that no one who had not come under discipline was capable of exercising authority over others when his time came. With what contemptuous scorn such an idea would be greeted by many of the youth of today—yet all experience shows that it is in fact true and that no good leader is likely to show himself unless he has first held a subordinate position. As a friend of earlier days wrote to me:

> The permissive society works in this way.
> I do as I like; you do as I say.

It is one, perhaps the chief, of the pleasures of university life that all subjects can be discussed and all views propounded, but it is clean contrary to university tradition that a militant minority should impose its will on the majority by acts of violence or the use of force. Here, I fear, university authorities have been partly to blame. When discontent was rife and such outrages as 'sit-ins' and the destruction of official files were common the duty of Vice-Chancellors should have been clear. Absolute clarity (as in industrial disputes) was essential. Undergraduates should have been told exactly what they might do and what they might not do and summary punishment should have been meted out to transgressors, whilst a deaf ear was turned to those who pleaded that others were more guilty than they and prated of victimization. It was a case for court-martial and not for a Nuremberg trial. It is easy to criticize and to advise, but I believe that any Vice-Chancellor who took such a line at the beginning of the troubles would have found that his university was the most popular and sought after of all the universities in the country.

How different it all was in the fifties! I close my eyes and think of those times wondering whether the undergraduates at Worcester really suffered from the tyrannical rule of their seniors. Unless all my memories deceive me they did not, and the College was a happy and harmonious place. When all is said and done, discipline and conformity have virtues not to be despised. Not that discipline was severe. A small number, and it was a very small number, failed in examinations and went down—for the rest I can remember one being sent down, but not by me. He was sent down at the instance of the Vice-Chancellor and Proctors for reasons which I privately thought inadequate. We did not think in terms of Students' Councils or Students' representatives on the governing body, but the links between senior and junior members were close. The J.C.R. was autonomous, and if it had complaints to make, it would bring them to the Dean or Bursar or even the Provost without feeling any need of special administrative machinery. Sometimes the President of the J.C.R. would come to see me to tell me of proposals which were to come up at a J.C.R. meeting or of decisions which the meeting had made, and this without embarrassment on either side.

For any Head of a House this sort of communication is of great importance and needs careful handling. The confidence and mutual appreciation which grows up between tutor and pupil are two of the great benefits of Oxford life and are the basis of the tutorial system. For the Provost there is no such easy method—he must create his communications for himself, and in doing so must avoid giving offence to the tutorial body. He must also, so far as possible, take an active interest even in those activities which do not naturally appeal to him. For these reasons I took any opportunity which presented itself of keeping in touch with the men. In the first week of each term every undergraduate came in to see me for a brief interview. A list was put up and each undergraduate could choose his own time, but even so (as I was well aware) this terminal interview must have been a tiresome chore for at least three-quarters of them. I felt, however, that for some men the procedure (or ritual if you like to call it so) was really useful. A man, for example, who wished to change his school but was unwilling to offend his tutor might ask me to open the subject, whilst another might wish to talk to someone who was impartial about his future career. For such the interview at the beginning of term was much more suitable than the formal 'collections' at the end of term when the tutors reported orally to the Provost about their pupils.

Leave of absence gave another opportunity. An under-graduate was required to get a chit from his tutor (or was it the Dean?) to allow him to be absent for a night or nights during full term and the chits were brought to the Provost for his signature. I cannot remember refusing leave, but the visit did give me the opportunity of a brief conversation with the man concerned, and sometimes even to inject a word of mild criticism or advice. Once a freshman in his first term came with a leave chit only a fortnight after term had begun. His reason? His father and mother would like to see him. Was he on a Government grant? Yes. Where did he live? At Hull. I signed the chit but suggested to him that the money spent on railway fares could have been spent (perhaps to greater advantage) on the purchase of books.

Entertainment was more difficult and here expense was not the only or the chief obstacle. The kitchen at the Lodgings was then in the semi-basement and the staff had to carry everything up a long flight of stone stairs. As a consequence I could not entertain undergraduates half as much as I should have wished and probably much less than I should properly have done. On the other hand I was able to throw the Provost's garden and paddock open to the College which was, I think, appreciated in the summer and I encouraged the men to visit the drawing-room where the best of our pictures were hung. On one wall was our greatest treasure—Jakob van Ruysdael's *Wooded Landscape*, a picture which the Director of the Rijksmuseum once told me was at least as good as any Ruysdael in Holland.

Then there was College Chapel. We had a system which was called 'compulsory' by the undergraduates but which was, in my view, not really compulsory at all. I could not disguise the fact, and had no wish to do so, that I lacked any strong religious conviction but that did not make me any the less convinced that it was right in a college, which was a place of 'religion, learning, and education', that its members should join in corporate worship. I therefore took the line that it was the tradition and practice at Worcester that undergraduate members of the society should attend at least one service on Sundays (week-day services being optional) unless they had got exemption from the Provost. If a reasonable case was put up I never refused, but the practice gave me the chance of discussion with those men who wished to be excused. Chapel was reasonably full for both Matins and Evensong right up to the time of my retirement, though it was necessary for me to set an example. I used, whenever possible, to go to both Sunday services and three times a week to the morning service on weekdays. Fortunately the music was excellent (though, alas, I was myself no musician) thanks to our long musical tradition— Buck, Hadow, Pickard-Cambridge, and Somerset and more recent organ scholars of the calibre of Mackie, who became organist at Westminster, and Dearnley, who held the same office at St. Paul's. A moralist might hold up his hands in horror at my attitude and accuse me of hypocrisy, but my own conscience was clear. If I could not pretend to any religious fervour I could at the least support the religious establishment, and could echo the thoughts of Lawrence Jones whose *Edwardian Youth* gives a vivid picture of Oxford before the First War. Of chapel services then he writes thus:

On Sundays it was the thing to go to Chapel once at any rate, and we went with a good will. The interior of Balliol Chapel in those days was lamentable to the eyes, and there was no visible source of the spell those short and austere services cast over some of us. But . . . worship or not Whom we might there, we came out of Chapel less divided, less self-occupied and more tolerant than we went in. Some unseen hand in that unlovely place could draw us, imperceptibly to a centre.

Admittedly it was a system of paternalism but it seemed to me then to be the right way to run a college. Now, looking back, I can see many deficiencies and some failures but still feel that all in all it was a good and acceptable way of life.

XXIV

PROVOSTSHIP AND PUBLIC SCHOOLS

It would surely be folly to abolish what has proved so successful for so long.

Sir George Pickering on the Grammar Schools

An autobiography is not the place where the history of a college can properly be told. Only the personal incidents are relevant and, curiously enough, it is only the personal details which remain clearly in the mind. Of the early days of my Provostship, for example, I think most often of a visit from Lionel Smith; a visit, I suppose, almost entirely forgotten by everyone but myself. His arrival presented difficulties. Somerset, our second historian was taking sabbatical leave and I persuaded Lionel, who had retired from the Rectorship of Edinburgh Academy, to come for a couple of terms to take his place. It was a task of great difficulty to persuade him that he could still teach at Oxford (he had been tutor at Magdalen before the First War), but I did overcome his scruples. Then the blow fell. The Foreign Office wrote to me and said that Lionel was needed urgently to take charge of education in the Middle East and that the interests of Worcester must give way to the national need. Lionel had been an outstanding success as Adviser on Education in Iraq from 1921 to 1931 and his heart was very much in the East, but he was already sixty-seven—a late age to undertake so important a job. I replied, therefore, that I should not withdraw my offer to him but that I should release him if he himself asked me to do so. The Foreign Office then put forward the argument that there was no other person who had sufficient experience of the countries concerned to fill the post. This, having regard to the number of those who had served in those parts during the war, seemed to me an untenable argument and I retaliated by pointing out that Sir

Kinahan Cornwallis, who had been Ambassador in Iraq till 1945, and Sir Reader Bullard (incidentally Lionel's brother-in-law) who had been Ambassador at Teheran till 1946, were respectively three and five years younger than Lionel and that it could hardly be said that either lacked the necessary experience. I did not add, though I confess that I wished to, that in my opinion the undergraduates at Worcester were of as much importance as many Arabs. A laconic message from the Foreign Office—'You win'—ended the correspondence, and Lionel came to us as we had arranged.

It was a year later that I realized how much he had helped us and learned something more of what the tutorial system could mean. Lionel had come to stay with me for a few days a year or so after he had left us. We were walking together towards the Lodge to get into a taxi which was to drive us out to lunch when Lionel with a brief apology ran across the cloister to start what was obviously an excited discussion with one of the scholars whom he had previously taught. The man in question was as reticent and as shy as a man could be; I had always failed to penetrate his defensive armour or to get him to talk. When Lionel rejoined me I asked him however he managed to perform what seemed to me almost a miracle. 'Don't you know,' he said, 'X is a tremendous fan of Hull City— I had to ask him how the players there were doing in training.' We got into our taxi and were just starting when Lionel looked out and waved his white handkerchief to another Worcester undergraduate who was standing on the pavement and who waved his own handkerchief vigorously in return. 'What does all that mean?' I asked. 'Don't you know he's a leading member of that Club that supports a Stuart restoration—the White Heather Club?' Again I didn't know and I felt humble. Once after dinner at Christ Church I had heard W.B. Yeats speaking of another poet and declaring that he felt humble when he read the other's work. I thought the remark showed that he was playing to the gallery, but now I felt that I was wrong. How unfair that anyone should be able to communicate so swiftly and so surely with his juniors as Lionel could! I could only watch and envy.

The adaptation of the old kitchen of the Lodgings as a War Memorial Room and the placing of the War Memorial caused much thought and discussion. What really suitable words could be found for the memorial which were neither arrogant nor yet too tender towards the whims and crotchets of pacifists and the internationally minded? Even Wilkinson was unable to suggest the appropriate quotation—but Seddon, our Professor of Ortho-paedics, came to the rescue with an extract from Milton's *Tractate on Education*: 'Brave men and worthy patriots, dear to God and famous to all ages.' The words were written not for a memorial but to describe the sort of men which a college should strive to produce, and to me they seem the most ap-propriate which could be carved on any war memorial.

More important than these things was the starting of the College Week-end and the foundation of the Worcester Society. The traditional College Gaudy was not wholly satisfactory as a means of keeping old members in touch with the College and with one another. A guest could normally only have a long talk with those on each side of him at dinner and might have little opportunity for discussion with many of his friends and, as numbers grew, invitations to a Gaudy could only be sent to an old member about every fourth or fifth year. On the other hand it was urged that at a Gaudy a man was amongst his own con-temporaries whilst at a week-end all different ages were present. It was some years later that this argument was shot down by our oldest member—Sir Harry Brittain, then in the middle nineties. 'But I *like* to mix the generations—besides, I *have* no contem-poraries.' At Christ Church, when the need for more festive evenings became apparent I had invented what was called the 101 Dinner (there being 101 men on the original foundation). This served as a kind of extra Gaudy and so pleased Dean White that he asked me if I could suggest an excuse for other dinners. My proposal that, since Henry VIII was our founder, we should celebrate his wedding day was not very well received. At Worcester, encouraged by several old members, I set about the establishment of a College Week-end, to be held annually a week after the end of summer term. Invitations were to be sent to all old members with the proviso that, if numbers proved to be excessive, those who applied first should have priority. The Week-end began with lunch on the Saturday, followed by cricket and lawn tennis in the afternoon, and a formal dinner in the evening. On the Sunday there were College services in

Chapel, games in the afternoon, and an informal dinner in the evening. Those who came lived for a couple of days as though they were still undergraduates and were put, when possible, into their old rooms. There were notable advantages in this plan. A Gaudy is expensive for a College; for the Week-end a modest fee could be charged to those participating and thus the expense to the College could be reduced. The fact that our ground is within the College precincts made the experiment easier for us than for most colleges, and it proved a success. The first Week-end was held in 1948, and has continued since then; other colleges at Oxford and Cambridge have followed our example with modifications and, I must suppose, with varying degrees of success and satisfaction. Given time, sensible men usually arrive at sensible decisions; Week-ends and Gaudies flourish at Worcester side by side.

If I studied the records and perused the newspapers I could, no doubt, reconstruct the history of my first ten years as Provost, but that would be an unrewarding task. Now it is all a blur— or rather a rich kaleidoscopic picture—a time of ups and downs, of successes and failures in which the happier moments overwhelmingly outnumbered the periods of discontent. College tutors are, thank God, incurably optimistic, as too are athletic leaders and coaches, and it follows that there were times when the results of Schools in the summer or of activities on the playing fields or on the river brought disappointment, but real tragedy hit us but twice. In 1951 an undergraduate, popular, well off, without (so far as anyone knew) a care in the world, left his lodgings in white tie and cap and gown on his way to the Schools for his final examination—and was never seen again. That mystery will now, I apprehend, never be solved; it remains only a hateful memory. About six years later the second torpid got into trouble on a swollen river and was swept into the weir at Iffley where one undergraduate was drowned. In neither case could any individual be blamed, but that fact did not offer any consolation. On another occasion there was a 'near tragedy', though perhaps the danger was really less than it appeared at the time. I had thought that one of the scholars was overworking before Schools and likely to spoil his chances thereby. I sent for him and read him the riot act. He protested that he meant to rest for a couple of days before the Schools, but I told him that this was quite insufficient. He ought to go away for the inside of a week and return to get acclimatized a couple of days before his Schools started. Had he, I asked, any special hobby which would keep him in the open air and away from his notebooks? Yes, fishing. Nothing, it seemed to me, could be better; he should go away at once and return as arranged at the appointed time. My advice was based on the experience of thirty years and I knew it to be sound. A final school at Oxford is the culmination of three years' work and the examination itself is very much like life. There is the candidate, all alone and dependent only upon himself, doing his best with the resources at his command in the short time available to him. If that is not like life in a modern society, what is? For such a test the mind must be fresh and keen enough to drag up from memory knowledge acquired perhaps a year or two before. The feverish last-minute perusal of notes and textbooks is no sort of use whatever. But can you persuade an undergraduate of this obvious truth? You cannot. Still, my scholar took my advice; and when a couple of days before the Schools a fine trout was laid on my breakfast table I thought that the patient had benefited from the cure. I was soon undeceived. Two days (or was it only one?) before the Schools there was a visit from Royalty, and after luncheon at Christ Church whilst on my way to a Garden Party at St. John's I looked in at the Lodgings to find my scholar fast asleep and breathing stertorously on the sofa in my study. I shook him without effect and then summoned the Senior Tutor, whom I had passed in the Quad, to my aid. It was clear to both of us that the scholar was drugged, and an urgent telephone call brought an ambulance from the hospital. How many sleeping pills he had swallowed I do not know, nor why he chose my study to stage an attempted suicide. Possibly because he hoped subconsciously to be discovered in time. When the stomach-pump at the Radcliffe had done its work he was transferred to the Warneford, which took in psychiatric patients, and there he was visited by the Senior Tutor and myself. He expressed the utmost contrition and apologized profusely for having abandoned his Schools, but he did not get the answer which he expected. Bryan-Brown, the Senior Tutor, was a man of Roman uprightness and I was not in the mood to sympathize with lamentations. 'Do you think', we said, 'that all this trouble has been taken for you for nothing? However miserable you feel, you will do your Schools at the Warneford. Invigilators will be sent up each day and you will write every paper whether you like it or not.' And so it was. In the event he had a long viva for a first class. He did not get it, but a very high second was not an unsatisfactory ending to a rather frightening episode. Modern psychologists might not approve of our handling of the case, but it was at least effective.

Such incidents were rare—for the most part the barometer was steady at set fair and the ship proceeded on her wished-for course. Picture after picture passes through my mind. New buildings to house more men in College, the cleaning of Chapel and Hall (though the munificence of an old member), the foundation of the Worcester and Somerville Musical Society (which added much to the musical life of the College), a series of well-chosen and successful plays produced by the Buskins, the appearance of new and exotic birds in the lake (which we would never allow strangers to refer to as a pond), often the gift of friends, the arrival of the wallabies. These last-named, the Worcester wallabies, had their little hour of fame but they caused me some disappointment and annoyance. They had been presented by the Boat Club to be a symbol of the Club's hoped-for and bounding upsurge on the river, and it had been thought that they would live happily in the College field. Had they been placed there, few of the growing trees and flowering shrubs would have survived, and it soon became evident that the paddock in front of the Provost's Lodgings was the only place where they could live. Accordingly the paddock was wired in, and there they lived and bred. The wallaby may be picturesque but to my mind it is an unsympathetic creature. The climax of their insubordination came when a couple of them escaped from their quarters and in the night devoured some twenty rose bushes, a diet for which they showed partiality, and also ate the bark of, and so destroyed, three promising young apple trees. Their deportation to the Ilfracombe Zoo ended their two years of residence, but the handsome birds which we were offered in exchange never reached us. Perhaps Ilfracombe, on closer acquaintance, repented of its bargain.

All in all it was a happy time. Possibly I gave less attention *a little self-criticism*

than I should have to the intellectual side of College life, possibly I rated character too highly as compared with the things of the mind when selecting candidates for admission, possibly I was too complacent, but be these criticisms true or not I felt instinctively year by year that the reputation of the College was growing, and growing in the right way—and I was content.

A large part of my life had been spent in teaching and lecturing and I should have liked to continue that work when the Second War ended, but I believe that I should have made a mistake if I had done so. Probably my teaching methods were a little out of date; certainly the keen edge which the teacher needs had been blunted; more certainly still the many calls which administration made on me left insufficient time to recapture enthusiasm for teaching and still less to keep abreast of new work and new publications. In addition, outside my College work there were a number of peripheral tasks which took up a good deal of time. Of these the earliest were, if not strictly College duties, more or less intimately connected with the life of the College, for they were concerned with other parts of the educational structure

As my Mother lived in Eastbourne, where I spent most of my vacations, I had become a Governor of Eastbourne College in 1926 and so remained until 1957. In 1935, at the instance of a friend on the staff, I had taken on the same task at Cranleigh. Later commitments included governorship at St. Edward's from 1944 to 1958, of Wellington from 1944 to 1965, and a Fellowship at Eton from 1942 to 1964. It amuses me, as I write down these dates, to observe that my services as a school Governor total exactly 100 years. Later on I was a Governor of the Atlantic College from 1962 to 1968, but that was an institution of a different nature from the conventional school and my connection with it was short.

Governing bodies of independent schools did—and still do—much useful and very responsible work, though this work seldom receives much publicity. In the past, no doubt, they had often been, consequent upon the terms of the school's foundation, bodies of men—local big-wigs and the like—not all suitable for the performance of their duties. At one great and deservedly famous public school the chairman who was faced with the necessity of appointing a selection committee to choose a new headmaster and who had run through the list of his colleagues to discover how many held university degrees—with disappointing results—was compelled to take the main burden upon himself. 'I too', he said, 'have no degree at Oxford or Cambridge but I have played polo for both.' By my time conditions had changed and all the Governing Bodies on which I sat were filled by hard-working and competent men. It is remarkable but not surprising that men of great ability and real distinction will give up so much time to assist their old schools. Colleges might well take this to heart and do more than they do to retain the loyalty of their old members—copying, perhaps, but with discretion, some of the methods of the alumni of American universities.

From this school work I learned much and profited greatly. It was not only that I formed links with many of the schools and that this was useful for the College but also that it brought me into touch with educational problems and into contact with interesting people. The truth was forced upon me that all the tasks of bodies of this kind were insignificant compared with the overriding importance of wise selection and judicious delegation. You can find the right headmaster and the most competent bursar if you take enough trouble, but you will have achieved little unless you delegate powers to both and make your confidence in them clear beyond the possibility of doubt. That is one side—another is that Governing Bodies, like Prime Ministers, must be prepared to be good butchers.

At my first meeting of the Wellington Governors I sat next to Ian Hamilton [1] and was fascinated by his conversation, which fluttered over the years from 1871 when he had passed out from Sandhurst. His left hand stuck out almost at right angles from his forearm, for he had been badly wounded at Majuba in 1881. 'This', he told me as he extended his hand, 'was regarded as the great surgical triumph of that time. Everyone said that my arm must be amputated but the surgeons determined to save it.' Wellington had been, as everyone knows, originally a military school, but it had carried out successfully the difficult operation of turning itself into a school which fed the armed services and the universities with equal proficiency. Much of its

[1] General Sir Ian Hamilton (1853–1947); commanded Mediterranean Expeditionary Force at Gallipoli, 1915.

success in the academic world in the twenties and thirties was due to Talboys, the most effective of history tutors and one of the most remarkable men of my acquaintance. When he retired as an assistant master he was appointed a Governor—an unusual compliment which underlined the work which he had done in humanizing a school which before his time had often been open to the charge of Philistinism.

Even so, Wellington was still in many ways a military school, and it was impressive to see how men of action (and there were many of these on the Governing Body) applied themselves to the problems of the academic world and to observe how effective they could be in helping to integrate the life of the school with the life of the nation, whilst retaining a wary suspicion of the intellectuals among their colleagues. When Wellington had a Government inspection and the inspectors asked for a meeting with the Governors before they presented their report, a Duke and a Field-Marshal drew me aside and begged me to sit between them and the inspectors lest the latter should embarrass them with inconvenient questions. That the inspectors were equally nervous when faced by a group of distinguished officers I have no doubt. It is interesting and often instructive to watch the meeting of individuals who live in different worlds and to see how they tackle a common problem. When we were choosing a new Master for Wellington, Claude Auchinleck, the most famous of living Wellingtonians, asked each candidate the same question: 'Do you believe in beating the boys?' At first I thought this a mistake, but I came to realize what a good question it was. It made no sort of difference if the candidate was for or against the practice; the manner of his reply made all the difference in the world. The man who raised his hands in pious horror at such a revolting suggestion was as surely damned as the thick-skinned extrovert who thought the more beating there was the happier we should all be.

I recall one dinner of the O.T.C. (or perhaps at that time it was the S.T.C.) when similar thoughts poured through my mind. The dinner was an annual and agreeable function, spoiled to some extent by the length and multiplicity of the speeches. On the occasion of which I speak one of the first speeches was made by Maurice Bowra, who, as always, spoke with a brilliance, wit, and urbanity which few could match. I began to wonder if those who followed could possibly maintain so high a standard, but the undergraduate who succeeded him seemed to have no difficulty in reaching the same high level. Other speakers, in their turn, performed with hardly less *bravura* and I began to feel anxious. One of the objects of the dinner was to popularize the O.T.C. and, in particular, to encourage men to enter the Army through the University. Field-Marshal Lord Alexander was to make the last speech and I was genuinely afraid lest his speech should fall flat after the fireworks which preceded it. I need not have been worried. When his turn came Alex gave us a clear and concise picture of the Army of the day—the number of divisions in Germany, the opportunities afforded in various branches of the Service, and so forth. Then came the peroration: 'Some of you, I hope, will be taking up the profession of arms—a not ignoble profession.' All the clever speeches of that evening have been long forgotten but that simple statement remains, 'a not ignoble profession'. I suggested that the Field-Marshal should use it again at the Academy Banquet where he was to speak shortly afterwards on behalf of the fighting services, but he did not. I wish that he had.

I learned much at Wellington and still more at Eton, where I became a Fellow in 1942. The Governing Body there consisted of the Provost and eleven Fellows—the Vice-Provost, the Provost of King's (who was Senior Fellow), elected representatives of the Universities of Oxford and Cambridge, a member nominated by the Lord Chief Justice, and another by the Royal Society, a member elected by the Masters to represent them, and four members chosen by the Provost and Fellows themselves. Naturally these four places were usually filled by men of experience in public life and ready to devote much precious time to Eton affairs. The office of Fellow was no sinecure. We had about a dozen meetings in the year, starting in mid-morning and usually continuing well into the afternoon. The small size of the body made it possible for all the members to take an active part and there was little delegation to committees or to the officials. Of course, the constitution was not ideal; what constitution is? The Provost lived, so to speak, on top of the Headmaster, an arrangement which could in certain circumstances lead to difficulties, though these were overcome through the good sense of the individuals concerned. When, for example, Claude Elliott was Provost and Robert Birley Headmaster it would have seemed impossible to us that either should pursue any course which was not, in his opinion, in the best interests of Eton, nor indeed could a body go far wrong which was guided by the sure hand of Edward Bridges. I have served on many committees and many Governing Bodies but none of them impressed me more than did the 'Provost and Fellows'. For most of my twenty years as a member I was, with the exception of the Provost of King's, the only non-Etonian present—a source both of weakness and strength. On many topics it would have been tactless for me to interfere but on others the opinion of an outsider (that is of a non-Etonian) was held to be of value. Perhaps it was. Be that as it may, I found the meetings extraordinarily stimulating. At one of the first which I attended I listened spellbound to an argument between Provost Quickswood and Maynard Keynes. Not only were they two of the finest intellects in the country but both were masters of the spoken word. It was for me an intellectual treat beyond price, a lesson in dialectic, and a model for the manner in which such a discussion (or disagreement) should be conducted. Seldom, I think, can so much wisdom have been concentrated in one room as was at a meeting of the Provost and Fellows.

The years during which I served as a Fellow coincided with the replanning of Eton, the restoration of the old buildings, and much new building. The history of all these things has been well and accurately recorded by J.D.R. McConnell in his *Eton Repointed*. I do not recall that we differed much over most of the changes, though all were discussed with the greatest care. Aesthetic questions caused the most debate, especially that connected with the windows in Chapel, where the painted glass had been shattered by the 1940 bomb. There was an acute division of opinion between those, led by Jasper Ridley, who wished to give the contract to Miss Evie Hone and those who felt that her Celtic style and vivid colours would be out of place and architecturally wrong in Henry VI's Chapel. Unable to agree the Fellows wisely decided to invite the opinion of three experts—Sir Kenneth Clark (Lord Clark of Saltwood), Lord Crawford, and the Dean of York—and to abide by their decision. The experts, in their turn, were divided but the two laymen supported the Hone party. The result was, by general consensus of opinion, a triumphant success, more especially when the design had been completed by the eight windows in the Chancel which were the work of Mr. John Piper and which linked up the Hone east window with the *grisaille* windows in the nave. The ancient buildings constitute much of the charm (I had almost written magic) which Eton exercises and that charm was enhanced by the notes and memoranda which Henry Marten[2] was wont to circulate among the Fellows; but, when all is said and done, the life and work of the College and the School were of greater importance even than the buildings. The special and most admirable feature of an Eton education was its freedom and versatility, and this caused Eton to wage an unending war against too early specialization and against outside examinations which were to be taken after cramming at an early age. Sadly it must be admitted that that battle was not won, though it was never wholly lost. For this result, in my opinion, the universities with their increasing demands for high examination marks and paper qualifications were chiefly to blame. They favoured in their admissions policy, though they would not admit it, a movement towards mediocrity and stifled the growth of individuality and all the exciting possibilities of the eccentricities of genius.

I cannot disguise from myself that the contribution which I made to all the schools which I helped to govern was small indeed compared to what I received from them. From theories of education and pure educational politics I kept aloof—indeed I have always felt a distaste for such things—but the human contacts and practical wisdom of my colleagues at all the schools gave me some of the richest and most rewarding hours of my life. At Eton I cannot forget Edward Bridges christening the new swimming pool by having the first pre-breakfast bathe there on the morning of a meeting, or Kim Cobbold[3] asking that item 13 on the Agenda might be taken before item 12 (in which he had no interest) so that he might catch his plane to Zürich to face the gnomes of that place. Equally in my mind's eye I see at Wellington the Duke of Wellington, a professional

[2] Successively Vice-Provost (1930–45) and Provost (1945–8) of Eton.
[3] Lord Cobbold, Governor of the Bank of England 1949–61, and Lord Chamberlain 1963–71.

and expert architect, clambering to the highest point of the buildings to examine the suspect roof or hear again Hugh Beaver[4] expounding the details of his Industrial Fund which was to give so great an impetus to the teaching of science. Yes, I gained much and gave, I fear, but little in return.

[4] Sir Hugh Beaver (1890–1967), industrialist, Vice-President of Wellington College.

XXV

OUTSIDE ACTIVITIES

Parergon. By-work, subordinate or secondary work or business; work
apart from one's main business or ordinary employment.
Oxford English Dictionary.

A clear difference can be observed in the life of a don in, say,
1910 and in 1950 or 1970. The first was with few exceptions always resident in Oxford during Full Term; in the Long
Vacation he might travel to Italy or Greece, to Scotland or the
South of France, but for the greater part of the year he was always in Oxford and his pupils would have been astonished and
perhaps outraged if he had taken a term's leave of absence or
exchanged with some foreigner from Germany or America.
Over Haverfield's mantelpiece in his rooms at Christ Church
was the legend—'Soul, thou hast much goods laid up for many
years',[1] a quotation which aptly described the attitude of
mind of some of the dons of those days. There must have been
many dons who did not miss keeping term for twenty or thirty
years, and whose work outside Oxford was confined to an occasional lecture or to some examining in another university.
After the Second War, and perhaps earlier, all this changed.
Sabbatical leave became the rule and not the exception and
after a time the right to it was laid down for all holding University posts. There was more and more interchange between
universities—a practice encouraged by the ease and speed of
air travel. Like most changes, this had its bad side as well as
its good. No doubt the college tutor was refreshed by contact
with a wider world and no doubt his teaching was freshened
and improved by visits to America and other seats of learning,
but on the other side of the account must be entered the admission that the tutorial system (that chief merit of Oxford) was to
some extent weakened. What don has not heard the bitter
lamentation of a pupil deprived of his tutor for the most critical

[1] Luke 12 : 19.

term in his course? On balance this modern habit must be judged of advantage, but a price had to be paid.

For the Head of a House, for example for myself as Provost, the case was somewhat different. By the Statutes I was obliged, unless the Visitor gave me dispensation, to reside in College for seven calendar months in each year, whereof six weeks at least were to be in each term—not that I had any wish to be absent for any long period at all. On the other hand I was less restricted than a college tutor by fixed hours of teaching and therefore more open to invitations to help in outside matters. It is a sad fact that once teaching is abandoned the former teacher becomes more and more immersed in administration and his time is absorbed by constant and always increasing committee work. Of these peripheral activities I must now say something, though they were, to my thinking, of very much less importance than my College work.

From the first I was keenly interested in examinations for the Civil Service and in the creation of C.S.S.B. (the Civil Service Selection Board). Prior to the Second War the Administrative Class had been filled after a lengthy written examination, a system which, though it produced many admirable officials, also let in a minority of candidates who lacked the personal qualities which were desired, and excluded a few who would have been of value to the Service. The conclusion of the war necessitated temporary arrangements, but very soon the First Commissioner, Sir Percy Waterfield, had a new system in operation. This was C.S.S.B., the constitution of which owed much to the W.O.S.B.s (War Office Selection Boards), which had proved their worth during the war. Put briefly, admission to the Administrative Class of the Home Civil Service could be obtained by either of two methods—by Method I, which was the old and lengthy examination process; or by Method II, which consisted of a qualifying examination, followed by three days at the C.S.S.B. centre, which preceded the interview at the Final Selection Board. The Foreign Service, under the influence of Ernest Bevin decided, for all practical purposes, to use only Method II. There was a residential centre at Stoke D'Abernon with a directing staff of ten, and there the candidates repaired for a board examination lasting for three days. They were divided into groups or syndicates of eight persons and each group was controlled by three examiners—a Group Chairman, an Observer, and a psychologist—who at the end of the course made up their list in an order of merit. The Director himself, Colonel Pinsent, was exceptionally well qualified for his job—an ex-regular Army Officer, he had taught at Winchester, had been Mayor of Winchester, and President of a W.O.S.B. At this distance of time I cannot recall who it was who asked me to inspect and give an opinion on C.S.S.B. but I think that it must have been Percy Waterfield. At any rate, soon after my Provostship began I found myself at Stoke D'Abernon charged with the task of reporting on a course, and there too was Harold Caccia[2] with a similar commission from the Foreign Office. We 'sat in' with different groups but had agreeable talks in the evening about our experiences.

I listened, of course in complete silence, to all the conferences, committee work, and discussions—in fact to everything except the tête-à-tête interviews—and to the final discussion held by the three assessors. When this was concluded—and only then—the Group Chairman asked me for my judgement on the system and invited my criticisms. I had gone to Stoke D'Abernon with considerable reservations in my mind, especially with regard to the psychologist, who turned out to be a woman, but my doubts had been dispelled thoughout the course during which I could only admire her judgement and perception. Like Balaam I had come to curse and stayed to bless. How, I asked, could I criticize when my own private list of the group in order or merit tallied exactly with that of the three assessors? Harold was also most favourably impressed and reported accordingly.

It must be remembered that C.S.S.B. was only advisory, though its verdict was seldom substantially altered. Decision rested with the F.S.B. (Final Selection Board), which was composed of the First Commissioner with four or five permanent members, one of whom was a woman, together with two or three members of a panel of extra or occasional members. The woman member played a significant part, and her judgement with regard to male candidates seemed to me nearly always accurate, but I have the fixed impression that with regard to her own sex she was often stern to the point of ruthless-

[2] Lord Caccia, Provost of Eton, formerly British Ambassador at Washington 1956-61, and head of H.M. Diplomatic Service 1964-5.

ness. 'That candidate', she might say of one who had charmed the male members of the Board, 'only wants to enter the Service to find a husband.' I had the privilege of sitting on the Board for two or three days for many years and under four First Commissioners, and this experience convinced me that the examination was among the fairest and most effective that I have met with, and that the criticisms of C.S.S.B. were for the most part unfounded. It was, for example, often said that the system was tailor-made for candidates of a particular type and that a good social background played too great a part in ensuring success. This criticism was not well founded. In the old written examination the syllabus was based on the various Oxbridge Final Schools, and probably Oxbridge candidates had some advantages over those trained in a different stable. In my view those from less wealthy or less aristocratic homes had a better chance under Method II than under Method I, and, if swayed at all, the Commission tended to over-compensate for lack of opportunity or for personal difficulties. Nor can this argument that a written examination is the only valid test be maintained. Candidates were seeking to enter upon a career where personal effectiveness was vitally important, and such a quality could be better judged by C.S.S.B. than by the perusal of a number of written papers. The years that I sat (as an 'occasional member') on the Board was a time when the really intelligent man (excluding those who entered such professions as the Law, Medicine, or the Church) could choose between an academic career, the Civil Service, and industry. From all three arose the plaintive cry that the other two absorbed more than their fair share of the best men. In fact there were not enough first-rate men to go round, and I believe it is true that in those years the Civil Service, even though it lowered its standards by ever so little, never succeeded in finding enough men to fill all the places which it had to offer. Later on with the growth of new universities the field of choice was enlarged, but the quality of the candidates certainly did not improve. I have read that an ex-Minister of Education has declared that no person of intelligence could subscribe to the doctrine that 'more means worse'. How wrong he is—or was! Taken in its context with regard to higher education the sentence is not a foolish slogan but a simple statement of verifiable fact.

All through my later life I have been involved in this matter of personal selection and—though I lay myself wide open to the charge of vaingloriousness—I believe that I became with time a good and judicious selector. To find the right man, or at least the best available man, for the job. It sounds so easy and is so difficult; it suggests a laborious task and turns out to be a fascinating problem. And the techniques of those charged with the duty of selection used to vary to an astonishing degree. As a young don at a scholarship examination I have seen Arthur Hassall creeping noiselessly behind the candidates in order to study the backs of their heads. He declared that this survey was a better guide than many papers, though my own opinion is that thumbs are the best of all physical indications of a man's abilities.

Such things are trivialities, but think of all the things which must be taken into consideration in process of selection. How much weight do you give to past performance compared with promise for the future? How much can character and determination compensate for lack of previous training or of opportunity? How far can intelligence above the average be held to be more important than some weakness of moral fibre? How far can you trust your own judgement in assessing the recommendations of referees? Can you be sure that the candidate himself has not darkened judgement by his ingenuity or his charm or because of the expert coaching which he has had? To answer all such questions you must have flair and, above all, confidence in your own judgement—a confidence which comes only through experience. One golden rule must always be observed. You must know exactly what you are looking for among your candidates, and here Aristotle gives the needed warning. The qualities of the good man and of the good citizen are not identical. Even in the Home and Foreign Services the qualities demanded are not exactly the same. Absolute integrity is essential to both but, for obvious reasons, some personal qualities are more important in the Foreign Service than in the Home, and vice versa.

Another commitment outside Oxford was the Chairmanship of the Army Education Advisory Board which I held for four years from 1952 to 1956. I was lured into this, rather against my better judgement, by Brigadier Wilfrid Pidsley, the Director of Army Education, who, after a fine record in the First War (D.S.O., M.C., Croce di Guerra), had joined the Army Education Corps in 1919 and risen to be its chief. He was the most friendly and persuasive of men, with whom it would have been a pleasure to serve, but I felt somewhat deflated when I learned that his retirement came at the same time as my appointment. In 1952 problems of the A.E.C. were considerable and it was not easy to see how some of them could be overcome. The Corps did a great deal of useful and essential work, notably in the training of illiterates and in its schools overseas, especially in Germany, but it laboured under two handicaps. In the first place there was an underlying prejudice at the War Office and in the Army against a Corps which some old-fashioned folk regarded as non-combatant and therefore inferior to themselves. Secondly the training of national-service personnel created a real difficulty. Education came under Training, and the military authorities naturally and rightly maintained that soldiering came first and that men could be ill spared for the fairly long periods for which the educational authorities pleaded. In addition there was an ill-defined but strong feeling in some circles that the A.B.C.A. productions during the war had been orientated too much to the left and had encouraged freedom of thought to the detriment of discipline.

I should like to be able to record that the Advisory Board under my Chairmanship swept away all these obstacles, for it was manifestly important for the country that the national-service men should profit from their period of service; but, alas, I have kept no papers and cannot recall any startling success. Some improvement we did, I think, secure—especially after 1954 when Jim Cassels[3] became Director of Training at the W.O. There was also one small victory for which I could claim a fair share of the credit. We succeeded, after a struggle, in having the post of Director of Army Education upgraded from Brigadier to Major-General, thus giving him equal rank with his colleagues in the Royal Navy and the R.A.F. This sounds trivial enough, but in the hierarchy of the War Office it was of real importance and certainly helped to push our educational

[3] Field-Marshal Sir James Cassels, later Commander of N.A.T.O. Northern Army Group.

interests. For the rest only a few faint memories remain to me: that room in the War Office where we habitually met and where a portrait of James Grigg seemed still to dominate the whole office almost as much as did John Reith at Broadcasting House; or again the Great Hall at Eltham Palace, which was the Head-quarters of the Corps. Dining there for the first time my host told me with pride, 'Here we celebrated victory in 1945—in the same Hall in which the victory of Crecy in 1346 was celebrated.' His remark was not strictly true for the Great Hall was built by Edward IV, but it is true that Eltham had been a royal residence since the reign of Edward II and without doubt the victory of Crecy was celebrated within its walls.

For some seven years (1952–9) I was a member of the General Advisory Council of the B.B.C. This was interesting, but truth compels the admission that I feel it to have been largely a waste of time. The Committee was large and the members were able, intelligent, and active, but the plain truth is that it did not meet often enough to be as effective as it should have been. An issue would be discussed and proposals made, but by the time the next meeting took place such proposals, if they had not been acted upon, were too often allowed to sink into oblivion. But at least I could feel that I had learned a great deal about the art of chairmanship from Cyril Radcliffe,[4] who presided over us for the first three years of my stint.

Very different was the next appointment which I must describe—the Chairmanship of a Government Committee on the political activities of civil servants. The Staff side of the Civil Service Whitley Council had pressed for this and Sir Stafford Cripps, the Chancellor of the Exchequer, announced in February 1948 that a Committee would be set up with these terms of reference: 'To examine the existing limitations on the political activities (both national and local) which may be undertaken by civilian Government Staffs, and to make recom-mendations as to any changes which may be desirable in the public interest.'

We were told that, whilst there was a case for investigation, the Government would be totally opposed to any radical change in the non-political status of the Civil Service, and

[4] Lord Radcliffe, Director General of the Ministry of Information 1941–5, Lord of Appeal 1949–64.

further that we were not called upon to consider the staffs of
the nationalized industries nor of the Local Government
Service. The Committee, ten in number, was a strong one,
especially because of the presence of its Vice-Chairman, Sir
R. Hopkins. He had retired only in 1945 from his position as
Permanent Secretary to the Treasury and Head of the Civil
Service and would have made an admirable Chairman but for
the fact that he was regarded as being too closely involved with
the politics inside the Service. As things were he backed me up
with complete loyalty and nursed me through my Chairmanship. His advice, always sage, could never safely be ignored.
One member of the Committee was Dame Myra Curtis, a sometime Civil Servant and Principal of Newnham College, Cambridge. Since she was the only woman member I was inclined
to treat her with special deference, but Hoppy drew me aside
after our first meeting to murmur words of wisdom in my ear.
'Don't forget', he said, 'that the lady is much the toughest
member of your team and treat her accordingly.'

In the course of our inquiry we had two vital principles in
mind. They were these:

(1) In a democratic society it is desirable for all citizens to
have a voice in the affairs of the state and for as many as possible to play an active part in public life.

(2) The public interest demands the maintenance of political
impartiality in the Civil Service and of confidence in that impartiality as an essential part of the structure of government in
this country.

Obviously these two principles conflicted; it was equally
obvious that some members of the Committee attached much
greater weight to one principle than to the other. It was our
duty to find, if we could, a central position in which we could
reach agreement. In the event our main recommendations were
that the Civil Service should be divided into two halves, consisting on the one hand of those free of any restrictions in their
political activities and on the other of grades where members
were to be subject to restrictions in the national, though not in
the field of local, government. The number of those who came
under consideration was 1,100,000 and the report gave 'freedom' to 450,000 more than had previously enjoyed it.

The work was strenuous, for apart from the study of memoranda from individuals, associations, and overseas governments, we interviewed a great number of witnesses, official and unofficial, including representatives of all the main departments, and held fifteen full-day sessions. To me, as Chairman, the outcome seemed wholly satisfactory; not only had we produced (unlike most similar committees or commissions) a unanimous report, but we had done so in only one month over a year's time. I should have liked to have given more freedom to the 'restricted' to take part in local government, but it was clearly worth while giving way on this point to secure unanimity. The Government accepted our recommendations and decided to put them into operation at once.

Then the trouble began. A storm was raised during a debate in the House of Commons in July of 1949, and it was not until I read the account in Hansard that I realized how ineptly the affair had been managed. The National Staff side had always felt—and felt passionately—that there should be no restriction whatever on the political activities of civil servants, except that they should be expected to behave with discretion and they complained bitterly that the Government had made a decision without due consultation with them. This was a curious objection, since a large part of the report had dealt with the claims and proposals of the Staff side who had raised the issue in the first place. It should also not be forgotten that entry to the Civil Service is a voluntary act and that there can be no reasonable complaint if conditions of service include some restrictions (as in the case of other professions and employments). In the debate the report was inefficiently defended by the Government.

But if the Government was inept the Conservative Opposition was both opportunist and obtuse. It was wholly in the interest of the Conservative Party to get the difficult question settled, for they as much as anyone needed a non-political Civil Service. Unfortunately they saw in the Minister's handling of the problem a chance to attack the Government, and this chance they seized with both hands. They were entitled to object that the Government had pushed through the settlement without having a debate on so important a subject but they showed less than ordinary common sense when some speakers fulminated against the imposition of restrictions when the report had in fact freed 450,000 more civil servants than before. In effect they aligned themselves with the National Staff side and attacked the Government for imposing restrictions when the whole tenor of the report had been to reduce them. There is something ironic in the thought that, whereas after most inquiries are concluded the Government is berated for taking no executive action, in the case of this report the Government was fiercely attacked for acting on the advice of the Committee without any delay at all.

The outcome was expected, for most governments give way, often feebly, to protests and objections. It was decided that the Government should have further consultations with the Staff side and in the House of Commons, but that immediate effect should be given to that part of the report which freed 450,000 civil servants from existing restrictions. The person most to be commiserated with was Edward Bridges, the First Secretary of the Treasury, who was keenly anxious to settle the thorny question. He did not despair and succeeded in 1953 in bringing the matter to a conclusion. The new settlement, whilst maintaining the 'general principles underlying the Masterman Committee's recommendations', introduced a third category between those above and those below the line which we had drawn—in other words a number of people who were 'half-free'. Edward's letter telling me of the settlement was generous. 'May I say that, although the recommendations in your report have not in the end been wholly endorsed by H.M. Government, I for one, and I know many of my colleagues, feel great gratitude for all that you did.' From Edward Cadogan[5] I received a *cri de cœur*. 'I cannot help writing to you to say how shocked I was to read in *The Times* this morning that a Conservative Government has gone right on beyond the recommendations of your Committee of which you will recollect I was a member. My own view was that we had reached the extreme limit of possible concessions.' Others took the same view and I was fortified in my conviction that we had found a sensible middle position when I read a leading article in *The Times* of 13 March 1953 which was headed 'Weakening a good tradition', and which

[5] Sir Edward Cadogan, M.P. for Bolton 1940–5, brother of Sir Alexander Cadogan.

supported energetically the settlement made in the Master-man Report.

The Chairmanship of the Committee taught me a great deal about the actual working of the Governmental machine and caused me to reflect on these committees and Royal Commissions. It seemed to me that their utility depended upon the availability of a sufficient number of qualified persons—many of whom must be of necessity retired—to man them adequately and this number was steadily diminishing as a result of inflation and rising prices. In 1960 the then Postmaster-General at the instance of the Prime Minister wrote to ask me to be Chairman of a Committee on Broadcasting (a committee which afterwards became the Pilkington Committee). That I was not a good choice for this task is irrelevant; I was to retire as Provost in the following year and it was utterly impossible for me to spend a couple of years doing an unpaid job. Another example which springs to the mind is that of General Sir Henry Pownall, who had been Chief-of-Staff to three C.-in-C.s and military adviser to Winston Churchill for his history of the war. After Henry's wife died we used always to spend Christmas together in Cornwall, so I knew his mind well. By general acceptance he was one of the outstandingly successful staff officers of the war and a man not only of great administrative ability but also of the soundest judgement. Who could have been better as Chairman of a Royal Commission or committee of inquiry? He was offered a governorship but he needed additional income and went into the Brewery industry. No doubt he was useful there but surely the country would have gained more had he been employed by Government. Sadly I come to the conclusion that the man-power for independent committees is inadequate and that tasks which were in the past carried out voluntarily must become paid—and well-paid—jobs. To use the judges for such purposes I think a mistake. However impartial and how-ever tactful they may be the suspicion is bound to arise that the Judiciary has become political, and we are launched on that slippery slope which leads to a position where the judges—as in the seventeenth century—'are lions but lions under the throne.' The Judiciary must be kept absolutely independent and it must be clear to all that it cannot be used, and much less dominated, by the Executive.

XXVI

WRITINGS

It is natural to fathers and mothers not to think their own children
ugly; and this error is no where so common as in the offspring of the
mind.

Don Quixote (trans. Motteux)

Another interest of these years was writing, to speak of
which I must go back to 1933 when my first book, *An
Oxford Tragedy*, was published. I had always hoped and intended
to write and had little doubt that I should find my field in historical biography, but other interests and events had always
prevented me. It was strange that I should have started my
literary life with a detective story, stranger still that I have now
no recollection at all of the reasons which led me to make the
choice, strangest of all that I cannot remember how or where I
wrote the book. My memory only carries me back to the time
when I had completed the story and had it typed. I showed it to
George Gordon[1] at Magdalen, who gave it his warm approval
and then sent it along to a friend—an old Oriel man—who had
joined the staff of one of the chief literary agencies. His first
response was encouraging but his second letter seemed to dash
all my hopes. 'I have now read your novel *An Oxford Tragedy*',
he wrote, 'but am very sorry to say that I do not feel we should
be able to do anything with it. I would very much like to help
you if I could, but I really do not feel confident of being able to
find a publisher for it . . .'

From this depressing situation I was rescued by Bob Sherriff,[2]
then an undergraduate at New College. 'Let me take it to my
publisher', he said, 'and see what he thinks of it.' He was as good
as his word and Victor Gollancz, the publisher in question,
took the book at once. I have often wondered why my first
approach to an agent was so firmly repulsed. Any publisher

---

[1] President of Magdalen College 1928–42.
[2] Author of *Journey's End* and many other books and plays.

may refuse any book for this or that reason but I am still surprised that a literary agent should have thought *An Oxford Tragedy* an unsaleable book. Its subsequent history has not confirmed the agent's judgement. Reviewers were almost unanimously kind, perhaps too kind, and Gollancz was delighted. 'A sale of 2,500 (this is what the first two editions amount to) for a first detective story is extraordinarily good; but a third edition *may* be wanted . . . I see that the papers are full of the possibility that you may become headmaster of Eton. If this should happen in the next two or three weeks we shall probably sell 20,000 copies!' What a commentary on the things which govern popular taste!

'L'appétit vient en mangeant.' My second book, *Fate Cannot Harm Me*, appeared in 1935. With it I was not so fortunate as I had been with my first. Reviewers, I think, are generally kindly towards a new author but less gentle when he writes a second book. Feeling that Gollancz had not made the most of the book, which he had not advertised, I wrote to upbraid him. In a very charming letter of reply he told me some of the hard facts of the publishing world. I had written a novel of social manners when I should have cashed in on my early success by writing another detective story; I had put off the booksellers by writing a lengthy introduction; advertising must be governed by expected sales—a small edition without advertisement would pay its way, extensive and expensive advertising would only be justified if the book would sell on a much increased scale; there had been no review sufficiently eulogistic to boost it; he had therefore only printed a small edition. In my own mind I felt sure that *Fate Cannot Harm Me* was a better book than *An Oxford Tragedy*, a view shared by those friends whose opinion I valued most highly. I had sent a copy as a private gift to Lord Tweedsmuir (John Buchan), then Governor-General in Canada and his enthusiastic acknowledgement gave me extreme gratification.

Your novel arrived safely, and I have read it with enormous interest, admiration and indeed astonishment . . . the epithet that comes to my mind is 'distinguished', both in the subject and technique. You have got completely out of the ordinary groove . . . You have adopted Joseph Conrad's manner and greatly simplified it. You have been very bold too, for you have dared to give examples of your characters' written work . . . and the examples entirely satisfy the reader. I cannot remember anyone else who has been brave enough to do this . . . The dialogue is often brilliant.

Could a young author expect (even after making all deductions for friendship) a more encouraging letter? When I showed it to Gollancz he said immediately that, if he could use it, he would have another edition of 5,000 copies. Probably I was foolish to refuse, but I was at that time full of high-faluting principles and over-fastidious in personal relations and I did not like using a private letter for public advertisement. I ought to have cabled John for leave to quote his letter—instead I told Gollancz that the letter was personal and not to be used. The title of *Fate Cannot Harm Me* (which I always liked) came from Sydney Smith's *Recipe for a Salad* of which the last two lines are:

> Serenely full, the epicure would say,
> Fate cannot harm me, I have dined to-day.

When the *Oxford Dictionary of Quotations* appeared in 1941 I noted with almost personal resentment that the phrase was attributed to Calverley, who had used it in one of his poems. Needless to say I made sure that in the second edition of the *Dictionary* justice was done and the lines restored to their author.

My third book followed in 1937. I was still experimenting to find the best medium for my writing and once again the experiment ended in a manner which I had not expected. For the purpose of my teaching I was spending much time on the French Revolutionary and Napoleonic period, becoming specially interested in Napoleon's Marshals. One day, working in the Codrington Library, Oman[3] came up and asked me what I was studying. I told him that at that moment I had gone back to the declaration of war in 1803 which had brought the brief peace made at Amiens to an end, and that I was interested in the 11,000 British people who were left in France during the subsequent war years. None of them appeared to have written of their experiences. 'It is a curious fact', said Oman, 'that a very large number of leading French people engaged English governesses during the peace.' He then, to my amazement,

[3] Sir Charles Oman (1860–1946), Fellow of All Souls College and Librarian of the Codrington Library, Professor of Modern History 1905–46.

rattled off the names not only of half a dozen Frenchmen but also the names of the English governesses whom they had employed. That no doubt was a useless piece of knowledge but it did bring home to me some understanding of the impact which great events have on the lives of individuals. I forgot the governesses and returned to the study of the Marshals.

Among all the figures of the time Ney came to fill my imagination and I pondered whether I could write something about the last part of his life. I pursued my investigations in the Archives Nationales and the Bibliothèque Nationale in Paris and, as I worked, became more and more impressed by the dramatic possibilities of the trial. In this way my projected article or monograph became a play—almost without any conscious intention on my part.

It was natural that I should discuss this with Bob Sheriff and for a time we contemplated writing the play in collaboration. In the event this plan did not come into being but Bob wrote a short but telling preface for the book version which Cobden Sanderson published in 1937. In *Marshal Ney* I clung to my principles and refused to deviate from the truth, as I saw it, even in non-essentials. Even the words of the chief characters are for the most part their recorded utterances. Perhaps this disqualifies the play for consideration as 'good theatre'; perhaps not, for fact can be as dramatic and compelling as fiction. And most certainly as tragic—for in the history of Ney's last years all the elements of tragedy are present. It is not only that 'the bravest of the brave' is condemned to death for treason, and shot; not only that the individual who strives for peace is led to involve his country in further war; not only that loyalty to an individual or to a cause is found to be incompatible with patriotism. Most of all it is because an honest and loyal man is driven by fate ineluctably to self-destruction; it is the inevitability of disaster which is the keynote of Ney's story. Surely the essence of tragedy is that it is inescapable; there is nothing the victim can do which can save him from destruction.

As a play *Marshal Ney* was unlucky. In 1938 Eric Dance was planning to open the new Repertory Theatre in Oxford— the Playhouse—which was to be transferred from the Woodstock Road. He was enthusiastic about *Ney* and wrote to me, 'I think it would be ideal for the opening of our new theatre.'

Incidental music was to be arranged by Dr. Thomas Wood, who had unrivalled knowledge of, and interest in, military and traditional music. Unfortunately the theatre staff and Eric's advisers were unwilling to take a chance. It was too risky to start a new theatre with an untried play instead of an old favourite, and in any case they needed a three weeks' run to put it on properly. In consequence the production was postponed for a year, and Eric undertook to start the autumn programme of 1939 with it. Then came the war; Eric died in a P.O.W. camp in the Far East; *Ney* with many other more important things was forgotten. *Marshal Ney* has had only one public performance—in March 1953 when it was adapted for radio by Helene Wood and produced by Peter Watts. Marion Crawford gave a splendid performance as *Ney*, but I could not but feel that the play was far better suited to the films, the stage, or television than it was to radio. Possibly a play written by an amateur ought never to go on the stage, possibly it should only be read and not acted, yet I have always regretted that it did not get its chance and obstinately, though perhaps erroneously, believe that it has some merit and some real theatrical possibilities.

At the end of the war, when I was released from service, I wrote a report on the double-agent system, but this was at the time 'top secret' and was not published until 1972. The account of the struggle which finally led to publication belongs to a later chapter.

After I had settled in as Provost of Worcester my mind turned again to writing, for I had come to think of myself as an author, though I still felt uncertainty about the form which my writing should take. *An Oxford Tragedy* had given me my start as a writer of detective fiction but I had no wish to become a writer of one particular type of book; *Fate Cannot Harm Me* was a novel, which owed much to better practitioners, especially Max Beerbohm. In my introduction I had been rash enough to write: 'Nothing obscures the truth so much as the attempt to cut a long story short; the art of the novelist is to make a short story long.' With *Marshal Ney* I learned a different lesson. A dramatist is engaged as it were upon a piece of intricate carpentry where every piece must fit into place—or, to put the thought in another way, where every word must tell. There is no room for digression or side issues. My *Double-Agent System* was a report, a piece of serious writing, and in its small way a primary historical-source document. All four books were of a different kind—where should I go next? I had thought often enough that my bent was towards historical biography, but *Marshal Ney* had cured me of this belief. Try as I would I could not prevent myself from becoming a partisan—I shared too much and too personally all the violent prejudices and emotions of one side. Nor could I easily disbelieve many of the stories and legends on which I had been brought up. That is no habit of mind for a serious historian; a historian therefore I could not be. And was there not, too, a gnawing suspicion that, at least with regard to persons, the imaginative partisan sometimes comes nearer to the truth than does the scientific historian?

What then ought I to be writing? No one can write with conviction except on subjects of which he has experience, even if that experience is vicarious. For me Oxford was a compulsive theme and in that mood I wrote *To Teach the Senators Wisdom, an Oxford Guide-Book*, which was published in 1952. Its arrangement gave me every opportunity of writing about Oxford scenes and problems and Oxford stories. I borrowed from *An Oxford Tragedy* my imaginary college and set the members of the Senior Common Room to compose a guide-book which could be used by them to entertain and instruct three American visitors—visitors whom they expected to be Senators and who in the event turned out to be young ladies, for whom the guide-book was hardly appropriate. The book owed something to Lowes Dickenson's *A Modern Symposium* and much more to Tuckwell's *Reminiscences of Oxford* and Daniel's *Our Memories*. Of the books which I have written *The Senators* gave me unquestionably the greatest pleasure—not only from the writing but because of the correspondence which it brought me from Oxford men and women. Stories old and new poured in upon me and I could well have written another book by collecting them together. One strange fact emerged. I had always taken many of the Oxford stories with a grain of salt, but time and again I received letters from those who had actually been present when the described incident occurred. A single instance must suffice. An eminent ecclesiastic who could write 'Domestic

Prelate to his Holiness the Pope' under his signature wrote to me:

I remember many years ago the Pope was seized with the idea of founding a University in England. This scheme filled me and other Oxford men with horror. Two eminent ecclesiastics were sent from Rome to inspect Oxford and Cambridge . . . I was entrusted with the task of showing them round. I took them to the usual spots of interest, and I noticed that their spirits seemed to be sinking, but the end came in the Hall at Magdalen, where the Butler who was doing the honours, pointed to a picture, and casually remarked— 'His Eminence Cardinal Wolsey, formerly Bursar of the College.' That was the end; when we got outside I said, 'Do you really think that you can found a University here in England?' They sorrowfully shook their heads, and nothing more has ever been heard of the idea.

I had heard before of the Butler's remark but the occasion when it was made had been unknown to me.

The illustrations gave me especial satisfaction for most of them were photographs taken by Reggie Weaver, the President of Trinity, whose photographs of Spanish cathedrals and other buildings were of superlative merit. The endpaper of the book purported to be a view from the tower of St. Thomas's College (my imaginary college) and many were the guesses as to whence it had been taken. Ronnie Knox, after examining the various possibilities, roundly accused me of cheating and using an aeroplane, but in fact Reggie Weaver had taken the photograph from the top of the Castle. It almost landed me in trouble when Sanderson, the Governor of the prison, had it pointed out to him that some of the prison windows were shown in the photograph and that this transgressed the regulations. Fortunately he was a Worcester man and was able to tranquillize his superiors, but both he and I were a little perturbed when a prisoner escaped from the gaol a few weeks after the book appeared. *To Teach the Senators Wisdom* was well received—the only discordant note coming from a temperance organization which accused me of the crime of excusing or even recommending undergraduate intemperance. I could have replied that I was not responsible for the views of all my characters but I deemed it wise not to reply—the more so because I held the opinion that the 'brisk intemperance of youth', which often removes inhibitions, is in many cases a salutary experience—

provided only that it is brief as well as brisk. Few things have given me more pleasure than the knowledge that the book has been used in a number of cases to give strangers and new-comers a picture of Oxford and Oxford Life. It is my contribution to Oxford and I am unashamedly proud of it.

In my next book, *The Case of the Four Friends* I returned to the detective story, but to a detective story with a difference. I called it 'a diversion in pre-detection'. There were four suspects for a crime which did not in fact take place, each of them meditating killing one of the others. To close the ring so that there were four potential murderers and four potential victims demanded some ingenuity if the tale was to be plausible.

In 1961, during my last year as Provost, I collected together some shorter pieces in a book which I called *Bits and Pieces*. Several of them, including *Marshal Ney*, which I always held had 'missed the boat' had appeared earlier but several were new. One piece in the book had produced some excitement—a story called 'The Gifted Amateur' which the *Evening Standard* had published in 1950. It was an extravaganza in which I made Lestrade, the professional detective, give his version of an untold adventure of Sherlock Holmes and Watson. To parody great writing (as the Sherlock Holmes stories are) seems to me to be a tribute to the greatness of the original author and I suppose Holmes and Watson to be as well known and famous as any two men in history or in fiction, but my poor little extravaganza did not appear in this light to the Directors of the Conan Doyle Estates. I received a frosty note which is worth quoting:

Sir. There is such a thing as honour in literature as there is in daily life. As a writer of integrity, my father would have felt it beneath him to have stolen the characters of another man's creation for use in a story of his own composition. We are instructing our lawyers, at once, to take whatever steps they may think necessary, both in regard to you and to the Evening Standard.

The Conan Doyle solicitors wrote to the *Evening Standard* to say that they would issue a writ. But there, not unexpectedly, but to the undisguised disappointment of my friends, the matter ended. Gavin Simonds, the Lord Chancellor, declared that he had ordered a false beard so that he might enjoy the spectacle of me in the dock. *Bits and Pieces* was my last book, for in the sixties I wrote only a few short pieces of which a pamphlet, *Theory and Practice in Industrial Relations*, was the most important.

Writing has always been for me a *parergon*—and often a relief from my real work—and for that reason alone I cannot claim to be a writer in the best sense of the word, for a writer to reach the heights must give himself heart and soul to his writing. But there is a place in our society for the minor poet, the competent but perhaps uninspired biographer, the writer of amusing and readable fiction. Beer and sandwiches fill a need as much as do champagne and caviare, or, to use another metaphor, there is a great deal of fun to be had in the second eleven, even if one can never aspire to be a member of the first.

XXVII

VICE-CHANCELLORSHIP AND LATER YEARS AS PROVOST

It is more correct, as well as more usual, to speak of a University as a place of education, than of instruction.

If a practical end must be assigned to a University course, I say it is that of training good members of Society.

J.H. NEWMAN

IT is difficult enough when describing my life at Worcester not to allow an autobiography to become a history of the College during the relevant years. For the short two years of my Vice-Chancellorship it is almost impossible to prevent the narration from becoming a short account of the University, but I must do my best to speak from my personal viewpoint.

In the course of my University life the relationship of the University and the Colleges underwent a slow but perceptible change. It is no exaggeration to say that, as undergraduates, the University meant little or nothing to us, except in the sphere of athletics. For the rest, the University was simply a shadowy body which matriculated us, examined us, and awarded us our degrees. If the University meant little, the College meant everything and even common speech indicated the relative importance of the two bodies to which we belonged. It would have seemed only natural to say, 'When I was up at Magdalen (or Trinity or Univ.)', whereas, 'When I was at Oxford' would have sounded stilted. In no other context could the Swiss proverb be more true, 'My shirt is closer to me than my coat.'

Among dons there was more understanding of the University but the majority—a very large majority—were dedicated College men who viewed the encroachments of the University with concern and usually with disfavour. Professors, for example, were useful in their proper sphere, but they must not be permitted to infringe upon the more important sphere of College teaching. The glory of Oxford was the tutorial system (in this they were wholly right)—the give and take of individual teaching—and Professorial lectures were only the sugar icing on the top of the cake. The Prof (Lord Cherwell), with his accustomed cynicism, spoke to me once of 'Professors Emeriti'. 'That', said he, 'is to suffer the indignity of the name without the compensating emoluments.' None the less it was essential that some dons should apply their energies to University affairs and University administration and many of the most able did so. I must not exaggerate but I think it is fair to say that in pre-First-War Oxford there was some disdain for University politicians who were considered as having deserted learning and teaching for politics and administration. 'So you have joined the busybodies', remarked S. G. Owen to a colleague who had just been elected to Council. With this disdain gratitude, on the part of many of us, was mingled. Though we felt that life and learning flourished in the Colleges we knew that tiresome problems of administration, finance, and external relations had to be handled by the University and that the Colleges must provide men to undertake these unwelcome tasks.

During the sixty-odd years during which I have known Oxford the balance of importance as between College and University has gradually but perceptibly shifted and the University has become more and more important. There are three main reasons for the change. The first is the growth in reputation and numbers of the newer universities. It was snobbish, but understandable, that being at the University in old days meant, unless some explanation was given, being at Oxford or Cambridge. Nowadays Oxford and Cambridge are only two, though admittedly the most famous, among many. The other reasons are more important. The growth of science has sensibly increased the sphere of the University. In the old days some of the larger colleges ran their own laboratories—a system of manifest inefficiency; nowadays the undergraduate who studies science must spend much of his time in the University laboratories and must depend upon many dons who are University teachers first and College tutors in the second place only. The third reason which tends to increase the importance of the University *vis-à-vis* the Colleges is a financial one. In the past it would have been unthinkable for a College to give a fellowship to anyone

not chosen solely by the College itself. Today financial considerations often make it necessary to appoint College tutors
who will be acceptable to the University and receive from the
University part of their stipend. All these reasons tell to some
extent against the College system—a system of fierce but perhaps parochial loyalty—which in the judgement of some has
had its day. Yet it can and should survive if only its adherents
hold fast to the need of maintaining a community which is not
too large to be housed for a proper part of university life in its
buildings and small enough to retain human relations and contacts between all its members. In universities, as in the industrial world, over-great size is the enemy of the good life. In this
context, more emphatically means worse. I surmise that those
newer universities which, by aid of student hostels, common
rooms, and such like, maintain the residential quality of a
university are more likely to prosper than those which are
merely teaching establishments open from nine to five.

What has already been said will explain my reluctance to succeed to the Vice-Chancellorship. When I became Provost in
1946 I had calculated the danger and come to the conclusion
that it was negligible. I could confine myself to my College and
avoid the frustrations and annoyances of University politics.
Fate decreed otherwise. I became Vice-Chancellor in January
1957 and this was the way of it.

By a convention which had been long followed, the Chancellor appointed as Vice-Chancellor the Head of House who had
served longest in *that* capacity. The system had great merit but
one drawback, in that Vice-Chancellors were often older than
was desirable when they assumed office. A series of accidents
depleted the ranks of those who were senior to me. A sad accident deprived Oxford of Stallybrass,[1] others had to decline
for reasons of health, others again, notably Keith Murray[2] of
Lincoln, passed to other posts. Suddenly and alarmingly it became clear that I might have to succeed in 1954, and the
Chancellor asked me unofficially if I was prepared to act. I
could not in decency refuse. There was, however, one obstacle

---

[1] Principal of Brasenose College 1936–48.
[2] Keith Murray, later Lord Murray, Rector of Lincoln College 1944–53, then
Chairman of the University Grants Committee 1953–63, and Chancellor of
Southampton University.

in the way of my succession or rather one person who had a prior claim. This was Alic Smith, the Warden of New College, but he would be seventy-one in 1954 and it was generally thought that he would either decline or be considered too old to take office. After all the Vice-Chancellor was *ex officio* Chairman of some seventy committees and boards in the University and no one was eligible for these committees who had passed the age of seventy. Which rule or which convention was the more important? The Warden himself was keenly, even passionately, anxious to be Vice-Chancellor and after many consultations with his advisers the Chancellor decided that he would follow the convention and appoint him, though I believe that he privately regretted the decision. So perhaps did Maurice Bowra, who wrote to me in May:

> My dear J. C.
>
> Veale has told me the Chancellor's decision and also reported that he has told you. As you know, I have no status in the matter and what the Chancellor decides must be right. But I had rather looked forward to you as successor, and must just record it. Otherwise you will, I expect, be relieved to go on looking after your College for a bit, since it is much more interesting than the University.
>
> Yours ever,
> Maurice Bowra.

At his last speech on relinquishing office Maurice gracefully stated that he felt that the time had come to give place to an older man! This brought a further difficult decision for me to make, for the Chancellor[3] was anxious that I should succeed in due course, even though—in 1957—I should be already sixty-six. It would have been very difficult to refuse without appearing to resent the decision of 1954 and a letter from the Chancellor of 4 June 1955 shows that I complied.

> I am very glad [he wrote] to hear from the Registrar that you are prepared to fall in with my wish, which I am sure would be also the wish of the University at large, that you should become a member of Council on my nomination next term . . . and in due course succeed the Warden of New College as Vice-Chancellor . . .

The character of Alic Smith is, for me, a fascinating study. First of all I felt the strongest personal affection and respect for

[3] Lord Halifax.

him because of the innate and endearing courtesy with which he treated alike those who agreed with him and those who did not. You might differ from him on fundamental issues, but it was simply impossible not to like him. His energy was tireless, the fecundity of his ideas remarkable, and his devotion to Oxford the guiding light of his life. But with all this he was also liable to be a storm-centre of dispute for he was prepared to push forward his own ideas and plans without taking much account of opposition. Almost, but not quite, he would have argued that the end did justify the means. From his imaginative plans and his practical work I gained much, but I also suffered from the controversies into which he had been drawn. I firmly believe that had he become Vice-Chancellor ten years earlier he would have been numbered amongst the greatest men who have held the office; as things were he left a balance sheet of good and ill.

Perhaps it was inevitable that at his age the strain of the office should prove too much for him, and so it did. Many in Oxford will have recollections of the visit of Bulganin and Krus-chev to Oxford in April of 1956, of the bomb which exploded in the Quadrangle at New College and of the joyous strains of the song 'Poor old Joe', the meaning of which was mercifully unknown to the guests, but few will now remember that the Vice-Chancellor himself led a party to Moscow in September and there contracted a painful and wearing illness. The University year begins in September and Alic Smith was deter-mined to fulfil his duties, but even so he was compelled to hand over to me, as his Deputy, half of the meetings of Council in Michaelmas Term as well as other duties. In December I was on holiday in Cornwall when the Registrar wrote to tell me that the Vice-Chancellor had had a couple of 'vascular fits' at a New College feast and that it was the opinion of his doctors that it was out of the question for him to continue in office. Still this indomitable man showed no intention of resigning and it was only the intervention of Sir Horace Evans[4] that per-suaded him to do so. He continued to act as Warden of New College and he gave me every assistance in his power, but the sad ending came in July when he died. I took office within a day or two of my sixty-sixth birthday.

[4] Lord Evans (1903–63), Physician to the Queen from 1952.

It was not a propitious moment. A writer in *Oxford* (the Oxford Society publication) at the end of my Vice-Chancellorship thus described it.

When he became Vice-Chancellor the University was torn by bitter controversy over the Meadows road. The Warden of New College had been a protagonist of the party which favoured a road through the Meadows, and on succeeding to the Vice-Chancellorship he could not help remaining a controversial figure. The controversy, in the manner of controversies, had cast its blight upon all sorts of activities in the University which were in no way connected with it. This darkened counsel and engendered suspicion. 'J. C.'s' first endeavour, then, was to remove the blight.

The writer went on to claim for me 'conspicuous success in his effort'; a verdict with which I am not likely to quarrel. But before I discuss the Vice-Chancellor's work in general it may be well to describe the constitutional change which was brought about in the office itself. I was determined that the University should not again be handicapped by the appointment of a Vice-Chancellor who was too old to give his best service to the University.

The appointment of a Vice-Chancellor was in the hands of the Chancellor, who habitually conformed to the convention that he should offer the post to the Senior Head of a House. The Chancellor, therefore, was the key to the situation, and here I had an advantage of overwhelming importance since I enjoyed the privilege of close friendship with him and could discuss any subject with him with complete freedom and the assurance of his sympathy and help. I therefore drew up a memorandum with statistical appendices which covered the history of the office for the preceding half-century. In those fifty years there had been eighteen Vice-Chancellors, of whom the average age on assuming office was almost exactly sixty. Exactly half had been nearer seventy than sixty in their last year of office. My memorandum continued:

It will be generally admitted that the two most vigorous and successful of recent Vice-Chancellors have been Lowe, who became Vice-Chancellor at 49, and Bowra, who became Vice-Chancellor at 53. It is a brutal but undeniable fact that there is generally some deterioration in the middle sixties, and that the strain of the Vice-Chancellorship is apt to accelerate this. For this reason I am forced to the conclusion that it would have been in the public interest if both Smith and Masterman had been passed over on the score of age.

My proposals for reform were two, and both were simple; the first that in future the Vice-Chancellor should hold office for two, instead of three, years, the second that the Chancellor should nominate no one who would have reached the age of sixty-five before his term of office ended—i.e. that he should be under sixty-three when appointed. The Chancellor agreed with my line of argument and instructed me to call a meeting of the Heads of Houses to obtain their views. At this meeting the scheme was approved without any negative vote and with only two abstentions. A letter was then sent to me from the Chancellor (which we had jointly composed) explaining the new procedure to Council and I was able to put an explanation of it in the *Gazette*. The change was made smoothly and I believe the plan to have been thoroughly sound. I was succeeded in turn by Boase (Magdalen), Oakeshott (Lincoln), Norrington (Trinity), Wheare (Exeter), and Turpin (Oriel). Each of them did his stint and was then able to return to full work in his own college for a reasonable period of time. It would be, I believe, acknowledged that they were all good, efficient, and active Vice-Chancellors, and subsequent history has, I think, reinforced the rightness of the plan.

The system was changed according to the recommendations of the Franks[5] Report in 1966. By my plan (if I may call it so) a Vice-Chancellor was Chancellor's nominee for a year, Vice-Chancellor for two years, and a member of Council for another year. He was, therefore, at the centre of things for four years, but only divorced—or partially divorced—from his college for two years. By the new dispensation he is designated at 'least two years' before serving for four years as Vice-Chancellor. Furthermore any member of Congregation is eligible for election; an election made by a committee consisting of six representatives of Council and the six most recent ex-Proctors who are still members of Congregation. Both these changes seem to me regrettable, though I was glad that the Commission retained my age limit by providing that a Vice-Chancellor should not be over the age of sixty-one at the time of assuming office.

[5] Lord Franks, Provost of Worcester College (1961–75), Chancellor of East Anglia University; formerly (1948–52) British Ambassador at Washington.

There are, no doubt, cogent reasons in favour of a permanent
Vice-Chancellor, but these are in my opinion outweighed by the
advantages of giving the office to Heads of Colleges in their turn.
I had been dubious about the advantage accrued to a college
from having its Head as Vice-Chancellor, but experience of the
office convinced me that the college did gain from the appointment. The Commission rightly rejected the plan for a permanent appointment, but the length of time which the Vice-
Chancellor must now serve makes it extremely difficult for him
to return to his former job. How, for example, could a Professor
resume his former post if it had been held for four years by
some other person, or, for that matter, how could the Head of a
House disturb a deputy who had acted for so long? Yet the
return to his college of a Vice-Chancellor, fortified by his
knowledge of his university and of other universities, is the
prime merit of the rotational system. In deciding that the office
of Vice-Chancellor should not be confined to Heads of Houses
the Committee would seem to have been guided by a mistaken
view that they were acting democratically. They declare that
the choice had been left in the past to 'the judgement of other
bodies, looking for other qualities . . .'. But is this true? With
the exception of Christ Church all colleges elect their heads in
a strictly democratic manner, and usually after long and careful
discussion. In my own College Statutes I read this: 'The
Provost shall be elected by the Fellows, who shall choose the
person most fit in their judgement for the government of the
College as a place of religion, learning, and education.' What,
I wonder, are the 'other qualities' of which the Commission
were thinking? I hope that they were not thinking only of skill
in raising money, a skill which seems to be the foremost desi-
deratum in some universities today and is also, regrettably,
often an albatross hanging round the neck of the Head of a
college. I think that the course of events has gone some way
to justify my criticism. When the election committee first met
they duly chose the Master of St. Catherine's (than whom no
better could have been chosen); he would have been Vice-
Chancellor under the old plan, for he was next in succession.
Had no change been made the Head of one of the Women's
Colleges would have been next in order for 1971, but after the
four years she was no longer eligible. The Committee chose

the Principal of Jesus to take office in 1973, and again that is what would have happened under the old rules. On the only two occasions on which the electoral committee has acted it has made the appointment which would have been made under the old rules. The new procedure may, or may not, have prevented Oxford from having its first woman Vice-Chancellor; apart from that possibility it has not interrupted the orderly succession. Often since 1966 I have regretted that I did not offer to give evidence to the Commission, for, though I do not think that my own advocacy would have had much influence, I do believe that some of the letters and statements of opinion which I had collected in 1957 might have led them, at least, to modify some of the changes which they made.

In 1957 the most zealous researcher, even if a good classical scholar (for a great part of the Statuta was in Latin), might have searched long and unavailingly to discover what powers the Vice-Chancellor possessed and what his duties were. The government of the University was legislative rather than administrative. The true governing body was Congregation, or in some cases Convocation, and decrees and statutes were brought by Council to Congregation. The Vice-Chancellor, though the effective Head of the University and its representative to the outside world, exercised his influence over its internal affairs indirectly, and was powerful mainly because he was Chairman of all the many boards and committees, of which Council was the chief. Next in importance to Council came the Chest, which dealt with questions of finance, the General Board, concerned with teaching, and a new body, the Building and Developments Committee, which had been the invention of Alic Smith and which in 1957 was becoming daily of more importance.

From another point of view the Vice-Chancellor could well be compared to a minister taking over a department and finding a body of experienced officials waiting to help him on his way. The Registrar was the linchpin of the whole organization, though this was a comparatively modern innovation. When I was an undergraduate Leudesdorf[6] the Registrar wrote all his letters in his own hand; there was not, I have been told, a typewriter in the Registry and his staff was minute. Things were

6 C. Leudesdorf, Fellow of Pembroke College.

very different in the days of Douglas Veale. Of all the men whom I have met in a long life spent in many different milieux Douglas Veale had the greatest administrative talent. There were murmurs in some quarters that his influence was too great—the current phrase was to speak of the Registry as the Hotel de Ville and the centre of power, but such criticisms were unjustified, for Douglas, in addition to his mastery of administration method and practice, also possessed the most prized virtue of the civil servant. Let me illustrate my meaning. Council met always on Mondays at two and on Monday mornings the Vice-Chancellor and the Registrar would spend about a couple of hours or more in going through the Agenda together. This briefing was essential if Council was to work efficiently and without undue waste of time. On important and contentious issues we hardly ever differed, but occasional disagreement was inevitable. When this occurred and the subject was discussed in Council I think that no member could possibly have guessed from word or gesture that the Registrar was not whole-heartedly in support of the Vice-Chancellor. A minister must be happy indeed if his permanent secretary supports him with equal help and loyalty.

I felt it as a great misfortune that Veale had to retire under the age limit at the end of my first year in office and I felt, too, that the choice of his successor was by far the most important appointment in which I must take a major part. My experience during the war, my time as Chairman of the Committee on the Political Activities of Civil Servants together with my observation of Veale's methods convinced me that the new Registrar must be chosen from the Civil Service, and it so fell out. Folliott Sandford came from the same stable and had the same virtues as his predecessor, so that I could, in my last Vice-Chancellor's speech, praise both with complete sincerity:

> This is the English, not the Turkish court;
> Not Amurath an Amurath succeeds
> But Harry, Harry.

The names were not quite appropriate but the sentiment was just. When in due course T. H. Aston's history of the University appears I have little doubt that Veale and Sandford will be recognized as among the chief architects of modern Oxford, but even then few will know how much they did to ease my own journey as Vice-Chancellor.

When I assumed office I had no high-faluting ideas about a programme of reform or any new development for the University. For such things I was far too conventional and conservative-minded. If I had been called upon to state what my policy was I think that I should have answered that I hoped to keep the University on an even keel and, during all the necessary changes, to retain the better part of the traditions of the past. I had often thought that Wellington ought to be numbered among the best of our Prime Ministers because he had made his over-mastering task to see that the King's Government should be carried on without disruption; change must come, but only after the need for it had been clearly proved. That opinion of Wellington I still hold today.

Yet this modest and perhaps humdrum policy still gave me much to do and was no easy task. The day-to-day business of the University was considerable and, when I took over, many matters were at a rather critical stage. For example the quinquennial grant which covered the years 1957–62 had, to the indignation of the University, been severely pruned, whilst the University Grants Committee, for its part, considered that it had been most unjustly accused of discriminating against Oxford and was incensed by the Oxford criticisms. It was the duty of the Vice-Chancellor, so it seemed to me, to placate the Committee without abandoning the case of the University. In other spheres, too, great projects had reached or were approaching fulfilment, for it was a time when Oxford was both expanding and refurbishing her ancient buildings.

Most notable of all the improvements was the creation and success of the Historic Buildings Fund. An appeal was launched in June 1957 to raise one and three-quarter million pounds to restore the ancient buildings, and its success was due primarily to the work of the trustees, of whom Edward Bridges was the chief. In America Oliver Franks was equally tireless and equally successful. In just over a year Edward Bridges wrote to me to tell me triumphantly that the target had been reached. But then I had a lesson which I have never forgotten. Lord Heyworth sent me a lecture on advertising which he had just delivered, in which the first sentence informed his listeners or

readers that in the year 1957 Unilever spent on advertising
£83,000,000! Our efforts, which had seemed to me prodigious,
now appeared to be only a puny affair. Unilever, I thought
bitterly, could have reconditioned all our historic buildings and
still spent £80,000,000 on advertising. All my sense of values
was upset. In spite of this the Historic Buildings Appeal was a
great start for a renewed and forward-looking Oxford. A little
later when it was seen that our target had been set too low we
asked for, and obtained, another three-quarters of a million. The
Appeal for the Historic Buildings fell entirely within my Vice-
Chancellorship and I felt legitimate pride in its success, but it
should be remembered that the original proposal for the appeal
came from the fertile brain of Alic Smith. It was without doubt
the happiest of his ideas and I like to think that he will be
remembered for it when other less fortunate of his projects have
been long forgotten.

Once a year the Vice-Chancellor makes an Oration which
together with the Report for the year is published in the
Gazette. It is his one opportunity of making his policy clear to
the University—of describing what he has done, or left undone,
in the past and what he hopes to do in the future. I make no
apology, therefore, for drawing freely on my two orations to
describe what, to my mind, was the central issue of the years
1957 and 1958. It was, in short, the maintenance of the college
system in the face of inevitable expansion of numbers and the
provision of new buildings and new amenities to meet the needs
of an increased University population. In 1957 I spoke of the
problem of accommodation for undergraduates as the most
urgent which had to be faced. In 1955 all the universities were
asked about the policy to be adopted in relation to the expected
increase in the number of applicants—an increase to be swollen
by the ending of national service. The need for an increased
proportional number of scientists was stressed at the same time.
The Colleges were asked whether and to what extent they would
be able and willing to increase their numbers, and their replies
showed that, for the most part, they were not prepared for very
much expansion. None the less the figure for those matriculated
steadily rose, and it appeared that a permanent increase of
about 10 per cent since 1954 had been generally accepted. It
was said that the increase of 718 for the year 1957–8 was to be

a temporary expedient, but experience has shown that when there has been an expansion to meet an emergency there is very seldom a later contraction to the original size. I went on to say that expansion of numbers and accommodation in colleges must go hand in hand. 'It is easy to see that the interests of any individual college imperatively demand that it should not permanently expand beyond its optimum number, for its teaching staff, its accommodation in college rooms, its domestic and administrative arrangements, and indeed its whole ethos are adapted to a society of a certain size. This is the College interest. It is not so generally realized or admitted that it is also clean contrary to the *national* interest for the Colleges largely to increase their numbers. If the college system has the merits which most of us ascribe to it, it is because it provides a way and manner of life which is built upon residence for a large part of an undergraduate's life in college rooms. In other words accommodation is the core and centre of the problem, for we should not increase college numbers without increased college accommodation ... If we are both to maintain the college system and provide for our due proportion of the enlarged University population, we must, we simply must, have the new College—and we are entitled to hope for generous government assistance in that project.'

In 1958, in my second and last oration I returned to the same theme. I pointed out that the Historic Building Appeal had been strikingly successful and that the new college—now to be called St. Catherine's—had ceased to be a project and had begun to take shape. Furthermore the new Engineering and Metallurgy building had been started on the Keble Road Triangle and the Manor Road site allotted to the Law Library, the Institute of Statistics, and the English Faculty Library. All this development was to be welcomed, but it did not remove the danger of over-great numbers. There had been a little over 7,000 in 1954 and an estimated 8,700 in the year 1958–9. In this fear of over-crowding I was not alone. The Vice-Chancellor of Cambridge was reported in *The Times* as saying: 'Time will show how well we can resist the creeping inflation of numbers which would be fatal to our system if it could not be controlled.' So I wrote: 'The real danger of this creeping inflation is ... that it is a threat to the College system as well as to University standards. The accommodation of undergraduates—and also of graduate students—for a large part of their University life within the walls of their college; the tutorial system; above all the mingling of men from different faculties in College life are the essential things . . . I have often quoted, and I hope I shall often quote again, what I think to be the central sentence in Newman's *Idea of a University*: "A University is an *alma mater*, knowing her children one by one, not a foundry, nor a mint, nor a treadmill. It is not and should not be an institution for instructing masses, or a factory for mass instruction."' And so to my conclusion: 'Does not reason suggest that, just as it is preferable to build new colleges rather than to overfill existing colleges, so it is better to build and develop new universities rather than to expand the old beyond their capacity?' The first need of a college is that its members should be carefully selected and that those chosen should be those who can best benefit from university life. No doubt the modern critic would snort that this is élitism and that all, however unworthy, should be treated alike. If indeed élitism means the selection of the best, then I am an unrepentant élitist. Today the area of conflict about admissions has changed and concerns itself with the problem whether women should be admitted to the men's colleges. On such a question the opinion of the elderly is of little importance, but I have no doubt in my own mind how I should vote on that issue. I think that for the purposes of learning men and women are better placed in their own separate colleges; I think that the proportion of women to men in the University is too low; and I think that the right answer is the establishment of another, and large, women's college. What an opportunity for some great new benefactor! But it is sadly true that childless and public-spirited multimillionaires are in very short supply.

With too great optimism I had hoped, and almost expected, to make a practical contribution towards the solution of the problem of accommodation, but in this I failed and failed completely. My proposal was to obtain financial aid for the individual colleges by including their building projects in the University claim for grants from the U.G.C. Colleges were providing extra accommodation to meet the national need for more places—why should they not receive government assistance to that end? The paper work connected with such a plan is enormous—returns to questionnaires and statistics from all the colleges, negotiations with competing claimants for grants, minutes of meetings of committees to discuss alternative methods of financing college building—and I suppose that University archives and those of government offices are cluttered with papers dealing with similar and equally unsuccessful projects. For my plan foundered. After I had ceased to be Vice-Chancellor but was still on Council the Buildings and Development Committee reported that it did not feel able to recommend an application to the U.G.C. for money for the purpose of college buildings and this refusal was endorsed by Council after a reasonable and well-argued debate. In this I took the line that since residence in College was an essential feature of Oxford life the scheme was more important than some of the other schemes which formed part of our programme for the next decade.

I have sometimes thought that my failure to carry this plan through was due to my success in shortening the period of the Vice-Chancellorship, for I was no longer Chairman of the Building and Development Committee or of Council when the crunch came.

19. J.C.M., aged 61, from the portrait by Edward Halliday
in Worcester College Hall

20. The Provost's Lodgings, Worcester College, from the painting by
L. L. Toynbee

21. Committee on Political Activities of Civil Servants, 1948. Reading
from left to right: F. C. Newton (Secretary), J.C.M., Sir Richard Hopkins,
William Cash, Sir Ronald Adam, D. N. Chester (later Sir Norman),
Sir Edward Cadogan, Dame Myra Curtis, H. Graham White. (Absent:
Sir John Stephenson and Sir Miles Mitchell.)

22. Censors of Christ Church: R. H. Dundas and J.C.M. about 1924

23. J.C.M. and Quelch in the Provost's garden

24. Provost and Vice-Provost: J.C.M. with C. H. Wilkinson, 1959

26. Harry Truman and J.C.M. at All Souls luncheon, Encaenia 1956

25. Part of the Encaenia procession, 1958. In front, Lord Beveridge, Harold Macmillan, Sir Owen Dixon and Hugh Gaitskell. The other Honorands were Sir Alan Herbert, Francis Poulenc, Dmitry Shostakovich and Professor Tiselius

27. Vice-Chancellor and Proctors on their way to Council

XXVIII

LATER YEARS AS PROVOST (Contd.)

I was then retired, much against my will, on grounds of senility,
having passed the age of 65.

STEPHEN LEACOCK: *The boy I left behind me*

Not least in importance among the Vice-Chancellor's
duties was his chairmanship of boards of electors to Professorships and Readerships. On these boards there are, besides
the Vice-Chancellor, six members nominated by various outside bodies, such as Council, the appropriate faculty, and the
college to which the appointee is attached. With strange and
irritating frequency these boards after eliminating all but two
candidates divided equally and the Vice-Chancellor's vote
therefore decided the issue. I developed a technique for dealing
with what was a really ticklish situation. So far as possible I
would not betray by any remark or hint to whom my opinion
inclined. Then when the almost inevitable 'three against three'
vote was taken I would address the Board in some such words
as these: 'After what has been said of the merits of these two it
appears to me that we must have a choice between two eminently, perhaps superlatively, good candidates. It is sad that we
cannot have both. I am naturally unhappy that I must decide
between them but I feel sure that, in the circumstances, both
sides will agree that, whichever way I vote we shall have an
excellent professor and that all will then wish to make the choice
unanimous.' As no one knew which side I was on the electors
usually hastened to express their agreement and I then found
some small fact to justify my vote—slight seniority, or more
experience of Oxford, or rather more published work.

Regius appointments were a different matter, for in their
case appointment is in the hands of the Prime Minister.
Naturally enough he consults the Chancellor, and the Chancellor in his turn consults the Vice-Chancellor, while the patronage secretary makes exhaustive inquiries amongst all the

interested parties. During my term of office two Regius Professorships fell vacant, Modern History and Divinity, and in neither case did the appointment coincide with the majority expectations of Oxford opinion. In the case of Modern History I was in an unusually delicate position since the candidate chosen, Hugh Trevor-Roper, had been my pupil at Christ Church, but on re-reading the papers, my conscience is clear. To one question from the Prime Minister to the Chancellor, and from him to me, I returned a clear answer. In this I said that I thought the office so important that it ought not to be held in plurality with the headship of a college—a choice by the person concerned must be made. From Hugh I had a long and impassioned letter urging me to use what influence I had to bring about the appointment of another person (who in the event would not let his name be considered). The Divinity Chair went to Henry Chadwick, now Dean of Christ Church, and no one, I think, would now contend that the Prime Minister had not recommended to H.M. the most fitting person to hold it. In both these cases I was impressed—I had almost said 'astounded'—by the care and trouble which were taken over them. Every person whose views were of value was consulted, and every reasonable opinion weighed and considered. This was a different procedure to that of even the most conscientious committee. No doubt appointment by the Crown is an anachronism, but it works. I must go on record in saying that, by and large, Regius appointments in my time were always as good and sometimes better than those made by a more democratic method.

Episodes like the appointment of a Regius Professor underlined the fact that, in the proper hands, the Chancellorship was by no means merely an ornamental office. On the contrary, especially when difficulty occurred with outside bodies of importance, the influence and help of the Chancellor could be of the greatest value. Of previous Chancellors some had treated the office as purely honorific whilst others were thought to have interfered too much. Salisbury in thirty-three years never came to the Encaenia and Curzon, though often accused of a wish to reform everything, attended only twice in his eighteen years. Edward Halifax, who to my mind was the perfect Chancellor, worked towards a compromise whereby he attended once in every two or three years. He always wished a Vice-Chancellor to have at least one Encaenia for himself. Much has been written of Edward Halifax, but, as is usually the case with national figures, the personal and intimate picture is often blurred, though it is the small incidents that most clearly show the nature of the man. So I write of him as I knew him. First of all he enjoyed a party and he liked seeing others enjoying themselves. Early in our acquaintanceship he told me with consummate tact to use his Christian name. 'I remember', he said, 'my own embarrassment when a Duke (I think the Duke of Devonshire) called me Edward and I did not know how I ought to respond.' His sense of duty was remarkable. Once, shortly after the war, we had both attended a Provost and Fellows meeting at Eton and were coming on to Oxford by train. He had had a long and tiring day and there was a long evening ahead of him so we agreed that he should put his feet up and have a sleep in the train. But on Slough platform there stood an American middle-aged couple, who advanced to tender him their good wishes. He had, as he told me later, met them only once but his response was immediate; he insisted that they should share our carriage and talked to them with animation all the way to Oxford. Much as he disliked the whole operation he consented at once to come to a luncheon which I gave in All Souls to the Heads of Houses in order that photographs might be taken by *Life* for an article which would encourage supporters of the Appeal for the Historic Buildings. When he presided at the Encaenia in 1957 I felt anxious for him about the long walk in procession from Worcester to the Sheldonian and suggested that he should go by car and form the procession in Bodley's quadrangle. 'Certainly not; that would be a confession of weakness', was his reply. As a compromise he agreed that he would halt for a short rest halfway when we reached the Martyrs' Memorial—an arrangement which caused a good deal of perturbation to those at the tail of the procession who thought, not unnaturally, that some horrid accident or misadventure had befallen someone in front. At the beginning of winter in 1957 I was obliged, unexpectedly, to have an operation and arranged to miss the last week of term and return to duty on 1 January. The operation itself was entirely successful but unfortunately complications occurred. The brief medical summary, given to me years later, runs as follows: 'You had a deep vein thrombosis in your leg with pulmonary embolism, after your prostatectomy in 1957.' I knew little of this at the time nor did I know that I was for some days very much on the danger list, but it was clear that I could not return to work at the time expected and I felt it my duty to offer my resignation to the Chancellor. His reply to my letter was characteristic, full of warmth and common sense. I was not to worry but set my mind completely at rest for 'it must be a very moderate show that cannot get along, if necessary, for a period without the day-to-day supervision of its executive head'. Of course, he was right. Maurice Bowra, my predecessor, and Tom Boase, my successor, undertook my work without a murmur and I very much doubt whether Oxford, as a whole, even knew that the Vice-Chancellor was *hors de combat*.

One incident during my illness has stuck in my mind. For the last three years of her life my mother had lived in the house of Mrs. Rashdall, the widow of Hastings Rashdall and sister of General Sir Ernest Makins. For her brother Mrs. Rashdall had the most profound respect; what he said was of necessity true and from his judgement no appeal could be made. She was distressed at my illness but was herself too unwell to pay me a visit in hospital and therefore sent her housekeeper to convey to me her condolences. I was too ill to understand easily what the latter said, but her last remark had been committed to paper and she delivered it with care. 'Mrs. Rashdall instructed me to say that the General always said that, if someone was really unwell, there was nothing like this to effect a cure.' When I became fully conscious I found a fat bottle of Benedictine by my bedside.

Writing of the Chancellor brings to mind the awarding of Honorary Degrees, particularly those given at Encaenia. On no other matter is Council more sensitive or more difficult to lead and this is as it should be. There are always those on Council who believe that degrees should only be conferred for academic reasons, there are others who favour rewarding benefactors but who reject the claims of public men, others again who wish to mark service to the State but who shrink from the danger of showing political bias. All, however, were united in one belief— that any interference or attempted influence from outside is intolerable and damns for ever the unfortunate person for whom the influence has been exerted. I came to the conclusion that no one in Council could be sure that any individual, however eminent, would be chosen, but that anyone could be quite certain, if he put his mind to it, that any individual would be rejected.

The day of Encaenia is a long and busy day for the Vice-Chancellor. It begins at his College at 11.15 with Lord Crewe's benefaction—champagne and peaches or strawberries—after which the Honorands and the Doctors proceed in procession to the Sheldonian. Here each Honorand is presented in a Latin speech by the Public Orator, and (if the Chancellor is absent) the Vice-Chancellor admits them with a few appropriate sentences also in Latin. My typed copy for these short speeches lies before me as I write; my pronunciation was that used in my preparatory school in 1900 but I did at least safeguard myself against false quantities for on almost every vowel I have marked a long or a short symbol. After the Honorands had been admitted extracts from the prize-winning compositions were recited and the Creweian Oration 'in commemoration of benefactors' delivered, in alternate years by the Public Orator or the Professor of Poetry. The Procession then left the Theatre and the invited guests moved on to the All Souls luncheon, which ended just in time for the Vice-Chancellor to return to his College to greet his guests at the Vice-Chancellarian Garden Party. That concluded, it was time to dress and proceed to Christ Church for the Gaudy—a happy and most enjoyable festival to which the Honorands were always invited. Since it was primarily the House Gaudy the Honorands played a secondary role, but the double celebration necessitated a full ration of speeches, followed by talk and reminiscence with many old friends. I calculated that the Vice-Chancellor was fortunate if his time on parade (if that is the right expression) was much under fourteen hours.

The only Encaenia at which I presided was in 1958 and I was singularly fortunate in my list of Honorands. It was not wholly accidental (and certainly it had caused discussion in Council) that Harold Macmillan, the Prime Minister, and Hugh Gaitskell, Leader of the Opposition, should come together. The other D.C.L.s were Beveridge, whose claims were over-

300 LATER YEARS AS PROVOST

whelming, Sir Owen Dixon, Chief Justice of Australia, and Alan Herbert, who, over and above his literary eminence, had been University Burgess for fourteen years. Poulenc and Shostakovich became Doctors of Music and Tiselius, Nobel prize-winner and biochemist, a Doctor of Science. It had been hoped that Picasso would have accepted the invitation extended to him but, predictably, after some havering, he refused. Each Honorand, after being admitted by the Vice-Chancellor, took his seat in the front row of the semicircle, going alternately to the right and left. Macmillan came first, Beveridge second, and Gaitskell third. After I had addressed the last-named as 'Vir potentibus adversando fortissime', I whispered to him, 'On this one occasion please place yourself on the right.' There were no loud-speakers then to carry my words to the audience. At the Christ Church Gaudy that night even the Prime Minister, notable orator though he was, could not steal the palm from Alan Herbert, whose speech was entirely in verse, a medium of which he was an acknowledged master.

The award of degrees not at the Encaenia gave the Vice-Chancellor somewhat more scope for exercising influence and one award give me especial personal pleasure. It was the conferring of the degree of D.Litt. on Dr. Surendra Sen. In this case the fairy godfather in the story was Richard Ramsbotham, a Magdalen man who had at one time taught me history at Dartmouth, and had later spent many years teaching in the East. Dr. Sen, as he told me, had come up to Oxford as a noncollegiate student and there had had his thesis for a B.Litt. turned down by the examiners. There may have been some technical hitch—I do not know—if not there must have been a clear miscarriage of justice, for Sen, even then, must have known a great deal more about his subject than did his examiners. He showed no bitterness and continued his work as a historian. In January 1955 he was commissioned by the Indian Government to write an objective history of the Mutiny which should be published in May 1957, the centenary of the outbreak. His book *Eighteen fifty-seven* is a remarkable achievement, remarkable both for its objectivity and for the evidence of the patient research of a historian's lifetime. Council acceded to my plea and Dr. Sen came to Oxford to receive the degree, though his health was failing fast. At lunch, before the ceremony,

I really feared that he would not live throughout the day. But he did and Ramsbotham wrote to me to say that 'his degree has given him the most supreme happiness'. Later came a letter to me from another source from which I quote. 'His [Sen's] achievement at Oxford has given the educated classes in Bengal great satisfaction and sense of pride. The press flashed the news and recalled that the only other Bengali Hon. D.Litt. was Rabindranath Tagore.'

It was the duty of the Vice-Chancellor to attend a number of lectures, as for example the inaugural lectures of Professors. This was not always a sinecure, for the Vice-Chancellor sat alone in front of the lecturer who at the end must raise his cap, and to whom the Vice-Chancellor in his turn would return the salutation. This was a danger moment for, if the lecture was dull or difficult of apprehension, the Vice-Chancellor might well be asleep. The 'inaugural' which I best remember was delivered by Edgar Wind, the first Professor of the History of Art. He used no notes, he never paused for a word, each sentence was perfectly composed and expressed, he spoke for an hour without losing the attention of any hearer—a true *tour de force*. More memorable, and alas! as sad as it was memorable, was the last lecture of Ronnie Knox. He had accepted the invitation to give the Romanes Lecture in 1957, but he was in failing health and it was known that his life was nearing its end. His doctors and friends urged him to abandon the task, but he was adamant in his determination to go through with it. He came to stay with me at the Lodgings at Worcester for a couple of nights in order that his energies be spared as much as possible. Always one of Oxford's favourite sons, half of the University seemed anxious to meet him and I was obliged to ration with the utmost strictness both the numbers of his visitors and the time which they could spend with him. At the lecture itself in the Sheldonian the delivery was, I thought, disappointing for the first part but brilliant towards the end. Of this I was not surprised for he had confided in me beforehand that he had forgotten to take what he called 'his pep pill' until an hour later than the appointed time. I think that it gave him great satisfaction that he had been able to give the lecture. He left the next morning to spend a day and a night with Harold Macmillan at 10 Downing Street and the Prime Minister accompanied him to the station for his return journey. When he had been settled in to a carriage and provided with books and papers the Prime Minister said 'Now I hope you are comfortable for your journey', and Ronnie, who knew that he was dying replied, 'It's a very long journey that I am making.' Most of us have had that sort of remark made to us and most of us have returned the usual hollow and fumbling reply. But Harold Macmillan was above that sort of artificiality, and his response came without hesitation: 'And no one, Ronnie, is better equipped for it than you.'

A small piece of patronage which was in the Vice-Chancellor's hands was the appointment of the preacher for the Assize Sermon. The Judge of Assize always attended a service at St. Mary's and the trumpets were blown as he left to start the Assizes. As timing had to be strictly accurate the sermon had to be completed in seven minutes and the fee, considering the shortness of the sermon, was generous. It was my custom to look quickly through the list of college chaplains who had not done duty before and choose one to invite and on one occasion I found that a quite senior chaplain had been previously overlooked. I asked him, he accepted, and I awaited the usual seven minutes of platitudinous praise of the virtue of tempering justice with mercy. Not so. Instead we had a fierce denunciation of those who would exempt the poisoner from the capital sentence, though poisoning was the most cruel and evil of crimes. As we proceeded down the aisle I wondered what the Judge would think of this, but I need not have been anxious. When we were only half-way down the aisle his voice boomed out—'The best assize sermon I've ever heard.' It was not until later that I learned that the preacher had been at one time a prison chaplain.

The official formalities and the social life of the Vice-Chancellor did not present so many difficulties as I had expected, nor was I unduly concerned by fear of making gaffes or falling into embarrassing situations. After all, young officials, new Proctors, or the like could be reminded of mishaps in the past, such, for example, as the occasion on which the Vice-Chancellor who, holding his 'square' or mortar-board in one hand, and intending to touch with a Bible the head of each newly admitted Master, succeeded only in balancing the Bible on his head and touching the kneeling supplicants with his cap.

Or again I could recall the first occasion when women received degrees and when some of the women from one college fell in with those of another college who preceded them. A plaintive cry or wail from the Dean of the first college was clearly audible —'She's got my girls.' Such mistakes appear at the time to the perpetrators as calamitous, but how much they add to the maximation of human happiness! Personally I felt no worry about ceremonial or fear of exposing myself to ridicule—with one notable exception—I could never rid myself of nervousness if I had to speak in Latin, especially if some unusual formula such as an incorporation from Trinity College, Dublin, had to be used.

The spate of dinners and lunches and the incessant speeches to every kind of audience were only one of the occupational hazards of my position and could be taken in the stride; but I did try, however unsuccessfully, never to make a speech without saying one thing which I felt to be worth saying. Sometimes I think that the shortest speech which I made was the best. Adlai Stevenson, after receiving the Honorary D.C.L., was made an honorary Fellow of my College. What could I say to such a man at such a time which had not been said a hundred times before? After much thought I simply greeted him in two sentences and then recited six lines from Rochester.

> Fame is not grounded on success
> Though victories were Caesar's glory
> Lost battles made not Pompey less
> But left him styled great in story.
> Malicious fate doth oft devise
> To beat the brave and fool the wise.

That was all—but it was enough.

From the Franks Report of 1966 I have culled two wise and pertinent judgements. The first is this: 'The most important services of a Vice-Chancellor, in brief, appear to be those of holding the University together and of giving its mind clear expression', and the second this: 'In addition, we think it an important duty of the Vice-Chancellor to keep in continuous touch with what is thought and felt about Oxford beyond the confines of the University.' I had reason to appreciate the rightness of both those judgements, even before I actually assumed office. In the spring of 1956 I was presiding at Convocation, in the absence of Alic Smith, when approval was to be given to those receiving honorary degrees at Encaenia. Normally this would have been a formality, but we had received notice that opposition would be offered to Harry Truman, and the Vice-Chancellor had decided in advance that, should it appear likely that the opposition would prevail, Convocation must be adjourned before a vote was taken. After I had looked over the House I felt certain that Council's proposals would be carried but I was keenly anxious that as little mud as possible should be stirred up, and I felt incensed when a woman member made an intemperate speech in which she described the ex-President as a butcher. I meditated vacating the Chair and speaking but thought it better to refrain and the moment came when I could put the motion to the House in the time-honoured formula, 'Placetne vobis, Domini Doctores, placetne vobis magistri?' Then came a stroke of good fortune. Had those in opposition, or a large number of them, shouted, 'Non', I should have been morally obliged to pronounce the words, 'Fiat scrutinium', and the Proctors would then have pricked the votes on the papers which they held. But luckily there were no shouts; either the opponents thought that verbal criticism was enough or (and, I fear that this was much more likely) they were un-versed in our procedure and missed their opportunity. So the decree was passed unanimously and much harm prevented. Had we been obliged to take a vote the Press would, quite properly, have seized on the incident and an act of discourtesy to an honoured guest of the University would have been perpetrated.

The degree when Encaenia came gave the greatest pleasure, especially to the recipient. I was talking to him in the quad-rangle of All Souls after luncheon and he was expressing his appreciation in terms which seemed to me exaggerated, or almost fulsome. It was the greatest honour ever done to him, the honour he appreciated above all others and so forth. I think that I responded rather coolly, and this he was quick to notice. 'You don't quite understand,' he said. 'When I was President I could have anything I wanted because people knew that I had every kind of thing that I could give them, but you have given me this degree when you know quite well that I can never give you anything in return. I think that means that you want to honour me, and that's why I appreciate it so much.'

A second case, which might have been more serious, occurred in the following year. The Vice-Chancellors' Committee had decided, unanimously that all the British universities should protest to South Africa about the proposal to enforce segregation on the universities. At the Committee when the document was discussed we learned that the South African Government had withdrawn the bill for minor amendments but that it was understood that no change of substance would be made. I held the view that, though it was highly unlikely that the bill would be much changed, it was at least possible that it might be and that our protest should not be sent until the amended bill was actually in print. I therefore refused to sign though, if my recollection is correct, Appleton of Edinburgh was the only other Vice-Chancellor who took the same line. Naturally when the protest was published, and Oxford was seen not to have signed with the rest, the fat was in the fire. A deputation came to me for explanation and to ask if Council could send a special letter to the South African universities, approved by Convocation, assuring them of our support for the objections which they were making to Government. I replied that I was in entire agreement and would, if need be, speak in favour at Convocation. I hope that it is not hubristic to say that more than one South African told me that Oxford's letter was as much appreciated and gave university opinion as much support as the letter from all the other British universities.

Keeping in touch with those in other universities and with university thought was made easy by two institutions. There was a fixed arrangement (which made one feel that Oxbridge or Camford was a reality) whereby one University visited the other each term. A deputation consisting of the Vice-Chancellor, the Registrar, the Secretary of the Chest, the Secretary of Faculties, and two or three members of Council would go over to Cambridge for the day and discuss matters of concern to both Universities, such as the salaries of professors and lecturers, the rating of college property, or the numbers desirable for admission. In my first year my opposite number was B. W. Downs, the Master of Christ's College, and in my second Adrian of Trinity. Sometimes strange and exotic cases would arise, as for example when the editor of the *Church of England Newspaper* asked that the ancient privilege of the two Universities to give licences to preach in the Provinces of Canterbury and York might be revived in his favour. The Archbishops had in the past been unwilling for this privilege, which had not been used for 250 years, to be revived, but after long-drawn-out negotiations both Universities determined to retain the privilege and Mr. Rhodes received his licence.

Of more consequence than the Cambridge meetings were those of the Vice-Chancellors' Committee which met in London once a month. It was thought by some that this Committee was jealous of Oxford and Cambridge, but I did not find it so. In fact these two Universities together with London were represented by two men instead of one, and, apart from the elected Chairman, the Registrar of Oxford, the Registrary of Cambridge, and the Principal (though not Vice-Chancellor) of London probably carried as much weight, even though they did not vote, as any member of the Committee. In those days the Committee was of a manageable size and worked efficiently; now that the number of universities has greatly increased I surmise that its work is more difficult—but of this I have no knowledge.

I learned much from these meetings as I did from the many visitors to Oxford from overseas, but I learned much more from a visit to America in 1958 for the Commonwealth Universities' Congress. The first Congress of Universities of the British Empire had been held in London in 1912; since then the sequence was interrupted by two world wars, but otherwise the Congress had become a quinquennial event. The 1958 Congress was the eighth in the series but it was the first to be held outside the United Kingdom. It was, therefore, something of a historic event—the more so because the Association of American Universities sent no less than twenty-four Presidents to Toronto and Montreal and because the A.U.B.C.[1] also invited representatives from Eire, Rangoon, Brussels, Dijon, Istanbul, Hiroshima, Leyden, Hamburg, and Milan. From the members of the A.U.B.C. itself there were delegations from places as far apart as Aberdeen and Ceylon or Tasmania and

[1] Associated Universities of the British Commonwealth, now the Association of Commonwealth Universities.

British Columbia. From India came fourteen Vice-Chancellors and from Pakistan five. The Oxford delegation consisted of Dean Lowe, Sir Howard Florey, the Principal of L.M.H.,[2] Sir Douglas Veale, and myself. In a word the Congress was representative of most of the world outside the Iron Curtain and its importance was recognized by the fact that it was opened by Vincent Massey, the Governor-General (who also entertained the visitors at Quebec), and that President Eisenhower returned to Washington for the express purpose of entertaining the Heads of Universities at the White House.

The arrangements, which had been started already in 1955, were admirable. The main Congress at Montreal was preceded by a series of meetings of the executive heads of the participating universities at Toronto (respectfully referred to at Montreal as the 'summit conference'), where about a hundred heads were present. At the end of the main conference we were taken by special train to visit Washington and Philadelphia, after which we were divided in groups to visit other universities in Canada and the U.S.A. As I was to visit Halifax I was attached to parts of two different tours, and had further the great privilege of being the guest of the State Department for ten days or so after the tours ended. Having opted for sea rather than air travel I left England in the middle of August in the *Empress of India*, a voyage made unusually agreeable by the company of the Adrians and the Mansfield Coopers of Manchester, and returned in the *Queen Elizabeth*, which reached Southampton on the last day of September, and in which I found, in spite of the luxury and comfort, that the company was manifestly less attractive than that in the *Empress*. So I had had seven weeks which had been not only enjoyable but in the highest degree instructive and beneficial.

Most congresses are alike—that is to say that the formal meetings are often disappointing but that the informal talks and the personal contacts are beyond price. I ended with a new appreciation of the merits, the problems, and the difficulties of universities all over the world. Probably the most interesting discussion was the so-called free session where among other things the problem of South African universities, and their attitude towards apartheid, was discussed freely but without rancour.

[2] Dame Lucy Sutherland.

Two honorary degrees were conferred on me—an LL.D. at Toronto and a D.C.L. at the University of King's College, and at both of them it fell to my lot to make the speech of thanks on behalf of the Honorands. It need hardly be said that neither the degrees nor the choice of orator had anything to do with my own merits but were simply a tribute to Oxford. On the evening before the ceremony at Toronto a number of us were talking after dinner and someone remarked 'I wonder who is to make the speech of thanks tomorrow?' An immediate answer came from an experienced American academic: 'You need not speculate—in this continent they always invite the man who least deserves the honour because he will be the one most grateful for it.' As I had toiled for some weeks to compose my speech I was not sorry to change the conversation. The speech was a statement of what I felt about universities—of the need for selection and the danger of excessive numbers, which could lead to depersonalization and a uniform mediocrity, and of the need to encourage a worthy social and cultural milieu. The occasion was suitable for what I had to say for President Bissell[3] had only recently succeeded Dr. Sidney Smith[4] in his office and Dr. Smith had, in his Presidential Report of 1957, inveighed against 'computer-populated lecture factories' and stated his conviction that universities should not be demoted to become institutions for instructing masses. In the course of my speech I committed a blunder which even now I cannot explain or excuse. Wishing to refer to the Canadian ex-President of Toronto I quoted four well-known lines of verse:

We are the chosen few,
All others will be damned.
There is no room in Heaven for you,
We can't have Heaven crammed.

and attributed them to Dr. Sidney Smith. What could have been more apposite or more fitted to the occasion? Not till a long time afterwards did I realize that the author of the lines was not Sydney Smith but Swift. No one then or later drew my attention to my blunder and I am left wondering whether this omission was due to transatlantic tact or only to ignorance,

[3] Claude T. Bissell, President of Toronto University 1958–71.
[4] Sidney E. Smith, President of Toronto University 1945–57.

but I shudder to think what my feelings would have been had any one of the hundred Vice-Chancellors present aired his literary knowledge by exposing me. Would anyone believe, in the circumstances that I had not done it on purpose? Perhaps some few liberal-minded spirits might have done so. Once when Alington was Headmaster of Shrewsbury a very junior master forgot twice running to attend a meeting *à deux* for which he had himself especially asked. When on the third occasion he did reach the Headmaster's study he could only say that he had simply forgotten on the two previous occasions. 'In your schoolmastering career', Alington replied, 'never forget that if a boy comes to you with the most unlikely excuse it *may* be true.' My innocence was genuine but I doubt whether any but a very few would have believed in it.

The degree of Hon. D.C.L. which I received at the University of King's College in Halifax gave me a different but special pleasure. King's College was the oldest university in the Commonwealth and in 1958, I think, probably the smallest. Its origins were interesting, and dated back to the eighteenth century. Bishop Inglis was ousted from Trinity Church, New York, in 1783 because he stoutly refused in those troubled times to stop praying for His Majesty King George III. Six years later he founded King's College at Windsor, whence it migrated to Halifax. The rump, if it may be so described without offence, remained in New York, where King's College, New York, had received its charter in 1754. In 1784 the charter was restored under the name of Columbia University. It added to my pleasure that the then President of Columbia, Dr. Grayson Kirk, was one of my fellow Honorands. What a change after two hundred years! There were, I suppose, almost as many thousands of students at Columbia as there were hundreds at King's College, so I could not with propriety speak of the danger of excessive numbers in universities! I could, however, enlarge on the importance of tradition and extol the merits of a residential university. I could, too, enlarge on my favourite themes—the value of cross-fertilization between those in different faculties and following different disciplines, and the need to produce 'giants' and not only competent but second-class men. The two addresses which I gave—at Toronto and Halifax —represented with clarity what my thinking about universities and university life really was, and after fifteen or more years I do not feel that it has changed.

Thanks to the generous hospitality of the American universities and of the State department I was granted a splendid over-all view of university life. In Canada I saw Toronto, Ottawa, Montreal, McGill, Carleton, Dalhousie, and the University of King's College; in the U.S.A. Harvard, Yale, Princeton, Columbia, Johns Hopkins where I acquired undeserved respect by claiming (as I could fairly do) that I had been at Christ Church a colleague of the great Osler, and Rochester, and stayed for a night or more at nearly all of them. It was a wholly enjoyable but very strenuous time and on two occasions I faltered. One was at Rochester on the last day of my visit there and was, I think, either a Saturday or a Sunday. My host, President de Kiewiet, asked me what I should like to see that day. 'What', I said, 'would you be doing if I was not on your hands?' With rather a wistful smile he answered that he would be playing golf with three of his colleagues. I could not think of a better way to spend the day and walked round the course with them, though I refused their pressing invitation to play myself. However, when we came to a long and devilish hole about the thirteenth or fourteenth they all insisted that I must play one hole during my visit and that this was the hole that had always been Hogan's bugbear. It was not disgraceful that in spite of infinite caution I took six, but I had to hole a very long putt to do so.

The second occasion was in New York towards the end of my stay there. I had had lunch with Dean Rusk on the 55th floor of the Rockefeller Foundation building in order to discuss the Rockefeller benefaction for the Law Library at Oxford; I had rushed round the museums and sights of the city; I had received hospitality on all sides and so I screwed up my courage and telephoned early in the morning to Mrs. Grace Belt, the kindly and almost incredibly efficient official at the Department of State reception centre. 'Could I have a quiet evening—perhaps at my hotel—instead of the dinner which had been planned for me?' 'Leave it all to me,' was the answer. 'I will phone you at lunch-time and tell you what I have arranged.' I spent that evening alone with Thomas Lamont[5] in his apartment, talking

[5] Thomas Lamont of J.P. Morgan, a great benefactor of Harvard.

of Oxford and of books. All Masefield's first editions were there, inscribed by the author and the evening was one of perfect relaxation. No form of hospitality could have been better devised or more appreciated by me.

My visit to America had a curious 'tailpiece', which I cannot forget. Dr. Advani, the Vice-Chancellor of Bombay, with whom I had made friends in Canada, paid me an unexpected visit on his way back to India, and found me at my writing-table in the Lodgings. He asked me upon what I was engaged. 'I'm trying to put together a few words for the freshmen when they arrive next week, and I'm not finding it easy going.'

'But how can you say that? It must be easy for you, for you have everything to offer them—wonderful colleges and beautiful pictures, playing fields, libraries, and laboratories, and learned men to teach them. You have only to speak to them of all these riches and tell them to use them rightly.'

'That is true, but still I find it difficult to find the appropriate words. What do you say to your men in Bombay?' His answer startled me.

'I always quote two passages from the Gospel according to St. John, "Work . . . while it is day: the night cometh when no man can work", and again, "Walk while you have the light, lest darkness come upon you". You see that, compared to you, I have nothing to offer them—nothing at all. How many teachers do you think I have for 40,000 students? All that I can say is that they have freedom to learn and time to study—everything else they must do for themselves.'

There are underdeveloped universities just as there are under-developed countries, and we cannot altogether disclaim responsibility in either case.

XXIX

LAST YEARS AT WORCESTER

A man may be in just possession of truth as of a city and yet be forced to surrender.

SIR T. BROWNE

To my own surprise I was sorry when my Vice-Chancellorship came to an end. Veale, who was Registrar from 1930 till 1958, thought that the Vice-Chancellor's office took up two-thirds of a man's working day and added, using the phraseology of the Civil Service, that the actions of the Vice-Chancellors of his day were 'as good as one would expect from a good minister'. Sandford, also in evidence given to the Franks Commission, regarded the Vice-Chancellorship as a completely full-time job over the next fifteen years. No doubt the work grew steadily year by year, but I think that both of them exaggerated the burden. It is a commonplace to remark that it is the busy man who can best find time to spare and much time was saved by intelligent use of the University car and still more by the efficiency of the Registrars themselves and their staff. Be that as it may I did not find it necessary to cut out any of my essential College duties, though I believe that my example has not been followed since. I always attended College meetings and committees and dealt as before with undergraduates so far as I could. Looking back I can see why I was sorry to give up the Vice-Chancellorship. Gradually whilst I was Provost, and much more speedily after I became Vice-Chancellor, I was gaining in confidence and no longer wished to avoid responsibility or the making of decisions. I began not only to trust my own judgement but also to be ready to act on my own decisions. Naturally lazy (and who is not?), I was compelled to live a very active and sometimes hectic life where one piece of business crowded on another and I found that I enjoyed the pressure. My chief regret was that I had not been Vice-Chancellor earlier—as I should have been under the new rules—so that I could return 'full-time' to the College for a reasonable term of years. I felt too that the University was working smoothly and I was therefore loath to leave an enjoyable if taxing task.

Naturally whilst I was Vice-Chancellor some matters had to go by the board in College. The need to exercise hospitality as Vice-Chancellor and constant official functions meant that hospitality in College had to be severely restricted simply through lack of time and opportunity. In addition, and this seemed to me the chief loss, I was unable to keep the same control or influence (call it which you will) over admissions which I had exercised in the past, and admissions were, as always, the most important factor in College life. The Committee which controlled admissions from 1956 onwards, and which soon led to the appointment of a Tutor for Admissions, worked always with thoroughness and devotion but I take leave to doubt if any such committee can be expected to take the same risks as can the Head of a House with candidates who have not the highest examination results to show. Committees tend to compromise and this tendency is exaggerated when tutors in different faculties are fighting to secure their full quota (but not more) of fresh entries. At Magdalen (and no doubt in other colleges as well) the President used to be given a few free nominations, or 'bisques' as they were sometimes called, and this allowed him to correct a too rigid adherence to examination results. That is private patronage—theoretically anathema and practically what could be described as 'a very good thing'. My old friend Kurt Hahn used to bombard me with harrowing tales of good men but late developers, kept out of colleges because of insufficient examination and paper qualifications. His ace instance was that of a Belgian, on whom his school reported that it strongly advised against his attempting the entrance examination for a university. He was ignorant of this report, went to a university, and ended as a Nobel Prize man.

At this time as in the University so in the College the number and quality of admissions was a burning question, and it was clearly tied up with the problem of adequate accommodation. In my first ten years as Provost the College had achieved a firm and settled shape, based on the assumption, with which there was general agreement, that the numbers should not exceed 240. This number seemed right in relation to our administration

set-up, our accommodation, and our tutorial staff. The actual
numbers of undergraduates and post-graduates who received
tuition were in 1947, 218; in 1948, 228; in 1949, 241; in 1950,
236; in 1951, 229; in 1952, 231; in 1953, 236; in 1954, 234;
in 1955, 227; in 1956, 238. It was after 1956 that the blow
fell and it is hardly necessary to explain once more why it did.
In brief the pressure to expand was impossible to resist. The
'bulge', due partly to the increased birth-rate of the relevant
years, the demand from the Government for more places for
scientists, above all the demand for more university places, all
worked together. The Education Act of 1944 and the Robbins
Committee were united—and properly—in their demand that
all those qualified to come to a university should have the
opportunity of doing so; they should, in my opinion, have
added that of those qualified a third at least would be wiser not
to come. A university education is not a necessary introduction
to life for all, and most unfortunately the insistence upon a
degree for all who can get one is a divisive element in our
society. Too easily it is assumed that the graduate is a superior
being and the 'two nations' division appears in a new form.

   The method of selection for places adds to the trouble. When
three A levels, of good standard, become the sole qualification
for a university place the schools are driven into a system of
cramming and the universities filled, not only with the really
intelligent, but also with the mediocre replete with information
but by no means well educated. For this the blame rests
squarely, not on the schools, but on the universities. The
generality of people are hopelessly misinformed about the
situation and believe that rigid examination standards have led
to a higher standard in intelligence among undergraduates.
Parent after parent has said to me: 'Of course I should never
have been able to get to the University myself nowadays.' That
is just a vulgar error. The intelligent man in the past who wished
to go to the University would have done so because he would have
taken the trouble to pass the examination test imposed on him.
One has not taught in a university for fifty years without knowing that the level of intelligence and of industry does not vary
over the years. The standard of a first class (in those schools or
disciplines in which I am competent to judge) has been maintained, sometimes with some difficulty, but the standard of a

second class has, on the whole, fallen. It was, for example, easier to obtain a second class in 1950 than in 1930. There is a measure of irony too, in observing that attacks on the independent schools and the grammar schools are, in this context, self-defeating. Largely because of the teacher–student ratio, the teaching at these schools is of the best and consequently if examinations only are to be the yard-stick for university entrance these schools will have an advantage over their competitors. Under the old system a college was anxious to attract the best men that it could and ready to seize on any promising man, whatever his examination record might be. There must, of course, be a written examination to show that a man has the necessary qualifications for a university but, when competition for places is keen that examination should not be the sole test, but careful choice should be made amongst those qualified. It is right that the State should spend freely on further education; it is wrong that the tax-payers' money should be spent on sending many to the universities who would gain more if they took a different course. Student grants could well be increased to an acceptable figure if only those who would benefit from a university career were admitted to it.

I must not digress too much but return to Worcester in the late fifties. It was not possible, try as we would, to hold to our maximum of 240. In 1957 the numbers were 254, in 1958 they were 268, though lip service was rendered to the theory that the increase was to be only temporary. Such a theory is seldom tenable—it is hardly ever possible to go back to the past. The increase of numbers brought into vivid relief the other side of our problem. We were all, I think, believers in the college system, but that system rested on accommodation as well as on numbers. If the full benefits of the system were to be obtained it seemed right that an undergraduate should spend two out of his three years in College or, at the worst, in a hostel closely adjacent to the College. Already in the middle fifties this was barely possible. Even allowing that residence in a few small hostels together with the old Riding School could be counted as 'living in College' we could only find places for just over 150 undergraduates and twelve Fellows. In a word it was imperatively necessary to build, unless the whole character of Worcester was to be changed.

My efforts to get assistance through the U.G.C. ended in failure and we were compelled to fall back on two other sources of supply—a College appeal and the help of private benefactors. In both the College was fortunate. Our appeal followed the usual course of such projects; old members were generous, but they were not a wealthy or very numerous body and we were driven back to depend on benefactors from outside. The need for money has been the common experience of most Oxford colleges, and too many Heads have found that pleading and negotiating for funds have become their major occupation. Not a few Heads have been elected under the impression that they will be adept at winning financial support—a totally unacceptable criterion for their choice. Here America has set us a bad example and to me at any rate it seems wrong and humiliating that the Head of a House should spend a great part of his time carrying round the begging-bowl to possible supporters. Probably the right policy is the upgrading of bursars. As colleges become larger and university life more complicated it has to be admitted that a college is akin to a considerable business and that demands a professional bursar, with business experience as well as innate ability. Gone are the days when one elderly clergyman could hand on the bursarship to another only slightly younger.

In our benefactors at Worcester we were fortunate indeed. The first was Lord Nuffield, who was the model of all benefactors. His first gift to Worcester was made during the Provostship of Lys and was one of £50,000, which was used to erect a new building in the garden now known as the Nuffield building. In 1945 he gave a further £10,000 for the foundation of a medical scholarship. So quickly does time pass that the extent of his munificence is remembered by few today, yet it was enormous. In his life by Andrews and Brunner, published in 1955, the total of his benefactions is given at £24,795,260. I have called him a model benefactor for a special reason. Though he gave the closest scrutiny and took the keenest interest in every donation which he made he never, save in one instance, interfered in any way once the gift had been made. This reluctance which he felt to interference did not in any way diminish the care which he took in arranging and organizing his benefactions. Nuffield College itself was a case in point.

Nuffield had bought the site in 1936 and had offered to endow a college for engineers, but when it was pointed out to him that a college for a single subject was contrary to the Oxford tradition he adapted himself to the prevailing view. The war stopped the building of the College and it was only in April 1949 that the foundation stone could be laid by Edward Halifax, the Chancellor of the University. Nuffield felt bitterly that he had been outmanoeuvred in the earlier negotiations and did not refrain from saying so. I walked with him and the Chancellor to lunch at Christ Church after the ceremony and heard the Chancellor (who naturally was imperfectly informed on the subject) express his satisfaction that Lindsay, who had been Vice-Chancellor before the war, had been praised for the part he had played in starting the College. Nuffield's reaction was immediate and decisive. 'Don't speak to me of that man,' he said, 'he lied to me.' On a much later occasion I realized how deep-seated his regrets were. An announcement was made about the foundation of Churchill College which came to his notice whilst I was talking to him. 'That', he exclaimed 'is what I wanted to do for Oxford. I would have given another million, or two million, or three million if they would have let me found the college I wanted.' In time, and largely due to the tact of Norman Chester, the Warden, he became reconciled to seeing his College as the centre of sociological and economic studies, and he did at least have the satisfaction of making that entrance to Oxford worthy of the city—an object that had been always in the forefront of his mind. Still it is sad to contemplate how often the wishes of benefactors are disregarded.

Of all the men I have known none was more straightforward than Nuffield, and few more modest and unassuming. Like many other great men he prided himself less on his great achievements than on his minor triumphs. When I called in on him at Cowley for a cup of coffee he would, almost invariably, point to the bicycle which stood in the outer room and on which he had won many races as a young man. 'They can't build a better bicycle than that.' His prowess at deck tennis on his voyages to Australia was another legitimate cause of pride. Strolling round the golf course at Huntercombe, usually in the company of Kennerly Rumford, he liked to give hints on how to play golf to Farquhar Buzzard and myself and he talked with enthusiasm of Mr. Gladstone whom he much admired. Though simple, straightforward, and honest in mind he was not I think, a happy man, for the wealthy, more than most people, always seem to feel unsatisfied. There was a peculiar benefaction at Worcester under the terms of which the Provost (who himself shared in the benefaction) was enabled to give a gift of £20 in books to each of the Honorary Fellows in turn. What can be given to a man who can himself hand out donations of a million or more without denying himself anything? When Nuffield's turn came I took anxious counsel with Cyril Wilkinson and with Lady Nuffield and chose some books which I thought would please him. 'Let there be plenty of illustrations' was the wise advice of Lady Nuffield. The outcome surpassed my hopes. Nuffield was delighted and in thanking me made me realize the loneliness of the very wealthy. 'Nobody', he said, 'has given me a present for the last twenty years.'

As I said earlier, he interfered but once with regard to his benefactions. This was in 1958 and was perhaps the most difficult question with which as Vice-Chancellor I had to deal. It concerned Nuffield's great Medical Benefaction of 1936. This benefaction had been made for post-graduate training and research, but when the war began Nuffield had immediately agreed that Oxford should undertake clinical undergraduate teaching during the national emergency. After the war he felt, and expressed, resentment that his trust funds were used in part for clinical teaching instead of for research, and finally in 1958 he wrote that he would welcome a reconstruction of the Nuffield Committee. The position was acutely difficult for, as in many such controversies, both sides were clearly, according to their lights, in the right. As the Medical Advisory Committee put it, 'Lord Nuffield's request is the first that he has ever made to the University in relation to one of his benefactions and there would, therefore, need to be an exceptionally strong reason for not meeting it if this could by any means be achieved without the sacrifice of a vital interest of the University.' On the other hand, under the leadership of the Regius Professor, the clinical instruction of undergraduates had shown itself to be of immense value and importance to the University. The details of the discussions which ensued have now no great interest; it is sufficient to say that both sides were composed of reasonable men, anxious

only to come to a right decision, and that a fair compromise
was reached, by which two new committees—one for the advancement of medicine and the other the Nuffield Committee
for Medical Research and post-graduate training—were
established. I felt throughout that the need to satisfy the wishes
of the benefactor was of paramount importance, and so it gave
me especial pleasure when Nuffield wrote to me on another
topic in the following year and concluded with the words, 'I
may add that I shall not forget my sense of gratitude to you for
all the work you did on behalf of my medical trust.' He was a
man of few words but he never wrote anything which did not
express his true feelings.

Another benefactor of Worcester was Antonin Besse, the
founder of St. Antony's College. For this he will always be
remembered, but it is too often forgotten that he also gave a
quarter of a million to the eight poorest colleges. His munificence to Oxford was based on his belief that the world had
gained greatly from the trust put everywhere in the word of
an Englishman and that the British businessmen had done more
to establish this trust than had governments or even colonial
services. To establish a new college, however generous and
open-minded the founder may be, is no easy task, and St.
Antony's had to wait for some years before it could obtain a
charter. In the early stages its affairs were managed by a committee and by trustees and it turned out to be difficult even to
get the funds for the College into the country. For reasons better
understood by economists and financiers than by me it became
necessary to put the money in the hands of trustees in Ireland,
whence it could be transferred to this country. At one stage
Besse felt that his legal advisers were not active enough in his
interest and desired that the committee should be strengthened
by the addition to it of three of his friends—a curious triumvirate of Rab Butler, the Bishop of London, and myself. In these
circumstances it was natural that he should take me into his
confidence with regard to his grant to the eight poorest colleges, and in this matter he showed both his benevolence and
his shrewdness. The colleges got together and agreed that no
one of them should do anything to increase its own share
at the expense of the rest, and this concordat was generally
observed. Besse was staying with me and we were going out

together to dinner at another college when he suddenly told me that one college had written to offer him an Honorary Fellowship. What did I think he should reply? This put me in a quandary and I had to answer with caution. I said that an Honorary Fellowship was the greatest honour that a college could offer and that everyone would agree that he was a deserving recipient, but I had to add that I felt sure that other colleges would wish to honour him if that seemed appropriate and agreeable to him. Besse smiled. 'I have already refused the honour, on the ground that I have said to the University that I will not accept an honorary degree until my College has proved itself. But do not be anxious, I promise that your College shall receive at least as much as any one of the eight.' I felt quite sure that he had only posed his original question to try me out.

The third of our building benefactors, if I may so term them, was to be Sir Isaac Wolfson. I tried hard in 1959 to gain his support for our appeal for a new building and had many meetings and discussed many plans with General Redman who then acted as Secretary to the Wolfson Trust. Both Sir Isaac and his son Leonard Wolfson were sympathetic but they felt at that time that they could not support an individual college. All the more, therefore, was I delighted when I learned in 1971 that the Wolfson Trust would pay for our newest building and thus bring our accommodation up to—or nearly up to—the required level.

It was, I believe, the inauguration of the Historic Buildings Appeal in 1957 which, partly by undertaking the restoration of the old buildings, started the wave of new buildings in Oxford. If that were the cause or not it cannot be denied that the late fifties and the sixties were a great period of building in the University. It is less certain that the buildings themselves reached the same level of excellence which had been reached in some earlier periods. In Worcester's case the Nuffield building was generally acceptable, but it was designed at a time when it was flanked by trees on either side and with the gardens in front. It lost something by the building of the two new blocks to the south of it. The Besse building was an addition to the College, built in the form of a gatehouse over the entrance to the Provost's Yard. As it was at the back of the College it made no pretensions to architectural distinction, but it could fit in well with the general scheme. It was, however, unlucky. The architect had prepared two plans, both adapted to their purpose. Unfortunately after stormy debates both were rejected by the College and a third version accepted. The fault of the accepted version was clear even to the most amateur of critics—it was out of proportion to that wing of the old Lodgings which had been turned over to the College. Had it been the same height as the wing it would have been inconspicuous and agreeable to the eye. This was another instance of the truth that architecture accords ill with democracy—are there any good buildings which have not been the work of an architect whose patron has given him a relatively free hand?

The next building—the Casson building—was also something of a disappointment because of its top storey, which had walls and roof of aluminium. In fact this storey was higher by some seven feet than as it was shown on the drawings. The Wolfson building had to be adapted to its position between the Casson and the Nuffield buildings, and this it does with some measure of success. On the whole our building has done little to add to the glories of Oxford architecture, but we have been lucky, for no part of it has attracted the full blast of Oxford disapproval.

That disapproval is easily aroused. There is no subject which causes such angry passions to arise and few on which everyone does not think that his own opinion is indubitably correct. I suppose that my own experience in this field would be not unlike that of many others. As a boy antiquity seemed a merit in itself and, when I reached Oxford, I was most impressed by the medieval buildings—Mob Quad at Merton, the cottages at Worcester, parts of New College, and so forth. Very soon the grandeur and comfort of Georgian buildings took the place of my earlier predelictions and that love I have never lost. Who could really wish to live in any other form of building who had once lived in the spacious warmth of Georgian rooms? Later I came to appreciate the better Victorian buildings such as Keble—whose chapel seems to me the most underrated building in Oxford. I could not have admitted to any such sentiment in my undergraduate days. Then all men of taste—and each one of us, privately or publicly, so regarded himself—agreed in pouring their scorn and indignation on three buildings, Keble, the Meadow buildings at Christ Church, and the new buildings of Oriel. Was it, I now wonder, only because these were the most recent? Since then I have seen building after building attract the splenetic criticism of the self-appointed guardians of Oxford taste. It seems as though each new building acts as a kind of lightning conductor to draw away criticism from its predecessor. I am irresistibly reminded of that purple (and magnificent) patch in Macaulay when he describes the growth of the National Debt. 'At every stage in the growth of that debt the nation has set up the same cry of anguish and despair.' At every juncture there is the same experience. The New Bodleian excited widespread disapprobation but who thinks of that now? In their turn the critics fell upon Rhodes House, Nuffield, the many new science buildings, St. Catherine's, and the major additions to existing colleges. 'Anguish and despair'—that would not be too strong to describe the feelings aroused by the new building which Magdalen put up on that precious and un-paragoned site by the bridge. Now surely, it was said, the end has come. But the Queen's College erected near by the Florey building, strange both in shape and colour, and all criticism was diverted to a new target. Is it to be expected that Wolfson, when finished, will take away the blue riband of unsightliness from the Queen's building? Hopefully not.

My own view of all these buildings was a personal one. By and large it seemed to me that the smaller buildings and adaptations were commendable—the beehive building at St. John's turned what had been a rather derelict-looking place into a lively and pleasing quadrangle. The changes at Pembroke, Univ., and B.N.C. were most acceptable. Of the larger build-ings Nuffield and St. Anne's in their very different ways, gave me the most pleasure—I think because both gave at once the impression of a college. Of St. Catherine's I hesitate to speak; probably I am too much rooted in the past to feel that anything so large can impress itself on me as a college.

The sixties were indeed a period when a new Oxford was built, and however severely the amateur architects of today may judge the results I believe that future generations will praise rather than blame. Oxford has a wonderful power of absorbing the new and blending it into the old. At Worcester we were lucky—we got our much-needed extra accommodation without exciting more than modified disapproval. Two great benefactions from old members after my time made it possible to make the number of scholars and of Fellows proportionate to the enlarged College.

In my later time as Provost one experiment connected with admissions stirred my interest more than any other. This was the establishment of the Trevelyan Scholarships. These scholarships owed their origin to the fertile imagination of Kurt Hahn, who in 1956 got in touch with Sir Walter Benton Jones, then Chairman of the United Steel Companies Ltd., and others in the steel industry. They felt that the supply of graduates to industry was not satisfactory and that opportunity to go to a university should be given to others besides those who had high examination results to depend upon. They felt that men were required 'of resolution, initiative, tenacity, and human understanding' as well as those who had only academic achievement at school to recommend them. There was strong support at both Oxford and Cambridge for this view and after the usual delays a trust was formed to provide scholarships at both Universities. Twelve companies, most of them in the steel industry, entered into covenants for seven years to provide for twelve scholarships at each University of £450 a year (later raised to £550). In all the Trust administered a sum of £312,668, and it is remarkable that over the eight years that the experiment lasted only £14,449 was spent in expenses. I say that this was a remarkable result because the method of selection was inevitably expensive. Candidates had to be interviewed locally, and the most promising brought to Oxford and Cambridge before a final selection board; their projects had to be judged by examiners; and there was a large correspondence with candidates and with their referees. The cost of all this was greatly reduced by the secretarial and administrative services supplied by United Steel without charge. In all, over eight years, ninety-three scholars were elected at Oxford and the same number at Cambridge.

The full history of the Trevelyan Scholarships has been admirably written by Ronald Peddie. I write here only of my personal involvement. The final selection board based its appointments mainly on two things—the careful personal interview and the 'project' which each candidate had to submit as evidence of his initiative and interest in things other than those contained in the school curriculum. The 'project' was the real basis of the scheme, as was shown when the first batch of scholars were chosen in 1958. Faced by the necessity of tackling some subject himself the candidate was limited by his opportunities. The last four of the selected scholars in that first year had, for example, chosen the most disparate topics. Here is the list: 'An account of a four weeks' stay by a school party of eight on the uninhabited Shiant Isles in the Outer Hebrides'; 'The Town Centre of Crawley New Town as an urban experiment'; 'A study and assessment of violins old and new and in particular the craft of violin making as practised today'; 'The last American Cowboys'. Other subjects chosen by successful candidates that year varied from 'The Teddy Boy problem as observed in West Ham' to 'A survey of Roman villas in the Darenth valley in Kent' or 'A translation in verse of Aeschylus's "Prometheus Bound"'. That initiative and adventuresomeness, even if they entailed some straying from the school curriculum, were no signs of intellectual failure was handsomely proved by the first year of scholars of whom three were awarded first classes and the rest seconds. Except for the first year I acted as Chairman of the final selection board, which was composed of the Chairman, two academics, and two industrialists. The last-named were unchanged throughout—Ronald Peddie of United Steel and Jim Parsons of G.K.N. Both were, in judgement and technique, as good as examiners could be and I learned from them something which was of much use to me in later years. Candidates, I found, were deeply suspicious of the academic members of the board; such clever men, they seemed to think, must always have an ulterior object in posing every question—they would lure you on by apparently harmless questions and then demolish you by an unexpected twist in their argument. Not so with the industrialists. Their questions were direct, factual, and could not be misunderstood. Consequently they could be answered without embarrassment and without consideration of what was to follow after them.

I enjoyed the business of selection, but there were many pitfalls to avoid. At the beginning we could not be sure that everyone we elected would be accepted by a college, and without a college he could not come to the University. In consequence I think that we attached too much importance to intellectual gifts rather than to character and also to the future prospects of the men. There was always too, a political angle which could not be ignored. Critics thought and said that the methods adopted gave an unfair advantage to the public schools and even that we were prejudiced in favour of conservatives. One amusing episode arose out of this wholly mistaken belief. The five examiners sat in a room on one side of a table, the candidate on the other, and while awaiting summons candidates sat in an outer room where they conversed with Donald Calder, an ex-Sudanese officer and an employee of United Steel. After the candidates had retired it was my practice to ask each examiner in turn his private opinion before we proceeded to give an agreed mark. On one occasion a promising candidate was shown by his school record and the letters of his referees to be very far, politically, to the left. When we had examined him and he had left the room I turned to the examiner who was sitting on the left of the row and said, 'Outside left', intending of course to ask for his verdict. Unfortunately the candidate had not gone out very quickly and the door had not been closed before I spoke. Outside the candidate told Calder and another candidate who were waiting that he had been ruled out. 'They think I'm left wing and that is enough to damn me.' In point of fact we had decided to elect the candidate, and Calder's report made it possible for me to write an explanatory note to the Headmaster. Political prejudice does much harm in education, but it is, unfortunately, very difficult to cut it out.

In one way the Trevelyan Scholarships were a triumphant success—in another they were a partial failure. The record of the scholars was admirable and showed beyond doubt that university entrance ought not to be confined to those who had scored heavily at previous examinations. That was the success side. The failure side concerned the donors. It had not been intended that the donors should derive any direct benefit from the scheme, which they considered as a contribution to education and training of men who could ultimately be of value to industry and commerce. They specifically agreed that Trevelyan scholars should be perfectly free to choose their own careers. Unfortunately only a very small percentage went into industry. The University gained from the scholarships and so did the country, but it cannot be denied that the donors (who had shown great generosity) felt that one of their objects had failed.

Towards the end of my Provostship I received the honour of a Knighthood. There are, no doubt, those people who look upon such honours with lofty disdain or with cool detachment, but I think that such people are few. In my own case I felt nothing but extreme pleasure, a pleasure which was increased by two small incidents on the day of investiture. My old friend, Henry Pownall, insisted that I should not go to the Palace in a hired vehicle and further declared that he would drive me there himself. To be driven by a General on an official occasion certainly improves the morale! Then in the room in which we waited before the ceremony I was accosted by a Colonial Governor who was to receive a K.C.M.G. 'We've not met since 1934,' he said, 'when you vivaed me in the schools.' Mercifully I seem to have treated him with compassion on that occasion and we spent an agreeable half-hour discussing the Oxford of a quarter of a century earlier.

The year of 1961 was my time of retirement from the Provostship and with the benefit of hindsight I can see that it was in the interest of the College that I should go just about that time. The numbers in Michaelmas 1961—the term after my retirement—were about 315. I had always clung to my belief in the small college, in spite of the accusation of paternalism which this occasioned, but I had to admit that the increase in numbers had brought some good with it. In particular the Senior Common Room had been reinforced by men of ability and character, and this undoubtedly added to the reputation of the College. I could, I think, have adapted myself to the new age, but I might well have used the brake rather than the accelerator. In any case the question of remaining for a few more years did not arise for I had made it known when I was appointed that I would not consider staying beyond seventy. As things were, my successor with masterly efficiency moved the College into the new world, and avoided most of the dangers which I had expected when Worcester grew from a small to a comparatively large college. In 1973 (as I write) there are 290 undergraduates and 95 graduate students—a total of 385. If I had been told twelve years ago that such an increase was possible without harming the ethos of the College I should not have believed in the possibility. Not for the first or last time I was proved to be wrong.

XXX

INDUSTRIAL YEARS

Life cannot subsist in society but by reciprocal concessions.

DR. JOHNSON

THERE is no part of this book which has given me so much difficulty to write as this chapter—and for a good reason. To write about persons in the remote past is simple and straightforward and my recollection of them is vivid and clear—nor is it possible (except in special circumstances) to libel or slander a dead person. To write about living persons is another matter. Is it then that I fear in speaking of recent events to denigrate people in a way that might bring me into conflict with the law? No, the exact opposite is true. In my long life I have had the extraordinary good fortune to belong to many bodies and associations and in every case I have found myself in tune with my colleagues and conscious both of their merits and of their friendship. There is no harm in that, but when I come to the last ten or fifteen years I begin to have doubts. Is it possible that all those with whom I associated were really such good men as they appeared to me? Is it not more likely that I have always turned geese into swans? Is it not even probable that I have indulged freely in self-deception and made heroes of those with whom I worked and with whom I agreed? Must not my personal comments of the living appear fulsome in their praise and therefore distasteful? Well, I cannot help it. You may think me naïve, or easily deceived, or just mistaken but not, I hope, an intentional or obsequious flatterer. I prefer to take an optimistic view of my fellow-men, for that view accords with my experience. Is it not true that the good far outnumber the bad, though they are less vocal? I can only describe men as they appeared to me, and that pleasant picture is, I believe, truer to life than critical sketches and harsh caricatures which are often accepted as showing insight and discernment. It is much too easy to accept the hostile and contemptuous estimates of diarists as the truth, especially when it is declared that diaries were never intended for publication. In many cases the reader needs a good deal of convincing that such was really the diarist's intention.

And so to 1961. Running true to form I had taken little or no thought about what I should do after my retirement from the Provostship. Vaguely I had wondered whether I could write more or even undertake again some sort of teaching; more practically I had considered examining work, reading for some publishing firm, or helping in selection for academic and other posts. Something I felt bound to do, if only for financial reasons. My pension from Christ Church was £1,000 a year, but this started only when I retired from Worcester. There my salary had been, for most of the time of my tenure, £1,650 but for the last few years £1,950 (of which £550 was tax free), together with the Lodgings free of rent and taxes. The size of the house made it necessary to keep at least two servants as well as some extra help, and my accounts showed that had I had no private income and done no writing, my loss on the Provostship in fifteen years would have been about £6,000. The lowness of the salary was reflected in the pension, which amounted to £463 a year or a lump sum (which I took) of £3,465. In addition I was now eligible for a national retirement pension, then £150 a year. The College, though poor, was always generous and gave me a College house in Beaumont Street free of rates and taxes. Ten years earlier this income would have looked like riches but in 1961 the outlook was not so rosy, and I had to consider how it could be augmented. An alternative would have been to give up my books, furniture, and suchlike and live in a small service flat or in some institution, but this I was unwilling to do. I wanted to keep a home.

From any difficulties of a financial kind, however, I was saved by Herbert Hill.[1] A year or so before the end of my tenure he had asked me at some College function if I would like to join Birfield—the group of companies of which he was Chairman. I did not pay a great deal of attention to what he said, but in 1961 he made me a straightforward offer of employment in his company. Enormously attractive though this was to me, I felt obliged to reply that I knew nothing about industry and could

[1] Chairman of Birfield Ltd. and of other companies.

hardly be expected to be of use to him. His answer gave me a new view of the broadmindedness of some industrial leaders. 'Of course', he said, 'you know little of industry, but that's not the sort of knowledge that I want. I shall be paying you for your judgement and your experience of men. Study the problems; I don't mind if you bring us nothing for a year; then we will see if you can help.' On such terms I was more than ready to accept. The directive which I received was typical of Herbert's generous attitude of mind. I was 'to carry out studies into the problem of human relations in industry', but I was to be 'free to accept other work which it would be normal for me to do, e.g. work for Universities and Schools and related associations, for public bodies and Her Majesty's Government'. My title was to be 'Adviser on Personnel matters' and this gave me a latitude of which advantage could be taken later. Five years later, reviewing my activities, I found that my time had been spent not only in studying industrial relations and advising in them but also in selection and appointments in management in the various companies, in assisting in training work at Goldicote, our educational and training establishment, and in recruiting graduates and school-leavers for the firm.

I started work with Birfield in October 1961, and only a month later a second job was offered to me by Norman Collins. This was the Chairmanship of A.T.V.'s Educational Advisory Committee. The responsibilities, I was told, were considerable but the duties were not onerous. The purpose of the Committee was to ensure that the educational programmes were of the requisite quality and that the programmes offered by the other companies were suitable for viewers in A.T.V.'s area. For this purpose a quarterly meeting was held in Birmingham. After consulting Herbert Hill I accepted the appointment and soon had come to feel that the decision was a right one since the work put me in touch with some parts of the educational world about which I was ignorant but of which the knowledge was useful in my Birfield work.

In the early sixties, therefore, I was a very busy man. Besides my work with Birfield and my subsidiary work with A.T.V. I was still a Fellow of Eton and a Governor of Wellington and of the Atlantic College. I was also a Governor of Ditchley and continued to sit occasionally on the Civil Service Final Selection Board, whilst for the Economic League I was Chairman of a subcommittee for industrial relations and training, which was centred at Birmingham. This, naturally enough, tied up with my Birfield work. None of these activities was in itself onerous but all took time and I could and did feel myself very fully employed. The material advantages were great. I had never known the hurtful impact of poverty, but all my life I had always been obliged to economize wherever I could—to count the pennies with as much care as many of my contemporaries counted the pounds. Now for the first time I was in receipt of an income which enabled me to spend freely and to save sufficient for old age—or, more accurately, for extreme old age.

How many people, I wonder, have entered a new world and started a new career at seventy? If some hesitate to do so I would recommend them to bury their fears and to plunge in at the deep end. My own experience was a wholly fortunate and happy one, for I found my years with Birfield as rewarding as any in my life. Naturally at the beginning I had qualms. On occasion, in church, I have pondered over the parable of the workers in the vineyard and found myself regretting that the workers did not have a union to secure fair play for those who had worked longest. Yet here was I working for the last hour only and receiving my penny none the less. The picture of industry in my mind was, I suppose, much like that of many old-fashioned academics. I thought of industrialists as a race of hard-headed men, intent on making their profits and in a curious way morally inferior to their fellows in the services and the professions; I thought of labour as composed in the main of honest but not very intelligent men, often led astray by a subversive minority; I thought of clashes between management and labour as unfortunate and unnecessary but had never really considered how the two could be reconciled. In such a world I must move very warily nor could I deny that I was nervous about my reception in it. Should I not be received either with (no doubt concealed) contempt as a mere theorist from an alien world or, still worse, with jealousy and suspicion as an unworthy protégé of the Chairman? It was not like that at all. From the first day I was welcomed at all levels and everyone seemed ready to talk with me, to tell me of their jobs and difficulties and to discuss the problems of a great business with reasoned criticism but always with the desire to further the firm's interests. Never in all my life have I felt more strongly the certainty and the value of belonging to a team. In other firms it may well have been quite otherwise but on the management side of Birfield we were a most happy and united team. George Blundell[2] used often to refer to Nelson's captains as an apt comparison.

Birfield, as for six years I knew it, was Herbert's creation and it was his thinking which had made it what it was. A short note from him, written much later, gives with admirable clarity an account of his aims and hopes. (Some part of this note I quote and the rest I summarize.)

On becoming Chairman in July 1950 it became clear to me that new policies were needed to achieve an organisation which it would please me to lead. I determined to make everyone in the organisation proud to serve it. To achieve this the following goals were needed:

(1) To make each person secure as possible in his job if he deserved well of us.
(2) To give each person an opportunity to feel to some extent the firm was his.
(3) To give each person the opportunity to achieve his or her full potential.
(4) To require of each person his or her loyal and whole-hearted service.

To this end what action had to be taken?

(1) In the first place a job-security scheme was adopted, whereby a week's notice was required from management for each year of loyal and uninterrupted service—without limit. Attempts were made to get this plan adopted by the engineering industry, but without success; none the less he applied the scheme and announced it in 1956.
(2) An employees' share scheme was introduced in 1952. Original holders' shares for which they paid £1 became worth nearly £200 per share. There were ultimately about 3,000 holders.
(3) Training had to be provided for all sections of the work force, and for this Goldicote (to which I shall come later) was

2 Captain G. C. Blundell, C.B.E., R.N., a director of Birfield's.

purchased and organized in 1952. There was to be training for all sections, though unfortunately the A.E.U. banned the special courses for shop stewards.

(4) Scholarships were awarded at the universities to attract graduates, and apprentice schools were set up at our two largest firms, Laycock's at Sheffield and Hardy Spicer at Birmingham.

(5) Pension schemes were constantly improved and working conditions kept under constant review.

(6) Joint consultation committees were introduced in the plants.

All these improvements are now common objectives but in the 1950s Birfield was at the head of progress, particularly in the Birmingham area. There was also another and most important side of Herbert Hill's general policy. He refused to sell off any companies which were not doing well, because this would have reduced confidence. Instead he built companies—not only in the U.K. but also in Italy, Holland, Germany, Sweden, and the U.S.A., where he had the enthusiastic support of First National Bank. His policy, in a word, was the opposite of the so-called 'lame duck' policy, which was to be adopted by many businesses in later years. For the rest, the rewards of top people were comparatively modest and expense accounts were taboo.

It may be thought that much of this was idealistic, and so it was—but idealism is never wrong, though often unrealized and a failure. One thing stands out—in Birfield, and especially in its top management, the human side of industrial life played a major role and the welfare of the organization was at least as much considered as the pursuit of profits. When, in 1961, I joined the company much had been already achieved and, as always, much remained to be done. At that time the central office was in Hill Street, London, and there were seventeen subsidiary companies, each of course with its staff of directors and management. The number of companies grew rapidly. Four years later there were twenty-seven companies in the group, together with two consulting and service subsidiaries and seven associated companies, whilst the operations of the group had spread as far afield as France, Belgium, Italy, India, Japan, Germany, Sweden, and Israel. The number of employees in our home companies was about 11,000. When I joined, the central directorate was small—Herbert Hill, Sir William Black, John Hooper (whose financial acumen and loyalty to the firm matched those of the Chairman himself), G.P.S. Macpherson, and Sydney Walker, whose life had been spent in the service of Laycocks. Of these Sir William Black (later Lord Black) reached the retiring age and was replaced by J.J. Parkes, the Chairman of Alvis, and later on George Blundell and Morris Moodie were added. The subsidiary companies were in the main producing components for the automotive industry, but also included companies with such diverse objectives as the production of blotting-paper (T.B. Ford at Wycombe) and various forms of filtration. When the history of the fifties and sixties is written economic historians will, no doubt, have plenty to say about the faults of management—faults of commission and omission and in their books it is not improbable that the virtues of private enterprise will not be recognized as they deserve—so much has the public sector impinged upon the private. Nationalization has won many victories—in my opinion often to the detriment of the national interest—whereas bad management or out-of-date methods in some independent companies has obscured the good work and the efficiency of others. Birfield, I am sure, was among the best of such companies and I wish that its history could be written for the enlightenment of the younger generation. It was strong, not only in its business and financial operations, but also in the atmosphere in which the operation took place. It was wisely directed, progressive, and successful without sacrificing the human interests of its members in a mad race for greater profits. To a newcomer it was soon apparent that its character and ethos had their roots at Goldicote, our training centre just outside Stratford-on-Avon.

Goldicote had a quality and atmosphere all its own. One writer has described it as 'a sort of miniature University'. The house was bought in 1951 and Colonel Pinsent, with whom Herbert had served in the original War Office Selection Board during the war, became Personnel Director. Courses and conferences were held throughout the year but, in order that the teaching and training staff might remain fresh, week-ends were sacred and no courses were held then. The background idea was to bring different strata of management and labour together and to treat all in exactly the same manner. In this way people from the different companies could meet in congenial surroundings and thus build up group co-operation and *esprit de corps*. Some of the courses were technical, others of a different type— ranging from one for the chairman and managing directors of the companies to background courses for apprentices. For me those which dealt with industrial relations were of the greatest interest—whether they were meetings of personnel officers or supervisors or a mixture of middle management and foremen. We had tried, but failed, to introduce special courses for shop stewards but the unions were too suspicious of our motives to allow these. Many of the courses gained when Jim Mathews, who had retired as Secretary of the G. and M.[3] joined us to play his part in the case studies of industrial disputes, which were based on actual disputes, suitably edited, which had occurred in the past. Jim, playing the part of a union representative, would have been a roaring success on film or television, and sometimes a foreman, promoted temporarily to the position of works manager or representative of the Employers' Association, would rival him in dramatic appeal.

The courses for apprentices had their special flavour. Participants, seventeen years or more in age and with at least one year's experience in industry, came for a week for a strictly non-technical course. Their indoor activities included discussions and case studies on world affairs, local government, industrial development, and suchlike; their outdoor activities included constructional work in the grounds, a gymnastic course built up among the trees, and what was called the 'Cotswold Walk', in which the apprentices were set down by bus in three parties and instructed to make their way by the aid of map and compass to a spot about 16 miles away. Apprentices are usually intelligent, nearly always good-hearted, often brash and self-confident but it was noticeable that many were strangely apprehensive about the Cotswold Walk until they had experienced it. Afterwards their morale was noticeably improved. The truth is that in our modern society many boys, if town-dwellers, have never walked properly in their lives and hardly know what it means to travel any distance except by motor transport.

[3] General and Municipal Workers.

The Warden of Goldicote, who in his own person exemplified its character and its merits, was George Blundell. A Captain R.N., he had gone into industry on retirement. He had insisted on learning his job and spent his first year as an electricity maintenance man at Hardy Spicer. No one, in all my experience, had a greater gift for understanding and getting on with every type and every sort of man. When, on occasion, I went with him to visit one of our smaller factories he would know every person there who had been on a Goldicote course and it was difficult to get him from one end of the factory to another. I think, too, that he knew the name of every telephone girl in the group. There is a classic tale of his early work at Hardy Spicer. He went one day to his foreman and asked for a day off in the following week on compassionate grounds. The foreman, who was much attached to him, sprang to the conclusion that he was in trouble with some woman and suggested that George should confide in him and take his wise advice. He was a little huffed when his help was declined but gave a reluctant consent to the request. And the real reason for it? George had to attend at the Palace to be invested with his C.B.E.!

Looking back over my six years with Birfield I am conscious of an unceasing round of conferences, courses, and discussions, not only at Goldicote or Hill Street but also at conferences arranged, for example, by the B.I.M.[4] and the I.W.S. (now I.S.)[5] and at meetings in the Midlands of the Industrial and Training subcommittee of the Economic League, of which I acted as Chairman. Interspersed with these meetings were visits to factories—our own and others—and a great deal of reading. No one can claim a full understanding of the complexities of industrial conditions who has not spent most of his life in industry, but I began to feel as time went on that I did at least understand enough to give me the right to form an opinion and even to offer advice not wholly without use to my Chairman.

In all this my subsidiary work for A.T.V. was helpful, though it added to the long list of meetings and involved a good deal of paper work and personal negotiations. Norman Collins, who had recruited me, was an ideal man to work with—clear, decisive, co-operative, and wholly determined to maintain

[4] British Institute of Management.
[5] Industrial Welfare Society and Industrial Society.

the high quality of A.T.V.'s educational programmes. If I am
not wrong, he had fought strongly to keep A.T.V. as least as
high on the list in educational matters as the other producing
companies—of which Granada and Rediffusion were the chief.
This was no easy job, for in independent television finance
plays a very important part and no programme could expect
to succeed without an adequate budget. It was also no easy
task to persuade Midland schools of the educational advantages
which could be obtained from television. When I succeeded
Mary Field[6] as Chairman of the Committee I found it a good
representative body—composed of members from all types of
schools (including John England, Chairman of the National
Union of Teachers), County Education committees, and the
Ministry of Education, together with the cultural attachés
from the French and German embassies who were useful in
criticizing our modern-language programmes. We met every
three months at Birmingham. The Head of the Education
Department in A.T.V. was the chief executive and acted as
secretary to the Committee; in Donald Carter we had a first-
class producer. Towards the end of 1962 our sphere of operations was greatly enlarged when responsibility for adult education was added to us. Norman Collins acted with speed and
efficiency and secured three new members—all active and
highly qualified—from the National Institute of Adult Education, the Universities Council for Adult Education, and the
Workers' Educational Association. Early in 1963 when the
Senior Education officer left us Norman Collins and I formed
ourselves into a selection committee and appointed James
Wykes, who became a tower of strength to the Committee both
in its schools and adult education work.

The Committee was a harmonious body and the programmes
which it sponsored were usually of high quality—especially
the modern languages programmes arranged by Mary
Glasgow.[7] In others, too, we aimed high; there was a series on
the English novel undertaken by J.B. Priestley and a series of
twenty-six programmes for sixth-formers on English drama, for
which Ivor Brown was our adviser and in which Sir John

[6] A personality in the television world.
[7] Mary Glasgow, C.B.E., Secretary-General of the Arts Council of Great Britain
1939–51, Chairman of Opera Players.

Gielgud introduced each programme. Meantime responsibilities did not diminish. In 1964 the Independent Television Authority decided that it needed better liaison between its Education Advisory Council and the Advisory Committees of the producing companies. Accordingly I was appointed to the I.T.V. Council to represent A.T.V. and found among my colleagues two old friends appointed at the same time—Sir Ivor Evans for Rediffusion and Sir William Mansfield Cooper for Granada. Our Chairman was Sir John Newsom. We did not always agree, notably over the question of a sex-instruction series which my A.T.V. Committee considered unsuitable, but the Committee was helpful and instructive and I enjoyed its meetings. The vexed question of the University of the Air was coming to the fore, but I did not survive long enough to see what attitude I.T.V. would take up towards it.

The end of my connection with A.T.V. in 1967 was unhappy, but I shall recall it. I think, though I do not know, that Norman Collins was taking less part in the management of our affairs and in 1966 James Wykes was appointed Director of the London Education television service. In consequence my relations with Management at A.T.V. House were less close than they had been. A new managing director, full of new-broom ideas and taking account of the new central contracts which were to come into effect in 1967, determined on a reorganization and proposed to disband the Advisory Committee in July 1967 and then appoint a new committee. I protested vigorously but without avail. Quite apart from the policy which I thought mistaken I objected to the manner in which the change was to be made. A letter was written to each member of my Committee which began thus, 'During the past few months, we have had discussions with Sir John Masterman . . .', and went on to say that it was the intention of the company to 'reshape' the Committee from July onwards. The 'discussions' were a myth, for they consisted of one short meeting, at which I had registered my dissent and a couple of letters from the new managing director which were muddled and not always grammatical. When I considered the skill and trouble which Norman Collins had exercised to persuade specially qualified persons to join the Committee it seemed to me ill advised in the extreme to get rid of them—particularly as the last two annual reports of

A.T.V. had stressed their success. For example the 1966 report recorded that the number of Midland schools registered with A.T.V. on regular series of our educational programmes had risen from 1,400 to 2,000 and that audiences for our adult-education programmes had grown consistently. In the 1967 report the number of schools registered appeared as 3,000. It may well have been wise to consider having a new Chairman, for I had served for five years and new blood is often a great advantage, but to get rid of the Committee was, in my judgement, plain folly. Of our thirteen members only three were invited to serve on the new Committee and among these the names of Sir Lionel Russell[8] (our latest acquisition) and John England (most forthright and loyal of members) did not appear. When I have so much good to say of those with whom I have worked it is something of a relief to criticize the managing director who made these changes. In the medical terms of my childhood there must be some powder to go with the jam. Though the end of my association with the Company came about in the manner which I have described I have many happy memories of A.T.V. I cannot think of A.T.V. House without recalling the immense length of Lew Grade's cigars, invariably offered when he came into Norman Collins's room, but always refused by me out of feelings of personal inadequacy to deal with them. Most of all I recall the satisfaction of having collaborated with Norman Collins. That was a cherished experience which I cannot rate too highly.

[8] Chief Education Officer of Birmingham 1946–68.

XXXI

INDUSTRIAL YEARS (Contd.)

Controversy equalises fools and wise men in the same way—and the
fools know it.

O. W. Holmes: *The Autocrat of the Breakfast-table*

In Birfield by this time we had gone through some hectic
days. The critical moment was in 1964 at the time of the
general election. Labour relations at that time were at least
good, as the low turnover of workers at Hardy Spicer clearly
showed. That there were occasional minor difficulties connected
with pressure for wage increases was inevitable. The strike
which led to the explosion of 1964 was one of so-called 'inspectors', about 130 in number, who could more accurately be
described as 'testers' or 'viewers'. The usual job of the inspector
was to take the pieces of metal off an assembly line and hold
them in front of a spectroscope or test them against a mould
to be sure that each piece was physically perfect. By no reckoning was this a highly skilled job! The claim of the inspectors
for higher pay was in itself a trivial dispute, but, as always
happens in the motor trade, a dispute in a small section could
soon lead to the disruption of the whole industry. The dispute
went through the whole of the engineering procedure for settling disputes—works conference, local conference with the
Employers' Association, and finally the Central Conference at
York—without reaching agreement. However, subsequent
negotiations led to a resumption of work, which, however, lasted
for only a few days. Another strike was declared and Hardy
Spicer closed down once more. It was in this atmosphere that
Mr. Wilson made remarks at a Press Conference which suggested that this strike was politically motivated, and that there
had been similar instances before in previous elections. He
declared that a Labour Government would hold a searching
inquiry with full powers to discuss the trade dispute at Hardy
Spicer and any other disputes that developed before polling day.

The timing could not have been more unfortunate. Herbert Hill heard the news on his radio as he was travelling south from Sheffield after a successful visit to Sweden, where Hardy Spicer had a virtual monopoly for the construction of propeller shafts for Volvo. Volvo had intimated to him that, owing to the prevalence of strikes in England, they could not rely on deliveries on time and were considering finding alternative sources of supply. Herbert had persuaded them that, as he was building a new factory in the North-East, they would be safe in relying upon Birfield supply. He was now told by radio that he was accused of fomenting a strike for political reasons in his own Company!

I was staying at Hill Street and accompanied the Chairman next morning to see Counsel and arrange to sue Mr. Wilson for slander and libel. At this meeting it was agreed not to ask for damages (which might have been very large) but only to restore the good name of the Chairman and the Company by demanding a retraction of all the allegations, a full apology, and the payment of costs. I have sometimes wondered since whether we were wise to be so moderate in our demands, but on the whole I think that it was right to act as we did. Most of the day was spent in interviewing journalists who poured into Hill Street. I was present nearly all the time, but not (unluckily) when Herbert had a conversation about the background of the strike with the Press Association, a conversation which he thought to be 'off the record'. In this conversation he used the phrase 'poor dears' in reference to the strikers—a remark which was thought to be patronizing and offensive. To anyone who knew him it was nothing of the sort. He was in fact only stressing his view that the strikers were cutting their own throats and those of their companions in the motor industry through ignorance of the facts of the situation. However, the expression was exploited and misrepresented and undoubtedly harmed him. I took a good view of the journalists who visited us that day and only once asked one of them to edit his report. 'Please', I said, 'leave out the word "malicious". It does not represent the tenor of the conversation and was certainly used in error.' He agreed at once and kept his word.

Much pressure was brought to bear on Herbert to withdraw his writ but to do so would have been clean contrary to his character. After a year the case eventually come into court and I think that quotation of *The Times* account is the fairest method of describing the settlement that was made:

PRIME MINISTER APOLOGIZES
Hill v. *Wilson*
Before Mr. Justice Thesiger

The settlement was announced of this libel action brought by Mr. Herbert Edward Hill, of Poulton Farm, Marlborough, against the Right Honourable James Harold Wilson, the Prime Minister.

Mr. Colin Duncan, Q.C., and Mr. David Hirst, Q.C., appeared for the plaintiff; Mr. Guy Aldous, Q.C., and Lord Lloyd of Hampstead for the defendant.

The Hardy Spicer Strike

Mr. Duncan said that Mr. Hill, at the relevant time was chairman of Hardy Spicer Ltd. and of their holding company, Birfield Ltd. Mr. Hill had, as was widely known, always played an active part in the management and direction of both companies.

At the end of September 1964, during the currency of the 1964 general election campaign, a number of inspectors and viewers in the employment of Hardy Spicer Ltd. at their Birmingham factory had for some days been on strike. That factory supplied propeller shafts to the motor industry both in the United Kingdom and on the continent, and the strike had already dislocated production throughout the motor industry.

On September 30th Mr. Wilson, as leader of the Labour Party gave a press conference at Transport House attended by many representatives of the British and World press.

During the course of that conference Mr. Wilson made a statement concerning the Hardy Spicer strike which bore the imputation that those responsible for the control of Hardy Spicer Ltd. were, or at least were reasonably suspected of being guilty of the fomentation of the strike for improper political motives. Mr. Wilson added that if a Labour Government were elected it would hold a full searching inquiry with full powers to get at the facts of the strike. This statement was widely construed as implicating Mr. Hill and his colleagues on the board of Hardy Spicer.

The press conference received wide publicity both in the British and World press, and on radio and television.

Any such imputation was totally without foundation. The very last thing Mr. Hill and his colleagues desired was a strike which harmed the general body of their employees, which gravely affected Hardy Spicer's home and export business and which would if continued disrupt the motor industry as a whole. At the time of Mr. Wilson's press conference they were doing their utmost to achieve a settlement so that the factory could resume normal working. Mr. Wilson accepted that this imputation was completely without foundation and he attended Court by his counsel today to express his sincere apologies to Mr. Hill and his colleagues for the injury and distress caused to them.

Mr. Hill for his part brought this action in order to clear his injured reputation and that of his colleagues and the company with no desire to profit financially out of the libel. His aim having been achieved by this statement in open court he had not asked for any payment of damages, but Mr. Wilson had agreed to indemnify him against his legal costs.

Mr. Aldous said that he associated himself with what Mr. Duncan had said. He (Mr. Aldous) desired on behalf of the Prime Minister to make it plain that, when he made the statement complained of, he had never heard of and had no knowledge of Mr. Hill and had no intention of making any attack on him. But he (counsel) had advised Mr. Wilson that people who knew Mr. Hill would understand the statement as referring to him and as bearing the imputation, which Mr. Wilson readily acknowledged would be baseless, that Mr. Hill and his colleagues were fomenting the strike at Hardy Spicer's Birmingham factory for political ends.

Mr. Wilson had accepted his (counsel's) advice, and, in those circumstances, welcomed the opportunity of expressing his apologies to Mr. Hill.

(Solicitors: Messrs. Linklaters & Paines; Messrs. Goodman Derrick & Co.)

A charitable critic might, perhaps, defend Wilson on the grounds that the heated atmosphere of an election leads inevitably to hasty and ill-considered statements and that the reports and suspicions of colleagues are too readily believed by the leader, but, as Nixon was to learn, the leader cannot escape the ultimate responsibility for his own words and actions. The case caused comment in America as well as in England. As many said there could not be much wrong with a country where a private individual could bring a case against the Prime Minister and be sure that he would obtain justice in the Courts. About the promised inquiry by a Labour Government into the strikes nothing further was heard.

Birfield expanded greatly in the sixties, especially overseas; sales increased from £6,000,000 in 1950 to over £40,000,000 in

1966, in addition to sales from European associated companies in excess of £30,000,000. This expansion had both its good and its bad side. Financially there was much to be said for the growth. In all its history the Company never reduced its dividend, indeed the dividends increased steadily; profits were always ploughed back into the business and depreciation was allowed for on a lavish scale. Economic pundits nearly always maintain that an industry cannot stand still—it must either grow or decline. In a memorandum which I wrote in 1964 I put on paper the facts as I saw them with regard to Birfield. Expansion must be right, for a business which stands still is usually doomed. A firm which remains small is likely fairly soon to deteriorate. If there are no opportunities for promotion except through stepping into dead men's shoes, those with initiative and drive in the middle and junior ranks of management will soon leave the firm and seek a career elsewhere. I went on, however, to question whether the organization had kept up with the expansion of the group—in other words that I felt that top management, though excellent in itself, was insufficiently staffed and the administrative machinery inadequate for the enlarged group. Something was done to correct this when George Blundell was moved from Goldicote to become a director and when Morris Moodie was added to the Board, but even so the burden on Herbert Hill was too heavy. I wrote in the memorandum which I sent to him: 'As I see it you had a decade ago a Brigade under your command; now you are a Corps Commander. You cannot run a Corps (much less an Army group!) with only Brigade Headquarters.' James Sandars was added to the board in 1965, and a system of regional directors was introduced, but this was scarcely enough.

Herbert Hill was a remarkable man and his life was dedicated to Birfield. His approach to problems in industry was paternalistic and every company suffered when he was not able to give it his personal attention. Everything in the group really depended upon him, though this was less evident than it might have been because he could delegate authority—and delegate freely and generously. When George Blundell left Goldicote to join the Main Board a successor as Warden of Goldicote had to be found and George, myself, and one of the Laycock directors were given the task of making a short list of selected candidates. It was a vitally important appointment and we spent much time on correspondence and interviews with candidates. Eventually we reduced them to three whom we were to present to the Chairman for his final decision. My recollection is that two of them fell out at the last moment, one accepting another appointment and the second falling ill or being for some reason ineligible. The candidate whom both George and I preferred remained and we decided to bring him up to London to be interviewed by the Chairman. The meeting was at twelve noon, on the supposition that we should conclude the interview by lunch time. We expected a long and searching inquisition, but it was not so. Herbert took a long look at our candidate and then said: 'So you are the man who is coming to help us at Goldicote.' He then gave a splendid exposition of the purpose and organization at Goldicote. I told him after-wards that, delighted though I was at the appointment, I was also completely surprised that he had made it without any examination at all. His reply was characteristic. 'I knew that George and you have taken a great deal of trouble to find me the right man. Of course after delegating the job to you I was going to accept your recommendation.' What a man to serve under! It is satisfactory to remember that Sam Stewart, the chosen candidate, was an outstanding success.

In spite of the changes which I have mentioned and in spite of his willingness to delegate, some of the British companies lost a good deal when Herbert was obliged to spend much of his time in negotiations abroad. There his reputation grew steadily—both in America and in Europe. He appealed to foreigners in European countries because he conformed to their ideal of what a British businessman should be—completely reliable, clear, decisive, and knowing his own mind, the embodiment of the figure whose 'word of an Englishman' could be relied upon without question. Had he been able to devote more time to the British companies our industrial disputes and difficulties would have been easier to settle, for it is the essence of successful paternalism that the leader should be in constant touch with his employees. 'Paternalism' was, too, very much out of fashion and this militated against Birfield when there came the question of a merger with a larger group.

To show Herbert, 'warts and all', it is necessary to draw

attention to his weak points. He held his own views so strongly
and expressed them so clearly and forcibly that those who did
not know him well regarded him as dogmatic—and reacted
accordingly. In fact he was not dogmatic and would listen
carefully to any argument and be prepared to change his own
view if he was convinced. It was, however, true that he could
not appreciate the fact that sometimes those who opposed him
might be actuated by completely honest motives and might
(quite unjustly) be mistrustful of him. To this extent he could be
intolerant. Furthermore he would not conceal his views even
when it was clearly best to wait for a more appropriate moment
to express them. This, I think, more than anything else, deprived him of the power of wielding political influence. It is
sad, but true, that politics in a democracy demands a full
measure both of caution and of compromise. Herbert would
never stoop to conceal his opinion either of men or matters.
His image (to use a distasteful word) was therefore a wholly
distorted one. Ironically, at the time of the Wilson trouble he
was pictured as a reactionary employer when in fact of all the
industrialists I have known he had the greatest measure of compassion. No one ever asked for his help in vain; if some people
had realized this at the time of the merger with G.K.N. they
would have obtained what they wanted far more effectively
than by any negotiation. In spite of the criticisms which I have
made, Herbert was one of the truly great men whom I have
known. Never once did I observe him doing or thinking anything mean or paltry; always he acted in the big way. In my
mind he is linked with John Reith; both in their different
spheres did great service to their country; both had they been
allowed might have done even more. It was not their fault that
the opportunity was not given.

The sort of paternal care which Herbert took for his employees ran counter to the general trend in industry which
tended to conform to computerized efficiency and in consequence to larger and larger units. Success in a small firm or in a
fairly small group depends upon the personal involvement of
the presiding deity. Though, as I said before, it is usually
necessary for business to grow or to fall back, it is also true that
sheer size is the enemy of business in the private sector, and to
go beyond a certain size is liable to change its nature and rob

it of many of its benefits. All this became clear when Birfield
and G.K.N. negotiated for a merger in 1966. The financial
policy of Birfield had always been eminently sound; the dividend had never once been reduced, much had been ploughed
back into the business, and no bonanza had been given to the
shareholders. The position made Birfield a very attractive
proposition for another company but it also tended to under-
value Birfield shares and, at the same time, make shareholders
favourable to a take-over or merger. From a business point of
view there was much to be said for it, but there was also inevitably a great loss. The G.K.N. system was highly developed and
stereotyped. In Birfield the boards and managers of subsidiary
companies had been encouraged to show initiative and much
authority had been freely delegated to them. In G.K.N. no
decision of any importance could be taken until the matter
had gone to an administrative board and subsequently to the
Main Board, and this often entailed considerable delay. It was
calculated (I know not if accurately or not) that the extra
paper work demanded of the Birfield companies would entail
an expenditure of £50,000 annually. Size is the enemy of
human links and human relations. Among other regrettable
results Goldicote was sold off to another company. As G.K.N.
employed almost exactly ten times as many workers as Birfield
our directors could not expect to exercise great influence on the
policy of the merged companies, and in fact in 1967 Birfield as
an independent company or group of companies ceased to exist,
though some years later it was generally acknowledged that old
Birfield companies were among the most successful parts of the
G.K.N. empire. With the merger ended my own involvement in
industry.

When I had been with the company for five years I wrote a
letter to Herbert Hill questioning whether I could be of any
further use to him and offering my resignation. I listed
those matters in which I had been able to help, giving myself
'the benefit of the most favourable interpretation' but pointing
out that these things did not add up to very much and that my
Chairman could decide that I had become redundant and that
my employment could be terminated without the slightest
embarrassment to either of us. The answer was flattering to my
self-esteem and I agreed to continue, but the merger, of course,

made any further prolongation out of the question. The retiring age in G.K.N. was sixty-five and I was already seventy-seven! Trying to evaluate my six years in industry I could easily see that I had myself gained enormously from it—in experience and knowledge of one of the most important parts of the national life as well as through the acquisition of many close friendships—but could I feel that I had contributed anything substantial in return? For those who act as advisers there is always a gnawing doubt whether they are really of much use to those who act in an executive capacity; they have a sort of inferiority complex which is hard to overcome, and I fear that, in political circles especially the theorist and adviser often does as much harm as good. I have noticed a similar feeling in my own profession; teaching is much more satisfying and better than administration, and administration is much more satisfying and better than protests and demonstrations. There is an old story of the parson, who, feeling himself ineffective in his parish, prayed in church with the words, 'O, Lord, make more use of thy servant, if only in an advisory capacity.' With regard to one part of my duties—the study of industrial relations—I came to the conclusion that executives and practitioners were of far more importance than theorists and advisers, and with regard to industry as a whole I came to feel that the importance of human relations was underestimated in comparison with the struggle for increased profits and business success. Much of what I thought—and think—about industrial relations is contained in an article entitled *Theory and Practice in Industrial Relations* which was published by the Industrial Welfare Society (now the Industrial Society) in 1965. It was donnish, no doubt, in tone—an elderly leopard cannot change his spots—but it was practical also. Apart from insistence on the theme that industrial relations were human relations, it contains four specific proposals for improvement. A decade later I feel no inclination to alter or amend my views.

XXXII

PUBLICATION OF THE DOUBLE-CROSS SYSTEM

Publish and be damned.

DUKE OF WELLINGTON

THE end of my employment by Birfield left me free to devote myself to a project which I had had long in mind—the publication of my account of the double-cross system during the war. When this report was written in 1945 there had been no thought of publication, but as early as 1947 Clement Attlee, then Prime Minister, had been anxious that the story, in some form or other, should be told. The Chiefs of Staff, though expressing disappointment that credit could not be given to those responsible for a very successful operation, made it clear that the time was not ripe. No doubt they were entirely right. At that time the names of those involved, officers as well as agents, could not be revealed without danger and there were technical secrets connected with wireless communications which might be put at risk by premature publication. I had many talks with my old chief, Sir David Petrie, whose view was quite clear; nothing should be published whilst any security risk remained but when the time came when this risk had ceased to exist the account of Double Cross might be made public for the sake of historical truth. In the later years there was always the same question to be answered. Do we gain more by improving the reputation of the Service by telling the story than we lose by any possible security risk? Clearly it was only a question of time when the gains through publication would obviously outweigh the losses. But when would that moment be?

In my judgement that moment came during the fifties when there was much renewed interest in the subject of secret operations during the war. H.M. King George VI had asked to see the book and it was, in fact, in his possession at the time of his death in 1952. In 1953 Ewen Montagu published *The Man Who Never Was*. I was myself opposed to this publication

on the grounds that it was a mistake to publicize a single operation when all the rest remained secret, but I did not know at the
time that other—and perhaps incorrect—accounts would be
published in any case and that it was clearly better to have an
accurate and official account rather than to trust to them.
Looking back I feel admiration for the skill with which Ewen
obtained official leave, for, as I was to learn later, the utmost
political expertise was needed to obtain the co-operation of a
number of different authorities. At the end of 1954, Peter
Fleming[1] informed me that he planned to write a book on
Hitler's projected invasion and hoped that I could give him
information about the agents sent over in the early days of the
war. I referred him to Dick White[2] at M.I.5 and at the same
time suggested that the time had come for releasing the XX
story. I envisaged an official but anonymous publication which
would set the record straight beyond possibility of refutation.
At the same time I consulted a number of those most intimately
concerned and found that a large majority of them agreed with
me, though most thought a publication under my own name
would be preferable to an official document. Unfortunately
my suggestion was badly timed. David Petrie's successor,
Sillitoe, had published his memoirs and raised a great deal of
criticism in so doing, and a committee had been appointed to
establish more stringent rules with regard to publication of
similar works. In the light of Dick's comments I did not press
the matter, though I thought and still think that an official
publication at that time would have been the best course to
take.

And so to 1961, in which year I made my first firm and prolonged attempt to secure leave for publication. On the advice
of Philip Swinton, who was always my strongest supporter and
without whose active assistance XX would never have been
published, I wrote a formal request to Roger Hollis, then head
of M.I.5, and had a long discussion with him and Dick White.
Once again the timing was inept and I had no success. I am,
at this distance of time, uncertain why I did not press more

[1] Author; High Sheriff of Oxfordshire (1952), sometime member of Christ
Church.
[2] Sir Dick White, O.B.E.; successively head of M.I.5 and M.I.6; sometime
member of Christ Church.

vehemently in 1961, but I think that the reason was that I retired from the Provostship of Worcester in that year and was much occupied in changing my home. Negotiations and consultations continued but without strong pressure and the situation, from my point of view, deteriorated when the Profumo case came to occupy the first place in the minds of those in charge of the Security Service. Roger Hollis was firmly against publication and in June 1963 Alec Douglas-Home, then Prime Minister, wrote to tell me that, though he sympathized with my aim of giving the service in question a better image, he could not contemplate going against the professional advice which he had received.

I did not abandon the struggle but in December, on Philip Swinton's advice, wrote to the Secretary of the Cabinet, Lord Normanbrook, and asked if I could discuss the matter with him. We had several meetings and exchanged several letters but the upshot was that he felt that, in view of Roger Hollis's opposition and taking into account the administration difficulties, a fresh application was unlikely to succeed. If I did pursue the matter further he advised a direct approach to the permanent head of the Home Office or to the Home Secretary, as the Minister responsible for the Security Service. Once more I was obliged to accept the inevitable. I wrote to Normanbrook in March 1965:

... Meantime I shall follow the advice which is implicit in your letter. I certainly should not have consulted you unless I had intended to abide by what you said. In other words I shall let the matter drop for the time being though I think that I shall revive it at a later date. Among other things I should be unwilling to embarrass Roger Hollis just at the end of his time.

By this time my own views had crystallized, and my conviction that publication would be beneficial had become stronger and stronger. Some might say that it had become an obsession. This was my argument. In the first place there is a strong argument for recording as accurately as possible the chronicles of the past, and no historian would hesitate to demand that such records should be available unless there were overriding reasons to the contrary. Moreover the work of the XX agents makes intelligible certain parts of the history of the war and of enemy operations which would otherwise be ignored or misunderstood. This, however, was not my prime motive. More than anything else I was depressed by the low state of the reputation of the Security Service—or, to use modern jargon—by the poor image of the Service. Up to a point this was inevitable, for any good work done by a secret service is usually unknown, whereas any error or failure—e.g. when a previously successful spy is uncovered—receives much publicity and criticism. Here is a real dilemma, well put by Hugh Gaitskell in 1961 when, speaking of the Lonsdale case, he stressed that secrecy was essential for the Security Service but that it was also imperative to restore confidence in the Service. No doubt in Westminster and Whitehall and among those in or near to the corridors of power the merits and efficiency of the Service were well appreciated, but with the generality of people the case was otherwise. It is impossible, for reasons which must be obvious, to release secrets about operations which are very recent or still proceeding, but with each year I felt more convinced that only good could come from releasing an account of the wartime successes.

The spy cases of the 1950s and 1960s did indeed serious damage to the image of the Service, which came to be regarded as expensive, inefficient, and unnecessary. A writer as respected and admired as Rebecca West wrote in the *Sunday Telegraph*, on 26 March 1961:

It is a tragedy on more than one level that the apparatus of security which costs us so much and so constantly impedes us, should not be more successful in preventing penetration by the forces of espionage; for if there were never another war, and they found no use for the information which they gather, they spread a moral infection, often among people not without value.

A leading article in the *Evening Standard* on the Philby case in 1963 takes the same line. 'The real culprit in this case is the Security Service. Our intelligence service has spent millions and achieved nothing but darkness.' A reviewer in the *Sunday Times* in December 1967, discussing the spy stories of the year, began his review with this sentence: 'This year saw British espionage in more than its customary disarray, hampered by the frailties of its operatives, the eccentricities of its high com-

mand . . . and a demoralising lack of belief in its own utility.'
Nor is it irrelevant to remember that in 1969 the Secret Service
vote was reduced by £250,000. The fact that in the public
mind espionage and counter-espionage were hopelessly mixed
up does not affect the issue; to most people they were simply
the Secret Service, and for this much misrepresented body many
people had no use whatever.

It was in these circumstances that I embarked in October 1967
on my final effort to secure leave for publication—an effort
which was to be at long last successful almost exactly four years
later. The omens seemed to me propitious. Dick White, who
had been Director-General of the Security Service, had moved
over to become Head of M.I.6 and had been succeeded by
Martin Furnival Jones at M.I.5 and I was sure that they were
the key men whom I must persuade to put forward my plan
to higher authority. I hoped that they would support me
actively or, at the worst, adopt a neutral attitude. From both I
could expect (and received) a sympathetic hearing. Dick White
had been my pupil at Christ Church and I had served under
him in M.I.5 during the war. His services in M.I.5 and in
M.I.6, as also his work in SHAEF with Eisenhower were outstanding, though known only to a small circle. I had kept in
close touch with him since the war and he had always shown
both interest in and sympathy with my plans. In October
1967 he wrote to me: 'As you know I have always been sympathetic with the idea of your XX book, though I have equally
always seen grave difficulties connected with its presentation.'
He added that he would contact Furnival Jones so that we
could all discuss the matter. Furnival Jones himself had been a
solicitor who had entered M.I.6 for the war years and had
stayed on when the war ended. I knew therefore that I should
get a fair hearing from both. Another circumstance made me
hopeful—the obvious diminution of any security risk. Twenty
years before it would have been culpable to have mentioned
their names—in 1967 not only their names but the position of
their offices and even their telephone numbers had appeared
in American publications. Furthermore, another security
objection had disappeared. In earlier days I had often been met
with the argument that the Russians were ignorant of our
methods and must so remain, even though all the secrets were

by now well known in other countries. Then came the unmask-
ing of Philby and the unpleasant knowledge that Russia knew
more about our Secret Service than any other power. It seemed
to me that the last security objection had disappeared. Philby
himself I had met once or twice in our office when he was
responsible for M.I.6 for the Iberian peninsula. Even at that
early date I was told by both my chiefs—Petrie and Liddell—
to treat him with caution and release as little information to him
as possible. Dick White always mistrusted him and was the
first, or almost the first, to be convinced of his treachery. Yet
Philby's own account of Dick is not without perception. I think
that Philby feared him instinctively and wrote of him: 'His
most obvious fault was to agree with the last person he spoke
to.' In this there was a measure of truth, for Dick was so fair-
minded and so responsive to the views of others that he tended
to agree too easily with views that were put before him. But I am
tempted to add that in his official capacity it was his only fault.

It was natural, then, that I should feel optimistic in 1967
and that I should set about arranging a meeting with Dick
and Furnival Jones together. The meeting did not prove easy
to arrange since Furnival Jones left for Ceylon and Australia;
but I had it fixed for 8 January. Unfortunately Dick White was
ill on this date and so I spent some three hours alone with
Furnival Jones—an interview that seemed to me highly satisfactory. He did not believe that the book would sensibly improve the image of the Service and he thought that it would
come better as part of a general history of intelligence during
the war, but he had some sympathy with the idea of making
the public aware of the achievements of B1A and the XX
Committee and was quite ready to send my proposal forward
to higher authority. The only detail on which we did not agree
was the form of presentation. Earlier I had thought of an anonymous production, but one adviser after another had told me
that this would be wrong and that I should write under my
own name. Personally either course would have been agreeable
to me, provided only that publication was allowed, but Furnival Jones was not convinced about this. A day or two after our
meeting I wrote a letter of thanks to him in which I said
'. . . in particular I was grateful to you for your generous proposal that you should yourself take the initiative and begin to

consult the authorities concerned. You may have been surprised that I did not immediately jump at this offer. My reasons for going slow were these.' I then explained that it seemed best to get the details about the method of publication settled and also to secure the agreement of Dick White. I felt reasonably confident that if all three of us worked together and put forward the plan it would get fairly quickly to the Minister and I felt, too, that if this happened it was more than likely that leave would be given.

It was not until May that the joint meeting occurred but it was agreed then that my case should go to Sir Burke Trend, the Secretary of the Cabinet, and Sir Philip Allen, Permanent Under-Secretary of State at the Home Office. Though I was pretty optimistic I felt that it was right to make provision for a refusal and I therefore constructed what I called Plan Diabolo, a plan which was only to come into operation if leave to publish was refused. Briefly the plan consisted in publishing the book in America. This, of course, would lay me wide open to prosecution under the Official Secrets Act, but of this I was not unduly afraid. At that time there could have been either a prosecution for a felony or for a misdemeanour and a study of the Act convinced me that I was only likely to suffer the smaller penalties of one guilty of the lesser offence. In fact I did not think that Government would prosecute me or that if they did they would get a conviction. I could clearly show that the main purpose of the book was to enhance the reputation of the Security Service and of M.I.6; I had offered 'any part or the whole' of the royalties to the department; I could produce letters from a great number of those most intimately concerned who were wholly in favour of publication in this country; the Security Service which would have been the prosecutor would have found it easy to show that I was guilty but what would be gained thereby? They would, if they did get a conviction, only give immense publicity to the book. I did not like to disguise my intentions from Furnival Jones and Dick White, but I could not well seem to press them too hard. I therefore adopted a different technique in each case. I had a talk with another old friend in M.I.5 John Marriott (who was himself consistently and bitterly opposed to my plan), and let him report to Furnival Jones. For Dick White I used Peter Fleming as an intermediary. Peter, who was one of my warm supporters wrote to Dick urging publication and telling him of what Peter described as my 'diabolic plan'. 'You can rely on my indiscretion', he wrote, adding that he hoped I should not have to put the plan into operation.

In spite of this pressure there was no progress, and I began to feel that both Furnival Jones and Dick White were becoming lukewarm. And why not? Even if they personally agreed that publication was eventually desirable they could not help feeling that all kinds of official and administrative difficulties would be avoided if my request was allowed to lapse and be forgotten. Then in October 1968 the blow fell. Furnival Jones wrote to me and told me that the Chiefs of Staff felt that they were 'insufficiently informed about the business' and that they had 'commissioned a study of the material available as a prelude to a decision'. Apparently it was felt either that my book was better kept to be incorporated in a general history of intelligence or that it should be combined with a projected history of deception. Not unnaturally I protested vehemently, both because my book was essentially a counter-espionage document and because the proposal meant an indefinite delay. In the autumn I had secured the invaluable help of Christopher Harmer (a solicitor and former colleague in M.I.5), who was ready to act for me as legal adviser but, as he was bound to do, advised me not to attempt an American production. I decided to press on with my attempt to have my proposal considered at a higher level, and in January 1969 I wrote to Furnival Jones and put to him two specific questions, which I quote in full.

(1) I am particularly anxious not to misrepresent your attitude in the matter, for you have been helpful throughout. Would it be fair if I said that you held a position of 'benevolent neutrality', that is to say that, though not committing yourself to support, you would have no objection to publication if higher authority agreed to it? Please let me know if my interpretation is correct.

(2) In 1964–5 Norman Brook . . . advised me to approach either 'the Home Secretary personally or Sir Charles Cunningham, for it is with them that the final decision would rest.' Is Normanbrook's advice good to-day? Would you advise me to go to Sir Burke Trend and/or to the Home Secretary?

As usual I sent a copy of this letter to Dick White. Furnival Jones was ill, so I did not receive his answer till April when I was told that the answer to my first question was 'Yes' (though there were misgivings about the obligations of the Department to some of its agents), and to my second question the answer was 'No', since Sir Philip Allen (Cunningham's successor) was already taking part in the business. Dick White had already written to me to say that he had no doubt at all that I must meet Burke Trend and Allen and that neither he nor Martin Furnival Jones would raise security objections to publication. He reminded me at the same time that both of them were only advisers and were as anxious as I was to have a firm decision made. A meeting with Trend and Allen was arranged for June— and I felt that a real step forward had been made. The meeting itself went off moderately well. Both of the officials were courteous and sympathetic, both emphasized the practical difficulties which they foresaw, both agreed that, though the outcome was very dubious it was worth 'trying it on the Minister'; both agreed that there should be no unreasonable delay. I felt complete confidence that they would give a fair chance to my proposal and I did not, therefore, ask even to see the shorthand record of the meeting. I do not think that I have misrepresented their views but I did underestimate the immense slowness and the complications of the Whitehall machine. Though Philip Allen wrote to me at intervals to tell me that my request was under active consideration it was not until April 1970 that I received an answer to my request—and that was that 'the final decision comes down against your request.'

I wrote to Furnival Jones and to Dick White. The former surprised me by his answer. 'As a matter of fact I did not, as you assume, know what was going on. Perhaps it is that those who adopt a neutral stance are thought to have no opinion worth hearing.' Dick's view was that I ought to use my own Memoirs for telling the story. Donald McLachlan[3] took a critical view of governmental action. 'If I believed that the motive behind the policy was security I would accept it. But I am convinced that the sole object of the F.O. is to avoid gossip, publicity, and administrative embarrassment.' My own view

[3] In N.I.D. during the war; author of *Room 39*.

coincided with his, with the exception that I should have sub-
stituted 'Whitehall' for the F.O., since I felt that the multiplicity of authorities which were expected to agree was the real
stumbling-block. Whatever the cause of the refusal I decided
at once that Plan Diabolo, formerly something of a pipe dream,
must now be put into operation. It was perhaps hubristic on my
part to set my judgement against the official view, but I felt
that I could not abandon a project which I had advocated for
so long. Security objections had diminished almost to the point
of disappearance and I was fortified by the growing support of
those individuals whom I consulted and for whose opinions I
had respect. These included not only many of the officers with
whom I had served during the war (of these the most important
in my judgement were Tar Robertson, who had been the head
of B1A and Johnny Bevan, who had been in control of
Deception) but also those who had concerned themselves with
intelligence work in the subsequent years, including the Chief
of the Defence Staff and those engaged on the official history. A
letter from Michael Howard was typical of many others. He
wrote:

Speaking personally, I would like to see it published for three
reasons:—

(1) As a historian, it seems to me *ipso facto* desirable that chronicles of the past should be as complete and accurate as human endeavour can make them; if only because it is misleading and possibly
dangerous to get things wrong. Your story not only fills in a gap in
the history of the Second World War, it makes intelligible a great
deal which is at present ignored and misunderstood, and will continue, until your book is published, to be ignored and misunderstood;
not only by the general public but, as the wartime generation dies
out, by those concerned with formulating national policy. This will
be, for obvious reasons, a Very Bad Thing.

(2) As an Englishman, I should like to see the full story told of
something which we really did superbly well. Our record in the
Second World War is not so glittering that we can afford to leave
this out of it.

(3) As a connoisseur of literature, I judge it a jewel of a book in its
own right: beautifully written, clear, witty and wise.

The argument that the story can be told as part of a broader
study of 'Deception' seems a very weak one to me. Your study is
something *sui generis*, even though it does overlap with Deception;

and it deals with something much more important than Deception. Please feel free to show this letter to anyone and everyone.

Philip Swinton, too, urged me to go ahead.

When I had decided on an American publication my troubles were by no means over. My literary agent wrote that he could not handle the book. He had recently been involved in the *Daily Telegraph* action and had no wish to tangle once again with the Official Secrets Act. I consulted Norman Collins and he persuaded A. D. Peters, his own agent, to act on my behalf through his representative, Harold Matson, in America. At the same time I sought the help of James Osborn, eminent bibliophile and author and a great benefactor of the Bodleian. In both cases I made it clear that I had been refused leave to publish in England. I asked Osborn to sound out the Yale Press and find out if they would publish. This was in May 1970. The next few months were a time of disappointment. The first nine publishers in America refused the book—some thought it 'too British', others were already committed to other books dealing with the same topic, others thought that it would not appeal to the general public. I came to believe that Matson was trying to sell it as a 'spy book' rather than what it was—a report of some historical significance—and I urged him to concentrate on Yale. I also sent the typescript to James Osborn, who undertook to approach the Yale Press (November 1970). In March I received a letter from Matson which offered a contract for the book, which I immediately accepted and agreed further that the Yale Press should have the Canadian rights. Chester Kerr, the Director of the Yale University Press came over to see me and thus started, for me, a close friendship with him and with Ronald Mansbridge, the head of the Yale Press in London; they, together with Jim Osborn, were to prove my staunchest and most efficient helpers in the days to come. Unfortunately Chester Kerr was only able to see his solicitors on the day before he left for America, and from them he received the advice, 'do not proceed at this time.' Accompanied by Christopher Harmer I had a long interview with Jim Sandars and presented our case to him. Jim, the senior partner of Linklater & Paine, was known to me as a Director of Birfield, but of course I had no idea what advice he would give to his clients. I had, though, an uncomfortable feeling that I was about to fail again, especially when Chester Kerr told me that his committee would not make a decision until 24 June. At the beginning of June I received a firm offer from a commercial firm to take the book for America and not to raise the question of government approval. I replied that I should certainly accept the offer unless Yale decided to carry on with their publication. Then, some ten days later, came an unexpected, but to me joyful, cable from Chester Kerr. His committee had decided not to wait for their meeting but agreed to publish my book. A contract was being prepared. It seemed that, at last, I had come to the end of the road. At the same time Chester told me that some members of his committee wished to make a direct approach to the Home Secretary and request that the book should be declassified so that it could be published simultaneously in England and America. When I first made contact with the Yale Press I had not known that they published in London as well as in New Haven and though I was convinced that no publication in England would be allowed I saw no reason why the attempt should not be made. In fact it was made and a letter went to the Home Secretary immediately after I had signed the contract.

On the day when I received the contract I wrote to Philip Allen to tell him of my action and sent a copy to Furnival Jones. Something of an explosion then occurred. Two days later Alec Douglas-Home sent me a telegram asking me to lunch the next day, so that he might take me on to see the Home Secretary. Papers, I was informed, had already gone to the Attorney-General in order that he might decide what action could or should be taken against me. I cannot know what Alec did to protect me but I do know that the meeting with the Home Secretary (Maudling) was wholly successful. I had expected that the proposal to publish in England would be turned down out of hand and that the Yale letter would be answered in that sense. I was impressed by Maudling, particularly because he had obviously read and understood the book and I think that he was impressed by the letters which I showed him and which clearly indicated that the objections to publication were based, not on security risks, but on interdepartmental and administrative difficulties. Accordingly he wrote to Yale and intimated that no leave could be given unless the official experts could be satisfied that all security risks could be avoided by the excision of certain passages. I should as a matter of course be involved in the discussions about what was to be excised.

This was the turning of the tide and at last it seemed probable that the Government would allow simultaneous publication in both countries and, in fact, give approval to the book. Why did the Government change its mind? It may well be that the responsible minister was influenced by the request from Yale; it is possible that my own talk with the Home Secretary helped to secure his agreement; possibly the knowledge that the book would in any case be published in America (either by the Yale Press or a commercial firm) impelled the officials to 'make the best of a bad job' and allow publication in England; it is likely that all these factors contrived to bring about the desired result. I like to think that the outcome was a victory for common sense and depended upon the readiness of all parties to show a reasonable willingness to compromise. Undoubtedly Alec Douglas-Home's view that simultaneous publication was the most reasonable solution was of paramount importance. One hurdle remained to surmount. To secure agreement both the Yale Press and the author (myself) had to agree to any changes or excisions proposed, and it was possible that these might prove to be so extensive that we should not be able to agree. After a three-cornered exchange of letters it was settled that Chester Kerr should come from Yale and that we should meet the Home Office party in September, when a week was set aside for the conference. Assisted by Christopher Harmer I attended for the first two days, and quickly realized that it was intended that the plan should go through. After those first two days the negotiations were left, on my side, to Chester Kerr and Ronald Mansbridge, who proved themselves admirable negotiators. The excisions proposed were not extensive and after consultation we accepted them practically in toto.

This, however, was not quite the end of the story. When the new text was agreed and it was settled that the book should carry the words 'Copyright (C) 1972 by Yale University— Crown Copyright reserved' H.M.S.O. entered the lists and asked for the whole of the royalties which would otherwise have been paid to me. I took no part in the negotiations which

followed but left them to the Yale Press and the lawyers.
Eventually it was agreed that H.M.G. should take about half.
All through I had envisaged that the Department should benefit, and had on at least three occasions offered it 'any part or
the whole' of the royalties, but my feelings changed when the
Department took into consideration the possibility of prosecut-
ing me. That I think was a natural human reaction. I was,
therefore, quite content that half should go to H.M.G. but a
little sad that H.M.S.O. and not M.I.5 should be the gainer.

The final settlement gave me the greatest satisfaction. If
small men may be compared to great I felt much as Gibbon did
when he finished the *Decline and Fall*. There were other thoughts
also. Looking back over the whole episode I realized how
strange it was that I, who all my life had been a supporter of
the Establishment, should become, at eighty, a successful rebel.
Perhaps, contrary to the accepted view, the old are more ruth-
less than the young. They have little time to spare and become
impatient. But the strongest feeling of all was simply this. Sometimes in life you feel that there is something which you *must*
do and in which you must trust your own judgement and not
that of any other person. Some call it conscience and some plain
obstinacy. Well, you can take your choice. I, for my part, was
convinced that I was justified to continue pressing for the
publication of *Double-Cross* and I have never had any qualms at
all about the rightness of my decision.

XXXIII

AMERICAN VISIT

Materialist, practical, and matter of fact as the world of America may be judged, or may perhaps rightly judge itself, everybody recognises that co-mingled with all that is a strange elasticity, a pliancy, an intellectual subtlety, a ready excitability of response to high ideals, that older worlds do not surpass, even if they could be said to have equalled it.

JOHN MORLEY: Recollections

THE Double-Cross book was published simultaneously in the U.K. and the U.S.A. in the middle of February 1972, and I was soon plunged into a mass of business connected with it. I decided at once and irrevocably that I would not go on television in England on any channel, in order to avoid recriminations. It seemed to me that the first question must be 'Sir John, why did you go to an American publisher?' to which the only truthful answer would be, 'Because I was refused permission to publish here!' Since peace had been restored and the Government had agreed to allow publication I was anxious not to draw attention to earlier disagreements. Old quarrels are best consigned to oblivion. In America the case was different, for there the battle over publication was of little interest and the licence from the Government in the U.K. would be accepted without reference to previous refusals. I did therefore have an interview filmed by C.B.S. in December for production in America after 16 February. Another offer gave me more cause for thought. Chester Kerr was most anxious that I should go to Yale for the day of publication and help in the promotion of the book. I hesitated. To go to America in February at the age of eighty-one for what promised to be a strenuous operation was a dubious proposition, and I wondered if I should be able to carry it out without failing either in health or in effective aid to the publisher. Yet it was difficult to refuse, especially when Yale offered me a Chubb Fellowship and when Chester

declared that he would take me from door to door and back
again to Beaumont Street. I asked if a later date was possible
and eventually we compromised on the first fortnight in March.
I accepted with trepidation and lived to be thankful that I had
so decided—for my fortnight in the U.S.A. (at New Haven,
New York, Chicago, and Washington), strenuous though it was,
gave me one of the most enjoyable experiences of my life.

In this day and age, when almost all one's friends and colleagues have visited the States, it must be a work of supereroga-
tion to describe and praise American hospitality, but I cannot
think that anyone has experienced it more fully than I did.
This I owed to Chester Kerr, Director of the Yale Press, and
to his wife Joan, who 'kept with me' (if that is the right expression) all through my visit, arranged everything for me, and
took all the tiresome details of making arrangements on their
own shoulders. Without their help I should, I think, have been
unable to carry out all the many engagements on my schedule.
Efficiency and administrative expertise are not rare, but when
these qualities are combined with sympathy, tact, and friendship they acquire much greater virtue.

My schedule was, for a man of my age, a heavy one. Old
men grow garrulous, but even in Oxford (where, thank heavens,
the young are still too polite to check the old in mid-speech) I
have never talked half as much as I did in the first half of
March 1972. Dinners and lunches and speeches, television
appearances and radio talks, meetings and discussions, talks
with journalists all crowded one upon another and only a few
incidents remain clear. At Yale I found that the Chubb
Fellowship entailed very few duties and many agreeable contacts. The Fellow was required only to make himself available
to talk about his subject to any members of the staff or students
who might be interested in it. It was a special pleasure to learn
that a Rhodes Scholar from Yale was to go up to my own
College in Oxford in the coming fall. I learned, too, what the
promotion of a book meant and became accustomed to signing
copies of the *Double-Cross System* with reasonable celerity and
amiability. I hope that it does not sound patronizing if I say
that I was delighted and a little surprised by the behaviour of
the television interviewers and journalists whom I met. They
all asked intelligent questions but they did not attempt to force

the answer—rather they asked another intelligent question arising from my answer to the first. Watching television at home I have often felt that the interlocutor repeats his question in another form in the hope of getting the sort of answer he wishes for—or, in other words he tries to lead his victim along the path where he would have him go. I have, myself, never suffered—either in England or America—from being harried unfairly or misrepresented by the press or 'on the air', but I doubt whether that is a universal experience.

On one occasion my appreciation of American publicity stood me in good stead. For my first evening at Chicago I had accepted an invitation to a small private dinner with three Yale alumni. All were enthusiastic sons of Yale, but I did not know that whereas two of them thought that Yale was prospering in every way, the third thought that the recent, or fairly recent, evidence of student unrest indicated that Yale was going to the dogs. The small dinner turned out to be a banquet for about seventy people and that meant an unprepared speech of thanks. I bethought me of the Scottish pastor who, owing to the death of the previous incumbent, was hastily summoned to preach what was in fact a probationary sermon. 'I have had little time', he began, 'to prepare this sermon, so today I can only speak what the Lord puts into my mouth—but next Sunday I shall do better.' It was easy enough to start my speech by saying how honoured I was to have been awarded the Chubb Fellowship and how much I had appreciated the warm welcome and lavish hospitality of Yale. After that I chanced my arm. All this, I confessed, I had confidently expected though like the Queen of Sheba the half had not been told me. But there were pleasant surprises as well. What I had *not* expected was to find so much intelligence and so much genuine courtesy among the undergraduates (or did I say students?). No remark, I was told after dinner, could have been more appropriate. Those who sang the praises of the Yale of today were delighted; those who thought that the student body had deteriorated since their day were inclined to believe a stranger more readily than one of their local friends. As a cynic remarked (but not to me), 'That speech will bring in a good many extra dollars to the Yale Alumni Association in Chicago.'

Television and journalistic interviews were easy, but I had

to give a good deal of thought to two other commitments. One was an address to the Council on Foreign Relations in New York, the other an off-the-record talk to some of the C.I.A. officers at their H.Q. in Washington. As Dr. Johnson put it, the knowledge that he is to be hanged in a fortnight concentrates a man's mind wonderfully. Much the same, I think, could be said of a man who has to lecture to an audience who know, many of them, more of the subject than he does. That was my feeling, especially in New York, where I felt embarrassed by the knowledge that I was regarded as something of an authority on espionage and counter-espionage, whereas my experience was confined to some four years in wartime and at a period a quarter of a century past. None the less the necessity of speaking to two audiences who were well versed in the subject and, in most cases, still practising in their profession, did clear my mind to a quite remarkable degree, and I tried to put over my own thoughts and conclusions about an admittedly difficult subject.

In the first place espionage and counter-espionage alike present few difficulties in a totalitarian state. Where you have a dictator a man can be arrested, detained without trial, perhaps tortured, and few if any can dare to intervene. In a democracy it is quite otherwise and here peacetime and wartime conditions must be sharply distinguished. In time of peace the task of a spy is not too difficult, provided only that he has ample time to settle himself in. He is probably an agreeable fellow who can ingratiate himself into any society and who, once accepted, can acquire gradually and without much risk the information which he seeks. In wartime, however, a spy who has worked quietly and successfully for some years is unlikely to be of much use to his masters and is wise to sink into obscurity and wait for the storm to pass. Counter-espionage is a different thing altogether. In time of peace (in a democracy) any security service is faced by an almost impossible task since it must operate, so to speak, with both hands tied and both feet fettered. It may have the gravest suspicions about an individual but unless it has indisputable proof it dare not take action. Cries of protest resound if anyone, whether foreign or native, is detained on suspicion. Those architects of misfortune, the well-meaning and liberal-minded theorists, raise the banner of individual liberty and hurl defiance at what they designate as a police state. If, in despite of them, a case is brought to court all public opinion as well as the law itself is marshalled behind the defence. Very, very seldom can a conviction be secured and the wicked flourish like the green bay tree. Venturing then, on a generalization I would say that espionage and counter-espionage have a natural affinity with states governed by dictators and that both are by nature alien to the spirit of democracies.

In wartime the case is altered. Suspicion rests on every foreigner, the wildest tales of spying circulate, and only the most hard-headed can resist the hue and cry which demands that all potential enemies of the state should be incarcerated or, at the least, subjected to the closest scrutiny and control. The middle-aged spinster who detects an enemy spy among her neighbours is a familiar phenomenon of wartime neurosis. So, to generalize once more it can be argued that, where democratic states are concerned, espionage may be productive in time of peace but is a 'dead duck' in time of war, whereas the exact opposite is true of counter-espionage.

From this argument it is inevitable that one should go on to consider whether secret intelligence (for that is what espionage supplies) is of any substantial use whatever compared to intelligence collected by more orthodox methods. Inevitably in the war histories 'intelligence' has not yet received the attention it deserves; the historians tell us with accuracy what occurred, and sometime 'how', but seldom 'why'. No doubt this omission will be rectified in the future—meantime we can only speculate as to the value of secret intelligence—that is to say, of the information brought in by spies. Fictional spy stories which proliferate on the bookstalls often give an impression of unreality and exaggeration and when in real life a spy is unmasked and punished one is often struck by the triviality of most of his information and one wonders whether the results achieved can possibly compensate for all the trouble and expense which he has caused his masters. Would the world—or, to bring it nearer home, would any nation lose anything at all of value if spies and agents were abolished altogether?

That is a pleasing thought but only a fantasy for espionage, especially industrial espionage, is a natural activity. Every government and every business wants to know all that it can of the plans of its competitors. But time is the essence of the matter, for without time there can be no confidence in the trustworthiness of the source of the information. The short-time coup is a myth, and only those spies who have worked long and patiently can hope to achieve success. It is true that, almost by accident, in the Cicero case the Germans had it in their hands to score a sudden success; they missed the opportunity because they could not trust the agent. The ineluctable conclusion is that the importance of spies is on the down grade and for this there are two main reasons. The first is the growth of technological devices and of inventions which supersede some of the old personal devices. The second is the vastly increased speed of communications. A consideration of the Trent case in 1861, which brought Great Britain and the U.S.A. to the verge of war, will illustrate the point. Lord Lyons, then Ambassador at Washington, often expressed his opinion that war could not possibly have been averted had the transatlantic cable been in operation at that time. As things were and in the language of industrial disputes today there was necessarily a cooling-off period between the dispatch of one note and the receipt of the reply to it, in which time tempers could cool. (What a narrow squeak, for the cable was laid and was in operation before the end of the sixties.) A similar case, but with a wholly different outcome, was that of Stratford de Redcliffe at the time of the Crimean War. His influence on the outbreak of the war is still a favourite bone for the historians to worry, but some facts are accepted. Certainly he advised the Sultan to refuse the Czar's demands. Had he been, as a modern ambassador is, in touch with his home Government by telephone or wireless it is at least arguable that that wholly unnecessary war would not have taken place. Nowadays when news is communicated all over the world in the space of a few hours and when ministers and even heads of states visit one another, sometimes only for a short week-end, the role and the importance of the spy (and indeed of the ambassador too) is sensibly diminished.

Does this mean that importance of the double-cross system as we developed it in the war of 1939–45 has been exaggerated? I do not think so, though in asserting this I am confining myself strictly to the war years. The reason for my confidence in the value of the system will be clear to anyone who has studied the subject. Straight agents can seldom be trusted and may themselves be deceived, but in the case of the double agent in wartime the questions asked of him are as important as the answers. When, for example, the agents were plied with questions about defences of all kinds along the coast it could be fairly assumed that the Germans were contemplating invasion; when the bulk of the questions switched rather abruptly to aerodromes, food stores, industrial centres, and the like it was certain that the plan to invade had been dropped. In the later, and equally critical days, of the major deception (in which only the most trusted agents could be used) the follow-up questions of the Germans gave the clearest indication both that they had swallowed the information provided for them and also what was their own appreciation of the situation.

The success of the *Double-Cross System*, especially in America, surprised me. How much this success was due to the imaginative cover, which was developed in the Yale Press, how much to the introduction written by Norman Holmes Pearson, I cannot tell. In any case the book was almost immediately on the best-seller list of the *New York Times* and held its place there for a number of weeks. It was taken up by the book clubs, and a little later translated into seven or eight languages. Of the hard-back edition 35,000 copies were sold in the U.S.A. and 10,000 in the United Kingdom. The American paper-back edition sold about 200,000 copies. Both in England and America the reviews were almost universally favourable and more than one reviewer put their fingers on the critical point. The book was not another spy story but a report written at the time, and consequently a serious historical document. Comparing it with another book published at the same time the reviewer in the *Times Literary Supplement* says 'truth wins another of its victories over fiction.'

XXXIV

SUMMARY

And not uncrowned with honours ran
  My days, and not without a boast shall end!
For I was Shakespeare's countryman,
  And wert thou not my friend?

WILLIAM WATSON

I T is natural that, in this last chapter, I should look back
and that I should return to the more personal side of my life.
Always, as I now realize, I have been a privileged person and I
rejoice in the fact. In what manner have I been privileged?
First and foremost I was fortunate enough to be born into that
best of all worlds, that which might be described as the world
of the minor gentry and at a time when my class was most
secure and most contented with its lot. There was no need to
struggle to assert that one was a gentleman, little jealousy of
those with higher rank and greater responsibility, but too little
comprehension of, and sympathy for, those lower in the social
scale. In fact we had few doubts about the future; our course
was set on conventional lines; we had to work and behave as
befitted those of our class and if we did so the future was bright
and secure. There is much merit in the Greek concept of the
golden mean and still more in the blessed quality of normality.
In a word we were confident and secure.

I sometimes think that domestic service was the greatest
privilege which we enjoyed. All through my boyhood and youth
my parents were supported by two servants—Sarah Maulden
and Clara Figgins, both an essential part of our family life.
Sarah Maulden had been in the service of my maternal grandmother before she joined us; when she died in my Mother's
house at Eastbourne a *Times* obituary notice contained the
words: '. . . Sarah Maulden, for 54 years loyal and devoted
friend in the families of the late Rev. J. Royden Hughes, of

Long Ditton, and of Mrs. Masterman, aged 81.' Clara Figgins
came, as a young woman to be nurse to my brother in 1889—
she died, retired, in the Provost's Lodgings at Worcester in
1949. When either of these stalwarts were away or ill a niece
of one or the other of them took over the vacant place. At
Christ Church it was customary for a Master's servant to be
promoted after a time to be a scout or to hold a position in
Common Room. All that I had were admirable—I hope that
their successors are as good today. Then at Worcester I found
a couple, the Quelches, to look after me. Quelch was a character, with the agreeable quality of delighting to welcome and
entertain my guests. He died suddenly after twenty-five years'
service, and, after a brief interval in which I was unselfishly and
most efficiently supported by my next-door neighbour, who
controlled a hostel for Worcester undergraduates, I was taken
charge of (a better expression than that of employment) by
my present friendly couple, the Woods. Surely I do not exaggerate when I say that domestic service has provided me with
one of my chief privileges. Once at a lecture I heard H. A. L.
Fisher ask the rhetorical question, 'What would the world have
lost if Edison had had to do his own house-work?' But that is not
the whole question. Domestic service has often been derided,
but unfairly so. I do not think that the life of a domestic servant
is more monotonous or more lacking in independence than that,
for example, of the worker on an assembly line or elsewhere in a
modern factory. Very much the contrary.

The third privilege which I have enjoyed needs some explanation. All through my life I have belonged to some body,
some association, some team, or some fraternity—and, to my
mind, the sense of 'belonging' is the foundation of happiness.
A married man may well be content in his family circle but the
bachelor is dependent upon his friends. More than most
people I have lived on the support and encouragement of my
friends. A bachelor is, almost by definition, at the worst selfish
and at the best self-centred; for him the company and sympathy
of friends is of primary importance. At the beginning of the
Second War someone (whoever was it?) gave me a card on
which was written some guidance for those troublous times:
'Be not solitary. Never be idle. Try to avoid giving offence.
Grieve not for that which has gone beyond recall. Fear not that

*Or Hodge his / her own
inventing?*

which you cannot avoid. Don't fuss. Don't argue.' If I were
allowed one, and only one, boastful remark I think that I
should say that only once in a long life have I lost (except of
course by death) a close friend. One of my friends and colleagues
during the Second War bitterly resented the publication of the
Double-Cross System; he could not or would not understand my
motives; and so he would have no more of me. That loss
grieved me, but it made me realize how much my whole life
was built on friendships.

Privilege is nothing to be ashamed of, and, indeed, nearly
everything which is good in this curious world owes its origin
to privileged persons. What is hateful is the abuse of privilege—
the ready acceptance of all kinds of benefits without making
any adequate return for the common good. That, as I see it, is
the 'unacceptable face of capitalism'.

Looking back over eighty years I become convinced that
egalitarianism is the enemy of all good things, and that this is
especially true in the University world in which, for most of
my life, I have lived. Egalitarianism is clean contrary to the
concept of a university. It leads to 'standardization, which is
often essential in the material sphere, but which should not be
allowed to invade the things of the mind'.[1] And standardization leads on to mediocrity. In generalizing thus I have no
intention of comparing the present unfavourably with the past,
though, as the Russian proverb has it, 'Age always commends
its own boldness.' I am convinced that the undergraduates of
today are as good as ever they were, though some of them seem
to take pains to disguise the fact. They have, as a body, more
compassion for others than we had, though they have, too,
perhaps less comprehension of what they owe to the past and
less belief in the need for authority. Was it Goethe who declared that, 'the most foolish error for clever young men is to
think they forfeit originality by recognizing an accepted
truth'? From that sort of error all of us have suffered in our
time, as too from impatience with the judgement of our seniors.
Platitudes are often tiresome but they are more often true than
false. Again every generation suffers from an over-strict adherence to slogans and theories. In a university and perhaps else-

[1] From a speech by Vincent Massey (1887–1967), Governor-General of Canada
1952–9.

where, intelligent nepotism is in practice a policy more advantageous than theoretical democracy.

Why have I written this autobiography? Excuses are usually accusations as well. Memoirs and reminiscences are easily defensible for they are the small change in the historian's pocket, but autobiographies invite criticism.

The most hateful word in our vocabulary is destruction, the saddest is loss—lost without trace—*spürlos versunken*. Who in moments of grief has not meditated on the extinction of all that goes to make up a man's long-garnered knowledge and slowly acquired wisdom? The destruction of a great work of art is perhaps the nearest we get to pure destruction, the death of a great scholar, with most of his work unpublished, the nearest to complete loss. I believe that the urge to write of oneself is tied up with an obscure desire for survival. As Hazlitt put it, 'For not only a man's actions are effaced and vanish with him; his virtues and generous qualities die with him also!—his intellect only is immortal, and bequeathed unimpaired to posterity. Words are the only things that live forever.'

There are other motives, some reputable and some barely respectable. The desire for self-justification is one, and one that few of our great men can resist although it is generally better to leave justification to others. How many statesmen or soldiers have gained in reputation from writing their memoirs? Very few! With lesser men self-justification implies an unexpressed self-criticism for we are more concerned with the lost opportunities—and might-have-beens—than with ordinary justification for our actions. Imagination plays a large part here. Was that undertaking rejected for reasons of altruism, or because a refusal was really in the general interest, or was there at the time a weakening of the will, a sheering away from responsibility, a desire to avoid error, stronger than the wish to achieve something good? Treitschke finely defends Cavour: 'An den rauchenden Trümmer des Vaterlandes sich die Hände warmen mit dem behaglichen Selbstlob: ich habe nie gelogen—das ist des Mönches Tugend, nicht des Mannes.' Yet self-justification often, almost imperceptibly, degenerates into self-laudation.

In spite of this danger a good case can be put forward for any man to write something of his own life, for he is adding (if by but a very little) to the sum of knowledge about the past.

Almost inevitably a writer exaggerates his own share in events, dramatizes his own actions, and over-estimates his own influence. So be warned. It was a pretty conceit of Aesop's, as Bacon said, to speak of the fly on the axle wheel and his cry, 'What a dust I do raise.' Perhaps Abstemius should have the credit and not Aesop, but the sentiment is cruelly true, as any writer of autobiography must sadly confess.

Yet perhaps we expect too much and overestimate the sternness of the judgement which will be passed on us. On Heine's deathbed his wife prayed that God might forgive him. 'Have no fear, darling,' he said. 'He will forgive me; that's his job.' Nor is the judgement of men always severe, for the majority follow the age-old maxim of 'de mortuis', and write pleasant things of those who have at least not done much harm. I recollect the judgement of the disgruntled rowing coach who declared that the only good oarsman was the man who did not manifestly impede the progress of the boat—still more do I treasure Tommy Strong's remark after a Governing Body meeting at Christ Church: 'That was a splendid meeting; I really think that we did very little harm.' May I hope, then, that when my account is added up I shall not be very much in the red or even, perhaps, just a little in the black? The last word is with Kurt Hahn. 'I was lunching with some Salem friends', he wrote, 'and said in the presence of their 10-year-old son: "My grievance against life is that it passes so quickly." The boy then said: "Yes, by the time you know the trick of it, it's all over."'

Or perhaps the last word but one. In 1973 an old friend wrote to me: 'We are all like a river nearing the end of its run, wider in experience, slower in movement, and approaching the loss of our identity in the great unknown ocean.'

CHRIST CHURCH GAUDY—JUNE 25, 1958

(Reply for The Guests—after the Prime Minister)

We thank you, Sir, for all the flowered jests
With which you crowned your glad and grateful guests:
And for a feast with such a grace and glow
As we poor Londoners can never know—
Where wit and wisdom match the mellow wine
And men, by women undisturbed, can shine,—
Bacchus in conference with Socrates—
Lucullus chatting with Thucydides—
Can there be better company than these?
    And you have added Cicero. But no—
For I was not so fond of Cicero.
It's an Augustus you have heard tonight,
Who knows as well the forum and the fight,
Who, strong in storm and positive in plan,
Seems to forget that he's a Balliol man.
    Then there is Hugh, who may be Caesar too,
Though who knows when the Nyeds of March are due?
    Boy Beveridge you duly decorate,
The Archimedes of the Farewell State,
Who did so well distributing the gravy
That poor Britannia can't afford a Navy.
    Sir Owen Solon I regard with awe;
For here we have a Bradman of the Law;
And let them contemplate, the friends of schism,
This proud example of 'Dominionism'.
    Then there's an Orpheus—two—more moving far,
But less upsetting than their statesmen are.
And one of them, we hope, may now contrive
An Oxford Symphony—and stay alive.
    We hail Tiselius, for Sweden's sake,
Though most of Science is a big mistake.
I wake at dawn each day and mutter 'Drat 'em,
Those careless Cambridge men who split the Atom.'
I've seen no Sputniks, and I shall not try:
I don't approve of litter in the sky,

I hate the idiots who threaten soon
To fire a missile at the common Moon,
And mean to mutilate the only face
That is beloved by all the human race.
I trust you'll never give a D.Sc.
Because of Atoms—or of A.I.D.
       And last, the one unworthy of the lot,
A well intentioned old New College swot.
It warms a man, however slight the cause,
To find himself a Doctor of the Laws
(Though, as the Proctor has become a Prog,
A Doctor, I suppose, is but a Dog):
And here's a circumstance to make him sing—
That his constituents have done this thing.
I thank you, friends, who let so small a mouse
Speak for a mountain in the Commons' House.
       My vintage? 1910. New College then
Was rich with Wykehamists and studious men.
We cared much more for Plato than for play
(Though always Head of the River, by the way),
But now and then, across the quiet morn
We heard whips cracking, or a hunting horn.
'Christ Church,' we said, 'are getting up at last,'
And bent our heads to Greece's glorious past.
'Christ Church,' we said, 'or Magdalen—almost worse,'
And jotted down some yards of Latin verse.
Yet oft I came to these congenial courts:
Your Doctor Carter taught—would it be Torts?
So here, unhampered by the horsey row,
I learned a little law—and look at me now!
       Most graduates are geese for sale as swans.
Let us salute our marketers, the dons:
Who year by year, spectators of the game,
Send others forth to fortune and to fame.
       And now, with terror treading on my tongue,
May I address the Less Contented Young?
I am not one of those who moan and mourn
'It was without our leave that we were born!'
And therefore claim the right to sit and wince
At almost everything that's happened since.
I do not love the literary line
Whose chief motif is, roughly, 'What's My Whine?'
No, no, with all the Bombs they bustle out,
This is a goodly time to be about.

Prime Minister, what wonders Man has done
Since you and I were little boys of 1!
We had no gramophone—we had no flight:
We cooked by coal, and read by candle light.
No moving pictures, boys; I saw them come:
And then—can you believe it?—they were dumb.
Yes, when the photographs began to speak
All England had hysterics for a week.
No radar nursed the steamer in a mess:
No radio could send the S.O.S.
No penicillin eased the doctor's toil,
And if you had a boil—you had a boil.
    You turn a tap, you poor frustrated kid,
And all the Elements do what you bid.
The siren and the sage of every land
Attend your dwelling place at your command.
All these delights you take for granted, rather—
And have the cheek to criticize your father.
When I was young, dear Mervyn, one would meet
The beggar and the blind in every street:
Nor could the humblest of the island race
Proceed to Oxford—or the other place.
Be glad, at least, you Angry Ones, I beg,
With such advantages you left the egg:
And every day, at lecture or the lab,
Repeat 'Thank God—I might have been a Tab.'
    Oxford! In all the catalogues of worth
There is no name like Oxford on the Earth—
The only name, they say, that sounds as clear
As Coca Cola in the cosmic ear:
A name of love on all the nations' lips,
As 'Greenwich' still is mistress of the ships.
Set sail, brave boys, Frustration left ashore,
The flag of Oxford flying at the fore:
And let us whisper, as we put to sea,
'I'll give the world what Oxford gave to me.'

A. P. HERBERT

APPENDIX II

BALLAD OF PHYSICAL SECURITY

At 58 St. James' Street
   The door is open wide;
Yet all who seek to enter here
   Must make their motives crystal clear
Before they step inside,
   That none may probe with fell intent
The secrets of the Government.

Beside the door which serves the lift
   A pair of sentries lurk,
Steel-helmeted and battle-clad,
   The lift itself, it's fair to add,
Is one which does not work,
   (A further check we thus secure
Which makes assurance doubly sure).

And woe betide the visitor
   . Whose business is not clear!
Not admirals nor belted earls
   Nor exquisitely lovely girls
Can dupe the scrutineer
   Who haunts the hall at 58
Like Peter at the golden gate.

For everyone must show his pass,
   And only those that know
The current form from day to day
   Can guess what sort of pass they may
Be called upon to show;
   We may be sure the guileless Hun
Would never have the proper one!

They vary with the personnel;
   For those in lower grades
A Sunday ticket for the Zoo,
   Adroitly shown, will often do;

Whereas the Ace of Spades
    Or else a cheque on Barclays Bank
Will pass a man of senior rank.

And some there are who do not seem
    To need a pass at all,
Like jobbing electricians' mates
    Whose frank demeanour indicates
The purpose of their call,
    (The principle of course extends
To plumbers and their lady friends).

But one who merely looks as though
    He's something to discuss
Of urgent import to the State
    Is naturally made to wait,
And if he makes a fuss
    Or tries to pass abruptly by
We know at once that he's a spy!

What more could human wit devise?
    From basement up to roof
The wire which hangs in festive loops
    And bristling bayonets of the troops
Supply yet further proof
    Of how intensely we accept
The rule that secrets must be kept.

                    CYRIL HARVEY

INDEX

Advani, T.M., 311.
Alexander of Tunis, Field-Marshal Earl, 256.
Alington, the Very Revd. C.A., 190f, 309.
Allen, Sir Philip, 354, 356, 359.
Allen, P.B., 37f, 42.
Amery, L.S., 136.
Amies, Hardy, 205.
Amory, Viscount, 152.
Anderson, G.R.L., 77f.
Anderson, John, Viscount, Waverley, 216.
Anderson, J.G.C., 85, 120.
Architecture, Oxford, 320ff.
Arkwright, the Revd. E.H., 28, 30.
Army Education Advisory Board, 264ff.
Arnold-Forster, Cmdr. H.C., 29.
Ashford, Sir Cyril Ernest, 26.
Asquith, H.H., Earl of Oxford and Asquith, 182f.
Assheton, Ralph, Lord Clitheroe, 152.
Atkinson, C.T., 150.
Atlantic College, 253, 329.
Attlee, Earl, 348.
A.T.V. Educational Advisory Committee, 329, 335ff.
Auchinleck, Field-Marshal Sir Claude, 255.
Authentics C.C., 160.
Baldwin, Stanley, Earl Baldwin of Bewdley, 179.
Balfour, Sir John, 95, 97f.
Bandaranaike, S.W.R. Dias, 152.
Barker, Sir Ernest, 79, 177, 239f.
Barrington-Ward, J.G., 124, 127.
Baskerville, Geoffrey, 91.
Baynes, R.E., 116.

B.B.C. General Advisory Council, 266
Beaver, Sir Hugh, 259.
Beazley, Sir John, 121ff.
Beresford, Admiral Lord Charles, 33f, 106.
Besse, Antonin, 319f.
Bevan, J.H., 357.
Beveridge, William, Lord, 214, 299f.
Birfield Ltd., 328ff, 340ff.
Birkenhead, 1st Earl of, 136, 166f, 177f, 183.
Birkenhead, 2nd Earl of, 152, 202.
Birley, Sir Robert, 257.
Blakiston, the Revd. H.E.D., 182.
Blundell, Captain George, 331, 335, 343.
Blunt, H.W., 85, 116f.
Boase, T.S.R., 298.
Borenius, Tancred, 134.
Bowra, Sir Maurice, 255, 283, 285, 298.
Boyle, Edward, Lord Boyle of Handsworth, 152.
Bratby, Michael, 205.
Bridges, Edward, Lord, 257f, 269, 290.
Bridges, Robert, 48.
Briggs, Asa, 236.
Brittain, Sir Harry, 249.
Britten-Holmes, Everard, 160.
Brown, A.B., 236.
Brown, Ivor, 336.
Browning, Andrew, 80.
Bruce, Rosslyn, 16.
Brugnon, Jacques, 165.
Bryan-Brown, A.N., 236, 251.
Buchan, the Hon. A.F., 152.
Buttery, Horace, 133f.
Buzzard, Sir Farquhar, 203, 217, 317.
Caccia, Harold, Lord, 262.
Cadogan, Sir Edward, 269.

Calder, Donald, 325.
Carroll, Lewis, 128.
Carter, A.T., 118ff, 142.
Carter, Donald, 336.
Casement, Roger, 105.
Cassels, Field-Marshal Sir James, 265.
Cave, George, Viscount, 183.
Cazalet, Victor, 145, 166, 203, 215f.
Cecil, Lord David, 152.
Chadwick, the Very Revd. Henry, 181, 296.
Chadwick, Sir James, 104.
Chamberlain, Neville, 203f.
Chauncy family, 5f.
Chaundy, T.W., 124, 140.
Chelmsford, Viscount (F.J.N. Thesiger), 231.
Cherwell, Viscount (F.A. Lindemann), 201ff, 281.
Childers, J.S., 58f.
Chubb Fellowship, 362ff.
Churchill, Sir Winston, 125, 168, 202, 206, 228.
Churchill, Lady, 167f.
C.I.A., 365.
Clark, Brigadier W.E., 196.
Cobbold, C.F., Lord, 258.
Cobham, Viscount, 159.
Collins, Norman, 329, 335ff, 358.
Commonwealth Universities' Congress, 306ff.
Cooper, Alfred Duff, Viscount Norwich, 224.
Coote, the Revd. R.H., 14f.
Cotton, R.L., Provost of Worcester, 231f.
Crawford, Marion, 275.
Cricket, 16f, 59f, 81f, 154ff, 198f.
Cruttwell, C.R.M.F., 153.
Cryptics C.C., 162.
C.S.S.B., 216ff.
Cumberlege, G.F.J., 62, 79, 101.
Cumming, Sir Mansfield, 211.
Cunningham, H.J., 50, 53f, 73.
Curtis, Dame Myra, 267.
Curzon, G.N., Marquess Curzon of Kedleston, 49.
Dance, Eric, 274f.
Daniel, C.H.O., Provost of Worcester, 45ff, 51, 231, 276.
Daniel, Ruth, 48f.
Davidson, Maj.-Gen. F.H.N., 209f.
Dawes, G.S., 236.

de Gaulle, General Charles, 216.
Dendy, Brigadier M.H., 207.
Deutsche Hockey Club (Hanover), 172.
Dillwyn, Colin, 151.
Doeg, J.A., 166.
Douglas-Home, Alec, Lord Home of the Hirsel, 152, 350, 359f.
Drake, W., 59f.
Dundas, R.H., 123, 130f, 142, 146.
Easthaugh, the Rt. Revd. Cyril, 152.
Ebbisham, 1st Lord, 215.
Eden, Anthony, Earl of Avon, 130, 136.
Eden, Sir Timothy, 94f, 97ff, 130.
Einstein, Albert, 72.
Eisenhower, Dwight, 307.
Eitel brothers, 91ff, 99.
Elliott, Sir Claude, 191, 257.
Elmhirst, William, 58, 64f, 74.
England, John, 336, 338.
Eton College, 189ff, 253, 256ff, 329.
Evans, D.M., 166.
Evans, Sir Ivor, 337.
Ewing, Sir Alfred, 23, 26.
Examination procedure, 40ff, 185ff.
Factory Club (Oporto), 162.
Farnell, L.R., 141ff.
Feiling, Sir Keith, 85f, 124, 150f, 153.
Figgins, Clara, 369f.
Firth, Sir Charles, 79f, 148f, 152.
Fisher, Charles, 85, 116.
Fisher, H.A.L., 182.
Fisher, Admiral of the Fleet Lord, 22ff, 45.
Fitzwilliam Club (Dublin), 165.
Fleming, Peter, 349, 354f.
Fletcher, C.R.L., 81.
Florey, Howard, Lord, 307.
Ford, A.C., 104.
Ford, Herbert, 135.
Foster, G.N., 63.
Fowler, R.St.L., 161.
Francis, E.L., 194ff.
Franks, Oliver, Lord, 286, 290.
Furnival Jones, Sir Martin, 352ff, 359.
Gaitskell, Hugh, 299f, 351.
Garland, C.S., 165.
Garnett, John, 143.
George VI, H.M. King, 348.
Gerrans, H.T., 50f, 75f.
Gielgud, Sir John, 336f.
Girdlestone, Gathorne R., 173.
Gladstone, W.E., 73.
Glasgow, Mary, 336.